Huma Abedin has spent her entire career in public service and national politics, beginning as an intern in First Lady Hillary Clinton's office in 1996. After four years in the White House, she worked in the US Senate as senior advisor to Senator Clinton and was travelling chief of staff for Clinton's 2008 presidential campaign. In 2009, she was appointed deputy chief of staff at the US Department of State. Huma served as vice-chair of Hillary for America in 2016, resulting in the first woman elected nominee of a major political party. She currently serves as Hillary Clinton's chief of staff. Born in the United States and raised in Saudi Arabia, Huma moved back to the US in 1993. She lives in New York City with her son, Jordan. *Both/And* is her first book.

Praise for *Both/And*

'An extraordinary memoir about the most private and public things. With candour, insight and courage, Abedin takes us boldly behind the scenes of many of the most important political events of the past quarter century and dazzlingly deep into the heart of the most poignant, powerful and painful moments of her life—as a daughter, mother, wife and top aide to Hillary Clinton. It's a story about loss and triumph, resilience and grit; about love, loyalty and letting go. The writing is just gorgeous. I was gobsmacked.' **Cheryl Strayed, author of *Wild: From Lost to Found on the Pacific Crest Trail***

'An inspiring roadmap revealing how a little Brown girl from Kalamazoo, Michigan grew up to become a powerful political force navigating unimaginable rooms, relationships and circumstances with incredible resiliency, stunning work ethic and unwavering faith. There is no doubt that Huma's personal and professional journey, told in her own words, is one of the most unique stories you will ever read.' **Cleo Wade, author of *What the Road Said***

'A gripping testament to the power of a woman finding her voice, owning her ambition and sharing her truth. Huma's humanity, tenacity and singularity draw us deeply into her personal and professional journeys – and we are left inspired by her will to fight for herself and the world.' **Glennon Doyle, author of *Untamed*, and Founder of Together Rising**

'I've long known Huma to be a compassionate and committed advisor and public servant. I've relied on h͟   ͟ounsel for a quarter-century. *Both/And* is the beau͟   ͟y, and I'm so delighted she's chosen͟   ͟h the world.' **Hillary Rodham Cl͟**

THOUGHT FOR THE DAY

As an American, a Muslim and as a member of a fairly decent family a commitment should be a commitment. Whatever the provocation it should not influence you to act in an unbecoming manner. You have to be fair, honest and direct. If you can't stand the heat, then as Truman said, get out of the kitchen. But your exit should be graceful, decent and above board.

Let others do what they will. You are responsible in the first instance to yourself, your principles and values and ultimately to Yahweh (Allah)

Your Loving Father

BOTH/AND

A LIFE IN MANY WORLDS

HUMA ABEDIN

**SIMON &
SCHUSTER**

London · New York · Sydney · Toronto · New Delhi

First published in the United States by Scribner,
an imprint of Simon & Schuster, Inc., 2021
First published in Great Britain by Simon & Schuster UK Ltd, 2021
This edition published in Great Britain by Simon & Schuster UK Ltd, 2022

1 3 5 7 9 10 8 6 4 2

Simon & Schuster UK Ltd
1st Floor
222 Gray's Inn Road
London WC1X 8HB

www.simonandschuster.co.uk
www.simonandschuster.com.au
www.simonandschuster.co.in

Simon & Schuster Australia, Sydney
Simon & Schuster India, New Delhi

A CIP catalogue record for this book is available from the British Library

Paperback ISBN: 978-1-4711-7299-1
eBook ISBN: 978-1-4711-7298-4

Printed in the UK by CPI Group (UK) Ltd, Croydon, CR0 4YY

For my parents—Saleha and Zain—
who taught me what it means to live fully.

For my son—Jordan Zain—
who taught me what it means to love unconditionally.

CONTENTS

CONTENTS

PART THREE

PART FOUR

PREFACE

We tell ourselves stories in order to live.
—Joan Didion

I grew up surrounded by stories. The shelves in my childhood home were filled with books of every genre, every period in history, by every kind of author. Hardcovers, softcovers, brand-new, secondhand, spines split from wear and tear. Every bedside table held piles more. By our couch, baskets brimmed with stacks of newspapers and magazines.

Then there were the stories passed down by various relatives, as I sat on shag carpets or in family backyards, about generations of my ancestors. The women in my family who defied the norms of their day and pushed against the constraints within which they lived. The men who refused to accept the concept of "otherness" and explored coexistence during a time when sectarian and nationalistic fervor overtook their worlds.

Before me, there came generations of public servants, orators, healers, educators. Their motivations, actions, and choices created the moment I would step into. They blazed trails which allowed me to walk right on past the barriers they had faced and build a life of my choosing. A life shaped by their pursuit of knowledge, their love of literature, their curiosity about the world, and their commitment to their family, their country, and their faith.

When I was a little girl, I believed that my life would somehow be different from the lives of everyone around me. I carried that sense of certitude until a combination of fate, luck, and hard work placed me at the center of an epic adventure.

I embarked on a career in public service inspired by and working alongside an American icon because I wanted to live the values I was raised with, and do justice to the examples set by my parents. I was proud to serve a country that gave my family the freedoms and opportunities they couldn't possibly have had anywhere else.

The pages that follow track the migration of a family over the course of generations: from the Middle East, through Central Asia, into the subcontinent of India, over the Atlantic to the United States, back to the Middle East, and then returning again to America. This is not intended to be a treatise on religion, but a personal reflection on the meaning of faith in my own life. It is not a sweeping record of women's rights, but follows the choices, opportunities, and obstacles I encountered and witnessed. It is not an encyclopedic dissection of immigration in America, but just one family's experience of the American Dream. It is not a dissertation on American policy in the Middle East or vice versa, but the view of one young woman raised simultaneously in both worlds, loving both, questioning both, and, more than anything, appreciating both. It is not meant to be a set of political analyses on any particular campaign or candidate or party, but the chronicle of a singular life in American politics. It is not a romance novel but there is love too—deep and true and heartbreaking.

My journey has taken me to more than 100 countries. From the desert of Saudi Arabia to the White House in Washington, DC. From erupting war zones to the shrinking Arctic Circle. From refugee camps to Buckingham Palace. From flying on Air Force One to hiding in car trunks. It is the tale of one person's walk alongside history. Honored to witness. Proud to serve. Humbled to be recognized. Shocked to be dissected. Grateful to have been loved. Hopeful for the future.

This is my story.

PART ONE

PART ONE

DENIAL

Happy is the man who avoids hardship, but how fine is the man who is afflicted and shows endurance.
—Prophet Muhammad (PBUH)

I was a newly arrived American in Saudi Arabia when I got lost in a sea of *abayas*. It was 1978. I was three. It was hot that night. Actually, it was always hot. My parents had taken us shopping to Balad, to look for curtain rods. Balad is Jeddah's old city—a labyrinth of winding streets leading to a myriad of alleyways where an explosion of sights and sounds meets your senses, emanating from small shops packed closely together. Brightly colored children's clothing, tight bolts of fabric in black and white, endless displays of lamps and dates and perfume, electronics galore with every gadget turned to maximum volume, gleaming jewelry shops with twenty-four-karat-gold necklace sets seeming to float in air-conditioned windows. Overhead, fluorescent tube lights made it seem like perpetual, garish daytime. The air carried layered scents of baby formula, musky incense, grilled meat from the *shawarma* stands, and *shisha* smoke.

Men wore long white *thobes* with pantaloons peeking out from below, and either white or checkered headdresses. All the women, including my mother, were covered in black *abayas*. Back then, *abayas* were loose robes made from black silk or polyester with small armholes on either side, and open down the front so one hand was constantly clutching it closed. Draped over the women's heads were black scarves. Some covered their faces entirely, so their world was always a muffled gray. Others had slits cut in the fabric across the eyes to allow them to see more clearly.

3

My mother only settled after haggling on a reasonable price with the salesman, mandatory for shopping in Balad. My older brother Hassan was helping my mother carry one end of the curtain rods, and my big sister Hadeel and I were holding on to her *abaya* as she led us through the confusing, crowded streets toward the car where my father was waiting. We stopped at a shop that sold dates. Before me, at eye level, lay massive round copper trays heaped with different varieties of the dried fruit, all stacked taller than me. Dark syrupy sweet dates, honey-colored dates that were tougher and chewier, dates dipped in nuts or chocolate.

As my mother bent down to sample one, she must have felt the pull of my hand on the back of her *abaya*. She turned to look at me, and I found her face oddly covered with a veil, which she quickly lifted. I was staring at a stranger. In this mass of identically clad women, I had grabbed the wrong "mother." I let go and she watched me back away, saying nothing. I was overwhelmed by grown-ups towering above, uneven cobblestones under my feet, lines of shops on either side, shopkeepers advertising their wares in singsong voices. After what felt like forever, straight ahead, through a parting in the crowd, I saw my mother's face. She was screaming my name and, when her eyes locked on me, she ran toward me and grabbed me tight. Her warm tears fell into my hair and down the side of my neck. I have only seen my mother cry during two periods in my life. That was the first time. She quickly ushered us to our father and into our waiting car and we returned to our temporary apartment.

We were visitors here. Kalamazoo, Michigan, was home. It was where I was born, where I spent my earliest years and every summer for years after we had left. There we took no evening trips to crowded bazaars. We lived in a suburban ranch-style home with a large picture window, a backyard with a lawn, and a small field of asparagus stalks. We spent weekends shopping at Harding's Friendly Market, picnicking at Milham Park, or driving two hours to a kosher butcher in Gary, Indiana, where the proprietor usually mistook our Muslim family for Sephardic Jews.

The year I turned one, America turned two hundred, and that summer was jam-packed with bicentennial celebrations—county fairs, small-town parades, and displays of fireworks, all honoring the triumphant spirit of the red, white, and blue throughout the country, including in our hometown. My brother ran around the neighborhood with kids named Brian, Benji, and Shannon, and my parents went to backyard barbecues with friends. We were surrounded by mostly white people in the middle of white America, and our family felt welcomed with warmth and curiosity. We adapted in ways that made sense to my parents, letting go of cultural traditions that were no longer practical while holding on to the customs and practices that were important to them.

Our home was always filled with visitors. According to tradition, my father's mother moved in with us as she aged so my parents could care for her. There was always a relative coming through town, some just having arrived from India or Pakistan—for dinner, a weekend, or a few weeks before they made their own new American homes or headed back to the motherland after their studies were complete. My parents hosted dinner parties for friends and colleagues where they would discuss literature, religion, and culture over heaping servings of *biryani*. They didn't consume or serve pork or alcohol, and no one seemed to mind. Thanksgiving quickly became our family's favorite American holiday. Christmas Eve we spent at our close friend's house helping with tree trimming and preparing family feasts, opening the door from time to time to listen to Christmas carols.

A few months before my second birthday, my father was diagnosed with progressive renal failure. There were unidentifiable deposits in his kidneys, and his creatinine levels were abnormally high. "Your kidneys are failing," the doctor at the Ascension Borgess Hospital in Kalamazoo told him. "At most you've got five to ten years, so you should probably get your arrangements in order." My father was forty-six years old. In response, he simply smiled, nodded, and thanked the doctor for his help. My mother almost fainted from shock.

Despite the news, my parents, both professors, decided to go ahead with a long-planned sabbatical year. My father had intended to spend the year in Italy, but as they weighed various options, Saudi Arabia became a more appealing choice. At the time, flush with oil money and a rapidly growing economy, the Saudi government was investing in infrastructure and education and recruiting teachers to come and support inaugural programs at new institutions, and King Abdulaziz University in Jeddah made an inordinately generous offer. My parents would both be given faculty positions, plus free university housing, a stipend to pay for school for all three children, free medical care at the university hospital, and first-class round-trip airline tickets twice a year back to Michigan. Also, they would pay no taxes. On any of it. Their only expenses would be food, clothing, entertainment, and gas. We could live comfortably off of my father's salary alone, because the cost of living in Saudi Arabia was a fraction of what it was in the U.S., and put my mother's paycheck in the bank so she could continue to use her own money as she saw fit just as she had done for my parents' entire marriage. Perhaps the most compelling reason they accepted the offer was the opportunity to teach us kids about our faith. My father thought it would be a great experience, and plus, it was just a year. His enthusiasm became contagious.

Somewhere there is a photograph of the road not traveled. It is of me in our Kalamazoo home at my second birthday party, a little "English rose," as I was nicknamed by an aunt because of my rosy newborn skin, in a long pink dress holding a miniature golf set I had just received as a gift. The girl in that photo might have led a quintes-sentially middle-American life of Michigan football games and senior proms and road trips to the Grand Canyon. But just weeks after that picture was taken, we were gone, not just to another country, but on a grand adventure. My parents walked out of that hospital in Kalama-zoo, and they just didn't stop.

The denial that kept my parents from ever sharing the details about my father's health with anyone was, in part, a refusal to let it become a burden. His illness never dragged them down. It only propelled us all forward.

My father was told he was dying, so he went out and lived.

CITIZEN OF THE WORLD

Where the mind is without fear and the head is held high;
Where knowledge is free;
Where the world has not been broken up into fragments by narrow
domestic walls;
Where words come out from the depth of truth;
Where tireless striving stretches its arms toward perfection.
—Rabindranath Tagore

My father was curiosity itself. Whether with a bellman or a prince, he would strike up unexpected conversations. Sometimes, he would hear someone's accent and tell them he had traveled to their country and had written about it and wanted to hear their story. Or he would tell someone that he understood the current political situation in their country must be troubling them. Sometimes he offered a turn of phrase in their language. People must have wondered why he was so interested in their life experiences, why he never seemed to be in a hurry. Who was this charming, cosmopolitan bespectacled green-eyed man with a shock of brown hair that never went gray years after his beard was salt-and-pepper, whose back was ever so slightly bent, and who was always dressed in a perfectly cut and pressed suit?

To some degree, he was a mystery to me too. Though a lover of history, my father rarely spoke of his own past. He would say the reason our eyes are in the front of our heads is to look ahead, not backward. As a scholar, he certainly believed we should learn from the past, but that it should be a platform for flight, not an immovable weight to which we are chained.

How did he arrive at this fundamental optimism, this relentless posture toward forward motion? This I learned from the stories told to me on visits with my aunts and cousins in Canada, England, India, and Pakistan. In these homes, where black-and-white photos and newspaper clippings adorned walls or jammed photo albums, I learned in bits and pieces, most of it long after I had lost him, about the man who came to be my father.

* * * *

Syed Zainul Abedin was born in the spring of 1928, in New Delhi, India. To me, he was Abbu, derived from the Arabic word for father, but in his official correspondence he was always Syed or Zain. "Syed" is the honorific title given to a Muslim man who can trace his lineage back to our last Prophet Muhammad, and his name was a reminder of the legacy we were raised to honor.

Zain's family was well regarded in their community in North India. His mother, whom we called Api, was the eldest daughter of the chief physician to the Nawab of Bhopal, a state which had been ruled by women for one hundred years starting in the early nineteenth century, so it was no surprise that though still restricted by her place in society—in those days, living in *purdah*, or seclusion, was the norm for women of her social status—my grandmother was independent minded. She was homeschooled by the wives of junior British army officers stationed in Bhopal. Api married a man from Delhi who, like her own father, was a government physician. They had twelve children, six girls and six boys. Three of the boys died in infancy, and two of them didn't live past the age of nine. That left Zain as the only surviving son. Losing one child, let alone five, might have broken most people, but Api was said to be tremendously resilient and never lost her faith.

Zain's ancestors originated in the Hejaz region of Arabia and traced their path over a few generations through Baghdad, then Central Asia, before finally settling in the area that would become New Delhi, now the capital of India. The story of their migration over the centuries is the story of how Islam came to India, culminating in the rule of the Mughal Empire in the mid-sixteenth century, until the 1700s when the British invaded. The next phase of the story was the movement for Indian self-government. On August 15, 1947, the Indian subcontinent gained independence from the British crown after two hundred years of colonial rule. Days later, amid growing sectarian violence between Muslims and Hindus, Sir Cyril Radcliffe, a British attorney sitting in his London office, demarcated the borderline between the two new countries, largely secular India and the Muslim states of East and West Pakistan. Immediately, Partition sparked a mass migration of 15 million people: Hindus to India, Muslims to East and West Pakistan. It also triggered unthinkable brutality and violence—tens of thousands of rapes and incidents of arson, dismemberment, and murder, resulting in as many as 2 million people dead within a year.

The turbulence that was the Indian fight for self-rule touched many Muslim families, including Zain's. In the bloody Indian mutiny of 1857, his father's brother was killed while traveling by train to Meerut for his government service when, despite his protests in their native tongue, his attackers mistook him for an Englishman.

Partition tore families apart and the question of whether the family should move to a newly formed Pakistan was left to Zain, a nineteen-year-old college student and the only son, to decide. Zain had been raised in a mostly secular manner, so he decided to remain in India on principle. "I don't need a country to tell me I'm a Muslim," he said. So, they stayed. He believed that India could flourish, and always had flourished, as a nation made up of millions of people speaking different languages, keeping different traditions, and practicing different faiths. Segregation based on religion would solve nothing. Unless people were willing to respect one another's identities and values, a border would lead only to more division, more violence, and more mistrust.

At Aligarh Muslim University, Zain worked toward his master's degree in English Literature, and wrote poetry, both in English and in Urdu. He played nearly every sport, and rode for the university's equestrian team, competing in show jumping events across the country. One summer day in 1948, just as he was about to graduate from university, Zain was jumping hurdles during riding exercises when his horse pulled up short, launching Zain forward, and the iron bar he was meant to clear, broke his fall instead. For a week, he told everyone he was fine, grimacing through the pain, crawling up stairs when he thought no one was looking. When his friends finally carried him to see a doctor, the surprised physician asked how it was possible that he'd been walking around for seven days with a fractured spine. And that, I learned from one of his sisters, was how my father broke his back.

A long and agonizing recovery began at home. Medical treatment at the time consisted of lying flat on one's back on a pile of burlap sacks filled with sand, which Zain did for a full year, spending the time reading novels, writing poetry, and delving into books on history, theology, and politics. The doctors had no sense of what a long period of being immobilized would mean for his ability to fully recover. Undaunted, Zain threw himself into researching alternative Ayurvedic and holistic treatments, which became a lifelong pursuit. He essentially willed himself to walk again, but his spine never healed properly. He would also learn he had a condition known as ankylosing spondylitis, a rare form of arthritis that causes stiffness in the neck as well as chronic back and joint pain. He was left with a permanent tilt, looking like he had bent slightly to pick up a paper at a newsstand, just a little tip forward, at the top of his back.

After his yearlong convalescence, having completed his master's degree, he then taught English Literature at his alma mater for the next decade. Eventually, he applied for and was awarded a Fulbright scholarship to study at the University of Pennsylvania in Philadelphia.

In the summer of 1963, when Zain boarded a ship in the port of Bombay to carry him across the ocean, first to Europe and then to America, he had no idea the journey would be one-way. He was expected to return when his studies were complete, to marry a woman his parents had informally promised him to. That particular ship's manifest consisted of other students who had received Fulbright scholarships. Zain's Hindu cabinmate woke before dawn every morning to perform his daily *puja* prayer, complete with beautiful chanting and ringing bells. Zain followed shortly thereafter to quietly perform his own *fajr* dawn prayer. The Christian students held makeshift Sunday services. The merging of religious diversity was seamless, and they were headed to the one country founded on the principle that whatever they practiced would be honored and protected.

At Penn, Zain developed interests in eighteenth-century American drama and the American slave trade, and wrote his dissertation on the Barbary Wars, America's first foreign conflict, fought against the Muslim nations of North Africa.

* * * *

A year later, another Fulbright scholar, Saleha Mahmood, arrived at Penn from the same part of the world: my mother had come to pursue her doctoral studies in sociology and demography.

Like my father, my mother never spoke of her own youth. I only got glimpses of the firecracker she had been from stories my sisters and I would drag out of my aunts during lazy summer afternoons in Queens or late nights in New Jersey. She was *bhaji* to them, the eternal elder sister, and they spoke of her with respect, wonder, and awe. They would open conversations about her with "You know your mother was the first woman to . . ." Then they would conjure a character so fiercely determined, so independent, I had trouble reconciling it with the mild, uncomplaining mother who slept in the bedroom next to mine.

* * * *

Saleha's ancestors originated in the Middle East, migrating from Iraq and Yemen before settling in Hyderabad, where her grandfather and great-grandfather served as civil servants in the court of the Nizam, then the rulers of Hyderabad. Her grandmother Fatima lived in *purdah*, like my father's mother. When women in Fatima's family did go out, to pay a social call at the home of a relative or another family, they did so veiled. Covered carriages would pull up to the main entrance of the house, and household staff would hold up two sheets, creating a corridor between the door and the carriage. Shielded from view, the women would board, ride to their destination, and disembark the same way.

Fatima loved reading and writing and wanted to study in a school, but that simply wasn't an option for her. Even if she had been free to travel the streets, in the late nineteenth century there wasn't a single girls' school for her to attend anywhere nearby. Formal schooling was available only to boys. The education that women received, in reading, writing, and especially in math—women managed the household

11

finances, so they needed to know how to budget—was done in the home.

Fatima begged her male cousins to share their lessons so she could teach herself at home. She went on to publish a book of poetry, which, for the time, was revolutionary. Still, any kind of formal education remained beyond her grasp her entire life.

By 1912, the year Fatima gave birth to her daughter, Mehboob, a girls' school had opened its doors in Hyderabad, attended by the daughters of a handful of progressive families. Like her mother before her, Mehboob demanded to be educated in a formal classroom. Fortunately, she was blessed with something few girls her age possessed: her own mother's determination and her father's permission. Mehboob would be taken to school in the back of a covered oxcart so long as it pulled around to the *rear* of the house, so that neighbors would not see a girl going out into the world. Each morning, she would slip through the barrier of sheets and be driven to school. When it was time for her and her male cousins to take the matriculation exam, she was the only one who passed.

Mehboob went on to be the first woman in her family to finish secondary school and the first to attend college. At the age of eighteen, she was engaged to be married to a man she had never met or seen. Her first glimpse of her betrothed, Sadiq, came on their wedding night when they sat side by side, looking not at each other but at mirrors they each held in their laps. Mehboob was thrilled to see that the twenty-six-year-old groom was movie-star handsome, with curly hair and chiseled features. For Sadiq, what mattered most about his bride was that she had gone to school. He came from a family of strong women, and when it was time for him to be married, he told his older sister that his only desire was for his wife to be educated. His sister, an accomplished poet herself, thought of her friend Fatima, from her poetry circle. Fatima's daughter Mehboob, who had famously demanded to go to school, would be perfect. The match was made.

A decade later, in 1940, Mehboob was pregnant with her third child, and Sadiq was praying for a girl. This was an unusual preference in early twentieth-century Indian culture. Sons stayed at home, brought wives into the household, took care of their parents, and inherited all the property. Daughters were considered guests in their birth homes, to be married off in a few years. In some traditions, the bride's family was responsible for paying for the wedding and for giving a dowry to the groom, making the financial burden of daughters even more overwhelming.

Sadiq's prayers were answered. His first daughter, Saleha, was born on a hot summer day, in the city of Hyderabad in the waning days of the British Empire. Coming after two older brothers, she would be the eldest of what would be five girls, fulfilling Sadiq's wish many times over.

In 1946, when Saleha was six, the family decided to move to Bombay so Sadiq could join his older brother's billboard advertising business. Once he was settled in the bustling metropolis, he sent word for his wife and children to join him. On the long journey from Hyderabad to Bombay by train, Mehboob of course wore her *burkha*. When they arrived at the train station in Bombay, Sadiq boarded the train car to help his family disembark, and there found his wife, swathed from head to toe in black. He gently lifted the fabric, and threw it out the window onto the tracks.

"This is not how you dress here," he said.

Then Mehboob stepped off the train into the bustling crowd, a woman in her mid-thirties, unveiled in public for the very first time in her life.

In Bombay, Saleha's family lived in the Great Western Building, located near the Gateway to India arch, right on the Arabian Sea. She watched the pageantry of the formal procession as Lord Mountbatten, the last viceroy of India, arrived to oversee the British relinquish the crown jewel in its empire and India win its independence.

In this new world of opportunity and possibility, nothing was more important than education, so Saleha and her sisters were enrolled in Catholic schools, considered the best schools, and Saleha thrived. She was outspoken, hardheaded, and fearless. She loved the nuns and the sense of order and discipline they instilled. Each morning assembly started with the same invocation, "In the name of the Father, the Son, and the Holy Ghost. Amen."

Mehboob and Sadiq saw no contradiction in sending their Muslim children to Catholic schools. Their family easily assimilated with the Hindu, Christian, Zoroastrian, and Jewish families surrounding them. Saleha's best friend was her Jewish next-door neighbor in the Great Western Building. That kind of openness and tolerance was commonplace in Bombay, one of the major crossroads of the world, where people of different religions and ethnicities lived side by side.

Then came Partition.

Despite the growing tensions, Saleha's family, like Zain's, decided to stay in India. They loved Bombay, and the unrest and sectarian violence along the border and in regions like Punjab and Kashmir hadn't yet had any direct impact on their lives. They were a proud Muslim family, and they were also Indian through and through. Until they weren't.

On January 30, 1948, almost six months after Partition, Mahatma Gandhi was assassinated by a Hindu extremist who believed Gandhi was appeasing Muslims too much by advocating for both Hindu and Muslim rights. Shock waves spread through the country as his death was reported. People waited fearfully for news that the murderer might be Muslim, which would only escalate tensions further. Riots broke out in Bombay and a general sense of unease and uncertainty prevailed.

In the months and years that followed, life began to change. Saleha's parents, who had never before felt the need to defend their Indian-ness, hung the flag of the ruling Indian National Congress party outside their door so that no one would question their allegiance to their country. Until that moment, Saleha had never felt like she was different from her Indian neighbors, but suddenly everything seemed to change.

The family's future in India grew more uncertain as Sadiq's advertising company in Bombay began to fail. With each passing year more clients were taking their business to his Hindu competitors. "You are Muslim," they would say. "They made a country for you. Go there."

Eventually, they did.

They packed up their belongings and boarded a ship for the three-day journey to Pakistan. Oblivious to her status as a refugee, Saleha thought exploring the ship and running from the wild waves thrashing against the deck was an adventure. Once they docked, all their worldly possessions were loaded onto an oxcart, the children bundled onto a public bus, and they made their way through the crowded streets to make a new home in Karachi.

Finding appropriate schools for Saleha and her sisters was difficult. Instead, tutors were brought in to homeschool them, and they were able to supplement their limited instruction with access to a relative's small library, where Saleha read everything she could get her hands on. As she got older, even her father recognized that her intellect was superior. If there was a big decision to be made in the house, Sadiq would declare, "Go ask Saleha what she thinks."

Saleha's excellence at her home studies propelled her first to college, then to graduate school. While at university she joined the American Friends Service Committee, a Quaker organization founded during World War I to aid war victims and promote social justice around the world, and became the Pakistani correspondent for their youth newsletter. At a Quaker meeting, she met a visiting American professor who encouraged her to pursue her studies in the United States. This planted a seed. She had already planned to sit for an exam that would award her a SEATO (Southeast Asia Treaty Organization) scholarship to the University of Manila in the Philippines. In the room where the exam took place, most of the other applicants that day were men, and Saleha could see in their eyes their resentment: *If this woman gets the scholarship, she'll only be taking it away from me and I have a family to support.* When the results were announced, out of the many students, male and female, who'd applied from all of West Pakistan that year, the recipient of the single scholarship was Saleha Mahmood from Karachi. Within weeks she learned that she had also been awarded a Fulbright to study in America and that she had been accepted at all the universities to which she had applied. While her advisor told her to choose the SEATO scholarship, as it was considered a national honor, she chose the Fulbright and University of Pennsylvania.

Scandal ensued. Local relatives were horrified that her parents had allowed this to happen. "You're sending your unmarried daughter *where*? For *what*?" Some of them tried to persuade her parents to marry her off before she went, to protect her honor as a woman living abroad, but Saleha refused. Marriage was no longer the only path for the women in my family.

When Saleha boarded the plane to Philadelphia, she was the first person in her family to travel to the United States. She had less than $100 in her pocket, one suitcase, and no winter coat. Just a determined spirit, a hunger for knowledge, and an open heart.

In all these stories, the one thing that stands out to me is this: the impact of one person's choice. That's obviously true in the case of leaders who make decisions that alter the course of world events: Cyril Radcliffe sits down and draws a line on a map, and six months later a million people are dead, families and whole cities have been torn apart, and the largest migration in human history is underway. That's astonishing. But on another scale, the decisions individuals make about their private lives, like a young girl's demand that she be taken to school in defiance of prevailing cultural norms, also have surprising—and long-lasting—consequences. It may have taken a few generations, but the path Fatima pioneered for her descendants took them—us—to places she likely never even imagined.

* * * *

When she arrived at the Penn campus, Saleha found a room in a row house that looked onto Chestnut Street. Lonely and still adjusting to this new world, she would stare out the room's little window. Whenever she saw two people walking together she would think, *Those people are so lucky. They know each other.*

At a dinner in the home of a fellow Pakistani student she'd met soon after she arrived, she walked into the living room and encountered an older couple and a slight man sitting in the corner who seemed to hold the attention of the whole room. As soon as this man noticed her, he said with a puckish look, "Sooo, you have come from Pakistan." *Clearly an Indian*, she thought from his tone. As the dinner wore on, she listened to him talk with both nuance and clarity even when discussing the most provocative issues like the complicated state of affairs between their two countries. By the end of the evening, she had concluded he was the most self-possessed, dynamic, and interesting person she had ever met. She was offered a ride home by the other couple, and as she was getting in the car, the elegant man approached her. He handed her a card that said: "In case of emergency." It had a phone number and the name Zain handwritten on it. He smiled and walked away. She was twenty-four years old, raised as a respectable Pakistani Muslim woman, and a man had never so audaciously approached her, let alone given her his phone number.

A few weeks later, Saleha walked out of a routine doctor's checkup with some unsettling medical results. She had been told that she might have heart issues in her future. On the sidewalk, "in case of emergency" Zain happened to be walking by.

"Ms. Mahmood, are you okay?" he stopped and asked.

Alone in a new country, with no family or friends nearby, feeling anxious and uncertain, she told him she was just coming from the student health center. Zain took the paper with her test results from her hands.

"There is nothing wrong with your heart," he said tenderly. "Let's go for a walk."

Saleha wore a whisper-thin chiffon sari every day, her long hair down to her hips; Zain, his Nehru jacket, and a short, neatly trimmed beard. Though they must have been an exotic sight on the Penn campus, by all accounts they were happy there and felt right at home. They took walks, had picnics, enjoyed nights out at the local Pagano's pizzeria, and talked endlessly.

When the time came to propose marriage, Zain asked an older cousin who had migrated to Pakistan after Partition to visit Saleha's parents in Karachi and ask for her hand in marriage. By then, his cousin Ahmed was not only a well-known author but also a diplomat, having established Pakistan's first embassy in China and served as its first chargé d'affaires, so his bringing the proposal carried some weight. The message he presented was simply "If you think anything of me, Zain is ten times better. He will make your daughter happy." In the end, that's all that mattered. But a Pakistani girl marrying an Indian man? That was complicated.

In 1965, less than two decades since Partition, there were distinct new countries, both untested democracies. They had been in a heavily armed military standoff, and now border skirmishes between India and Pakistan had erupted into full-scale conflict over control of the territories of Jammu and Kashmir. Neither country provided a safe haven for an Indian and Pakistani to live together in peace as a married couple. Saleha's parents must have known that giving consent meant their daughter could never return to live in Pakistan.

That summer, after marrying and settling into a new apartment on campus, Saleha and Zain sent a letter to the U.S. State Department. As recipients of the Fulbright scholarship, they applied for a waiver to remain in the United States, and it was granted. Years later, when I worked at the State Department in Washington, DC, it struck me that it was this very institution, and the values it embodied, that anchored our family in America, enabling me to have truly the most incredible life.

When Zain completed his doctoral studies in American Civilization at Penn and received an offer for a faculty position at Western Michigan University, he and Saleha loaded a tiny U-Haul trailer, hitched it to the back of their emerald-green 1967 Dodge Dart, and headed west out of Philly on I-76 with their newborn, my brother Hassan, off to make their new home in the American Midwest. There they would have two more children, Hadeel and then, eighteen months later, me.

A decade later, they were off to the next unknown—this time to start a new life in Saudi Arabia.

GAZELLE

Our home in Jeddah overflowed with houseplants. Each day my father would walk around and talk to them as he watered the soil or pruned withered leaves. Later, when we moved into a house with a garden, he planted pink bougainvillea and jasmine flowers. On the evenings when the jasmine bloomed, my father would pick a few and place them on my mother's pillow. "Thank you, *mere jan*," she would say, using the affectionate Urdu phrase that means "my life."

Even the small saplings Abbu brought back from other countries managed to survive the soaring temperatures, a humid ninety degrees Fahrenheit and higher many days, with brief winters when the temperatures dipped down into the seventies. He would tell us that people are just like plants, and that a plant is only as good as its roots. "If you cut off its roots and plant it elsewhere, however good this new location might be, the plant will wither away. If the roots are preserved, nourished, any change of environment—winter, summer, storms, and frost—makes no difference."

When my parents picked up and left Michigan for what was supposed to be a yearlong stay, it was 1977. In 1975, Saudi Arabia's moderate and popular King Faisal had been assassinated by his nephew for his liberal views; he had allowed girls' schools to be built and satellites to bring radio and TV stations into Saudi homes. So the Saudi Arabia we moved to was still convulsing, as was the wider Middle East. Throughout the region there were regime changes. Protests in the streets. More assassinations. Civil wars. Cultural revolutions slowly shifting the sands toward more conservative, fundamentalist outlooks and agendas.

The Hundred Days War in Lebanon would erupt in 1978, leaving much of Beirut, once known as the "Paris of the Middle East," in rubble. After being defeated in a war with Israel, Egypt became the first Arab nation to sign a peace treaty with that country in 1979, but that did not lessen the tension between Palestinians and Jews within Israel's borders. The Israeli-Palestinian conflict was ongoing, with attacks and counterattacks perpetrated by both sides. In 1979, Iran overthrew its last ruling Shah, and militant students overran the U.S. embassy in Tehran, taking fifty-two hostages. That very same year, we lived through the siege of Makkah, the holiest site in the Muslim world. The two-week-long assault by several hundred armed gunmen led to the slaughter of hundreds of worshippers and stunned the Islamic world. Makkah was only an hour's drive from our little apartment in Jeddah, a port city and Saudi Arabia's commercial capital on the country's western edge. My parents watched the siege from afar, horrified, along with much of the rest of the world.

Life in Jeddah was very different from what we were accustomed to in the U.S. In contrast to the freedoms of a typical suburban American childhood, my siblings and I now faced barriers of all kinds—physical, social, and cultural. Some we overcame, some we came to love, some were immovable. Because of the heat, we were shuttled from an air-conditioned home to an air-conditioned car to air-conditioned schools to air-conditioned malls or restaurants or friends' houses and then back home, falling asleep to the hum of loud air-conditioner units at night.

My parents lamented the amount of time we spent in artificial air, but we were limited in the places we could be outdoors. The patch of dust in front of our building was often visited by wild dogs, and there were few public playgrounds. My parents did take us often to the beach, where we ran along the Corniche, the longest uninterrupted strip of coast in the region. In the newer part of the city, the Corniche was lined with restaurants, gated mansions, and large shopping malls, as well as amusement parks, *shawarma* stands, and ice cream shops, and dotted with huge, modernist public sculptures by artists from around the world. By the time I was ten and Hadeel twelve, passersby would complain to my parents that we girls shouldn't be giggling on the swings, playing so freely in public, so we'd end up on a bench that abutted the beach, watching Hassan play in the sand. Hassan could grab a ball and run outside to find neighborhood boys to play soccer or ride bikes with, but women and girls didn't wander around Saudi Arabia without an escort and without a set destination. I would watch our pet cat, Tiger, come and go as she pleased, sometimes disappearing for months at a time, and wonder what it was like to have that kind of freedom.

Mornings in Jeddah began with the sound of the call to prayer from the nearby mosque piercing the stillness of predawn, then a short while later a second, briefer call. I would gather the sheets around me and catch some more sleep in the room I shared with Hadeel. Our modest, fully furnished two-bedroom apartment was brand-new faculty housing, the only building in the neighborhood that had Western-style kitchens, with a stove, refrigerator, and built-in cabinets; its windows looked out onto a looming privacy wall that surrounded the building. Hassan slept in the small dining room off the kitchen, closed off by one of the curtain rods from Balad. Two years after our arrival in Saudi Arabia, when my younger sister, Heba, was born, and my parents were able to hire help, they converted our small balcony into a room for the nanny. Some mornings, I would hear my parents rustle around in the hallway, the tap running as they performed the ablution before prayer, then the kettle whistling as my mom prepared tea, the juicer whirring as my father made carrot and apple juice. During the workweek, Saturday through Wednesday, we dressed for school in our gray wool uniforms.

When we first arrived in Jeddah, there were no English medium schools, so my father joined a group of parents working together to establish the fledgling Manarat Jeddah International School. The curriculum was based on schools in the UK, and additionally we had weekly Islamic Studies, Arabic, and Qur'an classes. My brother studied in the boys' English section and my sisters and I in the girls'. For most of the day, and in most environments, we spoke in English. Still, my parents were determined that we understand multiple languages. Some days, we would come home from school and our parents would say, "We are only speaking Arabic today." Another day it would be Urdu. On those days they wouldn't respond unless we spoke in those languages.

Every morning when Hadeel and I ran through the school's front gate, we would be surrounded by girls of all nationalities and backgrounds, for the school was truly international, as its name indicated. The English section comprised mostly the children of professional expatriates—doctors, engineers, professors—who came from around the world. There were no World History classes, but we did learn Islamic history and the story of the founding of Saudi Arabia. How Abdulaziz bin Saud created a sovereign nation state, an absolute monarchy, over the course of the early twentieth century, after forming alliances with tribal and Bedouin leaders across the Arabian peninsula. How his ancestor Muhammad ibn Saud had negotiated the agreement with the religious leader Muhammad ibn Abd al-Wahhab that allowed Abdulaziz to run the state affairs as both King and Custodian of the Two Holy Mosques, while it was left to the Wahhabi clerics, who adhered to a conservative form of Islam, to run all religious affairs.

In Qur'an class, we learned to memorize the text, to pronounce it perfectly, and to understand its meaning. In Islamic Studies, we learned about our Prophet Muhammad, the final messenger sent by God. We learned that Christians and Jews were our fellow "people of the book." We learned about the various principles of Sunni Islam and the specific teachings of the different imams who interpreted the scripture—Hanbali (from whom the conservative school of jurisprudence followed by the Wahhabi clerics was derived), Shafai, Maliki, Hanafi. When I asked my parents if we followed a certain imam, they told us none, just stick to the original text of the Qur'an, the narrative traditions, or *hadith* as we called them, and use your common sense.

I came from a family of practicing Muslims whose faith was central to their everyday lives. My parents didn't force us to follow as much as show us by example. Every month or so, we would visit the nearby city of Makkah. There at the Masjid al-Haram, the holiest mosque in the Muslim world, I would pray, prostrating myself in front of the Kaaba, asking God to bless my parents and loved ones with good health and then requesting whichever toy or doll I was longing for at the moment. I would perform *tawaf*, the seven circumambulations around the black cube, while repeating the same memorized supplications over and over again. Then we would go to the Safa and Marwa hills—two large mounds within the walls of the grand mosque, connected by long white marble walkways, walking seven times back and forth between them, which then completed the tradition of *Umrah*, part of centuries' old rituals based on the path walked by one of Islam's most respected matriarchs, Hajrah. These were motions I had learned when I was five or six years old, and they had been repeated so often they were almost instinctive. Close to the end of our visits, my little feet would ache, and my mind would wander to the chicken *shawarma* and fries we would be picking up on the way home.

One of the greatest gifts of growing up in the Middle East was always feeling a secure sense of belonging. We call it the *ummah*, the ever-present community. It is a living, breathing organism in Islamic societies. Everyone is family, and generosity is pro forma behavior. If you went to a party and admired your hostess's earrings, they would be pulled out and plopped into your palm. If you singled out a particular dessert as sensational, you earned yourself a doggie bag. You could protest and protest that you could not accept, and they would insist and insist that you must. Not accepting would be an insult. When there's a wedding, everyone celebrates. When there's a funeral, everyone mourns. For both occasions, your house is filled with food, company, and communal prayer. *Zakat*, a small percentage of your annual income that goes to charity, is mandatory. Whatever you have, you share. Standing in solidarity, both in joy and in heartache, is a social responsibility and from the moment we arrived we were embraced.

In my immediate circle, I knew girls who were Saudi, American, Indian, Pakistani, Bengali, Kuwaiti, South African, Afghan, Nigerian, Egyptian, Palestinian, Sri Lankan, and Turkish, along with girls like me with parents of different nationalities. For years, Saudi men had been traveling abroad to study, and some had brought home foreign wives. It was common to meet girls with Saudi fathers and American mothers, alternating between two worlds. They'd spend the school year veiled in public and peppering their speech with "*Insha'Allah*," which means "if God wills it," as reflexively as American girls use the word "like." Then they'd spend summers with their maternal grandparents in the United States, wearing shorts and going to church on Sundays.

Our teachers, also from all over the world, brought their diverse perspectives and languages into our daily classrooms. Our headmistress was a Black woman from Baltimore, Maryland, my Biology teacher Sri Lankan, my Math teacher British, and my P.E. teacher Egyptian. We all lived together in our own chaotic normalcy, all of us transplants who had made our new home in Jeddah.

After school, we girls would gather in the courtyard to play tag, braid one another's hair, gossip, and wait. The girls weren't allowed to leave school on their own, men weren't allowed inside, and our mothers couldn't pick us up because women weren't allowed to drive. When my father's car pulled up, I gathered my bookbag, covered myself, and ran out as fast as I could. He would say that his fondest memory from my childhood was seeing me leap toward him as he waited in the car at pickup time; that I reminded him of a gazelle.

My parents furnished our interior world with warmth and openness. Just as in Michigan, our home was often filled with guests. Anyone coming from overseas to travel to Makkah would land at Jeddah's international airport and pass right by our house. Some people stopped in for a meal, others for a few nights. Academics visiting for conferences my father was organizing would carry on discussions with him late into the night. Family members from the United States or Europe sometimes stayed months. My mom just reorganized our sleeping arrangements, moving mattresses onto the floor of my parents' room for us three girls and giving the guests our room. So long as I could avoid the cockroaches (which were ever present), the lizards (who were terrifying nighttime visitors), and the mice (who came and went depending on the time of year), sleeping on the floor didn't bother me one bit.

If somebody was visiting for tea or a meal, my dad would say, "We have a guest in the living room. Go greet them and talk to them about your studies and your poetry." I would shake walking down the long hallway from my bedroom. It felt too grown-up, too scary, to me. Other times it was, "Call the airline to see if we can change our flights from Bangkok to Tokyo and stop first in Jakarta. And don't forget to ask about the ticket prices." My eight-year-old self stuttered every time. But I did it. We all did. And over time, without even realizing it, I walked around with a certain confidence. While girls and women might have been treated as dependents by much of our extended universe, in the Abedin home, we were taught to depend first and foremost on ourselves. My father's home office was always a place where we were expected to contribute: first by just sitting quietly and reading while he worked, then by sharpening pencils and opening mail, and then, as we grew older, by filing, faxing, typing mailing labels or letters, and eventually proofreading the articles he wrote and edited.

Discipline and moderation were drilled into us from our earliest days. Our father always encouraged us to follow nature's path—to be outdoors as much as possible, to eat well, to try alternative homeopathic remedies for any aches before reaching for the medicine cabinet. We could have a sweet treat after dinner each night, but only after we had eaten an equal amount of fruit first. We could drink soda, but we were also expected to consume fresh juice, a handful of almonds, and a spoonful of honey every single morning. It wasn't ever one or the other, it was a balance of both.

The four of us had specific duties assigned to us. Mine was making my father's tea at 5 p.m. sharp every day. One day, I snuck out to a friend's house to play while my parents were taking their afternoon siesta. I figured there were plenty of other siblings around to make tea. While there, I got a message that my parents had called and I was to go home immediately. When I arrived, my mother reminded me that my responsibility was to make Abbu's tea at 5 p.m. and he was still waiting. I silently made the tea. My parents' lesson was clear. When someone expects something from you, you'd better come through.

*   *   *   *

So how did one year turn into forever? Well, after my parents' first sabbatical year came to an end, their university asked them to stay for one more year, offering the same generous benefits as they had initially. My parents agreed, and they would end up doing so again and again, long after the first sabbatical ended. It was a challenge, and an exciting one for them.

My father was assigned as an advisor to the president of King Abdulaziz University and was charged with developing and promoting programs and communications with academic and research institutions worldwide. He organized international conferences and lectures with visiting academics and professors, focusing on contemporary issues just as the Saudis were opening up to the world. He was able to launch a research institution, the Institute of Muslim Minority Affairs, head-quartered in England, with a home office in Jeddah, which studied the conditions of Muslims living as minorities in countries throughout the world and published a biannual academic journal with the straight-forward title: *Journal of Muslim Minority Affairs*. My mother taught Sociology courses, modernizing the required reading with up-to-date textbooks and creating opportunities for her female students to study abroad, then a rarity for Saudi women. Whenever we would run into my parents' colleagues or students, at an airport or strolling through a mall, they would often end their conversations by turning to us kids and saying, "You are so lucky to have him as your father," or, "Your mother is my inspiration." My siblings and I would shrug and go back to doing whatever we were doing. To us, our parents were just our parents. But hearing these comments made me walk with my back a bit straighter and a constant desire to make them proud.

My parents had lived across two continents and four countries in the span of a little more than a decade. For them this was just the beginning of exploring the world and exposing their children to dif-ferent cultures and languages. The moment school was out and final exams were turned in, we were off. During one summer vacation we toured Austria, where we visited the gazebo from the film *The Sound of Music* and my sisters and I twirled in the wind, arms open wide, belting out "the hills are alive!" in our best Julie Andrews imitation. Another holiday we visited Japan, where my siblings and I insisted on eating only American food, compelling my parents to take us to the McDonald's for fish filets in Tokyo's Ginza district every day we were there. We toured Thailand and Malaysia, Indonesia and Singapore and Hong Kong, the acropolis in Greece, the blue mosque in Turkey, and also Disneyland in California. Each summer holiday also included a long stop in London for Abbu's work and to see family. All through Europe, we visited palaces and gardens and churches and monuments and more monuments and museum after museum.

On our travels to visit relatives in India and Pakistan, I learned more about my family's history. The irony of my father's life was that he loved India so much, but because of his marriage and, in later years, his health, he could not go home easily. When he met my mother, he was the consummate Indian patriot, but they didn't raise us that way. Only Americanness would allow us, their children, to move forward. In conversations about our identity, Abbu was clear: "You are an American and a Muslim."

Though I loved the sightseeing and the round-the-world adventures, which were often work trips for my father, I was always eager to get to my favorite part of every summer. It seemed like it always took forever, after we'd packed up our suitcases and boarded interminable flights, hopscotching across the globe, stopping at four in the morning on a layover in Shannon, Ireland, or Paris, France, or Athens, Greece. Whenever we landed, I would wake up groggy and bleary-eyed, no idea where we were or what time it was, and the first thing I would do was turn to my mother and ask, "Is it America yet?"

* * * *

Between my parents, I have fifty-four first cousins. Much of my mother's family, including her parents, came to live in Elmhurst, Queens, which had something we didn't know back in Jeddah: a neighborhood.

For lucky New York City kids, summer meant leaving the city. For me it meant racing through it with joy, chasing after the ice cream truck each and every night, gathering for watermelon and pizza parties at my aunt's picnic table in the small backyard carpeted with scrub grass. Most nights we sat on the front stoop of the redbrick row house, one that didn't look at a looming privacy wall but straight onto 74th Street, watching my cousins play stickball with the Polish and Italian neighborhood kids as the sun went down, the streetlights came on, and the long summer evenings seemed to stretch forever. Then we were called in for dinner, sweaty and thirsty. We dashed straight into the kitchen for glasses of cold tap water; in Jeddah, drinking water from the tap was unthinkable. After our parents went to bed, we would sneak down to the basement to watch TV late into the night.

Some nights we would sit by the side of my maternal grandmother, Mehboob, who had moved to the U.S. in the early seventies after all her children had migrated already. We loved to hear her tell us stories about her eight children. She was small and delicate, with eyes that had grayed with age, and waist-length silver hair, always neatly braided. She wore a chiffon sari every day, with a lightweight sweater to cover her arms on cool nights. I never saw her disheveled or informally dressed. She was perpetually ready to host any guest who might pop by to pay their respects to her, the matriarch of our family. If, as a little girl, she had not insisted on going to school in the back of an oxcart, I doubt all these highly educated, accomplished children of hers would ever have made it to America.

Many nights, she would pull treasures from a box beside her chair: a black-and-white photo of her handsome husband who had died when I was two, a letter she had received from my mother in the 1960s updating her on her life in Philadelphia, news articles about the work she had done as president of an organization in Pakistan where she advocated for expanded economic and social opportunities for women. For most of my childhood, the so-called "treasures" included tins of cookies and wrapped chocolates that always seemed to be in limitless supply. While her English was flawless, she often spoke to us in Urdu and would read aloud verses in Arabic or ask me to read them for her. She was exceedingly polite and well mannered, and she expected proper behavior from us too.

One summer, when I was about four, my parents left us in Queens while they made a quick trip to Kalamazoo. My aunt, worried that we would be upset, planned a special trip for us to see the Statue of Liberty and get ice cream. There is a picture somewhere from that summer day. A row of carefree little cousins holding ice cream cones in various stages of melting, all lined up in front of a chain-link fence, Lady Liberty in the background, unchanging, watching over us just as she had millions of other immigrants and first-generation kids before and would after.

When I was ten, my mother's family moved from Queens to a suburb in New Jersey. The neighborhood was filled with comfortable detached homes and green front lawns. No one locked their doors. Every morning of our summer stay, we'd dart around from one relative's home to another like pinballs, for swimming, pizza, swimming again, bike riding, horseback riding at a local stable, and going to the movies at a movie theater—another American novelty unheard of in Jeddah.

Each year we spent part of the summer at home in Kalamazoo, where my parents had kept our house and rented it out during the school year, before we made a stop in Montreal to visit my father's sister's home, where we could walk by ourselves down the street and play in the neighborhood park. Unveiled. Unfettered. I would hop onto one of the blue plastic seats, chains jangling as I jumped onto the swing, and start soaring. I'd pump really hard and push myself to go higher and higher, as high as I possibly could. No one told me to stop, to protect my modesty, to get off. It felt like flying. If I could fly, I could do anything.

No matter where we traveled in the world, we landed as Americans. It wasn't just a place that the word America represented, but a feeling. Freedom. Self-determination. Choice. That was true even in Saudi Arabia. I loved living there, but I don't know if I would look back on it so fondly if it had been the only life I'd ever known, had I not carried my American roots with me while I was there and elsewhere, had I not been certain that freedoms I couldn't enjoy in my current reality were just a flight away.

DRESSING GAMES

There is a crack in everything,
That's how the light gets in.
—Leonard Cohen

My mother never left the house without a perfectly put together outfit and subtle makeup, a dab of powder and neutral lipstick. The kinds of high fashion that I often saw on women at the parties and weddings we were invited to were beyond her means—and also her interest. But I loved looking at these women. I would stand in the entrance of the women's section of the grand halls and gawk at the magnificent peacock parade before me. Women would arrive swathed in black, peep-toe stilettos flashing below, then remove their *abayas* to reveal extraordinary designer clothing. Couture Yves St. Laurent gowns, Christian Dior shoes, and Chanel handbags, elaborately coiffed hair, eyes lined with thick kohl and mascara. On the street the women all looked like identical, shapeless beings, but once they were unveiled, it was a whole different story.

I loved playing dress-up in my mother's closet, trying on her long dresses when my parents were out. I would open her closet and dresser and make a pile on the bed of whatever I wanted to try on. My favorite gown was of teal taffeta, bought on sale at Sears—her thriftiness focused her shopping almost exclusively on the bargain sections—which she wore paired with a long pearl necklace and matching earrings. The fabric rustled as I walked around imagining myself as Anna Karenina wandering through the streets of Moscow.

My father's philosophy on clothes was that one's wardrobe should consist of only a few outfits that were well made and of good quality.

His closet was just like him, compact and immaculate: a few rows of color-coordinated suits and ties, a few drawers of neatly arranged shirts and socks, and two pairs of polished Bally shoes—one black, one brown—lined up just so. Because of his back, he had most of his clothes custom made by local tailors. Even at home, he wore dress pants and button-down shirts. Traveling abroad, he'd add a coat, scarf, and hat. That was how he dressed, whether he was going to work, going out to get the newspaper—or even going to the hospital. Because that's what my long, magically unsupervised afternoons of playing dress-up were—my father's twice weekly dialysis sessions.

Dialysis entails being hooked up by IV to a machine that essentially serves as an external kidney when your own kidneys can no longer properly function on their own. The dialysis machine cycles your blood out, ridding it of impurities and draining off excess fluids that your kidneys are no longer able to eliminate naturally, before recycling the blood back into your system. If the machine removes too much fluid, you're left with horrible muscle cramps, nausea, and vomiting. If the machine doesn't drain off enough, you can choke on the fluid in your lungs, literally drowning. Like chemotherapy, dialysis is the treatment that can be worse than the disease; it slowly kills you even while it's the only thing keeping you alive.

Just as the doctor in Kalamazoo had predicted, my father's kidneys failed almost ten years to the day after he was diagnosed, and now my mother accompanied him to long dialysis sessions. The most my parents ever told us was that my father had "a doctor's appointment."

One afternoon when I was around ten, I got so involved in playing and posing in my mother's gowns that I lost track of time. When I heard my parents walking in the door, I looked around the bedroom in a panic at my mom's clothes strewn across the entire bed, shoes scattered all over the floor, drawers gaping open, the perfume I had spritzed lingering in the air, and realized I had no time to clean up the right awful mess I had made.

My father walked into the bedroom. He looked weary and particularly bent over, but he smiled and said, "Hi Huma," as though it were any other day, seeming not even to notice the chaos. Then he slowly made his way around to his bedside table, which was stacked with novels and homeopathic medicine bottles, and added his watch and eyeglasses to the pile. He took off his chocolate-brown blazer, hung it neatly in the closet, and went to lie down, gently nudging aside the gowns to make space for himself on the bed.

Still worried that I might get in trouble, I tried to deflect my father's attention from the mess. "So," I blurted out, raising the dress to my knees so I could walk toward him without tripping, "what did the doctor say?"

"The doctor said my daughters are very beautiful," he replied, easing himself into bed.

As he closed his eyes, my mother came in to shoo me out. "Come on, let Abbu take a nap," she said, as if this were nothing more than his typical afternoon siesta. She said nothing of what had transpired at the hospital. Nor did she say anything about the lipstick or the pearls or the crumpled clothes on her bed.

I certainly never thought of my father as someone sick. I knew that he got tired a lot, that he had lots of doctor's appointments, and that, once dialysis started, he seemed to spend a lot of time at the hospital with my mother. Late one night, in that groggy space between sleep and wakefulness, I heard hushed voices in the hallway outside my room followed by the sound of the front door closing, but fell back to sleep before even realizing that my parents had left the house. Later, I learned that they'd had to go to the emergency room because my father couldn't stop vomiting in the aftermath of a dialysis session. Since he was in no condition to drive, my mother woke my fifteen-year-old brother to take them even though he barely knew how to drive and didn't have a driver's license. When morning came, it was like nothing had happened. Breakfast table chatter was about news of the day and plans for the weekend.

My father never betrayed the often excruciating pain he was in. My mother aided and abetted the illusion. She made everything look so easy. Whenever we were at an airport, airport staff would escort my dad in his wheelchair through security and help settle him in his business-class seat, where he'd be more comfortable, something my mother insisted on. Meanwhile, she would manage the four of us and all the luggage she had single-handedly packed through security, and then into our seats in coach. Once she finally dropped into her own seat, she would turn to us breathless, and say, "We are going to have the best time!"—never betraying what an effort it must have been to manage all that on her own. We would take turns visiting my father up front, to sit on his lap, eat his meals, ignore the smoke, and play with the seat controls. Back in coach, when the flight attendants approached with the meal carts, they'd look at my sisters and me and ask my mom, "Ma'am, what can I get for your boys?" a confirmation that the identical bowl haircuts she used to give all of us at home were too short! And before we deplaned, my mother always made sure to stash any unused plastic utensils in her purse to use later.

When I try to piece together the clues to understand what was really going on back then, I do remember that as much as my father doted on me as a child, he never picked me up. I have no memory of being carried in his arms, ever. He simply didn't have the strength or the stamina.

Other fathers kicked around soccer balls with their kids, but mine had his own special way of connecting with us. He let my sisters and me help pick out his wardrobe in the mornings. We knew all his outfits by heart. After laying his things out, we would leave him to get dressed, comb his hair, and dab on his Old Spice cologne. To me it was always just a game that we played. I never realized that he was often in too much pain or too weak to do this himself.

In August 1986, my father got on the kidney transplant waitlist in New York, which meant he had to remain in the U.S. and could not come home with us at the end of our summer vacation. I was eleven. My brother had just left for his freshman year in college in Massachusetts, and all of a sudden our very united family was now just three girls and one woman—flying back to Jeddah on our own. In my diary, I wrote that my only dream was for our family to be complete again.

A few months later, when a kidney suddenly became available, family friends called and suggested we girls move in with them while my mother went to New York to be with Abbu for the surgery. My sisters and I begged to stay home. We had Medina, our beloved Somali live-in housekeeper, along with a driver who had been hired years earlier after it became impossible to depend on my father to drive us everywhere. At thirteen, eleven, and seven years old, we believed we were three self-sufficient girls. School exams were coming up and we had desks and bookcases at home that we studied at every night, so my mother thanked our friends, but told them it would be too disruptive without our things.

The next morning the doorbell rang. Medina came into the kitchen and said, "*Doctora*, the moving truck is here." We all asked in unison, "What moving truck?" We crowded behind my mom while she talked to our driver who was at our door. "They said they were sent to pick up the children's furniture, something about desks and bookcases?" None of us needed further explanation. This was a typical gesture of generosity in our community of friends. *The children need their furniture to be comfortable? Okay, let's move the furniture.*

By the time we had been driven to our temporary home, our furniture had been reassembled and our clothes were neatly put away in huge mahogany closets. Our hostess, "aunt" to us, made delicious eggs each morning before school, and nights sometimes ended with my "uncle" bringing in bags of takeout American fast food—the height of a treat in Jeddah—followed by Baskin-Robbins ice cream. Their house smelled of a comforting, heady incense. Most important, it was a home where everything seemed normal and safe. If Heba woke up scared in the middle of the night, she'd pad down the hall to sleep with my aunt, and my uncle would move to another bedroom. We had no sense of the trauma my parents were dealing with thousands of miles away.

That winter break, because my father was still not well enough to travel, Hadeel, Heba, and I joined our parents and extended family in New Jersey. Since we were to be there for a prolonged time, my mother enrolled us at the local public school after the New Year. The work was easy, all material I had covered the previous year in school; but the social adjustment was hard. I had become the kid in the class whose hand shot up every time the teacher asked a question, initially oblivious to the eye-rolling all around me. I dreaded gym, where I wore modest, loose T-shirts and pants, in contrast to the fitted gym outfits of the other kids. They played sports, like dodgeball, that were unfamiliar to me. I didn't know the rules and inevitably some other kid would yell, "Oh, come on, move!" A window, perhaps, into what life might have been like had we moved back to the U.S. permanently. I was relieved when my mom took us back to Jeddah a few months later.

After about six months, Abbu had recovered enough to be able to rejoin us there. His energy and color slowly improved, but the prescriptions and pill bottles on his bedside table only proliferated: steroids and painkillers and immunosuppressants. Next to all of his homeopathic medicines, his daily teaspoon of honey and handful of blanched almonds, he had a whole new medical regimen, required of all transplant recipients. I particularly remember ciclosporin, which he hated because it both burned his stomach and suppressed his immune system, making him more susceptible to catching colds or other viruses. He would line up all his medicines in the morning and take them one after another, often letting me measure and squirt the whitish liquid from the syringe into his glass of milk. One day, he raised the glass halfway, as though he was making a toast, and just stared at it.

"I am drinking this poison to save my life," he said in an ironic voice directed at my mom as she sat next to him. He swallowed it quickly and then went back to reading his paper.

HAVING CHOICES

Writing is one of the most ancient forms of prayer. To write is to believe communication is possible, that other people are good, that you can awaken their generosity and their desire to do better.

—Fatima Mernissi

The years following Abbu's surgery and return to Saudi Arabia were like those that preceded—filled with school and friends and books and our world travels. But then in August 1990 I spent the better part of the month sitting on the living room floor at an aunt's house in New Jersey, glued to the television, watching a war unfold in the region I was returning to in a matter of weeks. CNN International would become a fixture in our home, and its arrival couldn't have been timelier. After Iraqi president Saddam Hussein invaded his small oil-rich neighbor, Kuwait, on August 2, Saudi Arabia was on the front lines diplomatically and, potentially, militarily, as its northeast border abutted both Iraq and Kuwait. I followed the news of Saudi King Fahd meeting with international leaders, including the U.S. defense secretary, Dick Cheney, and the quick alignment of allies to push back against Saddam.

Once the United States and allies formally declared war in early 1991 and launched missile strikes and then ground movement, we found ourselves in the middle of Operation Desert Storm. Jeddah, on the western side of the country, wasn't in any immediate line of fire so, for the most part, life for us was unchanged. There were a few noticeable differences though. Adjusted school hours. Occasional evacuation drills. More American soldiers around the American consulate building, local government facilities, and palaces. Police randomly pulling over cars, checking identification.

We kept the news on all day and followed every update. Late one night, watching TV, I saw an attractive, dark-haired woman reporting from the ground in Iraq. She flinched from time to time when there was a mortar shelling somewhere in the distance but otherwise proceeded, seemingly unflappable, as she reported the news. I had seen female presenters on television in Saudi Arabia before, dressed modestly in black, with headscarves, always reading a script from a teleprompter. She was different; a real reporter bringing us news from the front, wearing khakis and a flak jacket, the only female I noticed among all the male reporters. She was confident and sure of herself.

Her name was Christiane Amanpour. I felt a kinship with her for reasons I couldn't quite articulate. If she had been a blue-eyed blonde named Mary Smith, I might not have had the same reaction, but she looked like she came from my part of the world. Right then I decided I was going to be a journalist like her, spotlighting injustice around the globe. I was fifteen and I felt like I had found my future path.

I always believed I would grow up and do something special, have a job that would have impact, that the world was wide open to me. This was not necessarily typical for girls in Saudi or South Asian Muslim families. Even with three daughters, my parents never prioritized saving money for weddings, as our friends' moms had done for years, but there would always be money for education. The message was "You can do whatever you want. You can live wherever you want. All we require is that you be educated." When Christiane Amanpour showed up on my television, she gave a real shape to my amorphous ambitions. She was also doing something else that captivated me: storytelling.

When Abbu would return from his travels to London and the U.S. several times a year, he always brought books back for us. He would number them in the order we should read them, L1, L2, and so on. *Great Expectations*, *The Brothers Karamazov*, *Portrait of a Lady*, *Pride and Prejudice*, *Tess of the D'Urbervilles*, *The Turn of the Screw*, *Anna Karenina*. I loved reading and devoured every book in sight. One year, when I was nine or ten, the book he labeled number one was *Silas Marner* by George Eliot. The material was beyond my grasp. When I read the introduction, I learned that George Eliot was the pen name for a female writer named Mary Ann Evans. Puzzled, I asked why she didn't just put her own name on the cover. Abbu told me that in the Victorian era, women weren't taken seriously as writers, so she used a male name. "Don't worry," he assured me. "When you write your book, you will use your own name and everyone will take it seriously."

As a teenager, whatever shyness I'd had when I was young evaporated. When guests were visiting, I would announce, "I have a new poem. You want to hear it?" I was already pulling out the folded paper from my pocket before my audience had the chance to respond. The poetry was neither good nor memorable, but my parents encouraged me by clapping loudly and saying "excellent!" while my siblings just rolled their eyes. Sitting in his armchair, smoking his pipe, my father would beam. He told me that the single greatest power I held was the power of my pen, if I used it wisely.

I also loved storytelling through collages of images I patched together from the Arab, American, and European magazines I collected. I covered my bedroom walls with these creations. A woman in a Dior gown pasted into the ruins of an Andalusian palace, alongside a quote from *Time* magazine. Arabic words glued onto Wild West landscapes, or Asian images onto a desert campsite. When we flew back from the U.S. to Jeddah, we'd pack as much of America into our suitcases as we could, and the magazines were part of that treasure trove, which might also include the latest Bon Jovi and Boyz II Men cassette tapes, videocassettes of the latest American movies, new books, and bottles of American shampoo, mousse, and lotions.

Landing in Jeddah, I would pray that the Saudi customs agents wouldn't search my bags and confiscate any of my precious acquisitions, especially the magazines. If the customs agents did find them, I would watch nervously as they flipped through the pages and ripped out any images they decided were offensive—women wearing bathing suits or outfits with a lot of cleavage showing—or sometimes just tossed whole magazines into the trash. As the years went by, perhaps they had to listen to too many women protesting that they were losing half an article every time a page was ripped out, so the agents resorted to blacking out the offending images with permanent markers.

Whatever the customs agents thought, my friends and classmates forged our friendships around most things American. We traded copies of Nancy Drew novels. We showed off our Trapper Keeper school binders, our new headbands, and the white Calvin Klein button-down shirts we'd wear with our school uniforms. Our bedrooms were plastered with the latest posters of American actors like Luke Perry, and we were always at one another's houses watching the movies and listening to the music we had brought back into the country.

My friend Summer, who had a Saudi father and American mother, was fun-loving and mischievous. She was always coming up with crazy adventures for us to try, and I was always her willing accomplice. Sumaiyah, half-American, half-Yemeni, was the beautiful one. I called her Sumaiyah with the cat eyes, and we imagined all our friends' brothers had a crush on her. My Nigerian friend Fatima was usually the responsible one, always saying, "Hey guys, maybe we shouldn't be doing this," with her teasing bright eyes. She wore thin-rimmed glasses and very shiny lip gloss. Her father had four wives, and she had lots of siblings, and they had their own family mosque on their property. Her house became our main hangout, a place of adventure, a place of security, a place filled with laughter and good food. It was a world of satin and gold and marble. Each of the mothers had her own identical floor, the only difference being the color of the drapes and carpets. A couple of times after school, we would look out the window and see a limousine pull up to the front entrance carrying one of the young Saudi princes, who would come to hang out with Fatima's brothers. We heard that the limousine was always stocked with Hubba Bubba bubblegum, which I had never seen in Jeddah, and every so often we tried to peek inside, but never quite managed to.

We named ourselves "The Four C's: The Culturally Confused Class Cut-ups," and like all teenagers, we rebelled. The rules we rebelled against were particular to Saudi Arabia, and as such—by Western standards at least—rather rigid and prohibitive. Probably my worst offense was experimenting with cigarettes, which lasted approximately three days, until I was caught smoking on the roof by a neighbor. When he reported my transgression to my parents, it was less about the fact that he'd seen a young woman smoking than about seeing an *uncovered* woman smoking.

Once we entered our teen years, we never went out in public without an *abaya*. But even that didn't prevent street harassment. It was part of everyday life. As we got older, my friends and I would go out as a large group, either to the popular Tahlia Street to eat fast food or grab an ice cream cone, or to wander through one of the newly opened malls. As we walked down the street, cars would pull up beside us with young men heckling and screaming and cheering. We'd ignore them, cover our faces, giggle, link arms with one another. If we were in a car, they would toss pieces of paper with their phone numbers toward our windows. Sometimes we'd toss the phone number back to show we weren't interested. Sometimes we'd keep it to let them think we were. It didn't matter, because we were never going to call or meet them. It was all just a game of pursuit, hormones raging without any other permissible outlet. We would roll our eyes or try to laugh it off. Nobody ever interceded on our behalf to make the young men stop or go away. And it was always incumbent on *us* to be the ones to leave, to find a way to simply disappear.

One day I got so fed up that I typed up a flyer advertising "counseling" services for girls. "CALL 1-800-TAHLIA-MANIA," it read, a very American joke because nobody in Saudi knew what a 1-800 number was. I handed it out in class and everyone had a laugh about it. That was really all we could do. What other options did we have to change the way young men behaved, or the way society tolerated their behavior?

From time to time, we endured the flip side of the coin, the *muttawwa*—the religious police whose job it was to enforce the morality laws. We'd be walking with our friends, and we'd hear a man or woman's voice reprimanding us, "*Cover your face!*" sometimes accompanied by a flick of the switch, grazing our ankles or shoes.

In private, though, we could be freer, test the boundaries of our behavior without scrutiny. I loved to go with Summer to her family's beach house in Obhur, less than an hour north of Jeddah. Being on a private beach was like being in a private home. We could wear less modest clothing there—some women walked around in bathing suits—and, more important, we could go into the water.

Tied to a narrow, creaking floating dock at the front of their house were a few Jet Skis and a small speedboat. From the dock I could see miles and miles of gleaming water. This was my pathway to freedom. If we wanted to go out on one of the Jet Skis, we had to ride on the back with Summer's brother or a male cousin driving; but soon we managed to convince Summer's brother to let us go by ourselves. Hopping on those Jet Skis was our one chance to just *go*.

One day when I was fifteen, Summer and I each took a Jet Ski and rode side by side at the fastest speed, straight toward the horizon. When we were far away from shore, we spun circles around each other. All of a sudden the sun was in my eyes and I couldn't see Summer. We collided head-on and were both thrown into the water. I saw stars blurring my line of vision. Summer's Jet Ski started sinking, and mine started to float away.

We could barely make out the shoreline—tiny dots in the distance. Reveling in the freedom of not having to wear *abayas*, we hadn't worn anything on top of our T-shirts, including life vests. We treaded water until I reached the point where I felt I couldn't keep going. Summer, who was the stronger swimmer, said, "Just hold on to me." I wrapped my arms around her neck, shaking uncontrollably, unbearably cold and terrified.

Out of nowhere, a small speedboat appeared, first a speck on the horizon and then growing larger. Soon, a life preserver was in the water, which we both grabbed onto, and Summer's cousin, who had come looking for us, pulled each of us into the boat. My body felt heavy, like deadweight. I lay on my back staring at the sky, feeling like I had just overcome something I didn't quite understand. From time to time, I would cough up the water I was convinced I would never rid my lungs of, my throat feeling the salty, raw burn.

If this was a visceral lesson that the freedom my friends and I so intensely desired came at a cost, it didn't exactly get through. The fact that I had choices about how I lived and what I would become was a constant in my upbringing. One that I appreciated more as I noted the lives of other girls I knew—some who had to do as they were told, others who had little choice about pursuing a higher education, or whom to marry and when. I also saw that for some, these paths were freely embraced. You never know what choice looks like.

There was a family my parents had known since their days in Philadelphia who had also ended up in Jeddah. When I was eight, my parents began sending me to their apartment for extra Qur'an lessons. The wife never left the house without being fully covered from head to toe, including her face.

One afternoon, I was with her in the living room reviewing some new verses when she opened the sliding door that led to the main hallway. Standing before her was a man who was not her husband. She let out a loud shriek, slammed the door shut, then took off her slippers and started slapping her face and the top of her head with them. She tried to compose herself, but our lesson was basically over.

I sat on the couch a few feet away, suddenly afraid of her. I understood the reason for her reaction but not the intensity, which seemed far out of proportion to the incident. There is a *hadith* that states "actions are but by intention." If you intend to do something wrong, that's one thing. But if it's an accident, which clearly this was, why would she think she did anything wrong? Why such an extreme reaction? I told my parents I didn't want to go back to her house after that incident, and they never forced me to.

Years later, when I was looking through old photo albums I saw a picture of my Qur'an teacher at my parents' wedding reception in Philadelphia. She was wearing a minidress, and black cat-eye eyeliner, and stared confidently right into the camera. In the same album, I saw aunts in college in Beirut wearing sleeveless shift dresses, midriff-baring tops, and short cigarette pants, women I had only ever seen in long blouses with loose-fitting pants. "Is *this* my Qur'an teacher? Are these my aunts?"

"Oh, yes," my mom said. "Back then, that's what everyone wore."

At the time, I couldn't reconcile how you went from wearing a micromini to hitting yourself over the head because a man saw you unveiled by accident. It was only later that I understood what a deeply personal choice this is for some Muslim women. Also that over the intervening years, there had been a concerted effort by conservatives to bring back the veil, which had succeeded particularly well in countries like Egypt, Turkey, and Syria.

Many women of my faith wear the *hijab*. The origin of the practice is rooted in a story from the early days when Islam was flourishing in Arabia as a new religion with an uncertain future. Some men alleged that Ayesha, the wife of Prophet Muhammad, had been unfaithful to him while they were traveling. An accusation against someone viewed as an important recorder of divine revelation and a leader in the community in her own right could potentially destabilize the entire nascent faith community.

Shortly thereafter, a new Qur'anic verse was revealed: "O Prophet, tell your wives and your daughters and the women of the believers to draw their cloaks close round them when traveling so that they will be recognized" (Qur'an 33:59). The Qur'an goes further, instructing that *both* men and women were required to be modest in their respective appearances. For women, "they should not display their beauty and ornaments except what must ordinarily appear thereof; that they should draw their veils over their bosoms and not display their beauty" (Qur'an 24:31). How to define beauty and what would "ordinarily" appear? For the Prophet's wives, it meant covering their hair and bodies and sometimes even their faces in loose garments, leaving only their hands and feet exposed. Since they were viewed as the best of women, many other women followed.

The verses in the Qur'an about modesty were not just about clothing and hair. They pertained to our code of conduct; how we talk, act, interact with the world. At its inception, the practice of *hijab* was designed to protect women from false accusation. I knew girls who were automatically expected to cover, who didn't even have the choice, and others who consciously made the choice themselves. Some took their *hijab* off after a few years or after moving abroad. Others still wear the *hijab* today regardless of where they live. To me, the key is having the choice.

* * * *

Since our school was British, it ended in tenth grade, and so I graduated from high school in 1991, just before my sixteenth birthday. I began taking some English Literature courses at my parents' university. Most excitingly, I started traveling overseas with my father for his work, serving as his scheduler and assistant. I also got my first part-time paying job as a photographer's assistant. One day the photographer mentioned that we were booked for an engagement party. The last name was a familiar one to me, a well-known large Saudi family.

When we arrived, the aroma of sandalwood greeted us along with the sound of ululating African women whose beautiful voices were part of every wedding celebration. We started setting up near the main staircase. After guests began arriving, the groom emerged and congregated with a few people at the bottom of the stairs. He was wearing a white *thobe*, a camel-colored cloak, and a formal headdress, a confident smile plastered on his face. Then the bride-to-be appeared at the top of the staircase dressed in a slim purple satin dress with poufy shoulders, hair swept up in a bun, and lots of dark makeup. She descended the stairs flanked by her parents, and was presented with a diamond necklace and earrings with stones the size of the nail on my pinky finger. In exchange, the groom was presented with a Rolex watch. Everyone laughed nervously as he slid off his old Rolex for the new one. Ceremony over, it was time to start moving people into their portrait positions.

"Let's go!" my boss called. I was paralyzed. As soon as the bride had come down the stairs, I realized I knew her. When she turned and noticed me, I think she was just as surprised to see me there *working*, in black pants, a black top under my *abaya* and scarf, carrying an extra camera on one shoulder and a light on the other. She looked so young—like a girl playing dress-up in women's clothes, too young to be getting married. After a quick congratulations, we went our separate ways. She turned to join her in-laws-to-be at dinner and I turned back to work.

We always knew that once school had ended, we would come to this fork in the road, that some of the girls would go to college while others would be engaged and married.

Summer graduated from high school a year after I did and went to university in Boston. Fatima moved back to Nigeria to study, married young, had five children, each of whom grew up to be accomplished students and professionals living the kind of international life between worlds just as I had.

Sumaiyah did not have the opportunity to get married or go to college. One ordinary Jeddah morning, an old classmate called crying hysterically, saying that she heard Sumaiyah was dead. I quickly hung up and rushed to find my parents. They were in their bedroom, their faces grim. My father told me in a soft voice that they had just spoken to some other parents who confirmed that Sumaiyah had been killed in a car accident the previous night. "Come here," he said. I sat on the bed and let him wrap his arms around me as I wept. He whispered the prayer you say when you hear someone has passed. "It is from God we come and to Him we shall return."

A group of us went to Sumaiyah's house that night to pay a condolence call on her family. Her house was filled with mourners sitting in the formal living room with her parents. Her mother sat in a chair with a floral scarf loosely tied around her head. We took turns hugging her. It was unclear who was consoling whom. Then we arranged ourselves on the overstuffed sofas and listened as the older women told us to accept this as God's will.

Even though I was so young, losing Sumaiyah awoke something in me, a sense of mortality, a belief that I needed to move on with my life. That I needed to pack in some purposeful work before my own time was up. Traveling with my father to Canada and London, going to his meetings, listening to his talks, typing up his notes, had opened a new window for me. And now that I'd spent more than a year watching Christiane Amanpour on my television screen, remaining just an observer suddenly seemed like I was wasting precious time.

A POINT OF LIGHT

Fear does not prevent death. It prevents life.
—Naguib Mahfouz

For most of my life, I took my mother for granted. If I needed to bring cupcakes to school the next day, I would fall asleep to the smell of baking from the kitchen. If I needed an outfit for a costume party, she sat down at her sewing machine and whirred away. If we got to a museum too late for a tour, she would figure out what we would do instead.

During our first year in Saudi Arabia, every time my mother looked out the window and saw an airplane in the sky, she would wish she was on it. The sabbatical to Saudi Arabia meant giving up the life she'd built in America, which included activities that had become impossibilities in her new reality, like driving. Yet she hung in there, year after year, and soon her passion for teaching and her commitment to her students overcame the physical, cultural, and social limitations that had chafed so much at first. Her professional responsibilities, demanding as they were, never got in the way of her domestic duties: cooking elaborate daily meals from scratch, ironing, sewing, doing laundry. While she was of a generation of women increasingly focused on pursuing their own career paths, gender dynamics hadn't shifted enough for there to be any expectation that men would share the household burden. As progressive as my father was, encouraging my mother in her work, never objecting to her increasingly frequent travels for academic conferences or to anything else she chose to do, in her own mind my mother must have thought she could pursue her professional goals only if she did so in *addition* to whatever would be expected of a wife.

My mother had a job outside the home from my earliest memories. At work in the university, she taught everyone from the daughters of shopkeepers to Saudi royalty. As many of her students spoke only rudimentary English, my mom taught herself Arabic so she could make her students more comfortable. She wrangled a rigid system and devised opportunities for many of them to go abroad to graduate school, as Saudi men had been doing for decades. Today there are scores of women thriving in their fields as a direct result of my mother's efforts. Whatever early hardships she had to endure were well worth it because she had found her calling: mentoring a generation of women to find their own purpose, whatever that might be. She was, in other words, a total badass, even if a teenage me could not see it.

Our relationship was complicated in a way that relationships between mothers and teenage girls often are. I was forever fighting with her and then finding refuge with my dad. I was often difficult, irrational, defiant. Still, my mother never lost her patience with me. She would try to reason with me or if that didn't work just hug me and wait for my sour mood to pass.

One day when I was seventeen I stood in the kitchen arguing with my mother about some small thing I've long since forgotten. I lost my temper and stormed out past the dining room, where my father was standing at the table holding his teacup and saucer, about to sit down for his five o'clock tea.

"What is going on?" he asked. Confident he'd take my side, I said, "Well, *that woman* won't let me—"

That was as far as I got. He slammed his cup down on the table, hot tea splashing out, pooling in the saucer and seeping dark onto the floral tablecloth. "*That woman*," he said, "is your *mother*. Don't you *dare* call her that ever again. Don't you *dare* treat her so disrespectfully. Go right back in there and seek her forgiveness."

Like my mother, my father didn't get angry often. When he did, it stopped me in my tracks; then it passed. He never let anger sit with him. But I had violated a very basic rule and my father wouldn't tolerate it. In Islam, your mother is the most respected elder in your life. As children, we were taught that heaven lay at our mother's feet. One of my earliest memories was looking at the soles of my mother's feet as she napped searching for any sign of "heaven." I went back to the kitchen, tensions still high, feelings still sore, apologized to my mother, and then sulked to my room.

That was the last time my father admonished me, because it was one of the last times we spoke.

* * * *

It was the spring of 1993 and life was good. We were living in a brand-new white villa with green shutters, in the suburbs. We each had our own bedroom, and my father had a large ground-floor office from where his journal work flourished. Hassan was now in England in graduate school, and Hadeel was there too, preparing to attend medical school. I was waiting to hear back from the American colleges where I had applied, and we were all excited about the big summer vacation we had just started to plan, a safari in Africa.

Hajj was coming up in May. It is the annual pilgrimage to Makkah that all Muslims who have the physical and financial means are required to make once in their lifetimes. My parents had gone many years before, but we children were too young to remember. That summer, my sisters and I were planning to go with my mother. A few weeks before we were supposed to leave, with preparations well underway, my father started having severe stomach pains. The doctors told him it was a stomach ulcer, likely caused by the side effects of all the medications he'd been taking or by an infection he might have picked up on a recent trip. He endured the pain for weeks, wincing occasionally when getting up or sitting down. If we asked "Are you okay?" he would always answer "I'm fine, has *Time* magazine arrived yet?" or "Can you bring me my pipe?"

He dismissed his pain, so we did too. It's only now, looking back through his medical records, that I see the stark reality. By that point, my father weighed ninety pounds. Yet there we all were, in relentless forward motion, plowing ahead like nothing in the world was wrong.

A few days before we were scheduled to leave for Makkah, my father's doctor told him that only surgery could resolve the ulcer. It sounded routine. In fact, we were all so confident about his quick recovery that my father insisted that our trip to Makkah proceed as planned. "I'll be back home recovering by the time you leave," he said. "You should all go." They scheduled the surgery for the following day.

The next morning, we gathered in my father's hospital room. He had changed into his surgical gown, sitting on the bed kidding around with the nurses coming in and out checking vital signs and making things beep. We were all perched around the room chatting about plans for the next week. When the nurses came in with the technicians and the gurney, my father greeted them with his usual jokes. "Please tell me the surgeon has had his breakfast today. I want to make sure he has the energy required to do this surgery." They all giggled.

One of the doctors walked in to check on us and said he would see us after the surgery. My father said, "Is it time already? Doctor, let me spend a few more minutes with my family. Just some more time with my children." I said, "Abbu, you should go now. It will make you better. It will be over so fast and then you will be back to one hundred percent." How I wish now I had not dismissed his wish so cavalierly. Had I known that would be our last conversation, I would have said, "Yes, let's just stay here together for a few more minutes." But to me at the time, this was just another of the medical interventions my father had experienced so many times over the years.

The nurses nodded encouragingly. The doctor stood by silently. My father smiled and embraced each of us in turn, including my mother, who was the only one who looked worried. He climbed onto the gurney and we followed him down the hall as far as they would let us. He sat upright and waved his hand, a thin IV tube dangling below his wrist, "I love you all," he said. And then the flapping doors closed and he was gone.

The operation was a success. The recovery was not. When my father woke up, they tried to remove his breathing tube, but the moment they did, he struggled to take in enough oxygen on his own. So the tube was reinserted. As his condition remained critical, he was driven by ambulance to a different hospital. There he remained on the ventilator, as doctors tried to manage the complications from an infection that his body was now fighting.

We arranged a schedule to keep vigil at the hospital while waiting for him to show any signs of recovery. Since we were off from school for the Hajj holidays, we were all able to split overnight shifts. A lot of the time he'd just close his eyes and rest. When he was awake, he would write notes on a hospital notepad and we'd joke around. "Your lunch today is three syringes of white gooey stuff and one syringe of pink stuff. Sound good?" He would nod and try to talk in response, but it was impossible with the tube. Sometimes he would scribble on the pad, handwriting shaky but still beautiful, and it would simply say, "Kiss me." We would lean over and kiss his hand or his forehead. We sat there chattering away, updating him on what was happening in the world, particularly in Bosnia, about which his journal was publishing articles, but mostly we were urging him to get well so that he could come back to all the important work left for him to do.

Every now and then he looked at me with his glassy eyes, the respirator still breathing for him. He would point at his chest and then up at the ceiling ever so slightly, in the direction of heaven. It was too much to bear so I responded the only way I knew. I would shake my head and say firmly, "*Come on!* You're not going *anywhere!*" Then I'd do my best to stay positive, going on about all the things we were going to do together when he returned home.

Our bedside vigil continued for a few more days. Even as we took shifts at my father's side, my mother rarely left. She ate in his room, slept in his room. In the very early hours of Saturday morning, June 5, 1993, my siblings and I convinced her to go home to take a shower and get some rest. She finally agreed to go, and Hassan and Hadeel, who had come back to Jeddah to be around post-surgery, drove her to the house.

Abbu waited until she was gone. That I know for certain. When she first left, everything remained the same. Heba and I were sitting in the large, uncomfortable chairs in his room, half-reclined, half-alert, the hallways dim and the windows pitch-black. From where I sat I could see him sleeping peacefully, the respirator making a deep rattling sound as it forced air into his lungs, the heart machine charting the same jagged scrawl, the blood pressure line appearing normal if a little low, when suddenly the call of the *fajr* morning prayer outside broke through. A minute later, one by one, the machines started going off like alarm clocks.

51

Doctors and nurses came racing down the corridor, and soon we were asked to move into the hall. We peered in as they dashed furiously around his room, turning on all the bright lights, ripping the sheet off his bed, pressing the paddles onto his chest. His body convulsed from the shock, lifting and lunging and then crashing back down. Then again. Finally a nurse wearing a surgical mask looked up and saw me, shell-shocked, staring from the doorway. She took a step toward me, reached up, and drew the curtain shut.

An uncle who was visiting called the house saying, "Come right away." Once the curtain closed, I walked out to the main hall outside the intensive care unit and sat on a bench, staring at the vending machine we had lived off of for a week, praying, bartering, making my pact with God. "Please let him be okay. *Please.* I'll be a good Muslim. I'll pray five times a day. I will fast every Ramadan. Please don't take him. Abbu, please don't leave me." From there the record skips. The next thing I saw was my mother. She walked in at the far end of the hall, Hassan and Hadeel on either side of her as a doctor approached them with his head slightly bent. She saw the look on all our faces and she knew. Her legs buckled and she started to fall, my siblings easing her into a nearby chair. Even though she knew, more than anyone, what Abbu had endured for so long, she was in shock, sitting immobile in the chair, tears silently streaming down her face, as the doctor assured her that they had tried everything. Even in that moment, the worst in her life, she was dignified as she thanked the doctor. Together we all went to say a final goodbye to my father, all the machines suddenly eerily still. Then she collected his things and went home. She was at Ascension Borgess Hospital in Kalamazoo all over again. This time though, without her husband's arm to steady her.

My mother went to lie down, and we took turns holding her hand, massaging her legs, lying on my father's side of the bed so we could feel close to him. Here in the privacy of her home, she allowed her grief to express itself without restraint. I could barely sit still. I followed Hassan into his room, out of my mother's earshot, and we started going through the list of everyone who needed to be informed. I sat down with my father's address book, started at "A," and Hassan and I took turns dialing, one by one, calling his colleagues, our relatives, and close friends with the news. "My father is in a better place," we repeated over and over again.

A few hours later, as the first day without my father was coming to an end, I sat on the floor of my brother's room listening to him make funeral arrangements, pivoting between English, Urdu, and Arabic depending on whom he talked to. Most significantly, we heard from one of my father's friends who had secured permission for the burial to be in Jannat al Mualla cemetery, in Makkah. It's no simple matter to be buried there. It is the cemetery in the holiest city in our religion, and many members of Prophet Muhammad's family are buried there, including his first wife, Khadijah.

As word spread, people began to arrive, and within a day our house was filled to capacity. Men shared stories about my father and recited joint prayers. Women flitted around upstairs in the family room and the dining room, making sure food was plentiful, urging us toward the table. Scores of relatives flew in from around the world, from India, Pakistan, Canada, New York, and London. We had mountains of food and more than enough people to eat it. Framed family photos were covered with cloth or gently turned over, as was tradition. The Qur'an was recited constantly, beautifully melodic and calming. Our family wandered around like automatons.

Every day more letters and faxes would arrive, and while the pile quickly became daunting, we couldn't wait to read them. From a minister in Malaysia, a friend at the Vatican, a scholar in Austria, a pastor in the Netherlands, even articles in the *Arab News* and *Saudi Gazette*, and so many more. A friend from Michigan wrote that his conversations with Abbu had inspired him to reaffirm his own Christian faith. One of the most touching letters came from our father's first foray into American life, an old friend at Penn: "He was a point of light—with patient smile, thoughtful pipe, and a shake of his head—always moving along the seams, illuminating proper distinctions and potentially connecting threads." Then, as now, we wanted to shout to the world that our father was amazing. When people's words came in, they validated what we already knew.

In Islamic tradition, the sons and the men in the family are encouraged to participate in preparing the body for burial when a male relative passes. Women are similarly encouraged when a female family member has died. It is considered an honor, similar to the act of pall-bearers in other traditions. We also believe that you don't immediately depart this earth when you die; that you can hear the footsteps walking away from your funeral and only then do the angels come to take your soul.

The next day, my brother brought my father home for the last time. The men, relatives and family friends, performed the Islamic *ghusl* cleansing ritual. They wrapped his body in the plain white cloth that all Muslims are to be buried in, a reminder, like the simple casket that is also traditional, that we are all equal in death. Only his face, which looked remarkably peaceful, was left exposed. When it was time to leave for Makkah, for the funeral and burial, we were called downstairs to say a final farewell. My father had been placed on the porch outside our dining room, overlooking the garden he had loved so much and tended so meticulously.

I don't know what took hold of me, but the moment I saw his face I was compelled to walk toward him. I bent forward and kissed his forehead one last time. I looked up, worried I had overstepped boundaries, and met my brother's clear eyes. He nodded that it was okay. Then he covered my father's face and the men very gently placed him in the coffin.

There was a sudden rush to get on the buses going to Makkah. I boarded the second bus and gathered my *abaya* close around me to fend off the air-conditioning, turning my face to the sun pouring in through the window. The normally quick trip seemed endless this day. I found myself staring out the window as we drove past mile upon mile of jagged coffee-colored hillsides strewn with dark rocks and the odd shrub here and there. I wondered whether my father was uncomfortable lying on his back for so long over these bumpy roads.

When we arrived at the mosque, the packs of other worshippers parted to make way for the casket, which was then placed in front of the Kaaba before the imam of Makkah led us in the funeral prayer. Thousands of people, many of whom had just completed the Hajj, made the prayer along with us. We then boarded the buses again for the short drive to the cemetery, and everything shifted into slow motion. Nothing could have prepared me for this part. In any case, I was just an observer, standing still, by the side of the bus, at the entrance to the cemetery, along with the rest of the women. It's not that anyone told us we couldn't enter, but none of the women did. We held hands, forming a line and reciting last-minute supplications, asking for mercy on his soul. The men hoisted the casket on their shoulders and started walking, my brother's back erect as they trekked up a hill and out of sight. And then it was all over.

REVOLUTION

A few weeks after my father's funeral, we received the official death certificate, which confirmed the cause of death as multiple organ failure. Raw and grieving, we turned our dinner table conversation to whether more could have been done to save him. Sometimes, late at night, staring at the ceiling, angry that my father had left me, I secretly wondered if there was anything more my mother could have done to keep him alive. Only now do I truly appreciate that he only lived as long as he did precisely *because* of her.

At the same time, I was also filled with guilt about the prospect of leaving her and Heba. The original plan had been for me to spend the summer visiting the colleges in America that had accepted me, make my decision, and then enroll in the fall, but then my father fell ill and the whole process halted. Now it was mid-July. I had yet to take a single campus tour in America, the deadline to make my choice was fast approaching, and it all felt like too much too soon.

I abruptly decided that I would defer another year. I had already taken two years off, so one more didn't seem like a big deal. Part of what led me to this decision were the piles of mail accumulating on my father's desk. Who would run his institute and edit the journal? In truth, my mother had been shouldering many of those responsibilities for years; she already had everything well under control. Yet, in my ignorance and my arrogance, I concluded I was the only one who could continue his mission.

My mother, meanwhile, even in her mourning, had not lost a step in making plans for the future—mine. She got busy planning a trip to visit all the colleges I had to choose between.

One afternoon while we were having lunch, I gently raised the issue.

"What if I take another year off before moving to America?"

"What about university?" she replied. "Have you thought about where you might want to go?"

"I don't know. Another year will give me more time to figure it out. Plus I could help you with the journal and the institute if I stayed here. I think it's what Abbu would want me to do."

There was the briefest pause before she replied firmly. "Abbu would have wanted you to study," she said. "He would want you to challenge your mind, to grow, to have new experiences of your own. The institute is his legacy, but so are his children. Keep that in mind as you decide what you want to do. In the end, it is your choice."

I walked downstairs after lunch and spent the rest of the afternoon in my father's office, sitting in one of the overstuffed armchairs across from his desk, sinking deep into the old leather seat, its springs long since shot. My father's desk was immaculate, everything in its proper place. The whole room was a testament to a life of nonstop activity, suddenly stilled. An article lay fanned out on the coffee table, in mid-edit. Journals were stacked up against one wall, waiting to be sent out, their address labels sitting in the typewriter. Freshly sharpened pencils were jammed into an old chipped teacup. Boxes filled with unopened condolence letters sat by the back door, my father's cream-colored letterhead stacked neatly beside them, ready for whenever anyone wanted to sit at the typewriter and type out our standard response of gratitude. I looked up to the wall where we'd hung an artwork a colleague had sent in tribute. The quote below it read: "Exhaled among Angels, a smile respires."

I picked up the pipe on his desk, cleaned out the tobacco, tossed the charred remnants, and pushed the soft pipe cleaner through the mouth until it came out gray and sooty. Then I set the pipe back in its place, never to be smoked again.

The prospect of abandoning my father's work and leaving my mother with this colossal responsibility combined with my fear of leaping into the unknown without him were leading me to paralysis. My mother knew this. She had laid the groundwork for my path forward, even if it was littered with the impediments of my grief. She must have believed I would come to the right decision. Education was her own legacy. A legacy passed on from a line of matriarchs before her, a right they had fought for, and a responsibility she was now passing on to me.

I had gone to my father's office to seek solace and refuge, and had received a clear answer. It was time for me to go. I climbed upstairs to begin packing, telling myself I would be back in only a few months for winter break.

Just before we left for the airport, I went into my father's still-meticulously organized closet, and grabbed one of his black-and-white wool scarves, which still faintly smelled of Old Spice. I went back to my room, folded it neatly, and slid it into my suitcase.

* * * *

We arrived in Washington, DC, for a tour of George Washington University on a sweltering August morning, and instantly I knew that school was where I belonged. It felt like the center of the universe—neighbors with the State Department, near the White House, and beyond that, just a little farther on, the U.S. Capitol, the Lincoln Memorial, and the Washington Monument. The line between where the city ended and the university began was invisible. It felt like a homecoming; even Washington's oppressive heat and humidity reminded me of being in Jeddah. Based purely on that gut feeling, and the words of a very persuasive sophomore campus tour guide, I turned to my mother and announced that I was now a GWU student.

The next day we walked from our hotel to the registrar's office, and I watched as my mom took out her checkbook and wrote out a personal check for $23,200. My hands felt clammy watching her turn over that much money, though she didn't even flinch. She had saved her entire salary for years for precisely this reason. Once she had secured a spot for me in the all-female dorm—the coed party dorm to which I had been originally assigned was a nonstarter—I was on my own.

Anyone leaving home for college has a learning experience in front of them, whether it involves learning to do their own laundry, to pay bills, to open a bank account, or to figure out how to feed themselves and manage their time without any parental supervision. In the months before he died, my father had sat me down to talk to me about what I was about to encounter. He said that the biggest challenge I would face in an American college would be managing the social and cultural change. It would be "like a revolution," and I needed to prepare myself accordingly. He said I would need to stay focused on my studies but not to neglect my social and extracurricular activities, because balance was important. He told me not to forget that the total liberty I was about to experience had to be informed by my values. No freedom, he said, is absolute. There were consequences to every decision I would make.

I was finally beginning to live my dream in America, but I missed my home, my friends, and more than anything, I missed my dad. I missed him so much that my entire freshman year, I referred to him in the present tense. It was always "my parents" or "my mom and dad think," and I was going to see "my parents" this summer. Casual phrases about family that no one would think twice to question.

One day, a few weeks after I arrived, I wandered over to Professor Seyyed Hossein Nasr's office in the Department of Religion. Professor Nasr was a well-respected Islamic scholar who my father knew. I had read a few of his books, had seen his articles and correspondence he and my dad had exchanged in my dad's office. I introduced myself to the woman sitting outside the door to his office, mentioning that I was Dr. Abedin's daughter. A voice from inside beckoned me in. The office was small but beautifully arranged, a jewel-toned rug on the floor and overflowing bookshelves. Elegant and welcoming, it stood out in an otherwise gray and unadorned row of offices.

"Come in. It's lovely to meet you, Huma. Are you a student here?"

"Yes, Professor, I am, and I am so excited to be here. I thought you might remember my father."

"Of course I know your father. How is he doing?"

Just two months ago, I had sat by the telephone phoning family and friends to tell them the news. I was an expert on how to have the grief conversation. Now, however, I could not. I had given up everything familiar in my life, but I could not give up Abbu.

After what felt like eons of silence, I said: "He is well." Subconsciously, I must have known I was in denial, but I just couldn't say the words.

"Wonderful, please give him my regards."

"I most certainly will, Professor."

I walked out of his office and circled the block half a dozen times trying to convince myself that I could go back and tell him the truth, but I never did find the courage.

* * * *

The first time I went to school in America, when my father was recovering from surgery in New Jersey, I was eleven and in fifth grade, and classes had been a breeze. So naturally, eight years later, I waltzed into Professor Puffenbarger's Journalism 101 class with a lot of confidence. *I'm going to be way ahead of everybody else*, I thought.

I was not.

I'd always thought of myself as well informed, but it took only a few days of college to learn that my education was oddly specific. I knew about the persecution of Uighurs in China and the Rohingya in Myanmar, the cause of the current turmoil in Somalia, who the OPEC secretary general was, and the name of the palace where a young Mozart performed for Empress Maria Theresa. But for a girl whose parents were academics, who had been spoon-fed book after book her whole life, who'd actually been born in the United States and was a U.S. citizen, I'd had startlingly little formal exposure to American history. Suddenly there was a hole to fill, and I began devouring every piece of reading material that my professors recommended. Much of American history was powerful, inspiring for someone like me, a product of immigrant parents. Some of it was shameful beyond words.

When I left for college, I'd had some unsettled feelings about how issues of race were in conflict with American values. I remembered my mother telling me a story about our early days in Kalamazoo when police with guns drawn came banging on our door because someone had seen one of the Arab students my father had hired to paint our shutters. Apparently, in 1970s Kalamazoo, the sight of a dark man on a ladder was enough for a passerby to call 911 and report a burglary. Nevertheless, I still had an idealized conception of America.

Many years later, I began to dig deeper. The final research paper I wrote for one of my college courses in Jeddah focused on the Arab and Muslim influence on American history. I read that one in every three enslaved people brought to the Americas from Africa was likely Muslim. Even though it's not certain in actuality how many were forcibly brought to America, if say 12 million people were kidnapped, as has been estimated by the Trans-Atlantic Slave Trade database, could it be that 4 million of them were Muslim? This was the beginning of my interest in the African American experience.

In Jeddah, my father's tattered, worn copies of African novels often made their way to my bedside. I read *From Zia, with Love* by the Nigerian author Wole Soyinka, *A Naked Needle* by Somali writer Nuruddin Farah, and *The Wedding of Zein* by Sudanese author Tayeb Salih. Tales about love and identity, about the colonized and the colonizers. On trips back from the U.S., my father brought back *Invisible Man* by Ralph Ellison and *The Color Purple* by Alice Walker, which revealed entirely different aspects of the Black experience. I was riveted by the characters and the story lines, so foreign to everything I'd experienced growing up.

My sophomore year at GWU, I took Literature of Black America Parts I and II. My junior year, I took a seminar in Black Studies. That was the first time I really studied not only the pain and degradation but also the pride, strength, and courage that informed African Americans' endurance, defiance, and struggle. I read James Baldwin and Zora Neale Hurston and W. E. B. Du Bois and Lorraine Hansberry. I watched *Gone With the Wind*, not romanticizing the story as I had as a child, instead feeling a deep discomfort.

I also signed up for Post-Colonial Indian Literature of India in an effort to connect with my heritage. The reading list exposed me to some of South Asia's preeminent authors: R. K. Narayan, Anita Desai, and Rabindranath Tagore. They each portrayed characters whose intense inner struggles were catalyzed by living in a time when social and cultural norms were changing and religious constrictions were loosening, the common line in all these novels: how to honor the past while embracing a rapidly changing future.

There was a novel called *Twilight in Delhi*, published in 1940, on our reading list, and I instantly fell in love with it. It told the story of an upper-middle-class Muslim family living in Delhi at the end of what had seemed a good century, the slow death of the Mughal Empire, in all its majesty and poetry, and the birth of a new era under British rule. Given my father's own connection to Delhi and his love for it, I was captivated by the book.

I was on the phone with my mom and told her I had settled on my senior thesis subject, the author of this book, Ahmed Ali, who had also translated the Qur'an into English and written other novels. And she laughed out loud.

"Mom! I'm serious. This author's work should be written about and I need your help doing research. He was so cool."

"This 'cool' author was your father's cousin. *Bhai* Ahmed is the one who brought the marriage proposal from your father to my family. I think we can manage your research." She reeled off the names of relatives in Pakistan who might be able to give me some more details.

"What?" I said, suddenly shocked and upset. "He was our *relative*? And he was a novelist? Why didn't Abbu ever tell us about him or give us any of his books?"

"I don't know," she said. "I think he wanted you to discover some things on your own. He was humble about such things. And, look, you did discover it on your own!"

She was trying to make me feel better, to save me from yet another instance that would make me feel cheated out of time with my father.

It was becoming clear that the idea that I could have taken over my father's institute at seventeen was laughable. His expertise spanned the globe: with a focus on the USSR and Europe but also the U.S., West Africa, and as far afield as Papua New Guinea, New Zealand, and Mauritius. The level of scholarship required was way over my head; but I do think my father and I were driven by the same sense of curiosity. He spent a lifetime exploring what comprised otherness—how to navigate relations between majority and minority populations was his central preoccupation, and a defining element of mine. For much of their early history—from the early caliphates in Medina and Baghdad to the glory of the Mughal Empire in India to the vast conquests of the Ottoman Empire—Muslims had been kings and conquerors, masters of their own fate. But the rise of Europe, the birth of the modern nation state, and the aftershocks of colonialism had flipped that history on its head. Moving forward, outside of the Middle East, more and more Muslims lived as minorities in foreign lands, often disenfranchised by and beholden to others. What would become of Muslims in this era? How were we, as a people and as a faith, coping with the shift from being rulers to being ruled? And how would the world react to us? These were the questions that had led Abbu to found the Institute of Muslim Minority Affairs, and start his journal.

Having watched as his own nation was torn apart along sectarian lines, my father realized early on that a failure to grapple with these questions might bring disastrous consequences, for Muslims and non-Muslims alike, as the world has seen in the massacre of Bosnians at Srebrenica, the persecution of Uighurs in China, the displacement of Rohingyas in Myanmar, and the alienation of young Muslim men in the *banlieues* of Paris and the council flats of London.

I'd had the benefit of being raised in a Muslim country where I could practice my faith without threat or suspicion. I'd never had to be the Brown kid in an American school who was teased for bringing "weird" ethnic food in my lunch box. Thanks to both my parents, as an adolescent I'd had enough confidence to carry on with my faith and cultural traditions once I landed in America, where I was suddenly a minority. Classmates asked questions like "Did you live in a tent?" "Did you go to school on a camel?" Always followed by the inevitable "How is your English *so good*?" I knew they were just curious, not malicious. I sometimes floated between an American accent, a British accent, and an Arabic accent, depending on whom I was talking to, but most people who met me didn't think I had any accent at all. I slipped in between different stereotypes and didn't fit neatly into any one category. I was never the "other" and found I could fit in everywhere.

When I was a kid, I read about how the American writer Washington Irving had traveled in Spain, studied the Moors, read the Qur'an, and stayed at the Alhambra. I tried to learn more about what intrigued this American man about Islam. What was that link and how far back did it go? Because I was both American and Muslim, the answer had personal significance, and it's probably why I took so many different classes and participated in so many different student groups— the Muslim Students Association, the South Asian Society, the Arab

Club, the Black Student Union. Whether I was reading Alice Walker or Anita Desai, I was never searching for the things that made everybody different. I was searching for what we all had in common.

*   *   *   *

In March 1995, in the middle of my sophomore year, my mom invited me to join her in New York at the preparatory session for the United Nations Fourth World Conference on Women, which would be held in Beijing that September. She needed an assistant to do what I had done for my father on his trips: make travel and hotel bookings, take notes at meetings, and so on. It had been a decade since the last World Conference on Women, and it sounded like some bureaucratic exercise. My mother's generation had struggled and fought for progress. Wasn't mine the one poised to reap the benefits? I assumed I could do anything I wanted, especially after leaving Saudi Arabia and coming to America. I didn't see it as revolutionary for women to meet to demand the very basic things that I now took for granted.

Yet I was awed the moment I stepped into the lobby of the United Nations, its grand entry hall flooded with natural light from a tall floor-to-ceiling wall of windows. The whole building was teeming with thousands of women. Turn this way and they were speaking Spanish; turn that way and they were speaking Dutch, and French, and Arabic. It felt like a place where things were happening.

The previous World Conferences on Women had resulted in a living document called "The Draft Platform for Action," about broad, far-reaching goals for the advancement of women, while also detailing specific milestones and benchmarks for each country and region. Delegations had come to New York to propose amendments to the document, and they would convene in different committees to consider and edit them, line by line and word by word. My job was to go with my mom and her nongovernmental organization to all these different meetings and take notes on the changes being made, then input them into the document so she and her colleagues could review them. The changes would ultimately be put to a vote, and the amendments that passed would be included with the final draft platform to be ratified in Beijing.

It was really exciting. Being there gave me a window into how diplo-

macy works, how countries have to bend their own priorities and nego-
tiate. It was also an eye-opening education in the ways women were
still being treated around the world, not just in the developing world
but everywhere. At almost every meeting, my mom would remind her
colleagues that nothing would change unless we urged men to the table.

Back at GWU, I ran for president of the Pakistani Students' Association after two guys snickered when someone suggested that I would
be an ideal candidate to lead our group. I won. Soon after, I invited
the Pakistani ambassador, Maleeha Lodhi, to the university, where she
gave a major policy speech about American-Pakistani relations. Our
group also organized students to lobby Congress. This small taste of
diplomacy and politics felt not just exciting but also right. Almost like
a beginning.

Over the course of my junior year, I began talking to friends
about an internship for my senior year. To apply to graduate school,
I needed some kind of work experience and I didn't have any. My
friend Roneith Hibbert told me about her incredible internship at the
White House, working for President Clinton's press secretary, Mike
McCurry. She sat right behind the podium and blue curtain, where all
the administration officials would make media appearances. "I think
you'd love it and it would be a great opportunity. I'll pick up an application for you."

I had never dreamed of working in the White House, or even in
government. I suspected it might be totally beyond my reach. But I
still carried the feeling I'd had as I walked around the United Nations
building, and I figured, *Well, what do I have to lose?*

* * * *

My sisters and I weren't segregated from boys in the way that many
of our peers had been. Still, by the time I left home for college I had
never been on a date, never been to a homecoming dance or asked
to a prom, simply because we didn't have those things. Usually the
first time a girl went out with a boy was after an agreement was made
between the parents or when there was a clear understanding the
intentions were serious and would end with an engagement. Sex was
not discussed until a woman was about to be married. Conversations

which took place behind closed doors in hushed voices. Until then, "sexual intercourse" was something we learned about in Biology class, described by our Sri Lankan teacher in a cold, antiseptic manner and in the same tone she used when we dissected a frog in the lab.

I had always viewed my parents as a single unit. I rarely saw them being physically affectionate with each other; it was not the custom for their time or in our culture. During their afternoon naps, they might fall asleep with their arms around each other. Sometimes my father threaded his arm through my mother's as they walked. Only in hindsight do I appreciate how deep their love truly was, how precious and, in fact, how rare. They were my model for marriage, and for the longest time, I took for granted that someday far in the future I too would have what they had. A man would walk up to me, say something brilliant and disarming, and the rest would be history.

In the meantime, I threw myself into an active campus social life with people I knew from my classes and then the people I met through the various student associations I joined. Together, we walked all over DC; along the Washington Mall, and then back past school and on to Georgetown to shop and eat dinner before it was time to walk back to Foggy Bottom.

That, typically, was where my evenings would end. After dinners, especially on weekends, many friends would head out to a club or a bar. I would grab a late dessert or coffee with other friends. I did the club madness a few times. It was dark, there was smoke everywhere, everyone seemed to be sweating, and the air was stale and dank with the smell of alcohol. It was so loud I couldn't actually talk to anyone. I just wasn't interested. My vice was, and still is, food.

During my freshman year, a classmate asked me if I wanted to go for coffee with him after class. I didn't exactly know how to handle a polite no, so the first time he asked, I told him I was late for something and slipped away. After he asked again, I couldn't think of another reason to turn him down so I said yes. On our way out of class, I asked, "You don't mind if Denise comes too, do you?" And that was pretty much it for that relationship. A few months later, I saw him across the street, on the opposite sidewalk holding hands with another girl from class and smiled to myself. Happy for him. Relieved for me.

I did all the things my parents expected of me in college. I studied hard, tried not to lose focus, experimented with different courses. I had a full social life and lots of fun. A guy who was dating an Indian American friend of mine began to call me Princess Jasmine, based on the character in Disney's recent *Aladdin* movie, and the nickname stuck. I didn't like it and, frankly, found it offensive, but I guess it was meant as a compliment. It was the first time anyone, aside from my parents, had suggested I was pretty. Heba was considered the beauty in my family; Hassan and Hadeel were brilliant and faithful. I was the skinny, awkward, loud one, forever skinning my knees and bruising my shins as I scampered around clumsily. As for men, I had only one significant relationship in college, and even then, it was significant to me, not to him. He was another Muslim student and a few years older than me.

I felt strange whenever he was around; conscious about how I looked, nervously avoiding eye contact, my heart fluttering when he spoke to me. As the months went on, I felt a certain tension begin to develop between us, and I found myself anticipating something. But what? I didn't know if he felt the same way about me. I didn't know what to do with these feelings, so I did nothing. Neither did he.

One night, after a group dinner on campus, he offered to walk me home. He followed me up the few steps from the sidewalk, down the longish brick path to the front door.

We stopped at the door and I turned to look at him. Could this be the moment when a charming man was going to say something brilliant and disarming? But, as I looked at him, he was barely making eye contact with me, twisting his body uncomfortably, kicking at a loose stone along the path that seemed to transfix both of us in the moment. Then, after what felt like an eternity, he said, "You are just different. You are not the kind of girl that boys date. You are the kind of girl that boys marry, and, uh, I am not ready to be married. And . . . I am sorry."

I didn't say anything. I think the most I could muster was an "Okay." He mumbled good night, abruptly turned around, and walked away.

I watched him leave, then I turned and went inside. Just like that, it—whatever "it" was—was over. Not long after, I saw him with a young woman on his arm, walking down the street. It hurt, the outright rejection more than anything else, but beyond that I was left wondering. Was this the "It's not you, it's me" episode I had seen in so many movies growing up? But he actually implied that the problem *was* me, so then what did that say about me?

I had always felt different, but this was not how I defined different. This meant not being special enough. I buried the hurt and turned back to my studies and my campus responsibilities, and quickly dismissed any foolish notions about romance.

As the school semester ended and I began to get ready to go home for the break, I finished up my application for a fall internship at the White House and turned it in, making sure to put my aunt's house in New Jersey as the return address so that none of the correspondence would get delayed in overseas mail.

I flew back to Jeddah for the summer, looking forward not just to long weekends with my friends but also to my summer job at the Saudi daily newspaper *Arab News*, where I would be editing, doing page design for the style section, and writing the occasional movie review. Late one evening toward the end of that long summer, I was reading in my room when the phone rang. A few minutes later, my mother called from the bottom of the stairs.

"I just got off the phone with your aunt," she said. "She says a large envelope arrived for you. It's from the White House!"

PART TWO

CALLING WHITE
HOUSE SIGNAL

A good life is a balanced life.
—Syed Z. Abedin

In the fall of 1997, on a rare weekend outside Washington, I found myself in New Jersey for the same reason I always found myself in New Jersey: a big family gathering. This time it was a wedding, a cousin on my mother's side. I was at an aunt's house, trying to find a formal South Asian outfit to wear for the ceremony, which was to take place the next day in Manhattan.

From somewhere beneath all the brightly colored silk and chiffon, my government-issued pager went off. It's insistent buzzing felt foreign sitting so far away in another state and immersed in another culture. I dug it out of the pile and read the message on the little screen. "Call WH Signal," it read. "Call holding with Katy Button."

White House Signal was an operations center that connected administration officials and staff by phone, and "call holding" meant that it was time-sensitive, with the caller on the line waiting. I dialed the 800 number, thinking it odd that Katy, a senior aide to First Lady Hillary Clinton's chief of staff Melanne Verveer, would be calling me over a weekend.

After a brief hold, I was connected to Katy, who apologized for interrupting me during my family weekend but quickly pivoted to the reason for the call. Would I be interested in advancing the First Lady's trip to Argentina? She was traveling with the President, and an official stop in Buenos Aires was on the schedule. Someone else had canceled, and there was an open slot. "Melanne thinks it will be good experience for you," Katy said. "But you'll need to leave from Washington first thing Monday morning. Can you make it?"

I was surprised by the request. I had never done an advance trip, and I was one of the youngest, least-experienced members of the First Lady's office, having been hired as Melanne's assistant and office manager when my internship ended just a few months before. My mind was racing with all the things I would need to do. I did the math on the flight times and realized that in order to make the plane to Buenos Aires on Monday morning, I would have to leave for Washington, DC, in the middle of my cousin's wedding on Sunday night. While everyone went upstairs to enjoy the reception, I would be on the Amtrak regional train back to DC, eating a stale bagel with cream cheese and sipping burnt coffee.

My heart pounding with excitement, I said yes immediately, thanked Katy for thinking of me, and we hung up.

* * * *

For all my uncertainty about applying for the White House internship program in the first place, from the moment I arrived on an impossibly perfect September morning in 1996, I loved every minute. I had walked the seven long blocks from the one-bedroom apartment I shared with a roommate, until I found myself standing in front of the North Portico of the White House, staring through the iron gates. Behind me, I noticed the cars driving past on Pennsylvania Avenue filled with government employees on their way to work, long inured to the view.

After a minute that was both nerve-racking and exciting, I turned back and walked up the steps of the stately Old Executive Office Building, now called the Eisenhower Building, where the majority of working offices in the White House are housed. A giant nineteenth-century structure built in the French Second Empire style, the OEOB is like the sister no one really looks at because all eyes are on the beauty in the family, but when you are forced to pay attention, you realize the "other" sister is quite impressive herself.

Inside, the building was a maze. Fifteen acres of office space connected by long hallways lined with identical arched doorways, peachy-white columns, and black-and-white marble and limestone floors so worn that some tiles had a permanent dip in them. After a brief orientation, I was assigned to the office of Melanne Verveer, then the First Lady's deputy chief of staff and chief policy advisor. If I had been an intern in any of the cavernous offices of the President, I would have seen only a tiny sliver of a vast operation. In this office, I was about to learn, it was all hands on deck.

On that first day, Melanne invited me to her office, which she shared with her policy aide Nicole Rabner. Behind their two large desks, elegant windows looked out to the Washington Monument. Melanne welcomed me by saying how excited they were to have me because the one-year anniversary event marking the First Lady's 1995 speech at the Fourth World Conference on Women was approaching, and she had noticed on my application that I had been at the preparatory conference at the UN. I told her about my mother's work, that she had watched Mrs. Clinton's speech in Huairou, that the applause was even more intense than at the Beijing conference *and* she'd even gotten to shake her hand.

Why did I say that last line? I thought. *These women probably have shaken her hand more times than they could count!*

"Your mother is probably right," Melanne laughed. "You will find that there is lots to do here and we are grateful for your help."

The American First Lady's job is completely undefined. Historically, most first ladies had chosen signature projects. Some worked on issues that wouldn't cause a stir, and beyond that they weren't involved in their husband's policy agenda. Others pushed the limits. Betty Ford was remarkably candid and prescient about both cancer and addiction, topics simply not discussed at the time, and Eleanor Roosevelt was revolutionary in just about every way.

Hillary Clinton took the role to another level. I caught a glimpse on day one when Katy handed me a stack of file folders filled with Melanne's incoming mail. My responsibility was to draft responses. Determined to do well, I picked up the first file on my narrow desk and read the little yellow sticky note with "FGM" written on it. Puzzled, I opened the file.

The next thing I knew, I was paging through letters and documents, absorbed in the details of female genital mutilation, the painful and sometimes fatal procedure of circumcising girls and women. Girls were being hurt, scarred for life, some dying. I knew that female circumcision was un-Islamic, and I learned as I read that FGM was not only still occasionally practiced in the United States, it wasn't even against the law. Calls to criminalize the practice in the U.S. had been growing ever since the Beijing conference, where the First Lady had called FGM a violation of human rights and urged countries to outlaw it. A vote to pass legislation would soon come before Congress. In the file in front of me was a stack of letters from NGOs, prominent officials, and everyday citizens, almost all of them supporting the First Lady's work encouraging congressional leaders to pass the bill.

I started rifling through Melanne's other mail and found letters about other issues Hillary Clinton had been championing for years: healthcare, equal rights for women, early childhood education, support for the arts, research on brain development in infancy, adoption and foster care, expanded family leave for all Americans. So many of the policy goals and accomplishments of the President's agenda flowed through the First Lady's office—*this* First Lady's office.

Some days I filed policy papers or updated Melanne's Rolodex or made requested edits to a speech or briefing. I was assured I could always go to Nicole or Katy if I had questions. Though they were only a few years older than me, they had an encyclopedic knowledge of the administration's policy positions. Their commitment and enthusiasm were contagious, and I soon came to share it.

Three weeks after I started, the Beijing anniversary event took place. On the day of the event, I assisted at the venue, programs in hand, and stationed myself outside the doors to help check people in. When the First Lady arrived, she came in through a back entrance, spoke, and left; I never saw her, just heard muffled voices coming from inside the auditorium room while I sat outside.

One thing I quickly learned was that being an intern in the First Lady's office entailed few interactions with the First Lady herself. For most White House interns, the President and the First Lady are almost mythological figures, constantly talked about yet rarely seen.

You might catch a glimpse of them surrounded by aides at the end of a long hallway, or join when interns were invited to watch a Marine One departure or a press conference in the Rose Garden, but our day-to-day interactions were limited. For the most part, I experienced President and Mrs. Clinton the same way everyone else did: on television.

On the day of President Clinton's reelection in November 1996, I traveled to Little Rock for the celebration with a few other interns and staff. By the time we arrived, a large crowd was already gathering for the rally, and for a while the other interns and I wandered outside the Old State House Capitol building, taking it all in and looking for the best spots on the rapidly filling lawn. The anticipation of results hung in the air like electricity. This was politics on steroids. At one point, the Reverend Jesse Jackson, Sr., brushed past us, surrounded by aides and trailed by reporters. Walking past the press risers where the news networks had set up, we giddily shouted "look!" to one another every time we saw James Carville or George Stephanopoulos make their way up or down the narrow staircase to perch on directors' chairs and update the world on what was happening in Florida or Ohio. Staring from time to time at the jumbotron screens that reflected the latest count of the electoral votes, we waited as it got closer and closer to the magical number of 270. Each update resulted in hoots and applause.

Hours later, the election was called, with raucous cheers diffusing from the front of the crowd to the back as word spread like a human wave at a concert. Finally, to the tune of "Hail to the Chief," three distant silhouettes filled the empty archway, and into the light emerged President Clinton, Mrs. Clinton, and their daughter Chelsea, followed shortly by Vice President Al Gore, his wife Tipper, and their children.

After the President gave his victory speech and a fireworks display lit the midnight sky, he and the First Lady came down to greet people on the rope line. As the First Lady moved through my section, I stretched out my hand as far as it would reach over the shoulders of the crowd of people standing in front of me. She leaned forward, took it in hers, looked right at me—just another face in the crowd, with no idea that I was one of the nameless interns in her office—smiled wide, and said "thank you."

It struck me then that she was more petite, more delicate in person

77

than the larger-than-life figure I had seen in pictures or on television. She was prettier too. This, I now know, is the single most common thing people say when they meet her in person.

I properly met Hillary Rodham Clinton—or HRC as we all referred to her internally—a month after the election, on the day the interns from our office were scheduled to take a photo with her in the residence. For the photo, we walked down a long red-carpeted hallway on the ground floor, and into the Diplomatic Reception Room, where we quietly arranged ourselves for a group photo and waited for the First Lady to arrive. The moment HRC walked in, chatting with an aide, the tone in the room shifted. It was as though every staff member around her projected an urgency suggesting that each minute of her time was precious and not to be wasted. She, meanwhile, seemed perfectly at ease and in no rush to be anywhere but with us. Stepping away from her aide, she gave us her full attention, shaking each of our hands, offering everyone a quick "Hi" or "Hello." She gave a short speech thanking us for our work, posed for pictures, and then seamlessly picked up her conversation with her aide as she breezed out the door. The whole experience was over in less than ten minutes.

Over the course of the internship, I had opportunities to go into the West Wing and the residence, sometimes delivering an envelope with Melanne's edits on a policy speech, sometimes to take a file with work for the First Lady to her small West Wing office. For someone who grew up in a country where power was projected through gargantuan palaces filled with marble columns, crystal chandeliers, and gold-plated staircases, the scent of *oud* musk pervading the atmosphere, the West Wing was modest in comparison. Small offices, many windowless, with simple desks, unadorned wall-to-wall carpeting, and cream walls. But it was no less intimidating for being so. The majesty of the place came from the power within its walls. Little ornamentation was required: American power spoke for itself.

* * * *

From the day I walked through the White House gates, I found myself in an environment where my background was not simply tolerated, but welcomed, where I had a sense of belonging and security, just as

I had had in Jeddah. Ignorant questions about riding to school on a camel were left behind in college.

During my first Ramadan as an intern, I observed it privately but shared my experiences with colleagues if they asked, which happened fairly often. I explained that Ramadan is the one month in the lunar calendar when, from sunrise to sunset, adult Muslims abstain from eating, drinking, having intercourse, or smoking. You reflect on your deeds of the past year and make your intention for the coming one. It's meant to be a test of your inner *taqwa,* or God-conscious self. Anyone who fasts knows hunger, the gnawing, disorienting, headache-provoking kind of hunger. It's a physical reminder both that there is always someone who has less than you and that you should be grateful for whatever you do have.

It was during that Ramadan, in January 1997, that I participated in my first official White House event—to greet the newly elected and first woman prime minister of Bangladesh, Sheikh Hasina, who was coming for tea with HRC and a meeting with the President. Knowing my background, Melanne suggested I welcome the leader to the White House.

The White House receives protocol guidance both from the State Department and the visiting country's embassy in advance of any visit. Still, a few days before the prime minister's visit, I got a call from the Social Office, an arm of the First Lady's office that produced every event that took place in the White House, asking how we could make her feel welcome. Since it was Ramadan, I asked if they were aware and had made preparations accordingly. "Send an email with any ideas, and see you then," my colleague signed off. At which point it clicked that this wasn't some theoretical conversation I was having about a meeting of world leaders.

I was going to be there.

That day the one other Muslim intern and I waited in the Diplomatic Reception Room to prepare for the official arrival. The room was elegant and oval-shaped. Its wallpaper, acquired by Jackie Kennedy, depicted scenes of America from a nineteenth-century French perspective. There was a fireplace behind us, the one President Roosevelt had installed for his fireside chats, a dark mahogany bookcase desk towering in front of us, and a pair of chairs covered in yellow damask silk on which I didn't dare sit, even though my head was now spinning. Our Social Office escort left us to greet the arriving limousine. My fellow intern and I were too nervous to talk even to each other, so we stood silently. Two Brown girls surrounded by a decidedly federalist America, standing in the room that was the very center of the most important house in the world, waiting to greet a head of state on behalf of the President and First Lady of the United States.

When the doors swung open, I heard a voice in the vestibule say, "Prime Minister, we have some interns here to meet you." The prime minister greeted us graciously and spent a few minutes asking about our backgrounds. I fell quite comfortably into a conversation with her. All the times my father had made me face and conquer my anxieties, the countless times he put me on the phone with the airlines, or sent me out to entertain his guests, teaching me to live without him, it had all been training for this moment. I just knew, instinctively, what to do.

A month earlier, before I left to visit my mom in Jeddah over the holidays, Katy had asked me to help plan the White House Eid celebration. Eid is the celebration which comes at the end of Ramadan, and the Clinton White House was the first to make it an annual event. I met with Mona Mohib, a Muslim staff member who worked down the hall from me, to discuss details and begin organizing. It was the first event where I felt I knew more than anyone else in the room. I had crossed the line from being just another young American Muslim to being a representative of the federal government who happened to be Muslim.

At the Eid celebration in 1999, I proposed that Professor Seyyed Hossein Nasr, from George Washington University, speak at the event. I had some important personal business to do with Professor Nasr. It was to him that I had lied about my father being alive when I walked into his office as a college freshman, still burdened by a trauma I did not quite recognize.

When he arrived for the event, I mentioned my father to him. "I was sorry to hear of your father's passing," he said immediately.

"Thank you, I was lucky to have him as long as I did."

"I am sure he is proudly watching you from above," he said with a smile.

* * * *

There was an intense work ethic in the Clinton White House. I was surrounded by people who were working. *All* the time. And I loved it. My internship was worth three college credits, and I was required to come in for fifteen hours per week to complete the course. Pretty soon I found that if I wasn't in class or studying, I was at the White House. I stopped going out for coffee with friends during the day so I could work longer hours, only meeting them for dinner and even then often making it just in time for dessert. I would stay at the office so long that I'd completely lose track of time until Melanne would come back from a formal dinner in the residence, notice me, and exclaim, "What are *you* still doing here? *Go home!*"

I stayed for a second intern session the following semester, not questioning whether that was normal. Nothing about this time in my life seemed normal. Everything existed on a more intense, more vivid plane than what I had known before.

Then, one afternoon in March of 1997 when Melanne was traveling in Africa with the First Lady, Nicole asked me about my plans after graduation, now less than two months away. I told her I was planning to apply to law school and would look for an internship at the *Washington Post*. As much as I loved working for the First Lady's office, I hadn't anticipated staying on in any capacity. It simply hadn't occurred to me it would be an option. "Melanne is going to need a new assistant," Nicole said, "a job we're combining with the role of office manager. We think you'd be a good candidate."

I didn't know what to think. I was stunned, excited, giddy even, at this prospect. In college, I had taken so many Political Science classes that I almost ended up with a double major, so perhaps this was a path I had chosen unconsciously. My father's family had been in government civil service in India for generations. I knew the stories about my maternal grandmother's work with a women's advocacy group hosting women educators and activists from around Pakistan and sometimes beyond, as when she had welcomed a group of Algerian women freedom fighters to the family home. Maybe public service was in my blood.

When you become a White House intern, no one asks you for

your political affiliation. There's no box asking if you voted in the last election or who you voted for. I think it's probably true that most interns who apply to work in a Democratic White House are Democrats themselves, but it wasn't something that was assumed. For my part, I hadn't been raised one way or another. There were no political parties in Saudi Arabia. And as engaged as they were on social issues, my parents didn't identify with Democrats, Republicans, or Independents. Many South Asian and Arab immigrants were socially and fiscally conservative that by default they automatically registered as Republicans. Still, Bill and Hillary Clinton were very popular in our home, even more so since I had started working for them; to hear my mother tell it to anyone who would listen, I was personally working side by side with the President and the First Lady on issues of global importance day in and day out.

In the end, my personal admiration and loyalty to the Clintons and their team held sway. I believed in the administration's priorities: the work that the First Lady was doing on behalf of women; the efforts the President was making on behalf of Muslims, which included intervening in the Balkans, hosting the ceremony for the Oslo Peace Accords between the Palestinians and Israelis, and paving the way for a recognized Palestinian National Authority. Where there had been an economic crisis only four years earlier, the general sense was that thanks to President Clinton, we were now enjoying economic prosperity and low unemployment. In short, these felt like good days, with lots accomplished, and much more to come. It was less a political party I was choosing to work for, and more like a cause.

When Melanne returned from her trip, I asked to meet with her. The interview did not last long. She told me I had impressed her with my work ethic and she offered me the job. I accepted on the spot, and on April 27, 1997, seven months after I first walked into the White House, and three weeks before I graduated with my bachelor's degree, I officially became a member of a lifelong club known as Hillaryland, the unofficial name for the First Lady's office.

In my very first full-time job, I was to be surrounded by smart, dynamic women working at the pinnacle of power, not just in America, but in the entire world, and I'd been given an invitation to join them, confirming everything I had ever believed about the incredible freedoms and opportunities American women enjoyed. When Melanne offered me the job, I was so excited I forgot to ask a single question about compensation or benefits. It was only later, sitting in the Human Resources Office filling out the necessary paperwork, that I learned what my salary was going to be. Twenty-seven thousand, five hundred dollars per year, they told me. To someone who hadn't even graduated college yet, it seemed like all the money in the world. What I didn't know then, what I didn't think to ask, and what I wouldn't have known to be upset about even if someone had told me, was that throughout my tenure, my male counterpart in the Oval Office made twice as much as I did.

A couple of weeks later, I sat in a folding chair on the Ellipse, just off the National Mall, among thousands of students graduating from George Washington University on a beautiful spring day. Covering my eyes from the glare of the sun, I looked to the right and saw the window to my office. I wondered how many of my peers had a view of work from their graduation ceremonies.

Most of my college friends were headed to graduate school, some to medical school, others to law or business school. That weekend we said our goodbyes and agreed to stay in touch, which I meant sincerely. I couldn't imagine my life without the first set of American friends I'd ever made. But those relationships soon faded into the background as I became consumed with the work that seemed to take up every waking hour. Gradually, my life just went another way.

* * * *

For all the twelve-hour days I had put in at the office during my first year on the job, getting that call at a family wedding in October of 1997 was something different. It was the first time I was forced to choose between work and family. It was, as they say, the fork in the road. It wasn't hard to see where one of those roads led. It was right there in front of me that weekend: the storybook wedding, a husband, children, holidays and weekends spent with friends and relatives—a fortunate, privileged life, one that anyone could be grateful to have. Down the other road was something else. A challenge? An adventure? A chance to change the world, maybe? I didn't know.

I also didn't know what the cost of taking that road would be, that it would mean twenty years of missed weddings, missed birthdays, missed funerals. Twenty years of sleeping on planes and perpetual jet lag. Twenty years of praying alone in strange hotel rooms and being the lone person fasting during Ramadan at official events, surrounded by people eating and drinking. Twenty years of downloading pictures of newborn nieces and nephews instead of visiting the hospital to hold them myself.

I couldn't possibly have foreseen any of that. All I knew was that whatever was down that road, I wanted it. I didn't even hesitate. That day at my cousin's wedding I told my family what I would tell them a hundred more times in the years to come: that I needed to leave early for work.

This time, at least, it was novel and exciting. "Argentina?" my mother said. "Traveling with the President and First Lady! Of course, you must go!"

"Well, I am not exactly traveling *with* them, Mom. I will be going in advance to set up their trip in one city."

"Oh, how exciting that you are going to Argentina with the President and First Lady."

"No, Mom, no. That's not—I'm not actually . . . Never mind."

I called the White House travel office and booked a Monday morning flight out of Dulles Airport. The next day, I packed my black gym bag with travel essentials; little of what I had with me in New Jersey would be needed in Buenos Aires. Then I joined the rest of my family in a caravan of cars into Manhattan for the wedding ceremony.

Traditionally, for most of our family gatherings in Queens or New Jersey, family members took turns hosting in their homes or backyards. Sometimes we gathered at the local Elks lodge, the only place big enough to accommodate our numbers. At those parties, a few things were always guaranteed: The guest list would be large, everyone invited along with plus-ones or -twos or -fives. People would be encouraged to help themselves from buffets that never seemed to run out of piping-hot chicken or rice. There would always be tea and a variety of too-sweet desserts, and never, ever, any alcohol. This wedding, however, was different. This one was being held at a Manhattan hotel on Central Park South, a decidedly more cosmopolitan setting for events than we were used to, and everyone was excited about it.

When I arrived at the hotel, the first thing I did was ask the concierge how long the ride to Penn Station would be, so that I would get there with plenty of time to catch my train to DC. To ensure I wouldn't be delayed at coat check later, I went to the room where the ceremony would take place and stashed my gym bag behind some heavy drapes, covering it with my gray wool coat and then straightening the drapes over the pile so that it wouldn't be visible. Then I found the bathroom closest to the ballroom and the exit so I would be able to quickly change from my gown into travel clothes. Finally, just before I walked into the ceremony, I called Amtrak to be sure my train wasn't late or canceled.

Unbeknownst to me at the time, I had just "advanced" my own departure.

After the wedding ceremony, I maneuvered myself close to the front of the crowd—my family, like many South Asian families, is not good at organizing in lines—and gave the couple a quick congratulations before slipping away, retrieving my things from behind the drapes, and racing to the bathroom across the hall. Cramped inside the small restroom stall attempting to change, I could hear women outside fixing their makeup and making small talk about the wedding. "What a beautiful ceremony. Didn't the imam do a wonderful job? Did you hear they are serving *alcohol* tonight? It must be because there are so many American guests." The chatter drifted in and out of my awareness as I focused on making a mental checklist of everything I needed to get done in the fourteen hours before my flight to Buenos Aires. When I finally stepped out, I was met by a group of suddenly silent women who stared as I stuffed all that taffeta into my suddenly too-small bag. I can only imagine what they said about me after I walked out and the door closed behind me.

As I raced through the lobby, I heard someone calling my name. It was my aunt, the groom's mother, a short distance away. "I wish you were staying with us," she said. This was the same aunt who had welcomed me into her homes in Queens and New Jersey for so many summers, at whose feet I used to sit to hear old family stories and legends. I could have walked back to hug her and given a proper, respectful goodbye. Instead, nervous I was going to miss the train, barely breaking my stride, I called back over my shoulder "Gotta go! Love you!" and made my way toward the revolving doors. I stepped outside into the weekend bustle of Central Park South, a bellman hailed me a yellow cab, I jumped in the back, and we pulled away.

Twenty-two years old and already always in a hurry to get somewhere, I rarely stopped to think of what I was leaving behind.

HILLARYLAND

You do not just wake up and become the butterfly—growth is a process.

—Rupi Kaur

The entire flight down to Buenos Aires, my stomach was in knots. The stated purpose of the President and First Lady's visit to the region was to "cultivate twenty-first-century partnerships" with Southern Hemispheric neighbors. In practical terms, this meant attending a series of meetings, conferences, speeches, tours, ribbon cuttings, receptions, formal meals. Advance staff is responsible for planning and executing each of those events. There were so many moving pieces on trips, it was unclear what my responsibility would be in relation to my colleagues, the embassy staff, and Secret Service.

My plane reading included the "First Lady Advance Manual." Would I be good at selecting the right venue for the message of the trip? Could I walk into a room and know how many bodies would fit just by looking at it? How would I know the dimensions of the stage I'd need to order for an event? Which lighting package was best? How to do the guest invitations and ticketing? Would I be good at writing briefings? What exactly was a throw? What was this mult box I heard my colleagues always worrying about? I didn't know the answer to any of these questions.

When I landed, a U.S. embassy official greeted me, took my tourist passport from me, expedited me through customs, and drove me to our hotel in the center of the city. When I walked into the hotel ballroom later that evening for the daily countdown meeting, among the sea of faces, I knew no one. *What am I even doing here?* I thought.

Thankfully, that night I met Leah Pisar, who worked at the National Security Council. She seemed to know exactly what she was doing and immediately took me under her wing. The next day, the advance teams visited the various sites to get a feel for each of the events, because any of us could be called on to build any event. Afterward, as Leah and I explored the city, eating Argentine pizza and dulce de leche ice cream, she answered all of my ignorant questions. I learned how to get the right contractor to build the site, how to properly light the President or First Lady, or any principal, design the right backdrop, and where to order it, that it took experience to know how many bodies fit in each room (you will get the swing of it), that a throw was the distance between the press riser and the stage to capture that optimal shot, and that without a mult box to plug in their equipment, the press wouldn't be able to hear a word, making the event semi-worthless.

In Buenos Aires, HRC was planning a major speech on women's rights. The demand for tickets was intense and we needed a venue that would accommodate several thousand people. Our advance lead, Pat Halley, selected the Teatro Colón, a historic and spectacularly beautiful opera hall.

Pat taught me that no question was too insignificant, that sometimes the biggest potential problems were discovered when the smallest question was asked, that you should always be direct in negotiations but step back to spare people's pride or feelings if necessary. When we were doing a walk-through in the halls of the theater, the staff was busy polishing every handrail and touching up every chip and crack in every wall.

In many places we scouted, if you so much as mentioned that the American president or first lady might be interested in visiting, the renovations would begin almost immediately. Pat turned to me and said, "Hillary Clinton must think the whole world smells like fresh paint!"

I was tasked with selecting an appropriate venue in case HRC might want to have a bite to eat or a coffee somewhere in the city. Armed with embassy recommendations and my Fodor's guide, I visited one café after another, just like any other American tourist, wandering in, ordering a coffee or a hot chocolate. I settled on Cafe Tortoni, a beautiful restaurant with dark wood columns, intricate crown moldings, and a stained glass ceiling. I made a reservation for the day of the speech, telling the manager that it was for the U.S. Embassy and nothing more.

On game day, an embassy colleague, a Secret Service agent, and I drove over to the café. I eyed an empty small, round marble-top table toward the back and waited nervously for the surprise visit. *What if she hated this place?*

Soon enough, we heard the commotion outside, the convoy of cars pulling up, packs of American and Argentine security, aides, embassy staff, and Argentine escorts, the unmistakable blonde head of the First Lady appearing in the front door, and the place erupting into cheers. She had barely sat down before people crowded around, asked to shake her hand, to take a picture of her. The coffee she'd ordered was left mostly untouched. In minutes, a sleepy, intimate café had been transformed into a circus of flashing camera bulbs, applause, squeals, and jostling patrons.

I thought of my mother seeing the First Lady in China; that she was among the throngs of people for whom this one handshake was the memory of a lifetime. Now I was on the other side of the invisible line, the one organizing the event, the one ferrying the First Lady through it.

*   *   *   *

Hillaryland was a miniature version of the President's staff. To illustrate, the President had a press operation that included an office in the West Wing consisting of the press secretary, the communications director, his or her deputies, briefing room wranglers, and traveling press staff. His press office in the Old Executive Office Building was even bigger. It included regional press staff, radio staff, television staff, web staff. A team of writers produced press releases, spokespeople chatted up reporters; there were news clip assemblers and media trackers. Major presidential offices like the National Security Council or the National Economic Council had their own press teams.

Hillaryland had a press operation too. It was very miniature indeed. Three people. To handle all interview requests, general media inquiries, press releases, and briefings, on top of traveling each day for a First Lady who was often just as in demand as her husband, sometimes more. This pattern repeated itself in every part of the operation. Though the White House complex has hundreds of rooms, in Hillaryland, most of us shared offices. On the road, we often shared hotel rooms.

However, "miniature" as everything associated with the First Lady was, she mattered, and this was reflected in her chief of staff's title. Typically, the most senior White House staff were given an "assistant to the president" preface to their job titles, the highest rank after cabinet officials like the White House chief of staff, the national security advisor, the press secretary. In the Clinton White House, the First Lady's chief of staff was made an assistant to the president too. Shortly after President Clinton's first election, Hillary Clinton had officially been named as the chair of the National Task Force on Healthcare Reform, a formal policy role on a top administration priority. For the first time, the First Lady's interests had a seat at the traditionally "white boys" table. So in Hillaryland, we just made do with less. We didn't think we were entitled to more. Everything in the White House is set up to orbit around the institution of the presidency. There's the commander in chief, and then there's everyone else.

For years, Christiane Amanpour had personified all my aspirations. In Hillaryland, I discovered other models for doing important work. Policymakers who developed detailed, exhaustive approaches to tackling big problems. Master negotiators who engaged with elected officials to turn policy into law. Communications staff in the press office and speechwriting departments who crafted the White House message on policy.

However, even the best policy, politics, and communications will not get through to the public unless you set the scene, building events that convey the symbolism of the White House policy agenda—and that was the work done by the advance team. In the nineties, with the explosion of twenty-four-hour cable news, a key imperative of advance was to create the "perfect shot" that would tell the whole story with a single image. Every detail was critical: the backdrop, the sign on the podium, what colors to embrace or avoid, where the principal stood or walked, who the greeters were, the order of the speaking program, and whatever gifts might be exchanged; all was negotiated and agreed upon in advance. If someone sitting in Austin, Texas, turned on their TV with the volume off and could say, "I see the First Lady is in Morocco talking about religious tolerance," the shot had succeeded. The advance staff also served as personal ambassadors for the principal. Usually the advance people were the first encounter a foreign dignitary would have with the U.S. delegation, and those experiences shaped the tone and success of each event.

The advance job also involved shepherding the principals through each visit, from the moment they landed until the moment they left. The staff member responsible for the logistics of every stop, in every country, for every trip, was the trip director, who accompanied the principal into the country and had to be ready at all times to brief on how the next few days were coming together. That usually meant that while an advance person was walking the principal through an event, the trip director was on the phone with teams in the next three countries. The First Lady's trip director also had to know what phone calls needed to be made in the car and have the phone contacts and briefing materials at the ready—most of the material in the voluminous briefing books having been committed to memory the night before. She had to know the President's schedule, where the first daughter might be, who to call to get the latest policy briefing in any given moment, what generally was happening in the news, and have a sense of the political sensitivities in any particular event or country. This trip director also had to know when to be loud.

Anytime HRC joined the President on the move, she was swallowed in the scrum that surrounded the leader of the free world, a small army marching in unison: cabinet members, senior staff, military aides, doctors, nurses, security. Every forward motion followed the stride of one man. Does he need to be briefed? Does he have his speech? Does he need a Sharpie? Some coffee? Some Tylenol? Is there a threat headed our way? Every human was there just for him. If he walked offstage after a speech or out of a meeting, twenty, thirty, people would move too. If you were traveling with the First Lady trying to get through that pack, you had to assert yourself. I watched our

91

trip director do it dozens of times. "Excuse me, gentlemen, can we please let the First Lady through!" Sure enough, from cabinet members on down, heads would turn and the crowd would part, betraying sheepish smiles. Once the President noticed she had joined the group, no matter what he was doing or who he was with, he would look up and smile, reach out for her hand, pull her toward him, wrap his arm around her, and kiss her cheek or forehead.

Most important, the trip director was "the bad guy," managing how much time the First Lady spent in one place, whether that meant interrupting an interesting tour or a fun conversation, or sometimes a serious session, or saying no to a VIP. The trip director had to know when it was okay to be late, when to let her sleep just ten minutes longer, when to give her bad news (never just before she was walking on stage), when to tell her good news (immediately!), and when to stay silent. Sometimes the role required having to make small talk with an ambassador, a senator, a former queen, while the First Lady was stuck on a call or making last-minute preparations for the meeting. Other times, the trip director had to assuage an indignant host who felt disrespected. The trip director had to be prepared for everything and anything.

When I started my job, I had no idea where I might fit into that vast flowchart of responsibilities. But HRC's trip director at the time, Kelly Craighead, did. She was already making plans to guide me into a role that I didn't yet see for myself, and to give me a chance to prove I was up to the challenge of taking it on.

* * * *

Six months after the Buenos Aires trip, I was slated to travel to Chile to support Kelly. I met other support staff at the appointed spot on West Executive Drive for the thirty-five minute drive out to Andrews Air Force Base. The paved tarmac seemed to stretch endlessly in both directions, with just two massive planes parked before us: Air Force One and the aptly named "support" plane, which carried extra staff not flying on Air Force One.

We were directed to a tidy lounge, offered warm chocolate chip cookies, and encouraged to help ourselves to coffee from the silver urn. When it was time to go, my name and White House badge were the only passport I needed. I walked back outside, bags in hand, and climbed the stairs of the commercial size 737 jet. It felt like a treat. What I didn't know was that it was a test.

By the time we landed and made it to our rooms at the Hyatt hotel, it was early the next morning. Shortly after we settled in, Kelly called and asked me to come up to her room. She smiled when I told her how excited I was to be on the trip. Then she looked at her watch and said, "Come with me."

Before I could get my bearings, we were headed toward the presidential suite. I nervously showed my temporary Secret Service–issued staff pin to the agent posted outside the door, who nodded and smiled. Kelly went right into the primary bedroom, quickly knocking and addressing the First Lady by her first name. Not knowing what to do, I stayed in the living room. A few seconds later, I heard, "Huma, come brief Mrs. Clinton about her day." *Brief the First Lady?* Kelly had tossed me into the deep end to see if I would sink or swim. I dog-paddled for as long as I could.

I approached the vestibule between the living room and bedroom, and Kelly directed me to stand at the open door. HRC had her back to me, so, mercifully, I didn't have to make eye contact with her. She wore a black-and-white checked robe, hair already done and sprayed to within an inch of its life, and was leaning over a table into a mirror, one eye half-closed as she applied eye shadow. I took her breezy "Hi Huma" cue, then launched into a quick skim of the schedule. I was nervous, stumbling through what I could remember. All the while, Kelly nodded encouragingly. When HRC started asking questions I didn't know the answers to, I didn't even try to fake it. I just said, "I don't know, I'll find out." Kelly piped in here and there, then mouthed "good job" to me on my way out. Her expression telegraphed nothing of what she might actually have been thinking. Humiliated at how poorly I thought I had done, I went back to gather my things, then waited in the living room until it was time to leave.

As we were departing the suite, with a long day of events ahead of us, I saw a few of the First Lady's bags by the door. I grabbed them to try to be useful, not wanting to bring more attention to myself after that sloppy briefing. I slung her purse over my shoulder and saw a hanging bag next to it, which I assumed was an outfit change. I put that over my arm too. I carried that bag with me all day, through five motorcade rides and one domestic airplane flight, transferring it from trunk to trunk, venue to venue, making sure it was on hand for the moment she needed it, although that moment never came.

About ten or so hours later, at the end of the evening, we had arrived back at the suite when HRC turned to ask me, "What's in that hanging bag?"

I turned to Kelly, who looked clueless. "I don't know," I said. "Isn't this yours?"

"I don't think so," HRC replied.

"It was with all the other bags by the door, so I assumed . . ."

"Have you looked inside?" she prodded.

"No."

"You have just been carrying it around all day and you have no idea what's in it?" Her eyes now widening.

HRC and Kelly looked at each other, baffled, as I opened it up. Inside was a tan trench coat. "That looks like Bill's raincoat," HRC said.

I had never heard anyone call him by his first name, so it took me a second to register that I'd been carrying the President of the United States' raincoat around all day for no reason.

"Huma, never assume anything. Always be sure you know why you are doing something before you do it."

Another screwup. I was starting to compile a mental checklist of lessons, and this was a big one: Don't undertake something when you don't know why, no matter if it's carrying a mystery bag whose contents you don't know or being told to build an event for a speech. *Why am I doing this?* Going forward I asked that question on matters both big and small.

In less than a year, I went from being an intern to being the office manager and assistant to the chief of staff. Through it all, there was one person who believed in me more than I believed in myself. Kelly Craighead was strikingly beautiful, with blonde hair and blue eyes that fixed on you like laser beams. She had been with the Clintons since the early 1992 campaign days and was queen of the road. She could conduct this moving orchestra without missing a beat. She taught me the phrase "Fail to plan, plan to fail."

When she was transitioning out of the trip director role in the second term of the Clinton administration, she was looking for a deputy who could first support and then potentially fill her shoes. Trip director was considered a glamorous, exciting job, and many young women in the administration were interested in it. We'd see one another being selected for trips on which we were being tried out for the deputy position, as had happened to me in Chile, and we knew that in the end only one of us would be picked. So we were very conscious that we were in competition with one another. Even so, in the beginning, I had trouble being assertive. When I was first on the road with HRC, she almost always had to say, "Huma, I cannot hear you," whenever I was briefing her on the events of the day. One of the first lessons I was taught was to make a decision and stick with it, and that if there were consequences, you dealt with them.

Despite whatever insecurities I had about my abilities, I wanted to be Kelly's deputy. She knew I had never led an advance team, had only one recent traveling aide experience in Chile under my belt, at which I had not exactly excelled, and needed many more hours of training. When I heard she was interviewing candidates, I asked to be formally considered for the job, and she said, "Great!" I was afraid she was humoring me. But even so I was encouraged by her apparent enthusiasm.

The day of the interview, I went into Kelly's small office and sat in the red leather armchair across from her desk. Her first question was: "Why do you want the job?" I could have said many things: that I was good at managing the interns, that I was well organized. That I could take the message guidance from the policy and communications teams, work with the scheduler to build out a strategic schedule, work with advance teams on how to develop and execute the directive, and then seamlessly take the principal through her day without being late and without causing any protocol mishaps. But I didn't. I gave the most straightforward answer I could think of. "I want this job because I'm committed to this First Lady and this team, and I want to do whatever it takes to support her and help her succeed in whatever she does." She nodded in response, asked me a few more questions, and the interview ended soon after. Then I left, walking past the next candidate waiting outside her office. This woman looked confident, was older, and had worked in scheduling and advance for years. I immediately regretted that I hadn't said more, but it was too late.

"Good luck," I whispered to the woman, as I wondered whether I had just disqualified myself for the job we both wanted.

Though I was excited to be considered for a travel slot, the prospect of leaving Melanne was bittersweet. She was smart, tough, warm, and indefatigable. She was also generous with advice, feedback, and, critically, food. Most junior staff didn't have a White House Mess account because those were reserved for West Wing staff, so Melanne often took care of us. It wasn't uncommon for her lunch order to be called in with something like five veggie burgers, five orders of sweet potato fries, four nonfat frozen yogurts, and one fruit salad.

Katy, who reported to Melanne and was my immediate supervisor, was equally generous. One day, Katy overheard me frantically calling friends to see if I could borrow a car to take my first driver's license test that afternoon. Without even hesitating, she offered me her car.

"Really? Are you sure? I have no idea if I will even pass!"

"Of course. I trust you. Take it. And good luck!" Then she tossed me the keys. I took the test, passed, then came right back to the office and put the keys on Katy's desk.

These were the women I worked with—those who climbed up the ladder but instead of stepping on the fingers of the women on the rungs below, reached their hands to pull up the lowest of us. Hillaryland is all about "What do you need?" and "Let's get this fixed." Hillaryland is "How is your mom feeling?" and "You should talk to my allergist." Hillaryland is "Happy Birthday!" and "Amazing job!" and "Get some rest." Hillaryland is all of those things because Hillary Clinton is all of those things.

No matter how often we get separated or how long we find ourselves apart, coming together is always like returning to a familiar place. Months or even years can go by, but no one in Hillaryland bats an eyelash if you call out of the blue and ask for something, for anything. It's a club that comes with lifetime membership, and the entrance fee is simply the shared scars that come from doing battle in the roughest game in town.

* * * *

A week after my interview, Kelly called me into her office and handed me some work. Offhandedly she said, "Congratulations, you have the job." I was so excited, I grabbed the papers before she could change her mind. Kelly broke into a wide smile. She seemed just as excited for me as I was for myself.

Years after the fact, on a long flight somewhere, I asked Kelly why she had picked me. "You had the job after your first answer when you said you were committed to the team. It's a job where you do whatever it takes to accomplish the mission. Where someone else's life takes precedence over your own. That's a commitment not everyone can make or chooses to make."

She continued. "Imagine if you and Hillary were in some far-flung place and she lost a contact lens before a big speech. What would you do?"

"I would get on the floor and look for it."

"Exactly. You would. I would. You get on your hands and knees on a disgusting, grimy floor and find that contact, because that's what needs to be done. If you can't find the lens, perhaps the speech can't be delivered, and that canceled speech leads to a domino effect of consequences. A disappointed audience, a speculating media, a frustrated administration, an offended host country. Find the contact lens and the world keeps turning."

"Kelly, did this actually happen or is this an example?"

She winked. "Have you ever heard of Hillary missing a speech?"

THIS IS NOT WORKING

White House jobs in any administration are never easy. The stakes are high, the scrutiny intense, there is a nagging and perpetual sense of urgency, a constant need for perfection. When I was sent on my first proper advance to Baltimore in January 1998, I planned, just as I had been taught, to be prepared for anything. Yet, while I was building my first event, something much bigger was breaking.

HRC was scheduled to speak at Goucher College. It was to be a day of meetings culminating in a speech on civil rights. The team and I were on-site by 7 a.m. doing final checklists when a colleague walked in and announced that we would need to accommodate more seats for press and additional guests. We didn't have a lot of time. As we began quickly unstacking chairs and creating new rows, I leaned over to the press advance and whispered, "What is going on?" He shrugged and responded with a single word: "Starr." Then he walked away.

Since I had spent the night in Baltimore and arrived on-site so early, I hadn't seen the news. Independent Counsel Kenneth Starr had been investigating President Clinton since 1994 about a series of "scandals," most recently a failed real estate investment from the late 1970s. From time to time, there would be a development, but it was confusing, and to me it mostly felt like noise. Nothing ever seemed to result beyond breathless headlines. The breaking news alerts about Starr's investigations were like a window into an alternate universe. Nothing about what was being reported from the outside matched what I saw on the inside.

Each of the events at Goucher went off without a hitch. I learned later, along with the rest of the world, that the President had awakened the First Lady with bad news that morning. I imagine that a First Lady mentally steels herself for all kinds of truly horrific news: middle-of-the-night calls notifying her spouse of terrorist attacks, natural disasters, or the loss of Americans in combat overseas. But this was news that no one could prepare for, a story HRC had been told wasn't true: that President Clinton had allegedly had an inappropriate relationship with a White House intern.

Nothing about the First Lady's demeanor that day at Goucher gave any indication that she might be troubled by what had transpired earlier that morning. She was business as usual. As she was shaking hands along the rope line, Kelly told me to get my bag; I was to return to DC with the First Lady on the train instead of going back on my own later. I didn't ask any questions and quickly grabbed my luggage.

By the time we arrived at Baltimore Penn Station, a large group of reporters was already waiting. It was my first experience with a press scrum—a cacophonous onslaught of questions called out by a swarm of reporters moving in unison as a single amoeba, and men with video cameras walking backward to capture every moment. Every few seconds there were blinding, stars-in-your-eyes flashes from the still photographers. The questions felt strident, insistent, and terribly invasive, about the President and his relationship with another woman. HRC categorically denied that there was anything to the rumors. I tried to keep pace with her while she maintained total composure in the face of this barrage. I wondered why she had to put up with it. Had anyone noticed she had just given a speech about civil rights in America? Little did I know then that this was the new normal.

When we got on the train, it was clear that Amtrak had reserved an entire car for the First Lady, her staff, and Secret Service detail. HRC settled into a window seat and started reading from a briefing binder she pulled from her bag for the events and meetings awaiting her at the White House. In her own quiet car, away from the shouting reporters and the solicitous crowds, she was sheltered in a private little sanctuary where she could just be.

* * * *

A week later, I was on the road again, this time to Switzerland to advance a speech the First Lady was delivering at the Davos World

Economic Forum. After a day of visiting event sites, jet lag and hunger were setting in when our hosts suggested dinner at the best fondue restaurant in town. In all our family vacations, my parents had never taken us to eat fondue, so I was curious. Minutes later, small pots of molten cheese were placed in front of us along with chunks of thick white bread for dipping. Our hosts lifted the thin fondue forks and gestured for us to dig in, which I did, wholly unprepared for the intensity and bitterness. I didn't like it at all, but, wanting to be polite, I continued eating. A few minutes later, our lead, Pat Halley, leaned over, pointing to the pot, and said loudly, "You know there is alcohol in here, right? A lot of alcohol."

Thus, did I learn why my Muslim parents had never taken us out to try fondue.

I mouthed back "thank you" and started dipping the bread into the small dish of butter instead while still insisting to everyone around me that I had enjoyed the fondue very much. Another indispensable lesson from Pat. That night I couldn't sleep. Whether it was real or psychological, something was going on in my pounding head, this being my unexpected first (and last) encounter with alcohol.

For this trip, the official schedule allowed HRC some wiggle room to sneak in a little early morning skiing with her staff, but she decided to stay in and work on her speech. My role in Davos was to manage all issues related to the hotel for the team, but as I realized that everyone was leaving, I wasn't sure what was expected of me. I still wasn't comfortable making small talk with the First Lady and didn't know what she might need.

"What should I do if she comes out of her room looking for all of you?" I asked Kelly, who was walking out the door, arms loaded with ski gear.

"You'll figure it out. Take any speech edits she has," Kelly said casually. "She'll tell you if she needs anything."

As usual, Kelly wasn't about to hold my hand. So much of the job was about following gut instincts and having good judgment. You either had it or you didn't.

After leaving a pot of brewed black tea, the latest draft of her speech, and a set of press clips on the small table in her living room, I went to work in the empty adjoining staff room. A few minutes later our press secretary pulled me into the hall and asked me to go back into the suite to remove an article that had updates about the investigation so that HRC could focus on the speech.

I had just been initiated into the tight circle of people making small gestures to manage the amount of stress the First Lady was dealing with from the constant barrage of news about the Starr investigations. The President had denied allegations of impropriety, as had Monica Lewinsky through her lawyers, but the press interest had only escalated, and Starr vowed to pursue Lewinsky. Updates from Starr's team that things were moving "swiftly" or that there was "significant progress" landed like bombshells. Days before we went to Davos, HRC had made a planned appearance on the *Today* show, where she said the accusations seemed part of a long line of attacks against her family and their agenda for the American people, a "vast right-wing conspiracy." It all sounded ominous and unsettling, but it lived in that alternate universe, far away from me.

I tiptoed back into the suite, praying she wouldn't walk out and ask what I was doing. I removed the offending article and slipped back out of the room. A few hours later, when I stepped back in, I saw that the speech was gone but the press clips remained in the same spot I had left them. I'm not sure she even looked through the packet.

Hours later, just before she got ready to leave for the speech, HRC had the team come to her suite to share their skiing adventures and mishaps. Eyes bright and smiling, she reveled in their stories. She even chided me for not having gone, insisting she would have been fine alone. It was something I would get used to. She was always defiantly, insistently trying to force her independence, as though she never wanted to become attached to the privileged lifestyle of the wife of the most powerful man in the world. Yet, there was always someone nearby: an aide, an usher, a butler, a Secret Service agent. Hillary Clinton was *never* alone, even if she wanted to be.

Later that day, she delivered one of her most important speeches. It was about the building blocks of a healthy civil society, how a properly functioning nation is essentially a three-legged stool; the economy and the government are two legs of that stool, but the institutions of civil society—schools, families, religious organizations and other nonprofits—make up a third and equally important component, and if all three aren't working in collaboration we cannot successfully foster a strong democratic society.

The speech received rave reviews, but the high was short-lived. As we flew back to Washington, we knew we were headed toward a pitched political battle, one which would, in the end, require the First Lady herself to jump into the fray.

* . * . *

During the second week of July, just as news broke that the Secret Service was being ordered to testify before a grand jury concerning what they might know about the President's personal behavior, the First Lady was scheduled to give a speech at a local event in DC. It was my first solo trip after my promotion from office manager to deputy trip director. Looking back, I can almost mark the milestones of my professional development alongside the breaking news developments in the Starr investigation.

To travel to local destinations, the First Lady's motorcade consisted of only a handful of cars—she in a large stretch limousine, me in a staff van several cars behind. When we arrived at the venue for that day, I placed the box containing the final version of the speech on her seat on stage. I was still learning to anticipate the First Lady's needs. Kelly had told me I would get to a point where I would need no instructions; I would simply know what to do and when, but I wasn't there yet.

Once the event got underway, I went and stood in the back of the room. As the speaker was getting ready to introduce her, HRC motioned for me to come to the stage. *Come to the stage?* This was not a scenario I had ever seen happen, which had to mean there was a problem. I approached, feeling the eyes of the entire room on me.

She leaned over and whispered, "I don't have the right speech." It was like the world stopped. She was to take the podium in a matter of minutes. I felt my legs go weak. "Did you take my copy from the limo?" Deep inside me, I quelled the nausea and said for the first time what became my standard response whenever there was a problem that needed fixing: "I got it."

That didn't mean I actually had the speech. I most certainly did not have it. I felt the heat rising through my body up to my ears as I walked away as calmly as I could. The minute I was out of public sight, I ran, grabbing a Secret Service agent by the arm along the way. We got to the limo as fast as humanly possible for someone in four-inch heels. While I had spent the long car ride holding and reading what I thought was the "final" copy of the speech, HRC had spent the entire time editing her copy, but had left it in the limo without mentioning it to me. Sure enough, there it was, sitting by her seat, handwriting on almost all the pages. Racing back with it, I entered the room to the sound of applause that greeted her after the introduction, and made it to the stage as discreetly as I could to turn over the speech. I then watched aghast as she spent the first few seconds standing at the podium putting the pages in order. It seemed to take an eternity.

Afterward, as she walked offstage to thunderous applause, she off-handedly said to me, "You should ride in the limo with me from now on." It was her way of acknowledging her own responsibility in the mix-up. It was also her way of showing me that she knew she could trust me when I said "I got it." That ride back to the White House was my first time in the limo with her, my introduction to the symbiosis that was essential to this relationship. Like the train ride from Baltimore, like the hotel room at Davos, this was one of the places where the First Lady was as close to alone as possible, where she could have the private moments from which she drew strength to face the public.

For the past seven months, the media and the public had relentlessly obsessed, scrutinized, judged, sneered, joked, and speculated about the truth of the President's relationship with Monica Lewinsky. Given all the manufactured stories that had come before this one—that the Clintons were murderers, thieves—it seemed very likely that this one was untrue. I knew from experience that interns didn't have that kind of access to the President; we barely saw him. Whenever I did see the President and the First Lady together, the way they looked at each other, the way he slung his arm over her shoulder walking down the corridor, the way they put their arms around each other's waist as they were being briefed backstage, they seemed a committed, loving, happy couple. So even though there was an underlying feeling of uncertainty as spring progressed into summer, fed by the constant driblets of news appearing in the press, I continued to believe that the President was innocent of any wrongdoing.

The most significant day was just around the corner. August 17, 1998, when the President himself was scheduled to appear before the grand jury. I was filling in for a staff member who wrote the First Lady's personal correspondence. I was now officially trip directing full-time, scheduling on days when they were short on womanpower, still helping the office manager who had replaced me earlier in the spring and approving Melanne's correspondence, which was now being prepared by a new intern. It seemed I was everyone's Girl Friday, and I didn't mind it one bit.

The desk phone rang. It was the First Lady, asking me to draft some letters for her. I got them ready and placed them in a large envelope and headed to the residence to drop them off, so she could review and sign them. Typically, whenever I had a package like this to deliver, I left it with the usher on the first floor of the White House residence. When the First Lady was finished reviewing and signing, she would send the package back down to the usher, and the usher would call me to pick it up. This time when I returned to pick up the signed letters, they weren't in the usher's office. Instead, the usher told me matter-of-factly to, "go on up."

I stared at the usher. Up? Up *where*? He smiled. "Mrs. Clinton instructed that you go upstairs." Political appointees like me (and the presidents and their families), came and went with every administration. The ushers, on the other hand, were part of the White House's residence staff, and they were just as much fixtures as the priceless treasures on the state floor. Seeing my paralysis, he said, "Come with me." Then he walked me to the small elevator and Wilson Jerman, one of the butlers, took me to the second floor, where the first family's private quarters were located.

I walked slowly, my arms tingling with goose bumps, my heart pounding in my chest. When I stepped off, I hesitated, not sure which way to turn. "Go on in. She'll find you," Wilson said encouragingly.

I had been deposited at the entrance to the West Sitting Hall, a graciously appointed room that was at once both elegant and inviting. Straight ahead of me, the central focus of the room was a large fan-shaped Palladian window, through which the late afternoon light was streaming. The window was framed by heavy silk yellow drapes, and the walls, carpet, and furniture were all in various shades of yellow and floral patterns. Vases filled with fresh cut flowers, family photos, and knickknacks covered every surface of the dark wood coffee and end tables. There was a tall white built-in shelf filled with books along the left-hand side of the room and a long dark table in front of it. Before stacks of papers and binders on the table, I found the First Lady at work.

My awe for the surroundings was matched only by my awe for the woman who lived there. This figure didn't compute with the hundreds of caricatures of her. She didn't appear to be the "scorned wife," and there was no indication in all the months I had been with her that she was Lady Macbeth.

She thanked me for coming up, handed me the signed letters, along with several binders and a few more assignments. She was a little tired-looking that day but otherwise seemingly unperturbed by the testimony happening simultaneously two floors below. As I would learn is her nature, she was using the time not to sulk or mope but instead to be productive.

When I had walked to work that morning, I did not know what the President's testimony would reveal or what it would mean for our collective destinies. I did not know that two days earlier HRC's husband had admitted to her that he had been unfaithful, that the reports over the last seven months about his affair were true, and that he would admit as much to the nation when he testified to the grand jury. If *she* was wavering in any way, it didn't show, even in the privacy of her own home. I felt reassured in her presence. I was not sophisticated enough even to speculate on what she might be feeling. I was years away from any serious relationship—or heartbreak—of my own and couldn't appreciate the magnitude of hers.

In any case, it was none of my business. In all the years of Islam classes, one of the lessons repeated over and over again was that slander, gossip, and exploiting people's personal weaknesses are among the worst forms of conduct for any Muslim. There was a *hadith* about

Prophet Muhammad asking his companions, "Do you know what backbiting is? Saying something about your brother that he dislikes." Someone then asked, "What if what I say about my brother is true?" Muhammad responded: "If what you say is true, then you have back-bitten about him, and if it is not true, then you have slandered him." Neither was permissible behavior. I didn't want to linger, not on those thoughts and not in that room. Even though she had invited me to come up, being there felt like an imposition. I was anxious to get back downstairs as quickly as possible.

When I reached the ground floor, I had just started to breathe normally when the door to the Map Room opened and the President walked out. I froze, not knowing whether to carry on or to stop until he passed me. I didn't know if he was done with his testimony or if he was taking a break; all I knew was that in that moment I wanted to disappear. He managed a sad smile and proceeded to the elevator I had just stepped off of.

Later that night, I walked home and into my Foggy Bottom apartment and watched on television as President Clinton acknowledged that he had misled his family and the American people. That perfect bubble of a world where I worked had just burst, and I was sad and angry on behalf of the woman who was now my boss.

* * * *

In all the frenzied speculation about why Hillary Clinton stayed in her marriage—that it was a political arrangement, that she did it so she could launch a political career of her own—skeptics tended to rush over the very obvious explanation: She did it because she believed it was the right thing to do for herself and her family—and her country. Looking back, I think about all she had to weigh in that decision. How hurt and angry she probably was. How unfair it seemed that the burden of her husband's mistake fell on her. But she didn't have the luxury of approaching this simply as a wife and mother. She also had to look out for the institution of the presidency and for the country. Yes, the President had committed a terrible error in judgment, but it was a moral offense, not an impeachable one. A mistake that was being weaponized by a minority faction of conservatives in an extreme effort to overturn a pragmatic and progressive agenda that the majority of the country had voted for and still wanted. However she felt as a wife, I don't think the First Lady, as a public servant, could have allowed that cabal to claim victory.

It was an impossible situation. Defending the institution of the presidency meant forgiving the actions of a man who, in different circumstances, she might otherwise not have chosen to forgive. The power to forgive was her burden alone. If she stood by him, then the nation would stand by him. If she didn't stand by him, then the nation might abandon him too, precipitating a constitutional crisis and sending the country into dangerous and uncharted political waters.

So, she didn't just stay. She stayed and she fought.

* * * *

The midterm congressional elections were a few months away and HRC was actively campaigning for candidates. While the President's approval numbers had stayed high despite the news in August, hers had soared, and her schedule was packed. Protecting the President from impeachment hinged on preventing Democratic losses in Congress, so they couldn't afford to lose a single vote.

Here too I followed her lead, as I had been doing for months. After I got over the immediate shock of watching the President's admission on TV that night, I put my judgments and emotions aside. What was at stake for the country was bigger and more consequential. Hurt feelings and anger weren't relevant. Only the battle mattered now. But being in the fight took a toll, most of all on the First Lady.

It made me all the more determined to spare her any worry about any of the practical problems it was in my power to resolve. Sometimes this involved near misses that verged on the comical. In September, the President and HRC traveled to New York City for a series of major events, flying in by a quartet of helicopters to the Wall Street landing zone. I was on one of the first helicopters to touch down. As the President's valets quickly unloaded the luggage that had been on my helicopter, suitcases and hanging bags sat precariously close to the edge of the pier when the empty helicopter was about to take off. Pretty soon, we all stood paralyzed as the propellers increased speed, the helicopter lifted into the air, and the prop wash from the rotors picked up one of the hanging bags belonging to HRC and flung it into the East River.

I raced to the edge of the landing pad to see the bag slowly floating away in the current, knowing it was already out of my reach. I looked up as Marine One was fast approaching. I ran into the terminal. "Do you have anything I can use to pull a bag out of the water?" I pleaded with the staff.

A crew member walked swiftly toward the water carrying a long pole that I think was in fact a broom and started fishing out the bag. "In all my years, nothing like this has ever happened before," he yelled, shaking his head as he lifted the sopping wet garment bag out of the water. Then I shoved it into the back of the staff van.

Once we had driven to the hotel and the two of them were safely deposited in their suite, I asked if the concierge could get the clothes cleaned within a few hours. The First Lady walked on stage the next day without a clue that her suit had been floating in the East River the night before.

A more significant day of reckoning for me came on October 6, 1998. Just the day before, the House Judiciary Committee had voted to proceed with impeachment hearings. But for HRC's schedule, this day was no different: a visit with the First Lady of Hungary, a speech on policy to prevent child abuse, an awards ceremony for the National Endowment for the Arts, a video recording session, a meeting with cabinet officials and senior staff, and finally two fundraisers to close the night. The day ended with a fundraising dinner for women who supported Democratic candidates, held at a gracious home in Washington, DC. A buffet was set up in the formal dining room; guests were making their own plates and then moving to the living room for the discussion, perching their plates on their laps, their wine glasses arrayed along cocktail tables as they filled the sofas and chairs arranged around the room.

The hostess pulled me aside and asked me if I was going to make a plate for the First Lady or if she was going to make one herself. Not confident that I knew what she preferred, but certain she must be starving, I decided to just ask her, interrupting her mid-conversation with a guest. She considered it for a second and then said she would just do it herself, seeming annoyed at the interruption. Everyone wanted a piece of her at all hours, and at this moment, so did I.

I followed her into the now empty dimly lit room, watched her pick up a blue-and-white plate from the stack, contemplate the food on the table, and suddenly set the plate back down on the stack with a clatter.

"This is not working." Her voice low, her tone firm and unmistakably frustrated. *What is "this"? Me? My work? My questions? My answers?* I said nothing, silence feeling like the only acceptable response. She skipped the buffet entirely, and returned to the living room to start speaking, her composure fully recovered as she passed through the doorway back into the public sphere. She gave her speech while everyone else ate, and didn't say another word to me the rest of the night.

Though I had instructions to ride in the limo with her, I made my way to the staff van for the return trip to the White House, feeling certain my presence would not be welcome. I spent the entire ride back sure I had lost my job.

When we pulled into the South Portico, I purposely stayed back, sad that my last experience with the First Lady had been such a failure. Seconds later, an usher popped out to say she was asking for me. I walked toward her, eyes downcast, biting the inside of my cheek.

I heard her voice before I saw her face. "I am sorry for what I said earlier," she said.

"We're all under so much pressure," she continued. "It wasn't a reflection on your work. I hope you know I'm incredibly grateful for all you do for me. I don't tell you enough, and I'm really sorry."

I was so unprepared for the generosity that she managed to evince, even in the midst of what must have been the most challenging period of her life, that I almost blurted out, *I would walk to the ends of the earth if you asked!* Every day in this job I was tested: to plan out and perfect every detail of a grueling schedule, to read the mind of a private woman who, in public, was carrying the weight of the republic on her shoulders. And I was forever anxious about whether I was succeeding.

This moment changed that. For the first time, she had told me that my efforts mattered, that they had been noticed and even valued. I now understood that I wasn't the cause of her stress; in fact, it was the very opposite. Just like that, my professional insecurity dissipated and I entered a new phase in my relationship with the First Lady of the United States. We walked arm in arm through the Diplomatic Reception Room onto the red carpet of the main hall to the small elevator.

"See you tomorrow," she said as the elevator doors closed.

* * * *

HRC relentlessly campaigned for just about every last candidate who asked for her help. California, New York, Illinois, Washington, Ohio, Nevada. By election night, she had headlined thirty-four rallies and more than fifty fundraisers in twenty states.

Conventional political wisdom dictates that the party controlling the White House will almost always lose congressional seats in midterm elections, and some believed that a weakened president would surely lose even more than usual. On election night, Democrats gained five seats in the House and held off any Republican gains in the Senate. Across the board, pundits and pollsters alike credited the victory, at least in part, to the efforts of the woman who had replaced her husband as the most popular Democrat in the country.

It was Hillary Clinton's effort, her struggle and her strategizing, her broken and open heart that had saved the presidency. For the first time since healthcare reform failed and the Democrats lost control of the Congress in 1994, Hillary Clinton was the savior, not the liability. She was now being encouraged to run for office in her own right, speak for her own potential, instead of just fading off into the background. For me, the background was just fine. More than fine. Plenty seemed to be happening there too.

NATIONS AND TRIBES

We should face reality and our past mistakes in an honest,
adult way. Boasting of glory does not make glory, and sing-
ing in the dark does not dispel fear.

—King Hussein of Jordan

I stood on the small balcony of my hotel room in Jerusalem, overlooking the Old City, the windy, ancient quarter where the world's three
great monotheistic faiths intersect. As the sky took on the golden,
orange, pink, and purple shades of sunset, I heard the call to the evening *maghrib* prayer. I closed my eyes. For a brief moment, I was back
in Jeddah enjoying the familiar melodic sound. I walked back into my
room to begin a letter to my mother. It felt like this trip was going to
be momentous.

It was December 1998, and while the U.S. House of Representatives was on the verge of impeaching President Clinton, I was part of
a team to help advance a historic trip. In addition to making a bilateral visit to Israel, an important ally of the United States, President
Clinton was going to be the first American president to set foot on
Palestinian territory. When we met with the Israeli Foreign Ministry,
on our side of the negotiating table the place cards reflected the names
of many of my Jewish colleagues: Engelberg, Steinberg, Rosenthal,
Shamir, Meyer, Stein—and Abedin. As a Muslim and an American,
even here in the Middle East, my home turf, I remained a minority.

My entire childhood in Saudi Arabia, I was deeply aware of the
ongoing conflict between the Israelis and the Palestinians. It dominated the front pages of our newspapers and nightly newscasts. Then
there were more subtle things. For example, I didn't care much about

what kind of soda I consumed. But I knew that in America, it was usually Coke. In Saudi Arabia, it *had* to be Pepsi because the Arab League nations, out of solidarity with the Palestinians, were boycotting the Coca-Cola company for selling its products in Israel. That boycott was emblematic of a way of thinking that had become prevalent in parts of the Arab world: us against them. Something as basic as a choice in carbonated beverage indicated which side of that war you were on.

For me, growing up in the home of Syed Zainul Abedin, that orientation was not tolerated. While his sympathies were certainly with the plight of the Palestinian people, just as they were with all fellow Muslims who were suffering, my father never allowed those emotions to translate into antipathy for the people of Israel. Some of the academics he met with cautioned him against engaging in dialogues with the "other," going places where even "angels fear to tread" they would say. But his willingness to engage was rooted in a deep love for and confidence in his faith. He believed strongly that for relationships between those of different faiths to progress, we had to accept one another, religiously and otherwise, as *equals*.

The trip to Israel and Gaza in December 1998 was the latest in the Clinton administration's efforts to bridge those divides, to walk where angels fear to tread. The Oslo Accords, signed in 1993, had outlined steps whereby the Palestinian Authority would be granted greater levels of international recognition, certain powers of self-government, and the kinds of infrastructure needed to be a more autonomous, fully functioning territory, in exchange for which the Israelis were to be given specific security guarantees and an end to the violence. The tentative progress made with the Oslo agreement had been all but derailed by the assassination of Israeli Prime Minister Yitzhak Rabin three years earlier. The current prime minister, Benjamin Netanyahu, representing the more conservative element of the Israeli electorate, had campaigned on taking a much tougher stance against Palestinian leader Yasir Arafat, but I was part of an administration committed to trying to bring the sides back into negotiation with each other again.

Seasoned negotiators in the White House were not always sanguine about the possibility of success, sometimes publicly noting "we cannot want this more than they do," where the "we" was an American government, the "they" was both sides in the conflict, and the "this" was some kind of détente in the hostilities. Yet to me, young and hopeful, this moment felt uniquely promising. The Cold War had ended, the Berlin Wall had fallen, democracy was spreading across Eastern Europe, the Soviet Union had peacefully broken apart, the world had stood united in the face of Saddam Hussein's invasion of Kuwait. Terrible problems still plagued us, but there was hope that as the world's sole superpower at the time, the U.S. was offering the right kind of leadership. In the wake of the Good Friday Agreement that President Clinton had championed to bring peace to Northern Ireland earlier that year, it seemed there was no foreign policy challenge not worth undertaking—at least in the view of this particular twenty-three-year-old. Every day the administration I was part of was propelled forward by policy goals that were translated into events and trips.

For this trip, Prime Minister Netanyahu would host the President at various meetings, stops at cultural sites, and a few message events. Chairman Arafat would accompany President Clinton to the inauguration of an international airport in Gaza, and to the speech the President was to deliver to the Palestinian National Council. His visit was in part an attempt to boost the Palestinian economy, to open it to international business investment and tourism. It was also an attempt to shift the perception of the Palestinian Liberation Organization, from being seen as a militia, based on its history, to being thought of as a functional governing body. The goal was to lift the Palestinians up as equal partners in order to keep them at the negotiating table.

We had three imperatives on this trip, as on every other. First and foremost, to carry out the policy goal; here, it was advancing the peace process. The second was to give the Clintons access to average people and nongovernmental organizations, and sometimes we had to push our hosts. On this trip, HRC wanted to visit Neve Shalom, an experimental village where Israeli Arabs and Jews lived side by side, to spotlight an inspirational model of peaceful coexistence. It probably was not the first choice of the conservative Netanyahu government, but she would also make a more traditional stop, visiting the Hadassah Medical Center in Jerusalem with Mrs. Netanyahu. The Clintons valued these events because they cut through the overly staffed and scrubbed depiction of a country and were often meaningful to the members of the public who were included. The third and last imperative was to visit cultural sites, in order to both deepen the principal's understanding of the rich history of a particular country and show respect for the country's traditions. Here, there were many such sites to choose from.

At meetings with officials from the Israeli Foreign Ministry, as a member of the advance who was also actually on the First Lady's staff, I was given more deference on what might end up on the final schedule, even though I didn't have the authority to make any final decisions. It was the beginning of my using the pronoun "we." "We" gives you a lot of latitude. "We" isn't my opinion, "we" keeps it one step away from "she" in case something needs walking back, and "we" doesn't put responsibility on any one individual. On top of everything else, no one can question "we." Who knows who the "we" actually is? But I will let you know what "we" want as soon as "we" figure it out. So, with all eyes turned toward me, I said I agreed with our senior lead advance and conveyed to the Israeli Foreign Ministry that yes, I expected that "we" would join the president at the grave site of slain former Prime Minister Yitzhak Rabin, as well as at the official state dinner with the Netanyahus.

The morning after I arrived in Jerusalem, our advance team toured the Old City; on the off chance the President, the First Lady, or a senior delegation member would want to go, we needed to scout potential sites. In Jerusalem, spiritual worlds collide, crammed together as closely as the cobblestones on the ground. For Jews, Jerusalem is the most important holy city and home to the Wailing Wall, all that is left of their sacred temple. For Christians, it is where Jesus Christ was sentenced to death, where he walked the Stations of the Cross, the Via Dolorosa, on the route to his crucifixion, and where his remains were entombed before his resurrection and ascension into heaven. For Muslims, the Dome of the Rock, which sits atop the Temple Mount, is the place from which Prophet Muhammad was taken up to heaven on a celestial horse brought to him by the Angel Gabriel. No matter your faith, or lack thereof, stepping into that setting is spectacularly moving.

The Old City itself evoked something out of an Arabian Nights fairy tale—the narrow limestone alleyways, the children playing in the street, the merchants selling their wares from sheets on the ground or in little one-room shops with bare fluorescent bulbs dangling from the ceiling, the scent of grilled *shawarma* meat and cardamom permeating the air. It reminded me of Balad in Jeddah, though here men walked by in black hats alongside women in hijabs. You heard Arabic from every second person, and to get basic directions we picked up a few Hebrew words. I couldn't really tell who was Muslim or Jewish or Christian or Arab or Israeli.

One of the first stops we made outside Jerusalem was at Masada. In AD 66, some nine hundred Jews fleeing the Roman siege of Jerusalem had taken refuge at the Fortress of Masada, built high up on a mountain overlooking the Dead Sea. When it became clear that their defenses would fail and the Roman army would soon capture them, rather than be taken as slaves, they elected, en masse, to commit suicide. Well known to both Christians and Jews in the West, it was a historic event I'd never studied in school. This was a perfect example of something that children growing up in my part of the Middle East, not so far from here, were not taught. And of course there were equally famous historic events with which we were intimately familiar, but that wouldn't have been taught to children here.

The very founding of my faith occurred when the Angel Gabriel appeared to Muhammad, who had withdrawn to meditate in a cave on Mount Hira, three miles north of the city of Makkah, and the angel proclaimed "Read! Read in the name of your Lord who created—created man of a blood clot. Read and your Lord is most bountiful. He who taught by the pen—taught man that which he knew not" (Qur'an 96:1–5). It was on this twenty-first day in the month of Ramadan that Islam came to be. Seeking knowledge, we are taught, is the message Muhammad was given. Yet there was much the two sides didn't know about each other.

Our advance team pressed on to Gaza. We visited the sites that the Palestinian Authority had proposed and met for lunch at an informal waterfront restaurant with Yasir Arafat's brother, a charming and gregarious man whom everyone called Dr. Arafat. He talked animatedly about the future, once the airport was open and Gaza was accessible to the world. He swept his hand out over the sea, describing plans to build hotels, amusement parks, swimming pools, and playgrounds where children could play. "You'll see. Everyone will come to Gaza."

The most emotionally intense stop was a visit to the Al Shati refugee camp, known as Beach Camp because it was built along the coast. The beach itself was gorgeous, mile after mile of beautiful Mediterranean blue. Turning toward land, however, was jarring. There what we saw was a squalid, exposed, concrete skeleton of a neighborhood, where doors and windows had been blown out by incoming shells, and several buildings abandoned mid-construction. It was home to tens of thousands of refugees sharing an area of less than one square kilometer, and living under the constant threat of violence. A striking contrast with Tel Aviv's skyscrapers, discos, and upscale restaurants, an hour's drive from here. We smiled and nodded our heads at the many people we passed, including little children, some with matted hair, a few wearing no shoes. The children were the same as children everywhere, happy and innocent, laughing and smiling—too young to understand all the ways in which they were being deprived. To them this life was normal.

Our team walked through the women's empowerment center, which was operating in a multistory building, one of the stops we were contemplating for the First Lady. The young man and woman escorting us took us to the roof as part of the tour. I looked out over the city, and other than the bright blue sea, most everything I saw was dusty, arid, and brown except, off in the distance, where I noticed a patch of vibrant green. There were nice buildings and what appeared to be trees and grass. It looked like a desert oasis, or a mirage.

"What's that?" I asked.

"That," our consul general said, "is an Israeli settlement."

"But it's so green. I thought you said there was very little running water here."

"That's right," he said. "There's limited running water *here*. The Israelis control the water so twenty times more goes there than comes here."

It was the first time I saw up close what it was like to live under the daily humiliation Palestinians had suffered for years. There it was, a better, easier life, staring right at them. It was our job to be diplomatic, but I was fighting to maintain a neutral expression in front of our hosts; in my chest, a flash of outrage. We walked back downstairs, and as we said goodbye to the children, I feared that in a few years their smiles would disappear.

Toward the end of the advance, our team gathered with our Israeli hosts for lunch at a casual outdoor restaurant on the outskirts of Tel Aviv. The head of the Israeli delegation, a senior official in the foreign ministry, invited me to sit next to him, and we dug into the hummus and hot pita bread that greeted us after we took our seats. All our business done, it was mostly a social meal. We chatted about our lives and families, our own origin stories, sitting there in that land where all our faiths intersected.

As we ended the meal, sipping on fresh mint tea, the official leaned over to me. "You know, we really like this American delegation," he said. "But you are our favorite because you are the most like us."

Thunderbolt moment. Growing up in Saudi Arabia, in the heart of the Islamic world, I might have thought that there was no one more "other" than an Israeli. We were raised on opposite sides of a vast divide and that difference was supposed to instill mistrust. I did and always will feel an affinity, an alliance with my Palestinian brothers and sisters. Yet in that very moment I knew he was right. Compared to most of my American colleagues, I did look more like them. I spoke more like them. I had a cultural connection with them. Intellectually, I knew that we worshipped the same God. Perhaps, most revealing to me, was that I felt very much at *home*. So what did that mean exactly? If we are so alike, then what would it take for us to stop killing one another?

*   *   *   *

When the day of the presidential visit finally arrived, it was clear that Gaza was like every other city the first family had ever visited; everywhere within view of the limousine was cleaned up, whitewashed, and painted. The motorcade route was festooned with ribbons on which dangled thousands of miniature American and Palestinian flags, the decorations seeming to string the entire city together. On billboards and buildings large banners read in English and Arabic: "We have a dream."

The airport inauguration ceremony was brief. Before the clicking of dozens of cameras, the President cut the ribbon once, then continued to cut it into strips, handing pieces to the First Lady and to Chairman Arafat and his wife, Suha, before slipping a fourth strip into his own pocket, a precious memento of his goals here. Could this be the true beginning of a new peace between the Palestinians and Israelis, a new prosperity for the Palestinian territory?

Most people we saw in Gaza on that trip talked so confidently about the future that it was hard not to get swept up in their enthusiasm. Even Arafat said to the assembled press corps that peace was possible with President Clinton's leadership. The air seemed alive with a palpable sense of promise. People genuinely believed, or were willing themselves to believe, that real progress was at hand.

* * * *

A year and a half later, the administration would remain dogged in pursuit of that hope, working to transform the magic of those historic moments on the trip, into lasting results. That was why President Clinton hosted Chairman Arafat and Israel's new Prime Minister, Ehud Barak, for last-ditch peace negotiations in July 2000 at Camp David. The President had asked for me to be a part of the team receiving the delegations from the Middle East. It was weeks before my twenty-fifth birthday and I could think of no better way to spend it.

The Clintons always seemed mindful of the symbolic weight of their presence. It showed in the way President Clinton had walked in the procession at the funeral of King Hassan of Morocco, shoulder to shoulder with thousands of mourners, defying both protocol and security. It showed when they both scrapped their schedules to attend the funeral of Jordan's King Hussein, a great champion of peace. It showed in how they publicly mourned the assassination of Israel's Prime Minister Yitzhak Rabin, to whom the President bid farewell with the simple Hebrew phrase, *shalom haver*, goodbye friend. Just as the Clintons used their time in the White House to achieve certain policy goals, they also used other tools at their disposal: words, deeds, and any skill, talent, or insight their staff might possess. Someone again saw that I had something unique to contribute, just as when

I'd been asked to greet the prime minister of Bangladesh, and to help with the White House Eid celebrations.

My role at Camp David was to work with the Social Office staff to ensure that the visiting delegations had everything they needed. If any delegation member had a question about the ever-changing meeting schedule, it was our job to guide them. If they were curious about what the other activity options might be, like going for a walk or bowling, we were there to advise. We made sure they knew where and when to go for meals, and then made small talk with them until the leaders arrived.

Even though the mood was often convivial during those days, there were also plenty of tense moments. Each side had come to the table courageously and without any specific preconditions on make-or-break issues. One day, the Americans spent a lot of time with the Palestinians because Ehud Barak was in his cabin with a few advisors for longer than expected, even when it was time for dinner. As everyone waited for Barak, Yasir Arafat seemed good-humored and chatty, and I spoke to him briefly. He seemed interested that someone like me worked in the White House. I mentioned a classmate from Jeddah who I believed was his relative. His eyes lit up. Of course, that was his niece's daughter. He adored her. This kind of casual chatter, on the sidelines of the negotiations, was why I was there.

Finally, Barak showed up. Dinner ensued and then the delegations immediately left for the one thing no one could argue over: the mandatory smoking break. I escorted them to a small back porch, the designated smoking section.

In the midst of small talk, I commented about the possibility of success in the coming week and what it would mean for the Arab world. Deep in my bones I held tight to what my parents had taught me—that peaceful coexistence was critical, that the alternative was a shared doom. Moreover, in the text of my own faith, God said he had created us as "nations and tribes" so that we might know one another, not despise one another. And what about the smiling kids I saw in Gaza? What about the optimism of Arafat's brother? What about the signs posted everywhere proclaiming "we have a dream"?

Some delegation members nodded politely when I spoke. One of the younger Palestinian members looked directly at me, eyes dark and intense, and said, "You think we are making peace here?" He shook his head and exhaled an ever so slight grunt as he put his cigarette to his lips.

The answer came soon enough. Both sides had been closer than ever to a deal, each on the brink of making concessions no other leader before them or after them was willing to make. Still, it wasn't enough. The talks failed. It was crushing. In the years to come, America would again and again be drawn into Middle Eastern turmoil and upheaval in tragic ways that no one could have predicted in that summer of 2000. I grew up a little that night. Still, I continued to believe that it was worth the effort. Or as the last two-term Democratic president before Bill Clinton, Franklin Delano Roosevelt, had put it, "It is common sense to take a method and try it. If it fails, admit it frankly and try another. But above all, try *something*."

ARCHIVES OF SILENCE

I walked into my office one morning to find a memo left on my chair. "March 1999, Memorandum for Advance Staff: Travel abroad in support of the President requires the highest standard of conduct by all. Everyone involved in an international trip is a representative of the White House, and in a larger sense, a representative of the American people. Any inappropriate behavior by members of the White House advance and traveling party reflects directly on the President and the United States government."

I was never a rabble-rouser, and when I did speak out, it was more with a whisper than a megaphone. But there was a smoldering agitation inside of me when *other* people were silenced or bullied. It was this agitation that drove me to my first, small act of defiance as a representative of the White House. At the time, I was on a trip to Tunisia, where HRC was traveling in support of the economic modernization efforts undertaken by Zine el-Abidine Ben Ali's government. She would also talk about the importance of empowering women through increased economic opportunity, specifically through micro-credit loans.

Ben Ali had been president of Tunisia for more than a decade, not unusual for a region with basically two types of government structures: absolute monarchies and presidents for life. A "democratically" elected leader, Ben Ali was also known to be a corrupt and autocratic dictator. His country exemplified the complexities of diplomacy: How should the U.S. interact with a government that was democratic in name, that was pro-engagement with the outside world, that claimed to prioritize issues like education and women's rights and economic reform, but that squelched the freedom of its people and enriched itself at their expense?

My advance colleagues and I were organizing several events over the course of two days. The president's wife, Leila Trabelsi, would be joining us for most of the schedule. Her office dispatched a representative to accompany us for the advance, both to support our activities and to weigh in on every minute decision. After a week of discussions between our ambassador, embassy colleagues, advance, and an often inflexible host government, the schedule was settled.

From the minute the blue-and-white plane touched down and we took the two first ladies through the events, I could see that my Tunisian counterpart was struggling in her role. Backstage at events, the Tunisian first lady would hand off her bag, speech, or shawl to the aide without even making eye contact, often scowling and dismissive.

When we arrived at the Palais de Congress for the women's speech, the first ladies were scheduled to meet with local women leaders before the program began. As we headed into the meeting room where the women were already lined up, all ready for their handshakes and photos, Trabelsi's aide suddenly pulled me over. She told me that two of the women who had been slated to join had to be cut.

When I looked at the list of attendees in my hand and compared it to who was in the line, I saw that the two women had already been excluded, women for whom meeting the First Lady of the United States would have been a once-in-a-lifetime experience, an honor to tell their family and friends about. I was upset on their behalf and attempted to convince the aide to bring them back.

By now our conversation had caught the attention of the Tunisian first lady. She probably had no idea who I was. She called her aide over and then summoned me herself and said that I should stop asking questions.

"But—" I started tentatively, thinking I could convince her if I could just explain the circumstances.

"*Bas, isquti!*" she snapped back at me. Enough! Be silent!

A moment later, HRC appeared and the meet and greet and speaking program proceeded as planned. In her speech, HRC highlighted all the progress she had seen at each of the events she had attended. She spoke of the struggle of Tunisian women in the years before independence when women had no legal rights. She said, "Silence has been a burden that women have suffered under for millennia throughout the world. . . . What is so amazing and wonderful to behold is that the silence has been broken in Tunisia." Toward the end of her speech, she quoted a Tunisian poet, Amina Said, who wrote "Host of the earth, we have crossed the centuries. With behind us the breath of the ancients, time also breaks us and destroys the archives of silence."

As the program wore on, I was still smarting from the exchange with the first lady. It struck me that representing my country well didn't have to mean staying quiet and polite. That asserting our values, even on a small matter like this one, was not "inappropriate"; that the urge to do the right thing should override my inclination not to ruffle any feathers.

At the end of the event, I found the two women who had been cut, and brought them to a hallway just outside so that they could have a minute alone with HRC. After almost two years of speaking only when necessary, of staying quiet in professional settings, I had chosen to break out of my own archives of silence. It was part of the process of coming out of the shell that I had crawled into when my father died, and was another turning point for me.

* * * *

I had found new footing back in Washington too. Just before I left for Tunisia, I began filling in as HRC's personal aide, often referred to as the "body person." The personal aide is responsible for all the principal's personal needs, making sure she is up and ready on time, that she has all the briefing materials she needs, that she has packed the right attire for any given trip, that there is food available whenever she is hungry, generally the all-round gatekeeper. I had already learned some practical lessons on the road. How to assert myself confidently, sometimes without even using words. How the distance between the powerful and powerless can seem vast, and that part of my job was to bridge that gulf when Hillary Clinton met the world. I had learned that if HRC asked a question to which I did not know the answer, a simple "I don't know" was the accepted, even preferred response—and that I was then to find the answer as expeditiously as humanly possible.

Now I was working out of the White House residence. By this time, President Clinton had been impeached by the House and acquitted by the Senate, resulting in a collective sigh of relief in the building, and yet our workload seemed to double.

No two days were the same, but each morning started with my walk through the wrought iron gates, past the guard in the West Wing lobby, past the Rose Garden, where roses were not always in bloom but which always looked perfect nevertheless, and past the narrow stone path leading to the Oval Office, down which none of us dared to wander. Finally, I would enter into the residence with its flawless red carpet, up the uneven marble stairs worn from years of people's footsteps, to the second floor, the space I had approached with such hesitation only months before. By my count more than four hundred of my days began this way.

In the early days, I glided through the residence in a trance. I gawked at the art that had lined the walls for centuries, like the massive portraits of President George Washington and his wife Martha in the East Room, and at more recent acquisitions like the first piece of African American art brought into the White House permanent collection, a large Henry Ossawa Tanner painting. My favorite, *Mountain at Bear Lake—Taos*, which was given to the White House by the Georgia O'Keeffe Foundation and other donors, hung in the Green Room. When HRC had procured it, it was the first time a twentieth-century female artist's painting was displayed on the state floor of the White House—but I didn't know that then and took it as a matter of course that such a painting would be hanging there.

My "new" office doubled as the White House hair salon, which meant my large computer monitor, phone, and small brown desk shared space with a white built-in beauty counter, a sink, a mirrored wall, and a heavy swivel chair like you would find in a barbershop. My desk sat right in front of a tall window looking out onto Pennsylvania Avenue, above the North Portico. Each morning, I made sure to arrive an hour before HRC started her day. Armed with my first of many cups of coffee, I never went up to that little office without having read the schedule, the briefing for the day, and the press clips. I shuffled speech drafts, to-do lists, and HRC's daily schedule, which had become my bible. I never agreed to anything, whether it was another trip or a dentist appointment for myself, until I consulted that schedule. And throughout the day, I scribbled all over it to make note of the inevitable additions that accumulated with each passing hour.

HRC might start a day with a White House conference on a policy issue—bringing together experts to combat childhood asthma, or spotlighting the importance of early education for infants and toddlers. She was putting these issues on the map long before they were commonly discussed, using the White House to amplify what were then considered niche issues. After that she might have to weigh in on suggested china and flowers for an upcoming state dinner, then make her way to some local events before returning to the White House for other meetings, and possibly an event on the state floor that would run late into the night.

Days when I was rushed, I closed the doors of the salon and quickly got ready before the beauty team arrived to do HRC's hair and makeup, which usually required setting aside ninety minutes. For my own regimen, I either let my hair air dry into a crinkly mess or did a quick blow-dry to straighten it as best I could. Soon after I took on more travel, I had cut my hair into a short bob and no one told me it was a mistake, even though it so obviously was. My entire makeup application, which consisted of black eyeliner and red lipstick, took thirty seconds. Didn't even need a mirror.

After HRC was dressed and ready, I'd remind her to touch up her lipstick and we'd take the slow elevator ride down to the state floor. At any moment I was prepared to answer every question put to me, just as on the road. Some days began at 8 a.m., others at 5 a.m.; some were eight hours long, others eighteen. After a state dinner or some other formal occasion that had extended long into the night, I would sit downstairs in the usher's office, slipping off my shoes from beneath my ball gown, and wait for the First Lady to call to say she was done for the night. Only then did I put my shoes back on and head home.

It wasn't lost on me that I was privileged to work there, that the White House was a national treasure. It wasn't lost on the Clintons, either, who wanted to make it as accessible as possible to the greatest number of people. HRC would often make annotations to the seating charts the Social Office had prepared for state dinners or cultural events, asking them to try to add more tables to the room. I would run these charts over to the Social Office in the East Wing to show the Social Secretary Capricia Marshall, who was the central nervous system of Hillaryland in the White House. Always the life of any party, she was also the one usually planning, organizing, and executing everything we did in the residence. Looking at HRC's additions to the charts she would exclaim, "At this rate, I will be seating people in the hallway!" I would shrug and say "good luck!" before I ran off again. Soon, there would be tents erected on the South Lawn to accommodate scores more people, and staff standing at attention to meet guests' every need.

There were arts and cultural events constantly, the White House being a stage like no other to showcase the best of American talent. Everyone from Nelson Mandela to the King of Morocco to Princess Diana to Maya Angelou to Bruce Springsteen walked through the portico doors, all of them figures of wonder in their own right. I was privileged to be present at a long lineup of extraordinary performances: Stevie Wonder, Lenny Kravitz, 'NSync, Wynton Marsalis, Aretha Franklin—it was complete sensory overload, day after packed day and night after spangly night.

At first I was thunderstruck by the sight of all these personalities I had only seen on television and in magazines wandering around among us as living, breathing human beings. Working one formal dinner, I heard a man say "excuse me," and when I turned, I saw it was the actor Will Smith holding the hand of his wife Jada Pinkett Smith, and my mouth dropped open for a second before I answered his question. A few months later, however, I didn't even flinch when HRC asked me to guide Jordanian Queen Noor through the residence to show her a blown glass sculpture the artist Dale Chihuly was constructing with his team. Eventually Jon Bon Jovi would seem like just another guest to show to his seat, like any other Jon at the dinner.

My role in these events was different from the pressure I felt on the road, where I was often responsible for building events from scratch. Here, it was more like being a juggler, helping with time management, relaying information to colleagues as they needed it, reading and understanding the briefing, the purpose of each event, being able to identify each guest in the room, on hand to answer any question posed to me by anyone. If something was wrong or went awry or needed to be changed, I was the bearer of the news, and increasingly the bearer and keeper of HRC's preferences.

Suddenly, and subtly, things began to change. In the spring of 1999, there were whispers of a nascent political campaign in the works, reports in the press that soon after Daniel Patrick Moynihan announced his retirement from the Senate, New York elected officials had begun urging HRC to run for his seat. The Democratic party leadership was trying to find a candidate who could compete with the likely Republican candidate, New York City mayor Rudy Giuliani. By this time I was privy to enough of the conversations and meetings in the residence that I knew this was a very real possibility. I saw the calls listed on her personal schedule, watched the heavy binders full of background material carried upstairs, and had advanced a walk in a Moroccan orange grove where I overheard HRC and Maggie Williams, her first White House chief of staff, weighing the pros and cons of a race as they strolled. But everything I learned, I kept to myself.

Once the news was public, Kelly asked me if I wanted to be considered for a position on the campaign, or stay at the White House. To me, the idea of a campaign was exciting. But instead of being direct with Kelly, saying that I preferred to go to the campaign, I said I would do whatever was best to support the team. Days later, I learned I would stay in the White House, and one of my closest friends from the road, Allison Stein, would be the campaign trip director. Professionally, she was respected as thorough and tough. I was disappointed I didn't get the job, but still called to congratulate Allison and tell her I would miss her on the road.

I would spend the rest of my time at the White House staffing HRC on whatever foreign trips she made, and additionally, traveling with Chelsea. Still studying at Stanford University, Chelsea would now, whenever her school schedule permitted, accompany her father on trips, where she would fill in for her mother at meetings, ceremonies, tours, and state dinners, sometimes joined by HRC's mother, Dorothy Rodham.

Chelsea was as approachable as her parents. I was struck by her friendly, casual manner and easy confidence. In all, we were together in Delhi, Agra, Jaipur, Hyderabad, Okinawa, Hawaii, Abuja, Arusha, Muscat, Bandar Seri Begawan, Hanoi, Ho Chi Minh City, Beijing, Canberra, Sydney, and Geneva.

On those trips, it wasn't unusual to find notes from Chelsea outside my door that read, "Whenever you have time, can we talk through my schedule?" Then at the end of the day, there would be a thank-you note with a smiley face left on my desk or atop a small tchotchke she'd picked up along the way. Most years, Chelsea gave me both a Christmas present and an Eid present, the first and last time any non-Muslim friend made that gesture.

* * * *

For about two months, I regretted not advocating for myself to get the campaign job. My misgivings, however, were overtaken by a much more personally meaningful opportunity, this one scheduled during a European trip that was to take place at the end of June. In addition to Paris, Palermo, Fes, and Geneva, the Clintons were to visit a refugee camp in Skopje, Macedonia. When we stepped into the hallway after the planning meeting, I grabbed Kelly. "Please send me to Skopje." She must have been puzzled, this being the least glamorous of the options, but she nodded her head yes without asking why.

On June 21, after flying to Aviano, Italy, I boarded a C-17 military transport plane with my colleagues, en route to the refugee camp in Skopje. In my bag, I carried a book from my father's bedside table called *Unveiling Islam* by Roger Du Pasquier. Inside the book I had placed a folded copy of an article, a warning call my father had written in 1992, titled "Let There Be Light." It was about the then-growing crisis in the former Yugoslavia, and ever since he stood at our dining table and read it out loud to us, his words had stayed with me.

For wherever there is slaughter of innocent men, women and children for the mere reason that they belong to another race, color or nationality . . . wherever the fair name of religion is used as a veneer to hide overweening political ambition and bottomless greed; wherever the glory of Allah is sought to be proclaimed through the barrel of a gun; wherever piety becomes synonymous with rapacity and morality cowers under the blight of expediency and compromise; wherever it be, in Yugoslavia or Algeria, in Liberia, Chad or the beautiful land of the Sudan, in Los Angeles or Abuja, in Kashmir or Conakry, in Colombo or Cotabatu—there God is banished and Satan is triumphant; there the angels weep and the soul of man cringes; there in the name of God humans are dehumanized; and there the grace and beauty of life is ravished and undone. When would men ever realize, in this game there are no winners . . .

Neither the book nor the article was specific to this trip, but still they were my guidebook of sorts. They both focused on the root causes of conflicts such as the one that had driven thousands of Muslims to flee their native homeland of Kosovo for the refugee camp we were about to visit in Macedonia. I wanted to do the Macedonia trip because in some small way I wanted to stand with my fellow Muslims, to see with my own eyes the reality of what my father had written about so presciently in so many articles—articles I had proofread and photocopied and retyped.

After we landed, we drove to the camp, which had been built outside of Skopje. As we pulled up, I could see thousands of stark white and blue tents densely packed together, set up on sand, dirt, and gravel. They seemed to stretch for almost a mile. There were more than thirty thousand refugees living here, and most of them seemed to be children.

The stories were hard to listen to. We heard from men and women who shared memories of being held at gunpoint by Serb forces, who'd been separated from and lost family members as they made their way from their homes into the unknown. Yet these were the lucky ones because they had made it out alive. Our advance team posed for many pictures with the beautiful children who clamored for attention and were eager to befriend us. One of the mothers wanted my business card so we could stay in touch and asked me to send pictures to her when I had processed them, which I promised I would try to do. Suddenly I was reminded of a chilling moment on a trip with HRC in Central America when, as we were about to depart from a meeting with democracy activists, a woman stopped my heart for a millisecond with a simple request: "They won't kill me if I have a picture with Hillary Clinton." Maybe the refugee mom standing before me now thought a photo with White House staff could offer her family immunity somewhere down the line. There we stood, communicating through a translator, two Muslim women, with an infinitely deep chasm between us of lived experience, of opportunity. Still we shared faith—religious faith to be sure, but also faith in the future. I could see that in all the pictures I took that day, in all the faces smiling at the camera. These were displaced people who were going to make it back home. When the Clintons arrived, they were received enthusiastically, and they both lingered longer than they were scheduled to, talking to families, playing with the children.

When we boarded the C-17 to fly back home, the President, who seemed equally moved by the entire experience, came by my seat and said, "I know it must have meant a lot for you to be here." He understood.

*   *   *   *

HRC formally announced her exploratory committee for the Senate in July 1999, and I watched it unfold on TV, like most everyone else. The campaign was in some ways a duplicate of the kind of office she ran in the White House. There was an intensity and focus, a schedule every bit as robust as the one she had maintained as first lady. HRC studied her briefing materials, traveled many of the state's sixty-two counties, took what seemed like every press request from New York media, and as she had stated she would from the outset, she listened a lot. Then she started to propose plans for how to revitalize the economy, particularly in upstate New York, bringing jobs and investment where they were most needed.

Meanwhile I was trying to figure out how to share my responsibilities with Allison. We had the same job for two different entities—she for the candidate, me for the First Lady. Our first joint event, a fund-raiser for the Democratic National Committee at a private home in Washington, illustrated the tensions between two young women with growing pains, each eager to prove herself.

Upon arrival, both Allison and I immediately went into trip directing mode. I directed HRC one way, Allison directed her another. We both called out the same instructions to guests as they made their way through the photo line. When I said, "I got it," she'd say, "I got it," and then we'd both shift to "Fine, you take it." This went on for half the event until finally we heard, "Both of you just stop! Only one of you can be in charge." It was HRC playing peacemaker, or at least sanity maker.

Afterward, Allison and I went out for a late dinner. It started out tense, each of us claiming our rightful place of authority in this world. Then we plotted out how we could operate more smoothly in these new circumstances and we came to a truce, which mainly involved my having to stop trying to control everything. We were able to draw the lines between where one's responsibility ended and the other's began. On days with a campaign schedule, I was responsible for getting HRC out the door of the White House, and then Allison would grab the baton from there.

Sometimes, though, just getting her to the plane was the most challenging part of the day. As my 8 a.m. days started inching minutes, then hours earlier, I would turn on the lights in the salon at 5 or 6 a.m. and then call the White House operator and make sure HRC got her wake-up call. One morning, after HRC had returned from a late night of campaigning, I received a predawn page from the White House operator with a surprise message. The First Lady had not responded to the scheduled wake-up call. I told the operator to wait fifteen minutes and try again. Thirty minutes later, Isabelle Goetz, the lovely stylist who came by several times a week to blow out HRC's hair, began looking at her watch. I asked the operator to try again, but still no luck. Should she call the President's side of the bed? No, I told her. Now I had to figure out how to rouse HRC without waking up the forty-second President of the United States.

I walked out of the salon, past the President's Dining Room, into the West Sitting Hall, and came upon Anita, one of the housekeepers, standing in front of the door to the sitting room holding a freshly steamed black pantsuit in one hand and a melon-colored sweater set in the other.

"Any signs of life?" I asked. Anita shook her head.

With Anita close behind me, I tiptoed into the narrow hallway, then stopped at the entrance to the bedroom. I opened the door to the pitch-black room, knocking lightly and whispering, "Mrs. Clinton . . ."

Once my eyes adjusted to the darkness, I inched toward the bed, leaned over, and shook her shoulder. Hard. She woke up with such a loud start that the President bolted up too, with a "What? What?" I cried out "Sorry!" and Anita ran backward down the hall. There was such a commotion that I could have sworn even the ghost of Lincoln had been awakened.

None of us could keep a straight face for the rest of the morning. HRC, in her usual direct manner, looked up from her briefing book as Isabelle rushed to fix her hair, and said, "Next time, just knock louder."

SPECIAL AIR MISSION 28000

Dreams are lovely. But they are just dreams. Fleeting, ephemeral, pretty. But dreams do not come true just because you dream them. It's hard work that makes things happen. It's hard work that creates change.

— Shonda Rhimes

HRC was campaigning for Senate in one of the toughest political and media landscapes anywhere, taking on two Republican rivals—first Rudy Giuliani, then Congressman Rick Lazio after Giuliani dropped out. There were days when I traveled in place of Kelly, who accompanied HRC on the campaign to ensure that someone from the White House would always be on hand to help the First Lady deal with any official government matters or emergencies that might arise. HRC always looked like she was having fun, and she seemed more energized than ever. She woke earlier, worked even longer hours, and kept going until even later in the night. At events, the crowds mostly cheered, but there were jeers too. She seemed unrattled by the occasional nasty chants at rallies and parades, the boos, the "go homes," the disapproving murmurs that she was a carpetbagger. I had been accustomed to people addressing her politely, deferentially, careful not to puncture the Bubble Wrap around any first lady in the White House; but she was clearly ready for a different kind of public service, and not intimidated by the rough-and-tumble.

At the first debate between the candidates, in September 2000, moderated by NBC's Tim Russert, there was a moment that made us collectively hold our breaths. Most of the debate had gone by without incident. She and Lazio parried on issues—they disagreed on pretty much everything—which had been expected. They did, however, find common ground on limiting the amount of money raised by outside groups to benefit both Republicans and Democrats. But then, in a move clearly designed to intimidate HRC, Lazio raised a piece of paper claiming it was a pledge to ban all soft money and dared her to sign it. When she demurred, he walked over from his podium to hers, shaking the piece of paper in the air, insisting again that she sign it.

She remained unflustered. She had already publicly called for a ban on soft money, but wasn't falling for his publicity stunt. Instead she offered a handshake, which he ignored. Backstage in the Green Room, there was a collective round of "holy shit!" Did it make him look strong and in charge to have demanded she sign? When she refused, did she look weak? I had never experienced anything like that up close professionally, a man confronting a woman in such a brash, threatening way. This was my first conscious lesson in what women were up against in the world of politics.

What I saw in that race was that nothing seemed off-limits, too sensitive to be weaponized for political purposes. A few weeks after the debate, the terrorist group Al-Qaeda attacked the USS *Cole*, an American Navy vessel in Yemen, killing seventeen Americans and wounding many others. Lazio's campaign then attacked HRC for accepting campaign funds from a Muslim donor who Republicans alleged was associated with a group that supported terrorism, which in turn meant she supported terrorism. Obvious, right? With this moment I observed how my faith could be used as a convenient bogeyman for certain dark voices in our country.

Our entire team, from both the White House and the campaign, pushed on, running on fumes and fueled only by adrenaline, ambition, and caffeine. Whenever I was in New York, there was a growing sense of confidence that HRC was going to win. In the days leading up to the election, the air was electric, the crowds ecstatic and large. We could feel the momentum on her side, invisible like the wind at our back, but palpable.

Election day started at 5 a.m. As HRC headed into the elementary school down the road to vote, I imagined what this experience must be like for her. She was holding a ballot with her own name on it. How did it feel to mark that ballot? I wondered. How much responsibility was about to become hers.

Later, I joined HRC to fly on helicopters from Westchester into New York City. It felt like victory from the minute we joined the Clinton friends and supporters who had gathered at the Grand Hyatt hotel in midtown Manhattan to watch election results. When the race was called, I followed Chelsea into the room where HRC was having her hair and makeup done and listened as Chelsea told her she had won. They embraced, and when she stepped out to join the rest of the staff, there was a chorus of quick "yays!" as she thanked everyone for all their hard work. It was such a big moment, so much to absorb, marked by nervous energy and a ballroom filled with cheers and popping champagne, which continued as news of other Democratic wins were announced. But the night was not over.

When a small group of us headed back to her hotel suite after the party, we were still on tenterhooks about the presidential contest between Vice President Al Gore and Texas governor George W. Bush. The presidential race was becoming a nail-biter, until the results rolling in seemed to indicate that Gore had lost. The President, who had been watching the race unfold with the rest of us in the suite, grew ever more unnerved as the night wore on, and began incessantly pacing and conferring with his aides. Talk about a night of mixed emotions. HRC's historic victory on the one hand, and then the gut punch of the Gore concession, followed by the whiplash when he took it back, which triggered efforts to properly tally the vote in Florida, the state that held the race in the balance.

The next day, the First Lady–slash-senator-elect went to Grand Central Terminal in midtown Manhattan to greet commuters and thank her new constituents for supporting her. I would be passing through there as part of my new daily commute in only a handful of months, though I didn't yet know it. HRC had casually mentioned early one morning before she left for a trip that she hoped I would stay on, but in what capacity was about as clear as coconut water.

I had begun to wonder where I might fit into this new world order. What was I going to do with my own life when all the intensity of the last four years—a job that had required me to remain singularly focused on one thing, on one human being—came to an end? I had thought about going to law school, as several of my friends, including Allison, were already planning to do, but I hadn't so much as signed up for the required LSAT exam. There were other staff who'd left during the final year to take lucrative jobs in the private sector, but that option hadn't tempted me. I decided that before contemplating my next professional move, I'd get through the here and now of the waning White House days. And then when I absolutely had to I'd figure out what came next.

*　*　*　*

By mid-November of 2000, transition materials on the rules of the Senate and lists with personnel suggestions started to proliferate, while decision memos about garden tours and spring art exhibits at the White House started to dwindle, then cease. A woman named Tamera Luzzatto was scheduled to come to the residence one day to meet with HRC to help her navigate the Senate transition.

HRC was preparing to fly to Israel that day for the funeral of Leah Rabin, the widow of Israel's former prime minister. By this point, I had seen my share of official funerals, and I arrived in the office that morning knowing I'd have to confirm which aircraft had been made available, that diplomatic staff passports had been collected and prepared, and that embassy officials were making all the necessary arrangements on the ground. I would be calling the Airlift Operations Office and faxing them the assigned seats for each staff member traveling. I knew who needed to be where, who wanted to be where, and who it would make HRC happy to have nearby. I would be confirming the order for the menu for the flight, I would be calling our protocol contact to confirm that HRC would not be taking any of the official gifts we usually arranged for any foreign trip, I would do a final check-in call with the assigned staff advance to be sure they knew the latest on HRC's needs and preferences.

As I was working, HRC walked into the sitting room and asked me to keep Tamera company while she took care of a few last-minute things. I found Tamera, a tall, thin woman with a shaggy bob, sitting on a sofa in the West Lobby and we made small talk as we headed back over to the residence.

We walked into the President's Dining Room, toward the too-shiny mahogany table where HRC held most meetings. I showed Tamera to the seat usually reserved for the most senior person when they met with HRC. She hesitated. "Where will the First Lady sit?" she asked. I pointed to the seat, and Tamera said, "Can she and I switch? This is my bad ear. I need to be on the other side."

"Of course," I said. If Washington was a town of saccharine niceties and opaque messages with hidden meaning, Tamera was exactly the opposite—direct, straightforward, clear in everything she said. When HRC walked in several minutes later, she barely seemed to notice that her usual seat was occupied, or if she did it didn't seem to bother her, and they got down to business immediately. They met one-on-one for a lot longer than we had scheduled, and when Tamera left, HRC turned to me and said, "I really like her."

I think it was in that very first meeting that HRC decided she wanted Tamera for her Senate chief of staff. I was learning that HRC was someone who did her homework before any new undertaking, but also that she had a gut feeling about certain things, and once she made a decision, that was that.

* * * *

I returned from Israel to a flurry of activity at the White House, joining the small team of staff who were helping the Clintons get ready to move. After nearly eight years in the White House, the Clintons being avid collectors and keepers of stuff, the number of things we were dealing with was overwhelming. The curator's staff walked through the residence putting small stickers on the bottom of items to distinguish which things belonged in the White House permanent collection, and which were personal. HRC's personal effects—books, clothes, decorations, and jewelry—were to be identified and indexed before packing them up. Some items would go to the New York house, some would be moved down the street to the new Washington house that was still not ready, some would be given away, and some would be sent to the eventual Clinton presidential library.

I had been officially asked to stay on for the post–White House transition, as the main point of contact of the soon-to-be former first lady. It was standard for all former first couples to receive support staff for six months as they set up their new offices or libraries. So even though there were several people working on the archiving and packing project, I knew that on the other end, I would be the one sitting in empty houses in Washington and Chappaqua and dealing with the consequences, so I wanted to be sure I knew what went where.

The formal President's Dining Room became the epicenter of this operation, where racks of clothes and stacks of books were rolled in on carts to be indexed and sealed away in boxes, only to be replaced by another rack. An endless caravan. Every so often, HRC walked in to exclaim at how much there was. Sometimes, she would look at an old suit or dress and ask if she needed to keep it or whether she should donate it, and I would remind her that she had worn it to some state banquet or other historic event. She would roll her eyes and say "fine" to it being archived instead. For the most part, she trusted me to work on my own, stopping in only occasionally to add to the piles or to make sure I had eaten dinner.

But one day, when the residence staff wheeled in a few racks with contents from the third-floor cedar closet, HRC happened to come by and started to find things that had been "lost," items that Capricia and I had intentionally hidden from her. Like the coat that looked like a carpet that HRC thought was colorful and fun; a tan suede jacket with extra-long strips of matching suede fringe hanging from the arms that she thought was hip. Then there was the worst offender of all, which we had hidden only recently: what I called the Michelin Man coat, a long, heavy, pleather thing with a stamped animal print and a thick faux fur lining that added considerably to the wearer's girth. Now HRC excitedly plucked these lost treasures off the rack and moved them back into her closet, remarking that she might find use for them in the weeks before she left. As I turned back to my index, I made a mental note to retrieve and pack them up where she wouldn't be able to find them.

I also accompanied the senator-elect to meetings for her new job on Capitol Hill. There I caught a glimpse of her future and mine. I didn't know what my title or my exact role would be in the Senate, but I was now the only person traveling with her. As we headed into a meeting, a

Senate staff member put his hand up to bar me from entering. I could no longer be the body who discreetly followed behind the First Lady wherever she went. I was staff to a new senator, one of one hundred, and very low on the totem pole at that. She turned around, completely unfazed, grabbed her bag and notes from me, told me she would see me later, and blended right into the crowd. It was like the first day of school—meetings and orientations about life in the Senate and its history—and she was really into it. When we returned in the evening, the new junior senator took off her student-at-school hat and transformed once again into her alter ego, First Lady, for a White House dinner honoring the new Senate, at which she effectively hosted herself.

The frenzy of the final White House days kept me intensely busy, even on New Year's Eve, when HRC was hosting a staff party at Camp David. As the afternoon turned to dusk, I looked around the room, then started walking down the hall and up to the third floor and saw how much stuff was still on the shelves that hadn't been archived or indexed, and I felt panicky. At this point, we had only twenty days left, and I had no idea how our little team was going to get everything done in time, especially since HRC was going to be sworn in as senator before the presidential inauguration. I decided to skip Camp David. I watched through the south windows as Marine One took off and the house seemed to empty of all life save for the low buzz of the usher's office and the shifting feet of the uniformed division Secret Service agents standing post. I rang in the New Year on the floor of the President's Dining Room surrounded by half-full boxes and holiday party leftovers.

* * * *

Inauguration Day arrived in all its inevitability on a dreary and cold January morning. The weather seemed to reflect the mood that had descended on the White House over the last few weeks. We had been on the last foreign trip of the Clinton presidency in mid-December, a farewell tour of Ireland and the United Kingdom. The crowds in Dublin, then Dundalk, and finally in Belfast, were jubilant. The rope lines were endless, with neither Clinton wanting to leave, each of them ignoring whispers of "we have to go" as they walked down the line.

The Clintons had been invited to spend the final night of the trip at Chequers, the British prime minister's weekend home, with Tony and Cherie Blair. The President's aide Doug Band and I were upstairs working when our phones started ringing simultaneously with calls from Washington. After weeks of recounts and lawsuits, political drama and uncertainty, the Supreme Court had required Florida to stop counting ballots, essentially handing the presidency to Governor Bush. Now we were being told that Vice President Gore had definitively decided not to pursue additional legal avenues and was preparing to call Bush and formally concede, despite winning the popular vote by half a million votes. The Vice President needed to speak with the President as soon as possible. Doug and I peered into the cozy sitting area where the foursome were chatting and relaxing after their dinner and realized what unwelcome messengers we would be. This was the only time during my years at the White House that I knew something important and historic before either the President or HRC. How dramatically the legacy of the last eight years was about to be altered.

Doug and I walked in together and instantly shattered the relaxed ambience. The President shot straight up and went to make calls: to his senior team, Vice President Gore, and Governor, now President-elect, Bush. HRC lingered for a bit but left for bed soon after. She was not going to stick around to watch the unpacking of "what went wrong" while the President, Doug, and I stayed up in a small family room glued to the television late into the night. It felt like only yesterday that I was a face in the crowd cheering from afar as the man on the couch next to me was reelected president.

The next morning was grim. We left Chequers by helicopter to fly back to London for a final tea with Queen Elizabeth. HRC wore a black suit instead of the periwinkle-blue Oscar de la Renta one we had packed. It was a decidedly more funereal outfit than first ladies typically wore to daytime tea with the Queen.

"This felt more appropriate today," she said.

An embassy colleague, who had asked in advance what color the First Lady was wearing so she could convey it to the Palace, raised her eyebrows when she saw HRC emerge from the helicopter in London.

"What can I say, it's muddy at Chequers," I told my colleague. I didn't need to share anything further and I didn't.

The tea HRC hosted at the White House on Inauguration Day for the incoming first and second family was brief, with polite smiles all around. HRC, though, seemed unburdened, and just before we left for the Capitol for the formal swearing in, she went upstairs to freshen up. She was wearing an old blue tweed skirt suit that we had kept out of the boxes for the day. There was an elegant matching navy wool coat to go over it. I waited in the West Sitting Hall, a place now devoid of all personal effects, save for the handwritten welcome note HRC had left on an empty desk for Laura Bush.

When HRC walked out of her sitting room for the last time, slung over her arm was none other than the Michelin Man coat, the black puffy monstrosity I had never managed to pack up. I started to tell her it would be better to wear the fitted, lightweight wool coat, that it would match the look of Mrs. Bush's slim turquoise coat, but I stopped myself. She was going to be warm and comfortable, and her sartorial choices would no longer be the center of attention, as they inevitably are for a first lady. She had not changed into the delicate heels, as planned, and was instead still wearing the comfortable flat black shoes that she had been wearing downstairs as she danced with the butlers. So I just said, "Great!" and we took the final elevator ride down to the main floor.

Two hours later, I watched as the Clintons, now officially former president and first lady, stood on the steps of the Capitol for their fare-well wave after President Bush had been sworn in. Then it was off to Andrews Air Force base to board Special Air Mission 28000, no longer called Air Force One, along with a few old friends and staff who joined for the final flight home to New York. For the first time in four years, the flight itself seemed missionless.

Just hours earlier, we traveled everywhere with a military aide, a doctor, a nurse, a traveling chief of staff, a press secretary, a valet, a trip director, a speechwriter, and a photographer. Now they were all gone. Even the Secret Service agents were new. The purposeful urgency, the slamming of multiple car doors, the sirens, the massive impact of a presidential movement—all that had disappeared. There was no one to clear a path for the First Lady, no hours-long rope line, no one working on speech edits or event preparation, no valets, or butlers, or ushers. As Doug and I climbed into the spare limo for the trip from New York's JFK Airport to Chappaqua, we looked at each other and simultaneously shook our heads. This was the smallest motorcade we had ever been in with the Clintons. A chapter had ended, one overwhelmingly stamped by my boss's husband, whose charisma, personality, priorities, and voice would no longer occupy the main stage. It felt both terrifying and liberating.

A NEW PROTOCOL

A few months after leaving the White House, HRC walked into my Senate office and asked for an application for a New York State driver's license. Her Arkansas driver's license had long since expired and she wanted new identification. From most people this request would be unsurprising; from her it seemed mildly absurd. The only ID she had needed for the last decade was her face.

"I think I might like to start driving again," she added.

Technically, all Secret Service protectees can drive themselves, but most don't. Holding my breath, I met with an apprehensive agent who politely suggested that perhaps she take a refresher driving course at their training facility in Beltsville, Maryland, just in case she was "ahem, a little rusty."

"Of course!" I assured him, laughing at the very thought of her behind the wheel of the huge party van in which we traveled all over the state.

The Secret Service had procured the van during the campaign, since the schedule required us to spend so much time on the road. It had two large captain's chairs, a reading light, outlets to plug in all our devices simultaneously, plenty of cup holders, and room for additional staff to keep HRC entertained or annoyed or informed depending on the occasion. She loved it. We coined it the "Scooby" van because it stuck out like a sore thumb when we rumbled toward events. While every other official stepped out of a sleek sedan or a Suburban, we lumbered around in a mini house.

The former president was not a fan. When he'd see the van pulling up to the front door in Chappaqua, he would say under his breath, "Oh, we are taking this again, huh?" When his wife was off on her own travels, WJC, as we now internally referred to him, would stand with his hand on the door of the van, waiting to kiss her goodbye, helping the rest of us grab hanging bags and suitcases one by one and stuffing them in the back.

"Is she running away from home?" he'd ask us every single time.

No, but her new job did keep her on the road a lot, either in Scooby, or on regular shuttle flights to Washington, DC, where she walked the halls of the U.S. Capitol to continue her decades-long advocacy for children and families, for women's rights, and for expanding access to healthcare. To these causes she added priorities like creating economic opportunity and addressing infrastructure challenges for New York State. She became the first New York senator to serve on the Armed Services Committee, a position from which she could shape defense policy, help service members and veterans, and support military installations in the state, bringing much-needed jobs to those communities. Though her new job did put her at the mercy of the Senate voting schedule, she had total autonomy over her agenda, unlike at the White House, where she had had to get permission from the State Department or the National Security Council or the President's Office, before going anywhere or speaking out on anything.

Right from the start, our team—including legislative aides, communications advisors, schedulers, correspondence staff, and interns, led by HRC's new chief of staff Tamera—helped HRC build a Senate operation that centered on substance, not flash, one that was accountable to 19 million New Yorkers and helped guide them through the maddening bureaucracy of federal programs, whether they were tracking down a disability check from the Social Security Administration or a proper discharge notice from the Department of Veterans Affairs or a Medicare reimbursement. While many public officials worked hard to call attention to their work, almost everything HRC did could make news simply because *she* was doing it. She tolerated the cameras that seemed to follow her everywhere but otherwise kept her head down and just got to work.

My new title was special assistant, and soon switched to senior advisor (my male counterpart in President Clinton's new office became counselor, but I wouldn't have dared to ask for a title that illustrious).

My job was a lot of everything: traveling with HRC and managing all that happened on the road, advising on the details of her schedule, and being the main interlocutor between HRC and the universe of people who needed to be in touch with her. To the new staff, I was the old-timer, the institutional memory of Hillaryland. To the numerous circles of the extended Hillaryland family—the archivists trying to decode my indexes of the former first family's stuff, the former White House staff looking for jobs, the world leaders and their spouses looking to reconnect, her personal friends and national supporters, the staff at the expanding post-presidential Clintonworld that was beginning to take shape in the form of the Clinton Foundation—I was now the primary point of contact. I also kept in close touch with HRC's new political operation, HILLPAC, being run by Patti Solis Doyle, her longtime senior advisor and scheduler. To make sure it was appropriate that I dip my toe in all these spaces, my salary was now split among HRC personally, the Senate, and HILLPAC. Acting as the fulcrum of all those moving pieces brought a lot of responsibility with it, and a steep learning curve.

As I sat in my new office in Room 450 of the Russell Senate Office Building, I had a whole new world to help navigate. How many junior senators needed to make time to interview an artist and schedule formal sittings for their official White House portraits? How many junior senators were asked to decide whether to sit on the inauguration dais up front, next to the most recent former president, or along with other elected officials? How many junior senators were now under a book contract to write a much-anticipated memoir? How many junior senators were marching in the Pride Parade and then running home to host a private dinner for former German chancellor Helmut Kohl, who happened to be in town? The answer to all these questions was none.

I kept a notebook to organize all the incoming. The pages on the right side pertained to everything I needed to get done, all the calls I needed to return. I kept a blank box next to each to-do item and checked them off when they were complete. On the left side were notes I kept with updates for HRC: decisions or FYIs, return calls, scheduling questions, the next bill up for a vote. One day, after my roommate had told me several times that my mother had left many messages at the apartment, I opened my notebook to find a new line in my notebook written in her perfect handwriting: "Call your family. They miss you!" Okay! Check.

For her part, HRC seemed to transition with few growing pains. As a junior senator, she waited in line and spoke in order of protocol, which often meant last at committee hearings. After one of the very first hearings she attended, she marched back into the office to say she didn't understand why we had scheduled her to get to the hearing late. The timing was intentional, her scheduler assured her. It was common for legislative aides to attend and take notes for their bosses; then the senators could come in just when it was their turn to speak. HRC was entirely unpersuaded and said so.

"Just get her there at the beginning," I told him. "It's not worth trying to explain what everyone *else* does."

My closest partner in this new world order was Heather King. She had worked on the campaign and was HRC's new executive assistant, the efficient air traffic controller for all goings on in the office. Together we adapted HRC's schedule to conform to her preferences, which meant that HRC would arrive at hearings right on time to sit and listen to all her colleagues ask the witnesses their questions before she got her turn. Out of necessity, we figured out a way she could make use of the slack time between votes: having walking meetings with guests as she went back and forth from the Senate floor to her office. Who knew she could move this fast? I avoided that trip as often as possible.

The only time I saw HRC truly exasperated in the first few months occurred after a long day of voting. I had been entertaining a guest from New York who had been waiting for her through the votes. After her last vote, she and one of her legislative aides had just made the long walk from the Senate floor back to our office when Tamera popped in.

"Senator, they're about to vote on another amendment," she said.

"Seriously?" HRC said, "There *has* to be a better way to organize this system!" and she rushed back out to record her yea or nay.

Tamera, still figuring out this woman she had known for only three months, looked over at me genuinely mystified.

"Does she mean change how the Senate votes?"

I looked right back at her. "Yup!"

* * * *

HRC shed the remnants of her former life like suffocating layers on a hot day. When she was first lady, someone—often me—carried her bags, mainly to eliminate the visual clutter in the photos that people were constantly taking of her. Now that she had reemerged as the working professional she had been before the White House, she carried her own bag. Toward the end of her first term in the Senate, she became adept at using a BlackBerry, calling and emailing people directly instead of having to filter everything through the White House operator.

Her getting a BlackBerry which, spoiler alert, would later lead to an epic headache, accomplished two things. First, it enabled her to find out about events in real time, instead of having to wait for a staff member to brief her, which was how the rest of the world was already operating in the early aughts. This in turn meant that she could communicate her decisions to us the moment she made them, which improved our lives immensely. Second, it allowed her to be free of the constant presence of her staff. It was welcome to me too, because I no longer had to go everywhere with her in order to keep her abreast of the latest developments. I could sit at my desk, participate in planning meetings, and interact with my colleagues in a much more focused, substantive way.

When the Senate was in session, we spent most of our time in Washington. I was still living in the crammed one-bedroom apartment I shared with a roommate in Foggy Bottom, a way station where I slept at night, stashed my clothes, and had a parking spot for my newly leased car. I started each morning with a twenty-minute drive to Whitehaven, our name for the house the Clintons had bought near Embassy Row when they left the White House. As soon as I saw her, HRC always made sure to mention there was a fresh pot of coffee if I wanted to grab a cup before we talked. From there, I would join her for the drive to the Capitol. Often, we would return to Whitehaven for a final check-in meeting after our long days at work. She'd open the fridge to find some leftovers for dinner, and we'd take turns at the microwave to heat them up. Then I'd collect my car and go home.

On weekends and during every Senate recess we were in New York. We'd fly up and spend Saturdays and Sundays traipsing from event to event. We worked, napped, and inhaled most of our meals in Scooby, but to the great relief of the Secret Service, she never actually attempted to drive it herself. Still, she never left home without her driver's license.

Every day, multiple times a day, I would overhear her on calls with her husband, calls that could be quite amusing. One afternoon, during a long drive, she called the house, and soon after they began talking I heard her tell him where he could find the Windex. Then, after another second, she repeated, "It's called *Windex*, Bill. No, *under* the sink." I don't know if he didn't hear her or didn't know what Windex was or just didn't know where it was kept. What I do know is that in his eight years at 1600 Pennsylvania Avenue, Bill Clinton had never had to rifle around under the kitchen sink for Windex.

We were all getting settled into our new reality, adjusting to new roles and responsibilities. Then, eight months in, an unthinkable tragedy turned our entire world upside down.

* * * *

When the plane hit the second tower, I thought my mind was playing tricks on me. That it was a replay of what I had witnessed just minutes before on the little white TV suspended from the corner wall in HRC's kitchen. One Twin Tower on fire. Now, impossibly, it was two. Still processing what I had just seen, I ran up the stairs to relay the news to my boss, my phone already ringing with multiple incoming calls.

It had been a beautiful September morning. Sun dappling green leaves on the cusp of autumn, a clear infinitely blue sky. When the first plane hit, I assumed it was an accident. Now there was a second crash.

"Okay, so it's a terrorist attack," HRC said, her voice low and serious, quickly gathering her things when I shared the news. "I need to get to the office now. Let's put in calls to George Tenet and Bob Mueller right way."

HRC had shifted so fast into action, so matter-of-factly, that while most of the world was still digesting the news, I was jotting down the names of the CIA and FBI directors and calling Heather to track them down. We called Chelsea, who was about twenty blocks north of the World Trade Center, to make sure she was safe, which she was, although I could tell HRC was worried. I then called Doug, who was on a trip to Australia with WJC. He was asking questions for which there weren't yet answers. While I was on with Australia, HRC was gathering intel from her Senate staff in New York. "I'll get there as soon as I can," I heard her tell her New York state director.

As I made my way back down the steps to the foyer of the house, eyes still glued to my BlackBerry for the latest news, Steve Ricciardi, the head of HRC's Secret Service detail, met me, his hand raised to get my attention.

"We should wait at the house until we know more," he said.

I never even got a chance to respond. HRC was bounding down the stairs behind me, bags in hand, saying, "Let's just go, we can talk in the car."

Steve hesitated, but the car pulled around, and soon we were on the twenty-minute drive to Capitol Hill, both of us making and taking calls, passing phones back and forth, trying to connect with officials in New York and the federal government who might have information to share. A call came in from Tita Puopolo, whose family had been supporters of HRC's campaign. Her mom had an early morning flight and Tita wanted to make sure she was okay, but she couldn't reach the airline and asked for our help. "It's American Airlines Flight 11 from Boston to LA," she said, her voice anxious.

Steve turned around in between calls. The Secret Service was moving First Lady Laura Bush, who had been on her way to the Hill to testify at an education committee HRC sat on, to a secure location. They wanted to move HRC too. Especially now that they were receiving alerts that there might be more planes, that Washington might be a target, and that they were about to evacuate the White House.

"Let me just get to the office and figure out what is happening."

"Yes ma'am," came the reply.

I didn't feel anxious about our safety, but as we got closer to the Hill, I sensed Steve's rising agitation. As we approached the Russell Senate Building, where our office was located on the fourth floor,

Tamera called to say that she was hearing that the building would need to be evacuated, and that her fiancé had a townhouse down the street where they could all relocate.

Steve turned around again. The Pentagon had been hit. "We need to leave now," he said. Our car was stopped at the front entrance, and we could see Hill staff and visitors streaming down the stairs.

"I am not leaving until I see all my staff is out safely," HRC said, eyes fixed on the entrance to the building.

Steve looked visibly uncomfortable. He made eye contact with me, but I was not going to gang up against my boss. Also, I knew she wouldn't listen. Besides, the idea that we might just drive away and leave our colleagues to face the unknown made me sick to my stomach. Whenever HRC saw a member of her staff leave the building and approach the car to greet her, she waved them in the opposite direction, toward the townhouse where they were to gather. Only when Tamera gave us a thumbs-up to confirm that everybody was out did HRC say she was ready to leave.

By that time, HRC had decided she would not be going to any secure location and we headed back to Whitehaven. Her most immediate concern was getting to New York to survey the incalculable damage from the now collapsed towers and to console people, and then get to work at the federal level to support the efforts to repair and rebuild. Foremost on my to-do list was finding a way to get her there since airports and train stations were shutting down. Along with my colleagues, I had reached out to contacts at the White House and coordinated efforts with fellow New York senator Chuck Schumer's office, but just getting calls through an oversaturated cellular network was a frustrating challenge.

In an awful revelation, we discovered that one of the flights that had gone down was American Airlines Flight 11. When I called Tita with the impossible news, I could tell from her voice that she already knew. I thought of her mother Sonia—vivacious, always wearing sweet-smelling perfume—as I handed the phone to HRC. She wandered into her living room as she spoke to Tita and then her father to express her condolences, assuring them she would do everything in her power to hold the perpetrators accountable.

As dusk fell, we loaded into the sedan again to head back to the Hill for HRC to join the members of the House and Senate for a statement of solidarity on the steps of the Capitol. The leaders were at the podium and the junior senator from New York was many rows behind and off to the side, singing "God Bless America" with tears in her eyes.

I was still trying to get the next day organized with our team when I got a message from my colleagues in New York. Since the recovery efforts were ongoing, HRC couldn't bring any aides, just the required Secret Service agents, in order to limit the number of visitors at the site. She hadn't been staff-less since her husband began running for president a decade before.

"That makes sense," she said without hesitation. She had adjusted to the circumstances instantly.

By midnight, in coordination with Senator Schumer's office, we had secured permission from the White House for HRC to fly on a Federal Emergency Management Agency plane the next day to visit what was now a pile of rubble and dust, and all that remained of an unknown number of victims. A makeshift operation of heroes was now on the spot, desperately trying to rescue anyone trapped in the debris.

From the minute she heard about the first plane, HRC had kicked into another gear, one I hadn't seen before. In any other emergency I had thus far witnessed with her, she may have been an important player, offering advice or counsel, yet she'd borne no official responsibility for anything beyond her own words. Now she was a United States senator, her home state had been attacked in the most profoundly grotesque and unfathomable way, and she simply, unflinchingly took charge.

The morning of the 13th, I arrived at Whitehaven early. In a hoarse voice, HRC recounted the devastation she had seen the night before.

"You just cannot imagine the carnage, the twisted metal, glass, and plastic everywhere. It is all beyond comprehension. We have no idea how many victims are buried in that mound. People who were just going about their lives and then . . ."

She looked out the kitchen window, coffee cup in hand.

"You know, we flew over the site in the helicopter to get a sense of the damage."

"What was it like?" I asked, not really prepared for the answer.

She paused a moment to think about her words. "It was like staring down into the gates of hell."

She described the exhausted and stunned people she'd met, the first responders she'd watched doing their grisly work. Along with volunteers and emergency workers, they were plowing through the rubble with bare hands, some with no masks, gasping through thick clouds: metals, toxins, and human remains, the smoke still rising.

"There are people who are just showing up, offering to help, working through the night. Can you imagine what they are breathing? It's got to be toxic."

Later in the day she joined Chuck Schumer and met with President Bush at the White House. Senate and House leaders had been negotiating an aid package to respond to the attack. HRC knew the only way to ensure New York would get the necessary recovery aid was if the White House was on the record supporting it.

While meeting with President Bush and Senator Schumer, she publicly thanked the President for pledging $20 billion to the rebuilding. A message popped up on my BlackBerry from our press office. Did I know she was going to say $20 billion on live TV? No, I did not. In fact, I didn't even know she had! I had been waiting in the West Lobby while she was first in the Oval Office for a private meeting, then in the Cabinet Room for a quick press conference. When we got back in the car, I asked her about the pledge, and she confirmed that she had come up with the number earlier in the day and told President Bush that's what New York needed when they met privately in the Oval Office.

"I am not even sure it is enough money, but I wanted to get a public commitment from him," she said.

The Republican whom many of us had viewed so skeptically when he walked through the North Portico doors just a few months earlier kept his word to her when he spoke to the press.

The trauma of 9/11 shaped us all in ways we never could have anticipated, ways that we are still wrapping our heads around. Intelligence officials confirmed early on that they believed it was an attack by Al-Qaeda. Their leader Osama bin Laden would later take credit.

Bin Laden was from a large and well-known Saudi real estate family, which had the honor of doing all the construction and renovation work at the holy mosques. Growing up, I had met women from the bin Laden family and there were bin Laden girls in my school, but Osama had long been stripped of his citizenship, unwelcome to return home. He left Saudi Arabia in the late 1970s, helping fund, train, and organize the Afghan Mujaheddin to fight against the invading Soviet army, and he'd welcomed support for that campaign from the U.S. The success against the Soviets validated his violent tactics. When the U.S. and Western alliance came to Saudi Arabia to repel the troops of Saddam Hussein in 1991, bin Laden determined to push the West out of the kingdom.

After the bombing at the World Trade Center in 1993, the first act of transnational terrorism on American soil, my father had stood in front of our TV in Jeddah repeating "*Astaghfirullah*," both an expression of horror and a warning cry for how the bombing might impact the broader Muslim *ummah*. "God forbid." Then came later terrorist attacks. In 1998 the U.S. embassies in Kenya and Tanzania were bombed, killing hundreds of people and injuring many hundreds more, and I saw bin Laden's name blaze across television sets at the White House. In 2000, Al-Qaeda suicide bombers attacked the USS *Cole*. And now 9/11.

I didn't experience the backlash that many other American Muslims had to endure, because I was surrounded by people who did not assume that if you came from the Middle East or happened to practice Islam you were suspect. History has turned the founder of our religion into a great warrior, which he was. But Prophet Muhammad was also a compassionate leader, statesman, and father, who built alliances peacefully. What bin Laden was doing had nothing to do with Islam, with the teachings of our Prophet. It was terrorism, plain and simple.

Later, I spent days and weeks with my boss, dealing with the aftermath of the devastation of 9/11. We spent time not just at the Lower Manhattan site, now known as Ground Zero, but anywhere there were survivors, family members, first responders, scared city residents. We went to hospitals and armories, support centers and churches. Wherever we went I'd take down people's phone numbers, promising to follow up on any questions, queries, requests for help. No one knew or cared that I grew up in the country fifteen of the hijackers came from. It shouldn't have mattered and it didn't.

A few days after the attack, HRC was back in New York visiting a downtown hospital to meet survivors and their families, and to show support to the hospital workers who had cared for the injured. I walked ahead and saw a door with a sign saying visitors were not allowed. I peered into the window of the darkened room. The patient was a specter—totally covered in white gauze and sheets. All I could see was a tuft of dark hair. As I rejoined the group, I asked one of the medical staff about the patient. She had been brought in as a Jane Doe, he said. Her injuries were so severe, she had to be sedated. I asked if she had any family we could talk to, and he mentioned she had a fiancé who was with her often but not here now.

"I'd like to come back and see her when it's appropriate," HRC chimed in, and we walked away without going into the room, no one commenting further on the woman's condition.

I didn't know it then, but my friendship with that sleeping stranger, totally dependent on the twenty-four-hour care of doctors and nurses just to stay alive, whose future was entirely uncertain, would teach me so much about strength and resilience, control and surrender. She could have been a victim, but as she would later tell me herself, she chose to be a survivor.

THE ART OF
THE IMPOSSIBLE

Overwhelmingly and overnight, HRC's efforts in the Senate shifted to rebuilding Lower Manhattan: visiting triage stations, hospitals, fire-houses, and victims' families; attending memorial services; and trying to help survivors as they fought their way out of the trauma.

HRC and I went back several times to visit the Jane Doe patient, Debbie Mardenfeld (now St. John). The first time Debbie was conscious for our visit, she smiled as I walked into her room. I was now the signal bearer that something big was happening, the advance before people's masks went up and they performed at their best. She attempted to raise herself fully from the pillow, smiling even wider as she saw HRC walking in behind me. Her fiancé, Greg, stood up.

On September 11, Debbie had been on her way to her office in the World Trade Center when she was hit by what she was later told was likely the landing gear of one of the planes. Both of her legs had been crushed, her backside had been partially sliced off, and she had lost a lot of blood. She didn't remember any of it happening. Now, she pointed to her legs, which were covered with a sheet, and said that one of the reasons she didn't bleed out on that street was because the heat from the metal was so intense that it seared the wounds on her legs shut.

We started visiting Debbie whenever we could, and our office advocated for her with federal agencies and the Red Cross to figure out what assistance would be available to her. Eight months later, in May 2002, she was still in the hospital, and often in excruciating pain. Her long-term recovery was far from clear.

Debbie always seemed to be smiling, even though I caught her wincing from time to time. In one of our bedside conversations, she told us how much she wanted and needed to hold on to the belief that she could one day have the wedding she had always dreamed of. Debbie and Greg were originally supposed to get married in late 2002, but that had to be postponed. Her old life had a future in which there was a wedding with a cake, a white dress—and dancing. And that's what she was still longing for.

"I just can't imagine getting married and not being able to dance at my own wedding!" she said a few months into her stay at the hospital.

HRC took her hands gently, looked right at her, and said, "You *will* dance at your wedding. And we will be right there with you."

At that point, no one knew with certainty what the outcome would be. But HRC was willing us all to believe the very best.

* * * *

While Debbie was fighting her way back to a new normal, my little sister, Heba, was preparing for her own wedding. My mother came to New Jersey that summer to help her shop for her wedding trousseau, and as we all sat on the floor, she very ceremoniously pulled out her "pièce de résistance," a brand-new heavily embellished cream-and-lace wedding outfit, from one of her suitcases. She hoped it would be the wedding dress or worn for one of the many formal functions. Heba modeled it for us, and from the look on her face, I could tell immediately that she hated it.

"Maybe you can save it for Huma," Heba offered offhandedly.

"Good idea," my mother said and nodded, soldiering through her disappointment and folding away the piece, stowing along with it the notion of a Huma marriage. I didn't mind. The idea of getting married seemed preposterous. I was twenty-six. My daily life was packed full. Plus, there was no one to marry.

On car rides between events, HRC would ask me about the wedding, offering suggestions on flowers and menus. Then, one day, on an endless car ride, she stunned me. "Bill and I would love to come to your sister's wedding," HRC said. And they did. They were mobbed and I was mortified, but it was a spectacular surprise and my entire family was honored and thrilled that they came. In Clintonworld, as in the Middle East, funerals, births, rites of passage, and weddings were a social obligation, whether it was my sister's first (and only) wedding—or Donald Trump's third.

HRC did not know Trump well, but they had had a few interactions and he had supported her Senate race. So when the invitation came, she figured, why not? When someone is getting married, you go. Plus, weddings are fun, and Trump's promised to be over-the-top. It also happened to be the same weekend as a speech she had already committed to in Palm Beach, making the decision all the easier. The Clintons flew down on a Saturday night, landing a few hours before the wedding, and decided to spend the night with their friends Jerry and Elaine Schuster. When I walked down the windy steps of Elaine's house in Palm Beach as the event approached, I was wearing the same thing I had worn all day: perfectly serviceable white pants with a turquoise blouse. Elaine stood at the bottom of the stairs, hands on her hips, looking on disapprovingly.

"You are going to Donald Trump's wedding dressed like that?" She was shaking her head and pointing me back up the stairs. "Come with me."

I protested that I was not even a guest, just the invisible body who always followed HRC, and that no one was going to notice what I was wearing.

"Listen to me. If you walk into a Palm Beach party looking like that, you *will* be noticed. And it won't be good!"

She led me down the hall to her large closet, and pulled out a long black slinky Giorgio Armani dress. I didn't dare protest further and walked discreetly behind HRC first at the church for the ceremony and then at Mar-a-Lago for the reception. I felt like I was at an Arab wedding back home. Marble floors, gold accents, large chandeliers. Big dresses. Big hair. Camera flashes everywhere. Trump met the Clintons as they arrived at Mar-a-Lago, introduced them to his new wife, Melania, and then escorted them around, giving them a tour and introducing them to guests before disappearing into the crowd, leaving us in a vast ballroom now filling up with hundreds of people.

After they'd spent a respectable amount of time milling around, I sensed they'd had enough. I broke into the crowd of people gathered around for pictures and said, "We need to go." We ended the night early and ate takeout standing at Jerry and Elaine's kitchen counter.

HRC's busy days and nights meant my days and nights were busy too, but I did try to squeeze in a social life of my own along the margins. I never knew exactly when work would end: 8, 9, or 10 p.m. Since our New York City days were typically on weekends, I would reach out to friends and join them for dinner or dessert at a new restaurant before crashing on one of their couches—usually Allison's. If I knew I'd have to get an early start for an upstate trip the next morning, I would take the last train back to Chappaqua and tiptoe up the creaky front stairs to the Clintons' guest room. Living in New York as a single woman, limited though my free time was, was as exciting as I had always imagined it would be. Even though I often ended up on a different couch every weekend, the city was already feeling like home. I rarely visited my family in New Jersey, and didn't book a ticket to Saudi Arabia my first summer in the Senate. My circle shrank to new friends I met through work and old buddies from the White House days.

The line between what was work and what was social was often blurry because so much Senate work involved unpredictable hours and long, late nights. HRC would sometimes meet up with colleagues for a drink or dinner in between votes, or we would order Chinese takeout for anyone still at the office.

One night, while waiting for some late votes to be called, a few senators and their aides made plans to grab a quick dinner at a nearby restaurant. By the time the votes ended, HRC had changed her mind about dinner but encouraged the rest of us to go. Afterward, I ended up walking out with one of the senators, and soon we stopped in front of his building and he invited me in for coffee. Once inside, he told me to make myself comfortable on the couch. I watched him take off his blazer and roll up his white shirtsleeves, and continue to talk about what I cannot for the life of me remember while he started to make the coffee. It was like any other day on the Hill.

Then, in an instant, it all changed. He plopped down to my right, put his left arm around my shoulder, and kissed me, pushing his tongue into my mouth, pressing me back on the sofa. I was so utterly shocked, I pushed him away. All I wanted was for the last ten seconds to be erased. He seemed genuinely surprised that I was rebuffing him and immediately apologized that he had "misread" me all this time.

My mind immediately went to problem solving: How do I leave without this ending badly? He asked me whether I wanted to stay, adding that he would understand if I wanted to leave. I tried to convey coolness, but my heart was pounding. Then I said something only the twentysomething version of me would have come up with—"I am so sorry"—and walked out, trying to appear as nonchalant as possible.

For a few days I kept away from the Senate floor so I could avoid him. But running into him was inevitable.

"Hey," he said casually when he spotted me a few days later in the hallway. "I've been worried about you."

I assured him there was nothing to worry about. "Friends?" he asked. I had no words to express how I felt, so I just nodded. As if she knew I needed rescuing even though I'd told her nothing about that night, the junior senator from New York joined us just then, and snap, everything went back to normal.

The senator and I did manage to remain friendly, and pretty soon I had buried the incident. I had wanted to forget it and I did. In fact, I had erased it from my mind entirely until the day, years later, when it was suddenly triggered. That was the day I read about Christine Blasey Ford being accused of "conveniently" remembering Judge Brett Kavanaugh allegedly assaulting her decades earlier.

*　*　*　*

Though she made a persistent, deliberate effort to work with Republicans, Hillary Clinton inspired strong emotions, often hostile ones, even among Democrats. This was not breaking news for me, nor for her. There was one woman, half of a couple—native New Yorkers, Democratic supporters, successful, well respected—who was always cool and distant to HRC and we couldn't figure out why. The husband was our primary point of contact in the relationship. Mutual friends advised that HRC shouldn't bother trying to befriend his wife, but HRC is so direct in all her relationships that avoidance didn't sit well with her. So, as we were planning a trip upstate for economic development meetings, she mentioned that the couple had a home near the site of our final event for that evening.

"Maybe we can stay at their house for the night," she suggested.

"You want me to ask the woman who does not like you if you can be her houseguest? Are you sure?"

She was sure. *Okay*, I thought. *Here goes nothing.* I called the husband's office and left a message with his staff. The reply did not come swiftly, but when it did, the husband called and said he would be delighted to have HRC stay with them.

So there we were, at the end of a long summer day, pulling into the private driveway of a lovely lake house at 7:30 p.m. Laid out in the kitchen was a simple buffet dinner of cold sliced chicken breast, a big mixed green salad, and hunks of rustic bread. The husband was convivial and charming as always, making up for the mostly silent presence of his wife. HRC asked the wife about having coffee together the next morning.

"Oh, I start every morning with a swim in the lake," the wife said.

"That sounds nice," HRC said.

"Actually, I don't think you'd like it, it's very cold," the wife said.

"I'd love to swim," HRC said. "But I didn't bring a suit. Do you have one I can borrow?"

Several hours later, after the wife had disappeared into her room and had not returned, we decided it was time to turn in. The husband said he would show us to our rooms and pointed toward a door that looked like it opened to the outside. Indeed, it did. HRC and I stepped out, waiting for our host to show us where to go. She looked at me with her eyebrows raised.

"Don't look at me! This was your idea. They are probably putting you in the outhouse."

Seconds later, our host returned with a flashlight and walked us toward an exquisite guest cottage by the water. Lying on the bed in HRC's room was what looked like a brand-new bathing suit, staring at us like a dare.

The next morning promised to be in the fifties, and I fell asleep in my room grateful there was no bathing suit waiting for me. The lake outside looked as forbidding to me as its mistress. When I woke up, I showered, piled on my layers, then went to check on HRC. As I approached her room, I saw the bathing suit hanging on the doorknob, still dripping. The door was ajar, and HRC was stripping her bed. She had been up for hours, and had already taken what she called a "refreshing" swim. We headed toward the main house for coffee with our hosts, who both stood up, wide-eyed, when Hillary Clinton walked into the house, arms full of her own laundry, before they all sat down to a longer-than-planned breakfast.

When I later brought my own sheets to the washing machine, the wife followed me in.

"She's not how I imagined she would be," she said.

As we chatted, she volunteered that she hadn't felt welcome at a White House dinner they'd been invited to, that she thought HRC hadn't recognized her, and that she had been given a horrible seat. Clearly, she had never forgiven HRC for what she perceived as a slight. It made me think of all the minute details we obsessed over for each White House event, our attempts to accommodate every need of every guest. When things went wrong, *we* wouldn't get blamed, *she* would, as I always told the advance teams and interns. While in this instance HRC's insistence on reaching out turned the woman into a valued friend, there were thousands of people she might never be able to reach. Still, she chipped away at whatever she could.

There were, however, plenty of times she had to succumb to extant reality. As her first term in the Senate was coming to an end, we took several trips around the country to raise money for her reelection and for the Democratic Party. Once, we got a ride back from California to the East Coast on the plane of one of her good friends and supporters, Haim Saban. We had just settled in for the long flight—me with my shoes off, HRC across the aisle reading a book—when all of a sudden we heard a strange sound and then felt the plane start to descend, first rapidly with a jerk, then slowly as if coasting. Haim and I exchanged worried glances. The flight attendant went to the cockpit to find out what was happening. HRC looked up, gazed out the window, then went back to reading. The minutes ticked by as we all felt the plane drifting definitively downward, fast then slow, then fast again, then slower.

"How can you be so calm?" Haim finally asked her.

"There are some things I can control and some things I have no control over," she said. "This is something I just can't control, so I am not going to worry about it. There is no point in getting upset."

With that, she went back to reading her book. Another agonizing minute later, the flight attendant reappeared, saying an engine had blown out and we would have to make an emergency landing. Everyone needed to buckle up for a rough landing. HRC looked up and said, "Thank you for letting us know." I started tapping out messages to our team on the ground to let them know we were coming back, busying myself with something I *could* control. Twenty unsettling minutes and one less than smooth landing later, she finally looked up from her book again when it was time to disembark from the plane.

* * * *

In November 2006, Senator Clinton cruised to reelection, as expected, though all year long our team had worked as if she might lose. When she told us she wanted to campaign in all sixty-two counties of New York State, it sounded impossible, but our team in New York mapped out a plan and managed to pull it off. As Election Day neared, she was so far ahead in her own race that increasingly we shifted focus to events for other candidates and for the Democratic Party. The election results were even better than in 2000. New York was her proving ground, and her reelection an affirmation that her dedication, hard work, and tight organization had paid off. Moreover, Democrats took back both houses of Congress. She would now be a senator in the majority party, which meant she could accomplish much, much more.

And there was one more thing that many clamored for Hillary Clinton to accomplish. From almost the very moment she won elected office in 2000, there had been rumors about her running for president. She would nod and smile and move on when people shouted it out on rope lines. Now, with her Senate reelection behind her, the drumbeat was even louder and she was giving it real consideration. But what kind of response would she get if she decided to run?

Presidential campaigns in America are marathons, not sprints, and she would need to decide soon if she was going to run. It would require a full year and a half to raise money, reintroduce herself to Americans after six years of being focused on New Yorkers, and share her plans for the country. I encouraged HRC to take some time off to think about it. After some pushing, I finally convinced her to visit the Mohonk Mountain House in the scenic Hudson Valley, known for its great hiking trails.

On the one cold morning we were there, we hiked a long, winding trail near the hotel. I had already been in several political meetings where the topic of a presidential run had been discussed, but this hike was the first time she raised it with me alone. It seemed clear she was close to a final decision.

"This might be madness," she said, the chilly air condensing her breath into little clouds. "We sure have a lot to do if we are going to try to make a difference in people's lives, don't we?"

When we returned to the hotel for hot chocolate before packing up to leave, the thing that struck me most was how good life was, right here, right now, in the present moment in the Senate. Status quo would have been just fine for me and maybe even for her. A fruitful and useful life. But it wasn't up to me. She was the one making the plans. I was just along for the ride.

There has always been cynicism about HRC, her apparent use of her New York Senate seat as a stepping-stone to the presidency, but I sensed she was ambivalent about the possibility of leaving a job she clearly loved, one in which she was evaluated on her own terms. It was in the Senate where her efforts had secured federal funds to screen and treat anyone impacted by Ground Zero's toxic air, rescued jobs by persuading companies to move upstate, fought off Republican proposals to dismantle the social safety net, among many other efforts. Where she broke through to conservative Republicans enough to achieve some concrete bipartisan policy victories, including a health fund for undocumented immigrants and expanding health coverage for military reservists.

HRC has never written her own story about those years in the Senate, but I believe it was her favorite job. By the end of her term, the Senate team tabulated a chart that depicted her time in office by the numbers, and the numbers were dizzying. She attended votes on the Senate floor 98 percent of the time in her complete first term. In the course of her years representing New York, our office received 280,000 scheduling invitations, 3.7 million pieces of mail, 6.5 million phone calls. She marched in 45 parades, delivered 88 floor speeches, attended north of 4,600 events in New York, ate Gianelli sausage at 8 New York state fairs, and did 1,000 events to support other Democrats. She secured $4 billion dollars in funding for New York projects in addition to the $20 billion originally promised after 9/11. She had been named Most Admired Woman in America by Gallup for most of the last decade. My favorite of the statistics told the story of her elections. In 2000, she carried 15 of the 62 counties in New York. In 2006, she carried 58 of 62 counties. If these were the results she achieved for her state, so my thinking went, imagine what she could accomplish if she were President of the United States.

In giving serious consideration to the prospect of the seemingly impossible—a woman president—she was blazing a new, uncharted path. But Hillary Clinton was never deterred by the lack of precedents or the appearance of apparently insurmountable obstacles. This was the woman who, in her senior class speech when she graduated from Wellesley College, said, "The challenge now is to practice politics as the art of making what appears to be impossible possible."

* * * *

Another impossibility, one that forever loomed large over us, was being able to envision a day when the smoke from 9/11 would clear, when the searing images from those days, the wails of the grieving families, and the acrid char of smoldering steel would fade from memory. Survivors, the loved ones of those who died, and the first responders would be permanently changed by the attacks. Their lives would never be the same.

Around the first anniversary of 9/11, Debbie had left me a message marked urgent, which caused me to fear the worst. But when I actually listened to the voicemail, she sounded full of excitement. She had made it one hundred feet with the help of a walker. She was making progress, literally one step at a time.

Now it was four years later, and HRC and I were invited to her wedding to Greg. The first time I had seen her, she was a white specter lying motionless. Now she was a beaming, lovely bride. We took our seats and watched as Debbie lived out each part of the wedding she had dreamed of. We had all promised not to cry, but some of us did anyway.

And by the way, we danced.

WHEN WILL THIS END?

*Living religion is actually like a spring; water continues to
flow from it, which then inundates and nourishes the fields
around it. It does not have to change, but what it does
have to do is remain a spring, to remain active . . . What is
important is to represent traditional Islam in a contemporary language, to write about the eternal truths in a contemporary language.*

—Seyyed Hossein Nasr

The first time I held a fishing pole, I was in Alaska on a large boat off
the coast of Seward, floating in Resurrection Bay, and flanked by two
United States senators. The sun shone hot and brilliant that day, the
glaciers surrounding us were pristine and otherworldly, the wind was
whipping so wildly we had to shout to be heard. John McCain was
teaching me to fish. McCain loved fishing and seemed delighted to be
teaching a novice. As I was about to cast, the other senator, Lindsey
Graham, piped up. "No, no, no, that is all wrong. Do it this way," he
instructed me. One of them told me to cast it far, the other to gently
lower it close to the base of the hull. One suggested I stay motionless,
"let the fish come to you." The other said to "jerk the line." *They should
be an on-camera reality show*, I thought.

Exasperated, McCain finally said, "Lindsey, her name is not
Heeyuma. You can't even pronounce her name right, how can you
teach her to fish?"

Graham was ready with a response. He usually was. "Oh, so you
know how to pronounce it?"

"Sure, it's Hooma," McCain said.

169

They were talking over me, as though I were not right there sandwiched between them. The truth is they were both wrong. I interjected that it is pronounced Huma with a short u, though I knew neither of them would get it right. So, we went right back to Heeyuma and Hooma, both of which I responded to. Just at that moment, mercifully, I felt a tug on my line and there was general jubilation. All of us eventually caught quite a few slippery gray salmon, which we then released back into the water, except for a handful that McCain saved to be sent home to Arizona. HRC had already caught and released her own batch of fish and was in the cabin working, playtime long over for her. This expedition was McCain's idea, and since he was the head of our congressional delegation, what he said went.

It was August 2005, and HRC was on her third congressional trip with John McCain and Lindsey Graham, this one a climate change research mission to Alaska. As with all previous trips, during the briefings from experts they took notes (well at least she did), asked questions, nodded their heads in unison. This trio of senators, all of whom served on the Senate Armed Services Committee, had traveled together on research missions to Iraq, Afghanistan, Ukraine, Norway, Germany, Estonia, and Iceland. In Iceland, HRC and I watched the men take a dip in the Blue Lagoon. In Norway, after checking into a small hotel in Svalbard, Graham volunteered that he was going to check out the hotel's outdoor hot tub and invited HRC and McCain to join, but they both remained stone-faced. They were up for adventure, but they had their limits.

HRC was considered potential presidential material by this time, as was McCain, so they were popular guests wherever we went, greeted with deference and excitement. McCain was intimidating at first, and gruff at times, but it turned out to be mostly bluster. In the many months I had watched McCain and HRC interact, it was clear they had a lot in common. They were deeply loyal to the people and causes they cared about. They both laughed loudly at cheesy jokes. They could hold their liquor, as evidenced by a vodka-drinking contest in Estonia. They were eager students of the world, and these fact-finding missions were undertaken in a genuine spirit of inquiry, none more somber than visits they made together to Iraq and Afghanistan.

In the wake of 9/11, the U.S. had sent forces into Afghanistan to destroy suspected Al-Qaeda sites and created a cabinet-level position for homeland security. An era of hypervigilance had begun, all a reaction to the aftershocks from the attacks. Over the course of 2002, the Bush administration began to switch their main focus from Osama bin Laden, whom they believed to be hiding in a cave somewhere in Afghanistan, to Saddam Hussein in Iraq. The Iraqi dictator was preventing the UN from inspecting his biological and chemical weapons stockpile, which was now viewed as the biggest threat the U.S. faced. We could not wait, the White House argued, for another terrorist attack on American soil.

In October 2002, the Senate was preparing to vote on a resolution giving the President authorization to go to war against Saddam Hussein unless Saddam complied with the demand for inspections by a deadline that was fast approaching. In the weeks leading up to the vote, HRC sought counsel from a broad array of people. She went to closed-door intelligence hearings, from which she emerged serious and pensive. She called on foreign policy experts and she polled her staff. When she asked me what I thought, all I could offer was what I knew from the perspective of my own background. Everyone in my community of nonwork Arab friends opposed going to war. They knew Saddam was an awful dictator, but they didn't see the point of attacking him. Many of us thought that Saddam was lying about his weapons capacity so as not to "lose face," considered a humiliation in the Arab world.

I knew it was not my vote to make. We could all dabble in our own opinions, but HRC had to make the tough call based on intelligence she was getting from the administration. Most people believed that the vote would give Bush the authority to attack, which it did, but HRC was arguing for trying diplomacy first.

On October 10, at 3:05 p.m., the House of Representatives voted in favor of the resolution, giving the President the authority to go to war. The bill would hit the Senate floor next. Restless, I paced incessantly, finally descending on HRC's press secretary, Philippe Reines. Philippe was always good for a distraction and great company. He was scary smart, with an acerbic wit. I plopped down into a chair across from his desk.

"What do you think is going to happen?"

Philippe did not mince words. "You know what is going to happen."

Tamera poked her head in a minute later suggesting HRC head home since it would be a few hours before the vote was called on the Senate side. We drove back to Whitehaven in silence and HRC went straight upstairs, holding the latest copy of her speech. As I waited downstairs, a Syrian American friend from college phoned to tell me she hoped that HRC would vote against the war. It was a gut-wrenching call. I had read the statement, and knew which way HRC was going to vote.

Well past midnight, HRC cast her vote in favor of the amendment, though she was clear about her reservations. When she delivered floor remarks, she said, "Even though the resolution before the Senate is not as strong as I would like in requiring the diplomatic route first . . . I take the President at his word that he will try hard to pass a United Nations resolution and seek to avoid war, if possible. . . . A vote for the resolution is not a vote to rush to war; it is a vote that puts awesome responsibility in the hands of our President. And we say to him: Use these powers wisely and as a last resort."

The following March, President Bush executed Operation Iraqi Freedom, and two months later declared "mission accomplished." In 2021, nearly two decades after boots were first on the ground, American forces still remained in Iraq.

As the years progressed, HRC's vote for the Iraq War, like that of every other senator who supported it, turned into an albatross. It didn't matter that the intelligence the administration had shared with members of Congress, and later the world, turned out to be faulty and in some cases manufactured from whole cloth. It didn't matter that her remarks on the night of the vote were nuanced, that she had cautioned against preemptive action. Those were words, but voting is a binary action—yea or nay—upon which senators are judged. She had made a choice, knowing from the beginning that it was fraught. It was a choice Barack Obama—who had not yet been elected to the Senate—didn't have to make.

* * * *

One day in the spring of 2004, Patti Solis Doyle, the director of HRC's political operation, called with a request from a well-known political advisor, David Axelrod, who had been a longtime friend of Patti's. Would she consider flying to Chicago for evening fundraising events for a Senate candidate running in Illinois? Patti wasn't sure we could pull it off after a full day of meetings and fly back to Washington late the same night. HRC had votes in Washington the next day and so making it back was a must. I hung up with Patti, promising to check on the logistics, making a note to discuss "Barak" Obama with HRC, spelling the name in my notebook the way I was familiar with it from the Middle East.

HRC happily agreed to add the events, and at each one she urged the party faithful to throw their support behind the dynamic candidate she had just met. When the events were over, she was so engrossed in conversation with Obama and Axelrod it was hard to get her out in time to catch the plane back to DC. She had been as impressed by Obama as the rest of the country would be when they heard him speak a few months later at the Democratic Convention in Boston, where John Kerry accepted the 2004 nomination for president. Obama's charisma, his story, the way he spoke, it was magnetic. She called her husband as we raced to the airport.

"Bill," she said, "I just met our first African American president. We did some great events together here in Chicago. You have to come out to help him too."

When we landed in DC close to 4 a.m., I pulled out my notebook to take down notes from HRC's usual trip follow-up. She ended with, "They asked and I really do want to host an event for Obama at White-haven as soon as possible. I want to get him what he needs to win."

Patti and her team organized a fundraiser for him a few weeks later. Before the speeches, HRC pulled me aside, saying she wanted to be sure Obama spoke last. Typically, at any event, the Clintons served as the closers, the ones making the most compelling argument for the candidate or the particular issue. And attendees would often stick around until the end to hear them, so many hosts preferred it that way. HRC had decided Barack Obama would be his own best closer. As guests assembled in the Clintons' garden for an evening of mingling, passed hors d'oeuvres and cocktails, surrounded by petite Japanese maple trees, tall hornbeams, rose bushes, and sleepy cascading wisteria vines, many were hearing of this new candidate for the first time. When Obama spoke, the warm air buzzed with the electricity and excitement he seemed to bring with him wherever he went.

That November John Kerry lost the presidential election to President Bush, and speculation about 2008 candidates for both parties started immediately. Barack Obama won his race and joined the Senate in much the same way HRC had: with a lot of fanfare and crazy high expectations. Like HRC, he appeared intent on keeping his head down once he got there. Like HRC, he found it virtually impossible. Our staff met and shared what we knew with the incoming Obama team, getting to know them over coffee in the Russell Senate Building basement's Cups & Company café.

HRC had been the next big thing for a long time. Now the latest big thing was informal, self-confident, and seemingly unburdened, though he too carried the weight of history. He was unaffected by protocol and just as comfortable hanging out with us kids as with his colleagues. When he joined us for a trip in 2005, along with a group of other senators, he crouched his way to the least coveted seat on the small plane, deferring the better seats to the more senior senators, including HRC—employing the kind of disarming tack HRC herself had often taken.

The event we flew in for that day was many hours long and guests regularly excused themselves to stretch their legs. Every so often, I checked in on HRC as she sat on stage, but I had conference calls, so I mostly paced outside by the motorcade, at one point moving in the direction of some dumpsters. As I approached, a tall lean man with his back to me turned his head and I realized it was Obama. Was that smoke wreathed around his head? Couldn't be. It seemed so incongruous with the image I had of him. Suddenly I felt like an intruder, so I turned away.

A moment later, as I was standing at the open door of our car, I heard over my shoulder, "Hey Huma, does Hillary have anything to eat in there?" If he had been smoking, there was no lingering evidence. We were all several hours away from a proper meal, but I figured HRC must have something in her bag since she was always prepared. I pulled her large black purse from the backseat and fished out two bags of Planters mixed nuts packets. I offered them to him and he took one.

"Save the other for Hillary."

He tore open the packet and casually strode back into the event where I would soon watch him bring the room to its feet.

When HRC had predicted that Obama would be our first African American president, she had simply called it the way she saw it. Did she imagine he would become the Democratic nominee only after a heated primary contest against her? Probably not. That's just not how her brain works. She doesn't dabble in hypothetical hand-wringing. When she said in 2004 that she wanted to do whatever she could to help Barack Obama succeed, that's exactly what she meant. And, in the end, even if the outcome was bitter at first, that is exactly what she did.

* * * *

By February 2005, HRC was growing increasingly troubled by the administration's prosecution of the Iraq War, two years after President Bush had launched it with promises that the Americans would be welcomed as liberators. At the end of 2003, Saddam Hussein was captured, but the war continued, and one year later, more than 1400 Americans had been killed in Iraq. Some 150,000 American troops were now stationed there, facing a brutal insurgency. HRC decided to join John McCain on a CODEL (congressional delegation trip) to meet with troops and examine what was happening on the ground.

I wasn't even supposed to be on this trip. Normally only Armed Services Committee staff are cleared for this kind of travel, but HRC had suggested that I would be value added and McCain signed off on my joining. On the flight over, I gave the same briefing I had become accustomed to sharing, prompted by HRC and encouraged by the others.

Even those who were well versed in the history and politics of the region didn't personally know many people who lived there, and fewer still had any grasp of the nuances of my culture: what it means to be Muslim, how it is a whole way of life, that the divide between Sunni and Shia Muslims originated centuries ago over disagreements about the line of succession after the death of Prophet Muhammad. How Islam is a faith that is broad and diverse, with myriad forms of cultural expression within it, not some monolithic dogma. Invariably the conversation shifted to Saudi Arabia. *Yes, I am a Sunni. No, I am not a Wahhabi. Yes, I know of the bin Laden family, but everyone in Saudi does, and no, I do not know Osama bin Laden.*

We flew first to Kuwait for a night, then hopped on a C-130 military plane to fly into Baghdad. Once we disembarked onto the tarmac, we were instructed to move fast to board Black Hawk helicopters that would fly us into the Green Zone, where the Americans were confined for their safety and, as a result, cut off from most of the Iraqi population. We landed at the Phoenix base for a briefing with General David Petraeus, then the commander of the Multi-National Security Transition Command for Iraq, where he was responsible for the training and equipping of Iraq's security forces, and for helping to build an entirely new security infrastructure.

The senators participated in a series of meetings with Shia prime minister Ayad Allawi and Kurdish deputy prime minister Barham Salih. The Kurds had been allied with the U.S. since the first Gulf War in 1991. The Shia Muslims in Iraq had been kept out of power under Hussein, but now that Saddam's Sunni Ba'ath Party had been toppled, they had opportunities simply not possible before. These were cultured men, educated in British schools. Determined. Optimistic. Gracious. They shared priorities, but didn't seem entirely aligned on how to achieve them. Throughout all the meetings with the leadership and also with community leaders, there was unanimous agreement on one thing: more. They needed more troop training, more money, more weapons.

Finally, we headed to the windy roof of the American Chancery building for satellite press interviews. As HRC sat in her chair, reviewing her notes, she looked over at McCain, with a flap of his gray hair blowing in the wind, and offered him her brush and hairspray. Like HRC, he didn't seem to care much about frivolous things, but being camera-ready was part of the job, so he took both of the offered items. I noticed him struggling to reach the top of his head. He never talked about the injuries he'd sustained during his years as a prisoner of war in Vietnam, but we knew it was difficult for him to raise his arms beyond a certain height. "Go help him," HRC whispered, and so with the cameras about to roll I did what I could.

"Thank you for fixing me up," he mumbled.

Time was tight and we were running late. While we needed to get the choppers in the air before the sun set, there were women waiting to meet with HRC in the chancery conference room, and there was no possibility she would cut that part of the schedule. With nightfall fast approaching, McCain agreed to wait while HRC did her meeting. We went into the small air-conditioned conference room where several of the chairs for participants were empty; those women had decided to leave to make it home before the curfew. The Iraqi women who remained shared their frustration at the lack of reliable jobs, the fragile security situation, the disruption of school for their children, the fear of being disappeared for political retribution as some of their friends had been. One of them said that in the old days, women had the freedom to be educated, to work in business and government, there had even been famous fashion houses, but now many of them were afraid to leave home. There was no judgment in their voices, they didn't seem to be blaming the U.S. for this predicament. Their point was simple and clear: life was getting worse and their fate was now in the hands of the coalition forces. "When will this end?" was the unanswerable question. If there was a light at the end of the tunnel, it was not clear to them, and it wasn't clear to us either. As we prepared to leave, one of the women put her hand over my arm.

"I never imagined I would live like this, in fear, scared to drive home after dark. You know what I mean?"

"*Aywah*," I responded, nodding that I did, even though of course I did not. I am an American. I was surrounded by soldiers from the most powerful military force in the world and by Secret Service agents, and I was in the company of the ranking member of the Senate Armed Services committee and a former first lady. As we flew out, low over the city, I was reminded how important it is to talk to a range of people on these foreign trips. They revealed far more than we could learn sitting in government complexes, talking to leaders determined to impress us with how well they were handling things.

I thought too of the twists of fate that had led me to a life that gave me so many advantages. How my parents left their homes, families, and cultures, and two countries at perpetual war with each other, to follow their dreams. How, just a few years before, I had thought I would move back to Jeddah, to live a far more constricted life with fewer choices. How I was offered an incredible opportunity to serve my country instead. How I outwardly blended in with the people we had just visited more than I did with the passengers on the chopper taking off. How privileged my own life had turned out to be, full of choice and freedom and self-determination. I prayed that these women would make it home safe. From time to time, I google their names just to be sure they are still alive.

*   *   *   *

A few months later we were on that trip to Alaska where John McCain taught me to fish. One night McCain suggested our group walk from our hotel to dinner. Somehow in the casual pairings, I found myself beside him. He asked me about my future plans, noting that I always seemed to be working.

"You know, Huma, there is more to life than your job," he said.

I confided to him that when this amazing opportunity to work in the White House, and beyond, came along I had seized it. That I had little time for a personal life. "My job is the thing I care about the most."

"Don't live a life without balance. Whatever you do, don't find yourself settling for less," he said, his words echoing what I imagined my own father would have said to me.

"There is more to life than work," McCain repeated. "Try to find joy elsewhere too."

Those words didn't mean much to me then. I had a full, active, exciting life, some would even call it a glamorous one. I had just celebrated my thirtieth birthday with two surprise parties, one in New York, one in Washington, both hosted by my boss and colleagues. Large parties filled with family members and more friends than I'd realized I had, all my favorite foods and music, a corner table stacked high with gifts. When I walked into Soho House for my New York party, I was presented with a large box. Inside was a custom-made Oscar de la Renta pantsuit. My very first designer outfit, made just for me.

I had job security, good healthcare, paid my small tax bill on time, had enough money in my bank account to not have to worry. I was healthy and genetically predisposed to not putting on too much weight even though I ate an atrocious diet. I had met more living legends and heads of state than I could count, had many conversations with women I admired and aspired to emulate, and had even met my childhood crush Luke Perry. I had not met the love of my life yet, and in the meantime, I was frequently a guest at interesting dinner parties and was certain that somewhere, sometime, I would meet the right man. I was in no rush since I could barely keep up with my current reality. Every day when I went to work there was a new challenge to solve, new people to meet, a new airplane or motorcade ride to some incredible, unique, or interesting place on some important mission. There couldn't possibly be much more to life than this.

IRON MY SHIRT

If you don't run, you can't win.
—Geraldine Ferarro

A peripatetic life commuting between Washington and New York had been my norm for years, but by mid-2006, I tried to live a little more like a grown-up, in DC at least. With my mother's help for the down payment, I bought a two-bedroom condo with a balcony and an underground garage in the Cardozo/Shaw neighborhood. Until then, my roommate and I had been sharing the same eight-hundred-square-foot one-bedroom apartment that we'd lived in since college. She moved with me to the new place, but now we each had our own room, and I started buying furniture and decorating with all the knickknacks I had collected from my travels around the world—the rug from Morocco, the tea set from China, the candleholders from Amsterdam, the woven baskets from Tanzania.

When HRC and I were in New York, I was still a nomad, staying at a hotel, or at the Clintons' in Chappaqua, or crashing with a friend. Some nights I stayed with my sister Heba. She was now living in midtown Manhattan with her husband, Sohail, their three-year-old son, and was pregnant with their second child. I ate out often and late. My life was as stable as it could be for any workaholic single professional. It was intense and all-consuming, but there was a routine to it that I'd become accustomed to. That was soon to change.

HRC had briefly considered running for president in 2004, but decided against it, preferring to complete her full term as senator from New York. In the intervening years a small team of us had been meeting to discuss what would come next, and we added a potential presidential run to the agenda, with no clear idea about whether she would decide to enter the race. No one with campaign experience thought it would be easy, starting with HRC herself.

The war in Iraq was deteriorating, our standing in the world was compromised, the economy was on the edge of a cliff, the housing bubble on the cusp of bursting, infrastructure crumbling—and the response out of the Bush administration was to implement tax cuts for the rich that exploded the budget that Bill Clinton had balanced. It seemed the country was ripe for change, and HRC thought she could make a difference. That's why she had decided to run.

HRC never asked me formally if I would want a job on the campaign. It must have felt like a given and it was. When we left the White House, I had promised myself that the day I woke up and didn't want to go to work would be the day I'd give notice. I had just passed the decade mark of my time in Hillaryland and each new undertaking felt like a chance to contribute to history. But nothing would be more history-making than a woman becoming President of the United States.

In the early days, before there was even a nascent campaign, when the meetings were just Patti Solis Doyle showing up with stacks of binders to sit in the dining room at Whitehaven, HRC asked me to join them at the table. She told me Patti was going to be the campaign manager and asked me to review the list of potential staff Patti had put together for the scheduling and advance teams. Patti offered me the job of traveling chief of staff, to coordinate with the scheduling office back at headquarters, manage the advance teams, and be the primary communicator with headquarters from the road. I accepted on the spot.

On January 9, 2007, I was one of the team of advisors HRC convened at Whitehaven. Most of the people sitting around the dining room table that day had been there before, having helped orchestrate her 2000 Senate win and her 2006 reelection. HRC knew them, she trusted them, they had delivered for her, and now they were preparing to help her run for president. At the top sat Patti, who was now the first Latina to run a presidential campaign.

The meeting that day was part of a series of strategy sessions we'd been holding to prepare for a late January announcement—

My mother was the first woman in her family to travel to the United States from Pakistan and the first to get a PhD.

1

My father in 1948 at Aligarh Muslim University in India shortly before he was thrown from his horse and broke his back. He had just turned twenty.

As newlyweds in 1965, my parents posed on the front porch of their first apartment. She in her whisper-thin sari, he in his Nehru jacket, they always felt right at home in Philadelphia.

3

4

Me at eleven months in Kalamazoo, Michigan. This girl might have had a whole Midwestern life ahead of her.

Celebrating my second birthday at home with an aunt, my father, and my siblings. A few weeks later, we would be off on a grand adventure.

6

With my older sister, Hadeel, and baby sister, Heba, at my mother's college in Jeddah. Mom not only worked full-time as a professor of sociology, she also cooked fresh meals for our family daily and made many of our clothes, including these skirts and tops.

My brother Hassan, Hadeel, and me at the beach in Jeddah. My parents encouraged us to spend as much time as possible outdoors and on hot days—which were frequent—we went out at dusk.

9

And here, Hadeel and I are in front of the Blue Mosque in Turkey. Flight attendants would often look at the bowl haircuts that my mom gave us and ask, "What would all your boys like?"

We were exposed to different countries, cultures, and languages from a young age. When I was four I posed with Hadeel after landing at Heathrow on one of our frequent trips to London.

Playing dress-up with a family friend in Malaysia.

10

In Austria on my thirteenth birthday. Behind me are the hills where *The Sound of Music* was filmed. This is me doing my Julie Andrews impression.

Doing cartwheels at Milham Park in Kalamazoo when I was seven. To me, America wasn't just a country. It was a feeling. Freedom. Choice. Self-determination.

12

Sitting on an aunt's crisscross staircase in Elmhurst, Queens, with a view of the neighborhood and worlds away from the privacy wall that surrounded our apartment in Jeddah.

Goofing off in Jeddah. Now a teenager, I wore an *abaya* and scarf in public.

14

During my sophomore year at George Washington University in 1995, Mom asked me to join her at the United Nations preparatory meetings for the Fourth World Conference on Women later that year in Beijing. It would change the course of my life.

As an intern in 1997 meeting the first woman prime minister of Bangladesh as she visited the White House. First greeting down, thousands more to go.

Hillaryland at the White House. It's a club that comes with lifetime membership. Each of our milestones was celebrated, and birthdays were no exception.

At the Taj Mahal on a 2000 presidential trip with Kelly Craighead. She taught me the phrase "fail to plan, plan to fail." My father's family briefly lived fifteen minutes away.

18

With Allison Stein at a refugee camp during an emotional trip to Macedonia in 1999. This group of children asked to have their photo taken with us. Many of these families would make it home to Kosovo.

I logged many thousands of miles from this perch on the military plane designated Executive One Foxtrot when the First Lady flew on it.

There were always exciting events at the White House. Day after jam-packed day. Night after spangly night. On this millennium eve in December 1999, some of us expected our computers to crash at the stroke of midnight. They didn't.

22

Conferring with legendary White House butler Buddy Carter while the Clintons addressed an audience on the State Floor of the residence.

Philippe Reines and me in the Senate. He kept us entertained or exasperated, depending on the day.

23

On the first anniversary of 9/11. The dust behind us is coming from the hole where the World Trade Center's Twin Towers once stood.

24

Typical day on the 2008 presidential campaign. HRC preparing to go on stage, me briefing her, Anthony hanging in the wings, bemused.

anticipating that an announcement from Obama would come around the same time. Early campaign research had shown that it would be a tough climb for any woman to win the presidency, so HRC wasn't running "as a woman," but rather as the most qualified candidate who happened to be a woman. But the seriousness of her presidential aspirations, and the fact that she *was* a woman, inspired a lot of people. Many of the top advisors around that table and in her orbit were women too—not just our campaign manager but the policy director, media strategist, senate chief of staff, campaign counsel, campaign scheduler. While this wasn't unusual for Hillaryland, people began to take notice.

Soon after she released a video announcing her intention to run, on January 20, half a dozen of us were asked to participate in a photo shoot and brief interview with *Elle* magazine. It was my first proper photo shoot and, while I enjoyed having my hair and make-up done, the minute we all arranged ourselves and posed, I wanted to flee. I realized how uncomfortable I was on this side of the camera. Still, I did what I was told and smiled wide.

A few days after the *Elle* magazine story, Philippe said the *New York Observer* was interested in a profile on me and he thought it was a good idea. I never knew him to steer me wrong so I agreed so long as I didn't have to actively participate in it. Philippe might as well have written the article himself, "Meet Hillary's Mystery Woman: Is Huma Human? Gorgeous, Ubiquitous Aide Has Special Powers." I was both flattered and agnostic. It was so over the top, it was hard to take seriously.

Ten days after the *Observer* article was published, I received a fax in the Senate office from Anna Wintour, the editor in chief of *Vogue*, asking me to participate in a profile. To me, this was next-level. This was the magazine I had spent years leafing through and obsessing over. For my job, I had to read the *Washington Post*, the *New York Times*, and *Politico*, but *Vogue* was the only publication for which I had a home subscription. For all my wariness of the press, I loved fashion as much as politics and this was a once-in-a-lifetime opportunity.

I had no idea what I was getting myself into. I wasn't prepared for the hours a photo shoot takes; two alone for hair, makeup, and manicure. The photographer, Norman Jean Roy, shot a portrait of me in a pretty red Vera Wang empire-waisted gown. I felt stiff and awkward the entire time despite Norman's constant encouragement that I was doing "just great." We then tried a few more outfits and traveled to a second outdoor location in Maryland. By the end of the day, I was wiped out.

Later, I spoke to the reporter, Rebecca Johnson, about what most inspired me in my work. I told her about the relationship HRC and I had developed with Debbie St. John, which for me exemplified the ways in which a life in public service could be meaningful. I also told her a bit about my background, and in the piece she described me as "a practicing Muslim born in Kalamazoo, Michigan, to a Pakistani mother and an Indian father." The combination of fashion and Washington politics was a novelty back then, so when the August issue came out, Philippe started getting press calls asking whether I would be interested in doing other interviews. He didn't bother to ask me before he turned them down.

Political campaigns are about telling a story—the candidate's story—to the public; building a narrative that gets voters invested and excited in the person running so they can hear her message. Staff should never be the story. You do your job, then get out of the picture so the cameras can capture the principal. A searing memory had stayed with me from an important White House trip when Air Force One landed to a phalanx of cameras and as the Clintons began greeting people on the tarmac, my pager buzzed. "Get out of the shot!" was all that ran across my small pager screen from an unknown colleague via the White House Signal operator. Mortified, I took ten steps back.

Political staff like me are meant to be rarely seen, and certainly never heard. For a long time, I did that job very well. When the TV cameras were swarming at events, I knew exactly where to linger to be close enough to help but just outside the camera's frame. On occasions when photographers did capture me standing beside the First Lady or Senator, if you scanned the caption, my name was nowhere to be found. I wasn't just anonymous—I was invisible. Now that I was traveling with the first woman who had a real chance of becoming the nominee of her party for president, it was harder to remain so.

With my fifteen minutes of fame now behind me, I went back to work preparing to spend the next year on the road. With Kim Molstre, our no-nonsense, smart campaign scheduling director, and our cheerful, sometimes scrappy advance director, Jon Davidson, we built out a schedule and a road team to help our boss navigate a very crowded primary season. Patti and I continued the pattern we had fallen into post–White House where she made big-picture decisions and ran the organization from headquarters and largely ceded decisions on the road to me. If there was a problem, I would call her to download or get advice, but over the years I managed mostly on my own, reporting in on political intelligence I had picked up or defused or, in some cases, lit.

There were all kinds of stories already being written about HRC's aura of inevitability. The last time a Clinton had lost a race was back in 1980, when Bill Clinton lost his bid for a second term as governor of Arkansas. So expectations were high. What I didn't appreciate then was how heavy a burden inevitability would prove to be. Between the challenge any woman in this position would face, the growing unpopularity of the war in Iraq, and the stench of being considered "Washington insiders," we were on the defensive right out of the gate.

To meet the challenge, HRC made the decision not to cede any state, to meet every voter everywhere she could. To raise the millions needed to fund our massive operation, we set aside an extraordinary amount of time for fundraisers. In the first four months of fundraising, we crushed the competition. While online fundraising was beginning to gain steam, and Obama in particular was beginning to benefit greatly, with HRC, we found that supporters wanted to see her, touch her, talk to her. On the road, we felt the energy in pulsing gymnasiums, packed auditoriums, and throngs-deep rope lines. Everywhere we went, we met women who were her peers and admired her as the realization of their feminist ideals, professional women who knew viscerally what she was up against, parents who brought their little girls to catch a glimpse of a possible future for themselves. For still others, HRC was merely an adornment, a bragging right, a curiosity.

For HRC, the way to break out of that bubble was to center her campaign on practical solutions. She opened her campaign asking Americans to join her in a conversation about the future they wanted to see. To that end, she rolled out detailed policy proposals. It was her signature in the Senate—to listen to people and try to solve their problems through policy, signaling with her pragmatism and nuance that her promises weren't empty.

HRC was considered the "establishment" candidate, the one to beat, and the other candidates did not hesitate to swing at her. One of her strengths, due largely to her discipline, preparation, and composure, was debating. Still, it didn't stop the others from trying to psych her out.

In April 2007, HRC was set to participate in her first presidential debate, in South Carolina, against the seven other announced candidates. As our team gathered in a large, spare classroom to review final notes with HRC, I received a message from an Obama campaign staff member asking if Obama could pop in and say hello.

"I'll let you know," I responded. It was more typical for candidates to stay in their own holding rooms, either meeting just before they went on stage or waiting until they were on stage.

I interrupted HRC's session.

"Obama wants to come by," I said.

HRC looked up, also registering how unusual this request was. "Okay, give me a few minutes," she said as she turned back to her notes. I stepped back into the hallway to buy some time, only to see Obama himself walking toward me. I turned back into the room, leaving the door open behind me.

"You are seeing him now," I said. To which HRC could barely get out, "Tell him . . ."

"Tell him yourself . . ." was all I could manage as Obama filled the doorway behind me. If his team had intended to surprise her, even unnerve her, it might have worked, but Hillary Clinton thrives under pressure. Not only did she do well in the debate that night, the reviews declared her the "clear winner." We were encouraged, but also cognizant that she was still 263 days away from anyone casting a vote.

By June, the gloves had come off. High-profile supporters from different campaigns began making negative statements. At the debate in New Hampshire the candidate Senator John Edwards attacked both Clinton and Obama for not having a strong enough plan to end the war. In July, WJC hit the road in Iowa. Obama outraised us by

$10 million in the second quarter, an exact flip from our first-quarter numbers. Suddenly, in the money game, our roles were reversed.

August brought more policy pitches, debates, and, most important, the Iowa State Fair, a mandatory pilgrimage for any presidential candidate. The ten-day-long annual fair is prime ground to court caucus goers. Aside from that, it's an assault on every sense. The day we visited, the sun was intense, the crowds were unnerving, but the smell of fried food, musty hay, and cheese was very tempting. It was a crush of two-way mobs—people trying to get to HRC and HRC trying to get to people—not to mention the crowds making their way to other candidates and, frankly, to the fried butter balls.

The Iowa State Fair, like many campaign events, was filled with food. On the road for a campaign, exercise is rare and sleep is even more so, but there is no end to pizza. HRC and I would put fresh jalapeños on our slices, and that would be our vegetable for the day. On nights our team went out to eat, HRC would order whatever the fish and vegetable options were on the menu, then wink at the server while pointing at me "and she's going to have a side of French fries." I knew full well who those fries were actually meant for. On days she was being disciplined, she would take a handful and push the bowl toward the rest of us. Most days, we just ordered more.

HRC isn't a picky eater, and our advance team usually found it pretty easy to find her something to eat on the road. At least, they made it look easy. Whenever we walked into a holding room before an event, I was amazed at how meticulously they had set it up, with the little things that made such a big difference. The brand of throat lozenges they knew she liked, an item that becomes a staple for anyone who spends ten hours a day, seven days a week talking. The water. The tea. The honey. The diet Dr Pepper, which she had asked for just once sometime in the past, and which had automatically appeared everywhere ever since.

The team would do calls after she left every event. What went right, what went wrong, what to bring next time. They traveled with all the staples the candidate might need: the food, the podium, the mult box, you name it. Every time she pulled up, they greeted her with a smile and walked her through the event they had sometimes created from scratch with only a few hours' notice. One thing Hillary Clinton never lacked for in all her years in public service: a loyal, enthusiastic, smart set of advance aides, each of whom grew into a MacGyver, with the unfailing ability to use whatever everyday materials were in her or his sight line to solve any problem thrown their way.

In the fall, we continued with our policy rollouts, doing the kinds of events we had been doing since the White House: tours of factories and farms, interviews with reporters, roundtable conversations with Iowans, speeches, and rallies. We had to convince the voters that these policies would help them *and* we had to get them excited about the candidate. Getting both right is harder than it looks. Though her proposals were as thought-out, considered, comprehensive, detailed, precise, and polished as she was, at times it felt as though she was trying to get the kids to focus on their homework, while everyone else was setting off dazzling fireworks.

We pressed on. A youth policy rollout, a rural tour, a comprehensive energy plan. As we closed in on the Iowa Caucus in January 2008, things got nasty from all sides. There were regular, constant judgments on her demeanor and physical appearance. At one debate, John Edwards turned to her and told her he didn't care for her jacket. At a later debate, HRC would be asked why voters didn't find her as "likeable" as Obama, and Obama would jump in to say that she was "likeable enough"—in a tone that felt jarring and uncomfortable, almost dismissive, and out of character for him. John McCain, who was running in the Republican primary, had a supporter at an event refer to HRC as a "bitch." Mitt Romney, another Republican candidate, suggested HRC couldn't even run a corner store.

No woman had ever been taken this seriously in a presidential contest, and it was as though she was expected to pay a toll to offset the threat her ambitions posed to the social order. The personal barbs came in every form, and from every direction: fellow candidates, including those with whom she had been friendly; the media; people at events. Anytime someone made a comment somewhere, anywhere, about how she looked, the tone of her voice, what she wore, how she styled her hair, it was met with nervous laughter—by HRC and whatever audience she was addressing.

I don't think at the time, we as a society knew how to deal with someone making a derogatory comment about a female politician. Laughing at it was a clumsy, unsatisfying way to deflect, defer, and defray all the uncomfortable and conflicting emotions it brought to the surface. So when conservative commentator Tucker Carlson said, "When she comes on television, I involuntarily cross my legs," there was no general condemnation, no *we are not going to tolerate this*. We simply looked the other way. It was the price we paid for being in the game, a way to show we could handle the attacks. It reminded me of the days in my youth when my friends and I were harassed on the streets of Jeddah and we just giggled through it. The behavior was taken for granted, and universally tolerated.

* * * *

The first contest of the campaign would be the Iowa Caucus, scheduled for January 3, 2008. We put our heads down and kept working hard in the Hawkeye State. In December alone, HRC spent nineteen days there hosting town halls, stopping in coffee shops, and doing interviews. Her supporters, the most prominent of whom was her husband, campaigned energetically around the state too. As much as possible, he would join her in whatever city she was overnighting in.

From the very beginning, it was clear that Iowa operated according to its own playbook. On our first trip there almost a year earlier, HRC had attended a breakfast for caucus goers. Soon after we arrived at the house party, a woman approached me and began to tell me how excited she was to meet HRC. She wore a "Ready for Hillary" T-shirt covered with Hillary fan buttons. In her arms, she carried a stack of copies of HRC's memoir, *Living History*, for HRC's signature. Finally, she took a picture with HRC, arm across HRC's shoulder, making a thumbs-up sign.

I suggested to our campaign videographer that the enthusiastic woman might be a good supporter to interview for campaign ads. But once the camera was rolling, the "Ready for Hillary" woman was quick and clear.

"Oh, I am an undecided voter. I have no idea who I am going to caucus for yet."

That, in a nutshell, was the Iowa experience. Totally unpredictable. You had to build a phenomenal field team and work the state from every angle. This wasn't a primary where you needed the *most* number of people to vote; it was a caucus, so you needed the *right* kind of people, engaged activists who could be counted on to show up and voice their support publicly and usually on a cold winter night. You either submitted to the rules or you didn't, but conventional political wisdom at the time suggested there was no path to the nomination without Iowa.

If the person who worked the hardest was meant to win Iowa in 2008, then HRC deserved to win. I am sure other campaigns feel similarly about their own candidates, whose paths crossed ours frequently in the frenzy of those last days of campaigning. With everyone out on the road simultaneously, it was inevitable that we'd sometimes find ourselves staying at the same hotel. Early one morning, I walked to the hotel gym and found a Secret Service agent standing post outside. I peered in through the glass door to see that it was Senator Obama working out with his aide, Reggie Love. Knowing how rare a candidate's personal time was, and even though the agent assured me it was perfectly fine to go in, I went back to my room. Although the campaigns did have these overlaps, this was one of the few times when I actually saw one of the other candidates, because by the time we got to the hotel, other campaigns had usually turned in for the night, and when we left early the next morning, they hadn't yet started their day.

On caucus night, after a full day of stops, we returned to our hotel in Des Moines at 7 p.m. to await results. I was already knee-deep in planning for the New Hampshire primary the following week. Every so often I would pop into HRC's suite with updates from our Iowa state director. From the start, the news was bad. She stayed in the bedroom while WJC watched TV from the suite's sitting area and stood up every few minutes to call someone on the Iowa team for minute-by-minute updates. At a certain point, I just plopped onto the beige sofa and waited with him.

Finally, the senior campaign team paraded in to announce that not only had we lost, we might be in third place behind both Obama (who later declared victory, having come in first) and Edwards. Everyone was crammed together on the couches, pale, stunned, and speechless.

It had never been a given that she would win. All polls had indicated it would be tight. But to come in third? No one had predicted that, in public or in private.

"Can someone explain what happened?" HRC asked.

The question was at first greeted with pin-drop silence. Soon there were feeble explanations, everyone doing their best to fill an awful void. We went downstairs so HRC could address her supporters, and then we immediately flew to New Hampshire. The show had to go on.

By the time we arrived at our hotel in Concord, it was 3 a.m., and we were all physically and emotionally drained. As I bid her good night, HRC called after me, "What do you think happened?" I knew nothing I could say could or would properly answer her question, so I grasped at straws and reminded her of the "Ready for Hillary" woman we met on that first trip. I was trying to come up with anything to keep her from thinking this was all her own fault. There was no time to unpack what had happened, but at this point HRC started to question everything.

*   *   *   *

On Monday morning, January 7, the day before the New Hampshire primary, I was already on my BlackBerry at 4 a.m. Patti emailed that she would be in HRC's suite at 5:30 a.m. with a report on our campaign budget and prospects. We had to leave the hotel no later than 6 a.m. because HRC had seven live satellite and phone interviews into various morning shows.

When Patti arrived, she was somber. There was no good news to share. Patti confirmed we were down in all New Hampshire polls by about eleven points. Given how we had budgeted resources, Patti said, we couldn't change the media plan or add many more staff than we already had. We had poured so much money into Iowa that we were strapped. A win there would have created momentum and made fundraising easier, but we were now in an uphill battle. It looked like we were about to lose New Hampshire, we knew Nevada would be hand-to-hand political combat, and South Carolina was an assured Obama state. By the time we got to the Super Tuesday map, there might well be more states favoring Obama than HRC. The future was murky.

Soon, WJC joined the conversation, and the Clintons pressed Patti with questions and ideas for reallocating resources, boosting field operations, and energizing donors. Patti took notes and answered where she could, but her tone did not change about the prospects.

HRC is someone who hires people she believes are best for the job and empowers them. She builds teams she has faith in and she trusts them fully. Once a particular strategy is agreed upon, she does not nitpick on the implementation, though she'll push us for answers and drive us to think more creatively, strategically.

No, she wasn't the most traditionally charismatic candidate—she would be the first to admit that. We also knew that she was vulnerable based on her decades in politics, taking hits on everything from her Iraq vote to the tone of her voice. And from the start, running against Obama sucked; he was a phenomenal candidate, most of us genuinely liked him, and she agreed with him on most issues. Maybe there was nothing we could have done to beat him in Iowa. Still, in this very moment, it was clear that we, as a team, had also failed her. What had worked so well in the Senate was our lean operation, laser-focused on very specific results. In contrast, our presidential campaign had felt like an ocean liner from the start: expensive, expansive, slow to turn, and now it had sprung a leak. Our bloated campaign was sinking.

A little before 6 a.m., my phone was ringing nonstop. Our press staff was up against a live hit in minutes. "We have to go," I interrupted, knowing the timing was terrible. Patti stood up to leave. She and I gave each other a "hang in there" hug. Her visit had felt more like a condolence call.

HRC and I climbed onto our big empty campaign bus, greeted by the faint scent of exhaust, to drive to the Common Man restaurant for her first set of live interviews. We had rented the bus weeks ago. It blared "Hillary for President" in bold red-and-blue lettering, a gas-guzzling, physical embodiment of all the money that we had been burning through, money she had worked so hard to raise. We had planned for the bus to be filled with surrogates, the advisors and supporters who spoke on behalf of the campaign, and with staff and reporters as we drove around New Hampshire. Instead, the surrogates were now fanned out across the state to cover more ground, and the staff and reporters boarded other cars. The bus was cavernous with just the two of us on it, along with one Secret Service agent sitting in the front passenger seat, silent as always, and National Public Radio playing on low volume before I whispered to the driver to just turn it off. If I was chief of anything on the road, it was chief of sanity.

"Isn't New Hampshire now a must-win for you, Senator Clinton?" a reporter asked in one of the interviews.

"Yes, it is, and I intend to win."

Her answers never wavered. The public Hillary Clinton was determined and confident, never letting on that she'd just received bad news from her campaign manager.

After the interviews, we had a long drive from Concord to Portsmouth, where HRC was scheduled to have a coffee at Café Espresso with a small group of undecided voters. She rested her eyes for the first part of the ride, her ability to fall asleep anytime and anywhere remarkable. As we got closer, she stood to pour herself coffee at the mini kitchenette built into one side of the bus.

She said she felt like now it was up to her alone to carry New Hampshire. She appeared to be right. There were hundreds of us around to support her, to help her win, but our strategy and implementation had taken a monstrous beating.

"Have you called Maggie and Cheryl?" I asked.

Maggie Williams, her first White House chief of staff, and Cheryl Mills, former White House counsel, were among her closest advisors and friends, and nothing big happened in our lives without some consultation with them.

"Not yet," she said.

"Why don't I call them and download Patti's news," I suggested.

"That makes sense," she said, and got off the bus for her event at the café.

I dialed Maggie and then patched Cheryl in. They had dozens of questions. Cautious, careful, neither wanting to step on any toes or be where they weren't wanted or needed.

While I was deep in this conversation, our advance person appeared outside the bus waving her hand furiously. I kept shaking my head, pointing to the phone, but she finally opened the door and climbed onto the bus.

"You have to come now. She is crying. We need you."

"I don't understand. *Who* is crying?"

Thrown for a loop, I told Maggie and Cheryl that if they wanted proof that the candidate needed them, there it was, although I couldn't quite believe it was possible. Hillary Clinton was crying at an event? In public? I left my phone on the bus sofa and ran inside. The event seemed to be going just like any other. A small coffee shop, people seated around tables with mugs and half-eaten donuts or bagels. HRC was at one end of the shop seated next to a state senator and talking. She was not crying. She did not even look like she had been crying. Nothing was amiss with one exception. The group of reporters at the back was more attentive than usual, furiously typing on their laptops or whispering on their phones.

Had she cracked? She never cracked. Jamie Smith, the traveling press director, and I looked at each other thinking the same thing: Was this really bad? I intently tried to make eye contact with HRC, to be sure she wasn't signaling that she needed anything, but she betrayed nothing. I decided that there were plenty of other people to take care of her and that the best way I could help her was to get back on the planning call with Maggie and Cheryl.

When she climbed back on the bus, she seemed exhausted, and I didn't press her for details. She joined the call and we continued making plans, acknowledging that there were some tough decisions about personnel and money that needed to be made, and made soon. They promised to do whatever they could to support Patti and navigate the months ahead and then we all hung up. I learned later from Jamie and our New Hampshire team that she hadn't actually cried, but what did happen was enough to make headlines. A woman had asked her, "How do you do it? How do you keep upbeat?" In her response, HRC's voice caught for a moment and her eyes appeared to moisten as she gave an emotional answer: that it was not easy and that she couldn't do it if she didn't passionately believe it was the right thing to do. That this country had given her so many opportunities and she didn't want to see us "fall backwards," but in the end she would present her case and let the voters decide.

The rest of the day remained a roller coaster. As HRC took the stage to deliver her stump speech at a rally in Dover, I ran into General Wesley Clark, the retired army general who briefly ran for president in 2004. He was a good friend of the Clintons and had been on the ground campaigning for her in Iowa and New Hampshire.

"How does it feel, General?" I wasn't looking for more bad news and immediately regretted asking. He beamed at me.

"She is going to win New Hampshire!"

In politics, you have to be clear-eyed about your prospects, and while ours felt cloudy in that moment, his enthusiasm was contagious. At the end of the event he said it to her with just as much conviction: "Mark my words, you are going to win here."

Despite glimmers of positivity, it was far from smooth sailing. Later that afternoon, at an event in Salem, about twenty minutes into her speech, a man stood up in the audience holding a sign and chanting "Iron My Shirt!" Another man followed suit. On stage, HRC addressed it head-on, first by saying "Oh, I see the remnants of sexism are alive and well." Then as the men were escorted out, she said, "As I think has been abundantly demonstrated, I am also running to break through the highest and hardest glass ceiling." She started the question-and-answer session that followed with a lighthearted "If there's anyone left in the auditorium who wants to learn how to iron his own shirt, I'll be happy to talk about that too." The room gave her a standing ovation.

"Can you believe what just happened?" she said afterward, referring to the hecklers.

"Well, I guess you just have to win tomorrow," I replied.

"Yes, I certainly do."

By the time we arrived in Manchester that night for our last rally, exhausted as she was, I could see that HRC was reenergized. When she asked, "Are you ready for an election tomorrow?" the crowd roared in response. Loading into our last car ride of the day for the long, slow drive back to the Centennial Inn in Concord, all I could think about was how cold and hungry I was. She, however, was animated. She had begun to feel something—a sense that the ground had shifted in her favor.

GET YOU NEXT TIME

I've learned that people will forget what you said, people will forget what you did, but people will never forget how you made them feel.

—Maya Angelou

Primary election day in New Hampshire started early and cold. We made a few stops at coffee shops and local TV stations before we hunkered down to wait for results. By mid-afternoon I was carrying two draft speeches, one a victory speech, the other a concession, but I decided not to give them to HRC; she would have time to formulate her thoughts later, and I suspected she already had. She didn't spend the afternoon torturing herself with each exit poll result. Since it was now truly out of her hands, she just settled in to wait.

When the final results came in, showing HRC winning by almost 3 percentage points, our staff room down the hall from hers exploded with such boisterous cheering that when the President and Chelsea opened the bedroom door to tell her the result, she already knew she had won. "Thank you all," she said as we hugged and high-fived and clapped. Impossibly, improbably, she was the first woman ever to win a presidential primary in the United States.

I cannot count the number of backstages and stage wings from which I had watched HRC speak, illuminated by klieg lights. History and Hillary Clinton were old bedfellows by now. But for me, as a young woman, there was no moment sweeter than standing on the sidelines of that stage at the Centennial Hotel when she received that victory—cautiously, carefully as perhaps only a woman would. To this day it is still one of the most inspiring moments I was privileged to witness with her. Anything felt possible in that moment—after all, just the day before we had been told our campaign was at death's door. I was not even dissuaded by news coverage that failed to acknowledge that she had made history, instead reporting she had "narrowly" won, just barely "edging out" Obama.

* * * *

For all the chatter of HRC being the "establishment" candidate, the "establishment" did not uniformly support her. Obama started racking up endorsements by some of the most powerful leaders in our party, including Senator Ted Kennedy. By mid-spring, the tide had shifted toward an Obama delegate victory but we were still hard at work. The media narrative that we were running on fumes had mutated into a drumbeat that Democrats wanted her out, but that belied our experience on the ground. At every event, in every state, she was received like a rock star, the crowds screaming "Don't give up!" "I won't," she'd always say. "I promise." And she didn't.

Then, on May 23, we were campaigning at Sunshine Foods grocery store in South Dakota, where HRC was speaking to voters about rising food prices amid cartons of milk and neatly stacked eggs. Since I was always on the road, grocery stores had become pretty foreign to me at that point in my life. It was Heba's birthday, and I texted her as I marveled at these mundane surroundings, when I saw Jamie heading my way. "We have a problem." I heard these words at least once a day, so I wasn't worried until she started to describe it. An hour earlier HRC had met with the editorial board of the *Argus Leader* newspaper. During the interview, she was asked why she continued campaigning this late in the race.

"My husband did not wrap up the nomination in 1992 until he won the California primary somewhere in the middle of June, right? We all remember Bobby Kennedy was assassinated in June in California," she said. Her point was that it wasn't unheard of for presidential primaries to go through June. It was intended as a statement of fact, an observation. A tabloid reporter picked up on the interview, insinuated that she was making a morbid calculus, and people ran with it, pushing the story out and inflaming hostilities between our team and Obama's.

Now the reporters in the back of the grocery store were asking Jamie if HRC was insinuating that Senator Obama could face a similar fate.

As soon as she was done speaking and started shaking hands, I whispered in her ear, "We have an issue with what you said about RFK. Don't talk to the press right now." She didn't seem to connect to what I was talking about, paused for half a second, then said out loud, "That is ridiculous, they can't believe that." With that, she continued shaking hands while still on camera as though nothing were wrong, but I sensed that a certain stiffness had descended on her, enveloping every movement until she was done and followed me out.

We showed her to the back of the store, where our entire traveling communications team had assembled, Mo Elleithee, Doug Hattaway, and Jamie. They repeated what I had told her and she stood looking back at us, frustrated, shocked, the equanimity she usually maintained seeming to falter. Then she looked away distracted, deep in thought, and started jabbing her index finger into the plastic wrap around one of the cases of water bottles stacked in front of her, like she was trying to plug a hole. When she looked up, she finally said, "I can't win. I just can't win." Her tone was resigned, angry, pained. Not self-pitying, just matter-of-fact. She couldn't win enough delegates. She couldn't win over the press. She couldn't win for trying and she wouldn't win this nomination.

For a brief instant, we all stood silently together amid fluorescently lit stacks of colorful juice bottles and cases of water, absorbing the looming reality. I emailed headquarters as soon as we got in the car. Patti was now the campaign's senior advisor, while Maggie had been installed as campaign manager shortly after that bus ride in New Hampshire, and Cheryl, who had warned HRC against running in the first place, had parked herself at the headquarters in Virginia and become our go-to advisor for everything. Maggie issued a statement saying that HRC had absolutely not intended to suggest something so outrageous and awful. A representative of the Kennedy family said the same, as did prominent Obama supporters. The *Argus Leader* went on to endorse HRC, and she would go on to win the South Dakota primary by ten points in early June. Jonathan Ellis, the *Argus Leader* reporter who had interviewed her on that visit to their offices in South

Dakota, would later write, "In this case, Clinton's opponents were bearing false witness against her. They were twisting her comment about Kennedy out of context and implying that she was staying in the race because she wanted her opponent to be assassinated. It was nonsense. It was actually worse than nonsense. It was slimy. Unseemly. As absurd as it was, Clinton was still forced to clarify the remark and issue an apology."

With every primary election or caucus night that came and went, we had been stacking up delegates, but so had Obama. Despite the often expressed opinion that she should have gotten out of the race as early as February, the primaries were actually neck and neck for much of the campaign after Iowa and New Hampshire. She ended up winning the popular vote in nine of the final sixteen contests, collecting 600,000 more votes than Obama and gaining 507 primary and caucus delegates to his 469 in that same period.

Even though HRC had had some major primary night wins, the Obama campaign from the beginning had focused on "delegate math," the political system whereby you win the required number of state delegates and superdelegates to secure the nomination. So while the popular vote was essentially equally split between the two, and slightly favored HRC if you counted Michigan and Florida, team Obama won the delegate math and, in the end, that's all that mattered.

A few days after the supermarket visit in South Dakota, we were on the road again, campaigning in Montana. My phone rang. It was Maggie. She had just hung up with a prominent donor in New York who was threatening to announce that he was switching his endorsement from HRC to Obama and publicly calling on her to drop out immediately. Maggie had tried to talk him down, but he was insistent on speaking to HRC himself to convince her to withdraw.

Right away, my phone started ringing from his number. HRC was about to make a speech, and I walked away from her so she couldn't hear me. He said he needed to talk to her immediately, this was "enough." His bullying tone, and insistence that she accede to his timeline, was offensive. I told him I would pass the message to her, making no promise that she would return the call. He called Maggie back, frustrated at what he viewed as my insolence. My phone rang. Maggie again.

"You can fire me, Maggie, but I am not putting him on the phone with her. Ever," I said.

We didn't need some guy calling from his fancy office in New York browbeating HRC to feed his ego, so that he could play peacemaker. When it was time to concede, she would do it as she always conducted herself: with grace.

*   *   *   *

A week later, HRC won the primary in Puerto Rico and then called Maggie, Cheryl, and me: it was time to meet with Obama. That was all the guidance we needed to set the inevitable in motion. By June 4, Obama had amassed the number of delegates he needed to secure the Democratic nomination, and I emailed Reggie Love, whom I liked and trusted, to set up a meeting. By then, the press had a stakeout at Whitehaven, with cameras keeping constant watch on HRC's movements for clues about her intentions. I knew the meeting would be tense and awkward for her, and I wanted to figure out how to get her to the meeting, which was set to take place at Senator Dianne Feinstein's DC house the next day, without alerting anyone. Before I left Whitehaven that night, I popped into the Secret Service command post at the house. Could they leave her car in the driveway and not park it in the garage? I had a plan.

On the morning of June 5, I drove my car to Whitehaven, parking as I normally would out front and just across from the press stakeout, which was even bigger than it had been the previous day. "Any updates?" one of the reporters called out as I walked by. Was she going to meet Obama? Was she going to make a concession speech? *It's going to be a long day*, I thought.

In the afternoon, I got an email back from Reggie saying the meeting at Feinstein's was on for 7:30 p.m. That's when the plan went into action. Bari Lurie, a friend from the White House who was now running the campaign manager's office and whom I trusted implicitly, came to the house under the guise of making a delivery. Once she was safely behind the gates, I slipped into the trunk of her car and she pulled out a few minutes later. She dropped me at Feinstein's where, after confirming there was no press stakeout waiting for them,

I kept watch for HRC and for Obama. HRC arrived first. In the blue minivan with tinted windows that they kept at the house for agents to go back and forth between shifts, the Secret Service had departed for Feinstein's house at 7:15 p.m. with HRC lying flat in the backseat. She had escaped detection. Our cars were still parked in front of White-haven, and the press's attention remained trained on the front door in expectation of any movement she might make.

Obama arrived at 8:45 p.m. after he too had figured out how to throw off the press. When their meeting was over, a little after 10 p.m., HRC and I climbed into the back of the minivan again and stayed low—she with a trench coat covering her—as we pulled back into Whitehaven's side gate for another "shift change" at 10:30 p.m. When I walked out of the front door to get into my own car late that night, just after our campaigns had issued a statement saying they had met, it looked like I had been there all day.

Two days later, HRC delivered her official concession speech at the National Building Museum. Our team had tried to think of the right image to capture this moment. Greg Hale, our genius production director who had taught me many invaluable advance lessons in the White House, suggested we put the stage in the middle of the room, surrounding her in a sea of supporters. It was a reflection both of the love for her and the main driver of her campaign: people. The room was charged with emotion—sadness, anger, and devotion. It was clear HRC needed to steer the mood, and she did. When she offered her endorsement of Obama, it was full-throated and unwavering. She now had to lead her diehard supporters along to the other side with her. Instead of allowing the pain to become anger or bitterness, she said, "Although we weren't able to shatter that highest, hardest glass ceiling this time, thanks to you it's got about 18 million cracks in it and the light is shining through like never before, filling us all with the hope and the sure knowledge that the path will be a little easier next time."

We held our first campaign event for Obama a few weeks later in Unity, New Hampshire, selected for its name and because HRC and Obama had split delegates evenly there. On the way from the airport to the venue, the two teams shared a campaign bus and peanut butter sandwiches. Both sides pushed through the awkwardness, HRC and

Obama like divorcing parents playing nice for the kids, papering over the months of tense exchanges.

As we headed into the summer's Democratic Convention, there were rumors that some HRC supporters, smarting from her loss, were planning some sort of symbolic vote on the convention floor. They had spent a year and a half volunteering, phone banking, door knocking. They had been inspired by the first woman to run for president who actually had a shot. This moment was theirs too, to claim something that in many instances felt personal. These people had wanted their efforts and their votes to count for something.

On our flight to Denver for the convention, foremost in my mind was: What exactly were we walking into? Would the Hillary supporters protest, cause some kind of commotion, fracture the peace we'd been trying to build with Obama supporters? We all got how it felt. God, did we feel the gut punch so viscerally. Each time we had walked into a rally those last few months, crowds screamed with excitement, oblivious to the impending reality, the shrinking delegate count. Who saw this coming? No one really, but in the end, everyone said they did.

After we stopped to talk to people waiting on the tarmac, I was scrolling through my emails when I accidentally walked into the airplane wing—my nose colliding with the hard, hot steel. Stunned and seeing stars in my eyes, I put my hand to my face and felt blood. "Am I okay?" I turned to ask HRC. The look on her face said it all but she said it anyway: "No!" This moment of distraction and clumsiness meant she was going to the hotel but only after putting me in a car that was headed to the hospital with a colleague who repeatedly had to field calls from HRC asking for updates.

A few hours later, stitched up and armed with ice packs, some pain medication, and a full bag of glucose in my system—turns out I was also rather dehydrated—I headed back to the hotel where HRC had convened a meeting with Minyon Moore and the senior team in her hotel suite to discuss the latest developments. Minyon was another veteran from the Clinton White House, where she had run the White House Office of Political Affairs. She was now a central political advisor on the campaign. She was always the voice at our table, in my ear, gently pushing us to think more creatively, more inclusively, expanding our circle, not contracting it. She was leading the political team managing whatever was brewing on the convention floor. After the meeting, our advance lead and I mapped out a logistical plan based on the strategy Minyon and the senior team had devised.

The next day, Tuesday, HRC addressed the convention after receiving a three-minute standing ovation. She told the crowd that Obama "is my candidate" and called on the crowd to work hard for him in the general election. The next day, when the roll call vote was to take place, she planned to announce that she was releasing all her pledged delegates to vote however they chose, essentially freeing them from their support for her.

The following evening, as HRC prepared to release her delegates on the convention floor, I noticed something I didn't see often in her. Was it nerves? Was this the final realization? She looked at her notes, handed them back, and then grabbed them again, as if she had been too distracted the first time.

"Just follow the lead and I'll be right behind you," I told her, mostly to prod her.

"Let's go do this, Miss Huma," she said, eyes bright, as she began her long descent down to the floor.

When she finally strode into the mass of humanity, surrounded by tens of thousands of delegates from around the country, it was like a prizefighter was making her way into the ring. The stadium exploded with sound. More than anything, it felt like relief. The Clinton supporters ready to join the Obama team. The Obama supporters glad to welcome her now that she was stepping aside.

* * * *

By the fall, we were settling into a steady rhythm of Senate events and surrogate events for the Obama campaign. Most days felt okay. The acrimonious moments were already growing blurry in my mind. On the plane, HRC tended to be matter-of-fact about the situation we were in. "I did the best I could. I lost." She wasn't pointing fingers or rehashing the past. This is how she and I were different. I was constantly living in the world of sliding doors. What if we had skipped Iowa? What if she hadn't voted for the war in Iraq? What if she had run in 2004? She, though, would never explore these conversations with me. "We have to focus on the future. Isn't it nice to have a break from the schedule?" She was right. It was a relief to not constantly have the alert button on. We could sleep till 8 a.m. and not feel guilty. We could put things on our to-do list, forget them, and it would be perfectly fine.

Though there had been brutal days, the experience was also inspiring, fun, and gratifying. I traveled a country I loved and saw places I never otherwise would have. I carried the fears, secrets, problems, economic and health challenges that people shared with me, and felt a responsibility to help them. So, she wasn't going to be president. There was plenty in life—and work in the Senate—to look forward to.

HRC campaigned hard for Obama and was greeted everywhere with enthusiasm, love, and gratitude. She gave it right back, slowly making her way around every rope line, shaking every hand, smiling for every photo, signing every campaign poster.

When she campaigned for Obama in Flint, Michigan, a group of African American women on a rope line called me over to confess that they would have voted for her if Obama wasn't in the race.

"You have to understand," they said. "This was not a vote against Hillary, it was a vote of tremendous pride for Barack Obama."

When HRC caught up to us, they all started cheering and posing for pictures and thrusting their posters toward her to sign.

"Hillary! We love you, we'll get you next time. 2012, baby!" It turned into a chant, with the women clapping and stomping, as we made our way to the exit. "Get you next time!"

When we got on the plane, both our feet up on facing empty seats in the quartet section on the charter, we chatted about the people we'd met on the rope line.

"By the way," I said. "Did you hear those ladies say they would support you next time?"

Without hesitation, she laughed and shot back, "I am *never* doing this again!"

PART THREE

A GLASS JAR

To be loved is sweet . . . whereas to love is full of sorrow and grief and pain.

—Ahmed Ali, *Twilight in Delhi*

"I'm sitting next to a really charming man and he asked about you," Capricia Marshall whispered as I was studying my notes in a corner. "You should go sit in my seat."

"Capricia! I am working!" A true Hillaryland sister, Capricia was always looking out for me, and this was another teasing if maddening example.

It was a balmy summer weekend in August 2001. We were on Martha's Vineyard for a Democratic National Committee dinner, and I was, as usual, working.

At the end of the dinner, I was standing near HRC as she was chatting with a few of the guests, when Capricia brought the charming man over.

"Hi," he said, "I'm Anthony," extending his hand.

I knew who he was, of course. He was not some random charming man, but a member of congress from New York, which meant he was my boss's colleague, and I treated him accordingly. He was tall, lean, with small black wire-rimmed eyeglasses, boyishly handsome with intense hazel eyes that looked directly at me.

"Nice to meet you, Congressman," I said as I put my hand in his firm handshake.

"A few of us are going to get a drink later. You should come."

He was then, in that first moment, the way I always experienced him, in both the brightest and darkest of days: breezy, confident, and smiling. I found myself smiling back. Still, I never took flirtatious asides seriously when I was working or, for that matter, almost ever. I was polite to men who approached me at work events, engaged them in conversation, tried to accommodate their requests or answer their questions. I was always conscious of the fact that I was representing the First Lady of the United States, now a senator, and work had to come first. This wasn't a night off on the Vineyard, it was a working one.

"Thank you, Congressman," I said in my most serious but polite tone, "but I have to work tonight." Normally, this would have ended the conversation, but not with this man.

"Work!? What exactly does the ninety-seventh most senior senator have to do at ten o'clock on a Saturday night?" he said loudly, referring to the fact that my boss had only been in elected office for seven months. Now, everyone around us was paying attention. I quickly excused myself and turned back toward HRC.

As the Clintons were getting ready to leave, I noticed the congressman standing by the motorcade, talking and laughing with HRC and Terry McAuliffe, then the chairman of the DNC and a good friend of the Clintons. Terry was always the life of any party, and I assumed he was sharing something funny. I went over to listen in.

"Hillary," the congressman said as I approached, "I asked Huma to join us for a drink, but she says she has to work. Can't you give her one night off?"

There was that attitude again: breezy, confident, and smiling. I stood behind him facing HRC, trying to get her attention, unambiguously shaking my head *No! No! No!* She said, "Oh, of course, all you young people should go have a good time!"

I was mortified. *The* gall *of this guy*, I thought. Now I was stuck.

Next thing I knew I found myself in a staff van with a largish group of colleagues, DNC staff, and other dinner guests on our way to the Colonial Inn Bar in Edgartown. I followed the crowd into a low-lit room with wood floors, a few tables, and a bar along the back wall. The congressman was already there. He had taken off his tie, was holding it in one hand and the top button of his white shirt was unbuttoned. He casually gestured toward one of the tables near the back, separate from the crowd gathering around the bar. I joined him at the table, ordered a hot tea, and while he was ordering, I excused myself to go to the ladies' room. It's not that I meant to be rude. I just didn't know how to extricate myself from this situation. On my way back to the table, I conveniently got waylaid chatting with various people, and by the time I returned, the congressman's seat was empty, my cup of now-tepid tea left solitary on the table. The congressman now stood in the middle of an animated conversation at the bar with a drink in his hand. He looked at me, nodded, and smiled with an expression that seemed to say, *I get it and it's okay.* I stayed for a while, sticking to the comfort of familiar friends, until we all walked across the street to the Kelley House, where most of us were staying. I watched the back of the congressman as he climbed up the stairs to his room, while I continued on to my room in another part of the hotel.

Had I been struck by lightning? No. Was it love at first sight? Certainly not. Still, I had never met anyone quite like him. So self-assured and so clearly interested in me.

After that, from time to time, our crazy overscheduled lives would intersect—two high-speed trains coming at each other from opposite directions, slowing down for a bit to acknowledge each other without veering off course, continuing on to our respective destinations. Those moments were fleeting but always memorable.

Many months after our first meeting, we ran into each other at a restaurant in Queens, at an annual event. He had just finished addressing the local civic group, walked offstage, shirtsleeves rolled up, big smile on his face, backslapping and joking with everyone he passed, and HRC was no exception. As the more senior elected official at events, she was often the last to speak. "I warmed them up for you!" he joked as he walked past her. HRC laughed; his exuberance seemed to charm her. He noticed me, said a quick "Hello Huma," and I responded "Hi Congressman," and we both continued with our day.

Thereafter I often saw him yelling or, as people tend to describe male politicians with loud voices, "speaking passionately," about all the causes he cared about. There he was at the annual Salute to Israel parade breakfast before the kickoff, and the St. Patrick's Day parade and the National Puerto Rican Day parade and the September 11th Victim Compensation Fund press conferences and his regular Sunday press conferences. He brought an equal amount of "passion" to whatever he spoke about and sometimes I just rolled my eyes at his shtick. Still, it was hard to ignore his personal charisma and the energy in the air when he was around. I stood by HRC on rope lines and watched him charm his constituents, goad his colleagues, and provoke his perceived adversaries. While I ran from reporters, never wanting to say anything wrong or accidently be caught on the record, he seemed to enjoy every exchange with them. I never saw him approached by a microphone or a camera without stopping to engage, always managing a clever sound bite. He knew exactly what he wanted to communicate and he nailed it every time, without a note in sight.

I was still living in a glass jar. Just one moth hovering along with dozens of others around the brightest flame. When your life entails traveling with a Clinton, it is hard for any other star to shine. Only when you pull away can you see that there is light elsewhere.

* * * *

After the aborted attempt at drinks on Martha's Vineyard, the next social outing the congressman and I shared came a full six years later, at President Bush's State of the Union address in January 2007. HRC and Obama had just shown their cards, after almost a year of fevered speculation. So everyone was watching to see how the two current Senate colleagues and now newly minted presidential rivals would interact with each other.

As I left HRC at the entrance to the chamber, I saw Congressman Weiner slip past us looking for a seat. In the first-come, first-served seating protocol for members of Congress from both houses, the congressman ended up sitting next to HRC and behind Obama and Senator Ted Kennedy. I don't know if either senator/candidate noticed that they were making their way toward each other, and I never asked. Every camera was focused on the brief exchange between Clinton and Obama, but none caught the actual words exchanged. Only those surrounding them, including Anthony Weiner, of course, could hear whatever was said.

The speech was barely over before my inbox filled up with messages from colleagues and friends asking what their interaction had been like. I had worked for HRC long enough to know that this was an instance where everyone was dying to know what had transpired, but no one really needed to know. If there was something relevant, she would tell me or more likely call Patti. I wasn't going to press her and she didn't volunteer anything. I didn't even bother riding back to Whitehaven with her because I had told Heather King and a few colleagues I would catch them for a drink near the Capitol.

Amid the flurry of messages in my inbox, one appeared from Congressman Weiner. It said he had the craziest experience sitting with HRC and Obama, would I want to hear about it over a drink?

I had to admit I was curious, so I invited him to join us at the restaurant. When he walked in alone in a gray suit, green tie, and eyeglasses, without any staff of his own, Heather looked at me with raised eyebrows. I threw my hands up defensively and said, "What? He actually does know what they talked about!" He shook hands with everyone and joked, "You're welcome for staffing her while you guys are out on the town." We all chatted about the speech, and the newly launched presidential campaigns. Weiner, in fact, betrayed very little about their conversation aside from saying that he had ribbed Obama that he had HRC's back so not to try any false moves. "Did you actually say that?" Heather asked. He smiled and winked, and no one could tell if he was joking or serious.

Nothing in Washington stayed open very late back then, so we were there only briefly before we were asked to leave. "Have you eaten yet?" the congressman asked as we made our way to the door. I was several years into a daily diet that included coffee for breakfast, coffee and a protein bar for lunch and then a carb-heavy dinner. So, at 10:30 p.m., yes, I was very hungry for my one meal of the day. There were only a handful of places still open so I suggested the all-night diner in Adams Morgan, closer to where I lived, and about a twenty-minute drive from where we were.

"Sure," he said, not mentioning that we were in his neighborhood. "We can go with Percy."

"Thanks, but I'll take a cab and meet you there." I didn't know who Percy was, and I barely knew the congressman; I wasn't about to get into a car with them.

As we walked outside, Heather whispered, "Are you going to be okay? Want me to tag along?"

"I'll be fine," I assured her. "I'll take a cab back to Whitehaven afterwards to get my car."

I arrived at the dark, retro-style diner before he did. It was crowded for a weeknight. The hostess seated me at a small table in the back near the bathroom, next to a few crowded tables. The congressman walked in a few minutes later, and I saw him talking to the hostess animatedly. They walked over to me, and the hostess picked up our menus and asked us to follow her to the front of the restaurant, where she seated us at a large table in front of the window. "What did you say to her?" I asked. "Nothing," he said. Had he tipped her? Asked for a table closer to the front? Did she recognize him and decide to give him a better spot? This was my inaugural night witnessing an Anthonyism. Things just happened when you were with him. He didn't spend a lot of time explaining; it was all just taken care of. I ordered a large plate of French fries and a milkshake. He ordered a grilled cheese sandwich and a beer, then immediately called the waitress back and said, "Actually never mind the beer, I'll take a Coke. The last time I ordered a beer in front of this woman, she ran away and never came back." It was the first and last time I witnessed him order, or almost order, an alcoholic drink.

For me, the conversation began tentatively. I was guarded because I didn't know him. I viewed him as a member of Congress, someone I should hold at a respectful distance. Not the case at all for him. Right away, he engaged with ease, confidence, and an ability to carry on a conversation about anything—and everything. Provocative, interesting, veering from topic to topic seamlessly. Talking about the State of the Union speech, our conversation shifted to the Iraq War. He had voted for military action, and he told me it was one of the issues that had come up most frequently during his last campaign, and that he had publicly said it was a mistake.

"Do you regret you voted that way in the first place?" I pushed, no longer hesitant.

"It was a terrible vote, of course I regret it. It was obviously a mistake, and anyone who hasn't said it yet knows better or is getting bad advice from their consultants." He warned that it was going to be impossible for HRC to get ahead of this issue in her presidential campaign.

He also had very strong feelings about Saudi Arabia. In Congress, he was the most vocal opponent of military funding for Saudi Arabia, arguing that the government had turned a blind eye to its financial support for Al-Qaeda, while tolerating its aggressive exporting of Wahhabism. I found myself in a heated debate about his oversimplification of a complicated history, arguing that it was unfair to malign an entire population because of the actions of its extremists. When he pressed that all Saudi school textbooks taught Muslim children to hate Jews and Christians, I retorted that I had studied no such thing, ever. He was an unabashed defender of Israel's right to exist as a democracy, and I shot back that it couldn't be at the expense of the Palestinian people's right to basic human dignity.

Still, he always managed to get the last word in, on just about every topic we discussed. I had never been one for confrontation. If a professional conversation veered toward disagreement, I, like most people, disagreed politely, often deferentially. Not this man. He never stopped asking, never stopped pushing, which made him like no man I had ever met in a professional social setting. Having grown up in a family where no topic was off-limits, I enjoyed the exchange. Even though I had worked at the White House and now in the Senate, my colleagues and friends and I rarely debated fundamentals. We argued over strategy and tactics for sure, but this was different. Anthony pressed me to defend the basics underlying my beliefs.

When we started talking about our personal lives, he listened more than he shared. I told him about my family, how we all lived in different cities, how I loved being able to spend so much time in New York. He told me he was born and raised in Brooklyn and lived in Queens and they were the greatest places on earth. He knew exactly where in Elmhurst my family had lived, even down to the local bodega we frequented that I had been meaning to visit again. "I think that place shut down years ago," he said. When I asked about his parents and whether he had siblings, he joked that he had been a jackal pup, raised by wolves, and then switched the topic.

Leaning forward in his seat, his eyes squinting ever so slightly, finger jabbing at the air in quick motions, he said, "Hillary should come out for gay marriage." In 2007, few, if any, politicians had come out in support of marriage equality and that included anyone running for president on the Democratic ticket that year. I hesitated. At the time, this was considered a rather fringe position.

He continued, "This is a change election and there is nothing changeier than a Black guy from the Midwest named Barack Hussein Obama."

"Isn't having a woman president also change this country has never seen? Plus, she is more qualified than he is."

I bristled that the historic nature of her campaign seemed ignored. As much as I wanted to find something negative to say about Senator Obama, I couldn't. So I didn't say he wouldn't be a good president, just that she would be better.

"Have you thought about your own position?" I added, long accustomed to people saying HRC needed to do or say something they weren't prepared to do themselves. He was ready. "I supported gay marriage publicly in 1998, when I first ran for Congress. Besides," he added, "it's the right thing to do, and in five years, everyone will be for it. You might as well do it now."

The right thing to do. Words my father had lived by. As a Muslim, I knew there was nothing in the Qur'an that explicitly addressed marriage between people of the same gender. There is the story of Prophet Lot in Sodom and Gomorrah where God wipes out the town for their transgressions, but it is unclear what the transgressions were that were in fact being punished. Ultimately, the primacy of human dignity and acceptance in Islam led me to question why anyone would deny people of the same gender the same covenant that I take for granted as a heterosexual. As Muslims, we are cautioned against stigmatizing the "other" and instead encouraged to reflect on our own actions because we are ultimately responsible only for ourselves. The stories I had heard from friends who were just coming out and struggling to find their true selves, and ultimately to love, weighed heavily with me too.

I told him I would raise his suggestion with campaign colleagues, then looked down at my BlackBerry, and saw it was almost 3 a.m. I was meant to be back at work in a few hours. The crowded diner had emptied out, leaving just us and a few stragglers at the bar. I let him drive me back to my car. On that drive in Percy—which I learned was the name he had given his Pathfinder—I knew I had enjoyed being with him. Once I had seen past that first glimpse of his brash, cocky persona, I found him smart, really interesting, never boring.

After that evening, walks became the thing that connected us, an extension of life from my college days. I always presumed Anthony was busier than me—after all, he was an elected member of the House—so usually I waited to hear from him. He would text me in between votes and we would walk around the Capitol complex.

One evening, after a long round of late votes, Anthony asked if I wanted to grab something to eat once the House and Senate adjourned for the night. I was running late because I never left the office until HRC left and certainly never for something personal. Once free, I raced through the hallways, heels clicking on the century-old marble, underground, then up again, through the Capitol and out the doors to the House side. I saw Anthony standing outside. He wasn't stewing that I was late. He seemed totally lost in thought.

"Are you okay?" I said out of breath.

"Yes!" he said as he stood straight, snapped out of his reverie. "Sometimes, I can't believe I am actually here. Let's go. I'm starving." Ever since I had entered the world of politics, I often found myself in awe of the power and privilege I was exposed to. Seeing Anthony, an elected congressman, eleven years my senior, who was regularly appearing on TV interviews multiple times a day, just as humbled, made me feel more connected to him.

For months, our friendship remained simply that. It wasn't a significant part of my life and I don't think it was of his life either. We were two busy people, grabbing moments to hang out whenever we could. Anthony was someone I felt safe spending time with. I wasn't worried he would push me to do anything I wasn't prepared to do. Many of my closest friends were men. We would go out for group dinners and spend the evening debating, arguing, commiserating over any number of topics, all over good food and lots of desserts.

But I knew that I was not one of the women these men would ever leave the dinner with, and I was okay with that. I don't know what made me ever think the perfect Muslim man was going to be easy to find, but somehow I was certain of it. Professionally, I almost never interacted with any Muslim men aside from annual iftars or Eid celebrations on the Hill or at the White House. On occasion, aunts in New Jersey would say they knew of a nice Pakistani boy who was studying to be a doctor or a dentist or an engineer, and they told my mom that the mother had "asked" about me. My mother almost never mentioned these inquiries to me. I can only imagine her saying to these families, "You want my daughter to give up her job and move to Ohio to be a doctor's wife? Good luck with that." Once, when one of these families came to New Jersey for a visit, my fourteen-year-old cousin came down the spiral staircase at the end of the evening spewing her wisdom after witnessing my interactions with this particular man: "Huma, I think if you are ever going to be married, you have to talk less. Maybe sound, you know, like you don't know so much about politics and Hillary and Iraq."

Who was talking about getting married? I had an ideal of love in my mind, the kind my parents and siblings had. The reasons I felt so strongly about marrying a Muslim man were rooted in my faith, my cultural upbringing, the commitment to the kind of future I envisioned for myself and the *ummah* I imagined joining. Many Muslim families allow their sons to marry outside the faith without hesitation—but not daughters. That is because in Islamic tradition, all children borne of the union automatically take the father's religion. For my eventual grown-up life, I wanted someone who shared the same values and beliefs. That meant someone who shared the same faith tradition, and would pass it on to our children. Because being Muslim is so much a way of life, it was hard to imagine a partner I couldn't pray with, fast with, someone who couldn't visit my father's grave. It felt as though a part of my very being would be cut out of my core without that.

I had gone on dates with five or six men since I left the White House, introduced through friends or at parties and, on occasion, at work events. Those encounters entailed coffees, dinners, walks, movies, Broadway shows. I kissed a few of them, but never allowed anything beyond that. As was expected of any girl with my background, I would lose my virginity to the man I would marry. My parents hadn't been particularly explicit; my mother never sat me down and said, "you'd better not sleep around with boys." It was, in the true form of all my parents' lessons, ultimately my own choice.

One night, I went to the home of a man I'd been out with several times and whose company I really enjoyed. The minute I walked into his apartment, after a long Italian dinner and a walk to get dessert, expectation filled the air of his dark living room, and I immediately felt the thick navy velvet curtains closing in around me. I told him I needed to leave. Extricating myself from such situations and rebalancing relationships so we could remain friends almost always proved successful. Some men, as soon as they learned my "limitations," ran away. Keeping men at a distance also kept things simple. I hadn't had my heart broken anyway since the Muslim boy from college told me I wasn't the type of girl men dated.

Even if I had been actively trying to find someone to settle down with or just have fun with, I knew it would affect my ability to do my job, which was my top priority. I noticed that male colleagues often brought their girlfriends to events the Clintons hosted, but few of my female colleagues ever brought dates unless they were married. One man came to a couple Clinton events as my plus-one, but I had to leave him in a corner to fend for himself because I was working. After a few of these evenings he told me to just call him when I was done with work. Anthony, however, was different. When he came to events with me, I would see him out of the corner of my eye with a small group gathered around him or deep in conversation with someone. I didn't have to worry about offending him if I had to cancel meeting at the last minute. He seemed happy and self-sufficient wherever he was.

On October 21, 2007, Page Six, the gossip column in the *New York Post*, reported that Hillary Clinton's "right-hand woman" was seen with "one of D.C.'s most eligible bachelors," chatting as we strolled through the halls of Congress. I had, in my previous seven years on Capitol Hill, strolled through the halls with hundreds of men—senators, congressmen, other aides, security details—all in the regular course of doing my job. I had never before been fodder for gossip columns. But now there was a story to tell.

The story was far more about who Anthony was than me. When

Anthony and I first began spending time together, he always seemed restless and hungry for action. He had been in public office since he was twenty-seven years old. In 2005, he ran for mayor of New York City and made a surprisingly strong second-place showing, and the world began to pay attention. By 2007, his name was regularly being mentioned as a candidate in the 2009 mayor's race. For me, that precious thing called anonymity was still my normal, but there were little mentions of us all through the winter of 2007 and into the next spring. On January 27, we were "spotted" going into the Maritime Hotel in the Meatpacking District, around the corner from one of HRC's fundraisers. On March 18, we were seen "standing side-by-side" and "whispering" at the swearing-in ceremony for the incoming New York governor David Paterson. By May 16, 2008, we were "dining *à deux*" at a restaurant in East Hampton. What on earth made this interesting to anyone? Going from invisible to visible just because of who I was *with* was not something I relished.

Somewhere in that mess of nonstop 2008 primary campaign travel, a Senate schedule, a trip to the hospital to visit my newborn nephew on Thanksgiving, Anthony had kissed me late one night in a Washington, DC, park after dinner. My head started spinning and didn't stop. I began to look forward to seeing him, to sharing the latest goings-on in my life with him, thinking about him more when I wasn't with him. The benefit, or maybe the curse, of our lives was that our schedules permitted only brief spurts of time together, which made those moments all the more intense and more precious. We were never in each other's presence long enough to have to reveal our warts or insecurities. The penny was always returned to the jar when it was still shiny.

I knew I was falling for him. I knew it when he started picking me up at the airport whenever I landed in DC after a long trip—at 3 p.m., 11 p.m., 2 a.m.—just to drop me off at my apartment. I knew it when I would forget and leave my shoes in his car because one of them had a broken heel and find it fixed and both of them shined the next time I got in. I knew it when I had a flat tire and he came to help me, then took the car to be serviced and cleaned and drove it back to my garage. I knew it when at the end of a long day at work he drove me straight to my favorite restaurant, fed me, and made me laugh the entire night. I knew it when I would vent to him about the challenges of the campaign and he cheered me up, told me not to give up. I knew he believed in HRC's candidacy because he was right there with us on the campaign, traveling, stumping, and canvassing for her anywhere he could be useful, from Iowa to New Hampshire and beyond.

Fresh off the emotional roller coaster of the crushing loss in the 2008 Iowa primary and a surprise comeback in New Hampshire, our campaign was preparing for the Super Tuesday contests. Late one night in February, the motorcade arrived back at the Hyatt hotel in Cincinnati after a long day of punishing events. I was too tired to even take off my coat when I plopped into a chair at the dining table in HRC's room to download on the day and prepare for the next. The table was bare, without the briefing books that normally would have been there. After a day of not eating, it appeared that the room service we'd ordered on our way back to the hotel hadn't arrived either.

Avra Siegel, our hotel advance, volunteered that she had left the briefing books in my room across the hall because there was something I needed to review in advance. HRC asked me to go get them.

Hungry and exasperated, I stood up and dragged myself to my room at the end of the hall, convinced that room service would never arrive. I pushed my door open and almost had the wind knocked out of me. Straight in front of me, at a little round table, sat Anthony surrounded by candles, a small vase of red flowers, and domed stainless steel dish covers—it was Valentine's Day and he had come to have dinner with me. Just the sight of him released an avalanche of stress. I fell into his arms and let all my worries pour out, feeling an immense relief to share the relentless burden and intensity of the campaign with someone who would understand, and who made me feel special. We ate pasta and spinach and French fries and a chocolate dessert and laughed about the madness of our lives.

What I didn't tell him, what no one on the campaign ever knew, was that this was my first-ever Valentine's Day date. In past years, I would go out for dinner with a group of friends or stay at work. My first year in college, my mom and sister sent me flowers because they didn't want me to feel lonely. I had never been anyone's valentine in DC or in New York or anywhere for that matter. Anthony had worked all day in Washington, jumped on a plane to Ohio, and arranged to surprise me with a meal of assorted comfort food—my favorite. When he was there, he was laser-focused on me, my life, my problems. When I was with him, I thought nothing bad could ever happen to me.

A few months later, in the spring of 2008, traveling on our campaign plane to Puerto Rico, one of our press secretaries told me that Anthony had made some news. Chatting with the press at the back of the plane and asked why he had been so active on the campaign trail, he was quoted as saying it was "largely because I'm dating Huma." His public announcement instantly made me uncomfortable because what exactly this relationship was neither of us really knew.

Our genie was out of the bottle, hovering wherever we went. The pressure of the campaign, along with the secret feeling that I was falling in love with him even though I knew I couldn't end up with him, heightened my feelings all the more. The highs were amazing. The lows we endured by catching a late movie, picking up mint chocolate chip ice cream from the local Baskin-Robbins, or just walking and talking late into the night. So much of our life was informed, infused by our work. Even our first fight was about HRC.

With the first Tuesday in May came the primaries in North Carolina and Indiana. After a resounding primary win in Pennsylvania, the momentum now briefly on our side, Obama publicly said he would win North Carolina and that Indiana would be a tiebreaker. When the polls closed at 6 p.m., we knew that we were on track to win, but there were local advisors who didn't want to jump the gun and claim victory until it was certain and the Associated Press officially called the race. "We need to wait for Gary to report," someone shouted from a desk, referring to the city in Indiana. Anthony and I stood amid the madness in the boiler room, where campaign staff tallied returns, as aides worked the phones with field staff in Gary or kept hitting the refresh button on news websites to try to capture updates. Everyone was agitated, knowing how badly we needed this victory. Anthony grabbed my wrist and pulled me into the tiny hallway.

"What the hell are you guys doing?! You need to get her out there *now*! Obama is going to claim the night," he said, the words coming through his clenched teeth.

"Why are you yelling at me? No one knows if we will even win yet."

"In ten minutes, it's not going to matter." He was agitated and frustrated. I was annoyed that he was inserting himself.

"Let me do my job," I said as I brushed past him to rejoin my team.

Of course, I knew we needed to set the tone for the night, but I was also cautious. If the first visual was HRC on stage claiming victory, it would provide momentum to carry us to the next primary, which we desperately needed. But if we lost, and had falsely claimed victory, everything we had worked toward would crumble. Every precious minute that went by was one minute closer to Obama walking onto his stage and claiming victory in North Carolina, a chance for him to frame the day's contests.

Anthony went back inside and grabbed Terry McAuliffe. They both started badgering anyone who would listen, "Get her out there!" I was furious with him. I didn't want to be the person whose boyfriend was pushing her around. Soon it became clear that there was no way for Obama to pass HRC at this point and our state director said it was time. I don't even remember anyone telling her she had won Indiana, I just said, "We need to get you out there." She picked up the speech box with the victory speech in it and said, "Okay, let's roll!" As we started to walk rapidly up dark stairs to the stage, we heard Obama's voice on TV. He had beaten us to the punch. Again. It was a deflating moment, but HRC didn't stop to listen. She kept climbing and stood backstage, her head bowed, and waited her turn, until the networks were done carrying his speech and would hopefully stick around to cover hers.

It was her last victory rally in the fifty states.

HRC delivered her concession speech at the National Building Museum in Washington, DC, a month later. It was not easy for any of us, but there was little time to lick our wounds. The disappointment over HRC's loss shifted rapidly into a massive team effort to elect Obama.

Throughout the summer, I saw Anthony as often as I could. While I had always found great personal reward in doing my job, and my job always came first, so much in my professional environment was uncertain. Anthony's very presence was the opposite—he was uncertain about nothing. He became my rock.

After a historic night in November when we elected our first African American president, I knew I had to face the reality of being in love with someone who was not of my faith, someone whose life in the spotlight made me uncomfortable but someone I wanted to be with in spite of it all. Still, I held out hope that maybe we could just go back to being friends again. I decided to see what life was like without seeing him, hoping I would feel liberated and independent, recapture the old Huma. The experiment was a failure. I was miserable and lonely. He had become core both to my social life and my happiness. Without him or my colleagues from the campaign, I was home alone watching TV or going to bed early, barely making it through a page of whatever book I was reading before falling asleep.

On a trip to New York that winter I confided to a friend at dinner how overwhelmed I was by my inner conflict. "I feel sorry for you," he said in response. "I think missing out on love, waiting for something that might never come, when it is staring you in the face, is something to think about before you walk away. To me, it seems you are afraid and being just plain stubborn." Was this mystery man I was saving myself for ever going to come? At thirty-three, that certainty I'd carried with me for my entire adult life began to buckle under the weight of the unknown. The election was over and HRC was not going to be president. The dull ache in my heart was no longer just about her losing.

I left to powder my nose and when I returned to our table, three chicly dressed young women were chatting with my handsome friend. As I reclaimed my chair, one of them leaned over to mouth, "you are so lucky." *I am*, I thought, but not for the reason she suspected. Later that night, sleepless in my midtown hotel room, I pulled out my BlackBerry and found the draft response I had started to send to Anthony's last email asking if I wanted to have dinner. It began with, "I don't know." I erased it, wrote one word and hit send. "Yes."

* * * *

The marriage proposal came late at night on the Friday of the Memorial Day weekend in 2009. Whoa, wait, what just happened? We went from "what are we?" just months earlier to a marriage proposal, zero to

120, in no time. Anthony was never paralyzed by indecision, and our marriage was no exception. He had told me how much he loved children and how he couldn't wait to be a father. I had told him I would marry but not until sometime in the future, and he stayed silent or smiled. We never had a conversation about our religious differences being a barrier to marriage, although I knew my being a Muslim wasn't an issue for him. He dealt with our differences by just powering through. I dealt with them by not dealing with them.

On this particular Friday night, he had planned the perfect Manhattan evening. Dinner at my favorite Greek restaurant in midtown and tickets to *West Side Story* on Broadway. During the show, I noticed he kept looking over at me furtively, so I finally whispered "What?" and he responded with a silly "Get it? Sharks and Jets? That's like us." After the show, he suggested we go to Gramercy Park. A friend had loaned him a key to the private park and we walked inside the beautifully manicured gardens. We sat on a bench and I pointed out all the flowers I loved planted around us. He mostly stayed quiet. It got chilly after a while, and he suggested we go inside the Gramercy Park Hotel for coffee. It had a recently renovated cozy, dim, ornately furnished lounge with art all over the walls.

We ended up in an unremarkable room near the lounge. It had velvet furniture, dark floors and walls, small spotlight lamps shining down on the dark rugs so I could see the minuscule specks of white dust float into the air when Anthony knelt on one knee mouthing words that my ears were too busy ringing to actually hear. Before me was a black velvet box opened to reveal an oval-shaped diamond with tiny little diamonds circling it. The setting was identical to an emerald-and-gold ring that belonged to my mother, given to her by my grandmother, which I had long coveted. It was the most beautiful piece of jewelry I had ever held and it was meant for me. I don't know when I stopped shaking. I do not remember what I said. I didn't know if any of it was real. I took the ring, we embraced, and I closed my eyes feeling a euphoria I had never experienced before, and wanting to share it all immediately with those I loved the most.

Anthony called his parents and brother and then I called my mother, my brother, and each of my sisters. The first thing each family member said was congratulations. I had met his parents and his brother one Thanksgiving and they had been warm and welcoming. No one had raised an eyebrow when I walked in as Anthony's "friend" at a time when our relationship was new and exciting yet still very much undefined. But in the calls with my family, after the congratulations, there hung an unmistakable hesitation in the air. Anthony had spent time with my mother when she had visited Washington the previous summer, and had met Heba on several occasions because she lived in New York, and he'd been his usual charming, confident self with both of them. From the beginning, he appeared to adjust seamlessly to our culture, eating our spicy food and seeming unfazed when my mom started speaking in Urdu during meals. But these were casual meetings, not meet-your-future-in-law meetings.

I knew there was still one big challenge for us to actually be married. Anthony arranged to make a trip to meet my brother in England and get his blessing. But Hassan raised the same issues my father would have raised. You are joining a family where faith is core to who we are, he told Anthony, where we hold certain values and codes of conduct that have passed through generations. Although Anthony tried to reassure him that he understood and accepted how central my faith was to me, the trip ended without resolution. So he took a second trip to see Hassan. "You are sure this is what you want?" Hassan asked me afterward, reluctantly telling me he would support any decision I made but not exactly giving us his blessing.

The rest of my family, in conversations that were often compressed and fleeting because of the great distances that separated us, seemed somewhere between resigned to our marriage and happy about it. "Have you done the *istikhara* prayer?" Hadeel asked. "What would Abbu say?" my mom kept repeating, picking at the still-open wound of his absence at the very moment in my life when I most needed him. For Heba the question seemed simpler: "If he makes you happy, I like him," she said.

The proposal, the existence of a ring, had forced the religion conversation. I told Anthony he had gone from being my best friend to the only man I had ever loved, and still I could not reconcile how to marry outside my faith. If we were to be married, I needed to know that he was someone who would accept and respect my God and my faith traditions—which in fact he had shown every sign of doing. He wasn't asking me to give up anything, in this or in any other aspect of our relationship. That I appreciated. I was the one asking him to bend, to change, to embrace a new way of life. And from almost the very first day we went out, he had. He stopped eating pork, he stopped drinking alcohol, he continued to meticulously give a percentage of his income to charity every year, he had even started fasting with me from time to time during Ramadan. Still, I could not force him to personally accept my faith beliefs—there is no compulsion in Islam.

A few weeks after the proposal, he told me he wished he had a do-over. His original plan had been to propose to me inside Gramercy Park, but when the moment arrived, he couldn't. After the fancy restaurant and expensive Broadway tickets, he was trying so hard to make the evening special, but the idea of embarking on a life together in an exclusive, private park was something he could not stomach. "I'm sorry. That is just not who I am," he said. This made me even more sure he was right for me. I admired his idealism, his simplicity, the fact that he had almost no material attachments. His apartment was minimally furnished and immaculate. His only indulgence seemed to be the bulky equipment for his weekly midnight hockey games at Chelsea Piers. I knew that if we got married, as two public servants we would probably never be wealthy, which was fine with me. He then said he was prepared to do what was necessary for our marriage to be acceptable in the eyes of my family and me and asked only that I approach his value system with the same open heart and mind. His work ethic and principles appeared to mirror mine and it was more than enough for a good life.

After spending so much of the past year filled with both intense love and deep uncertainty, my heart and mind now felt aligned and at peace, and I knew I was making the right decision. I was thirty-four years old. It seemed as though after prayer, reflection, and yes, some degree of stubbornness, I was finally with the only man I had ever loved and the only man who had ever told me he loved me.

BOOTS AND
KITTEN HEELS

*America will always win the war. It's a superpower that
no one can challenge. The real challenge is for the United
States to win the peace.*

—Christiane Amanpour

Not a week had gone by after Obama's victory when Philippe sent
HRC an email, cc'ing Maggie, Cheryl, and me about a rumor that
the President-elect was considering HRC for his cabinet. After noting
that he thought she would be a great cabinet pick, Philippe added, "I
know, I know, you're all going to reply that 'it's not going to happen.'"
Philippe knew us well.

Two days later, on Sunday, November 9, at 5:17 p.m., an email
appeared from HRC. The subject line read: "For your eyes only." I
hated when Philippe was right. WJC had just hung up with Obama,
who mentioned he wanted to meet with HRC. She wanted me to discreetly follow up. I went straight to Reggie Love, who confirmed the
request for a meeting in Chicago. On the commercial flight over, every
so often HRC volunteered that she didn't believe Obama would ask her
to serve in the cabinet. I don't know if that was a wish or an assumption,
but from what I observed, she was not savoring this. She talked more
about what she was looking forward to doing back in the Senate.

Whether she wanted it or not, she was offered the secretary of
state job after their one-on-one meeting. She didn't commit that day
in Chicago. Over the next week, there were calls scheduled and then
canceled, then postponed and then postponed again. Each time, I did

all kinds of verbal gymnastics to avoid putting my boss on the line to say no to a job she insisted she did not want. We were all pros at awkward phone calls by this point. Throughout the campaign, we'd stuck to the tradition of the loser calling the winner after each primary or caucus election. Some nights, when our team was receiving the call, were nice; other nights, when we had to place it, considerably less so. The very last call to Obama had been after his primary win in Montana, assuring him enough delegates to secure the nomination. When I handed the phone to HRC, she had said, "Barack, congratulations on Montana. And everything else." That about summed it up.

On a day when I postponed a call three times, my final excuse was that we were ending very late that evening and didn't want to bother the President-elect in the middle of the night. The response came from Obama directly. He would be waiting up for HRC's call. So, finally, at 12:31 a.m. on November 20, they talked and she said no. They later talked again. This time she gave him an almost no. Before their third call, she told me, "There isn't anything he can say that will convince me to take this job." Eventually, she said yes. He had decided that she was the best person for the job and he was unwavering.

I joined HRC for her first transition meeting at the State Department and left feeling really excited about this new adventure. I didn't know exactly what my role would be, but from the many conversations in which HRC told me about all the things "we" needed to do to get ready, it seemed clear that there would be a place for me if I wanted one. Everyone in my family was flourishing. My mother was creating a new college in Saudi. Hassan was in England completing his PhD, happily married with three beautiful children. Hadeel was now a medical doctor, also living in England, with her husband, Saeed, and their three sons. Heba and her husband, Sohail, were living in Manhattan with a weekend home in New Jersey, and their third son had been born in the midst of the campaign and was the only of her children's births I had missed because our campaign plane landed late. I wanted to feel that sense of flourishing too. After a hard year I was ready for the new one—2009—to begin.

As I considered what serving at State might mean, I thought about this country that I had loved from afar for so much of my life. I thought of the simple fact that without this institution and the waiver that allowed my parents to remain here, I would not even have this nationality that I carried with such pride. I thought about all the trips to the U.S. consulate in Jeddah when I was a little girl, where the USIA officer held keys to the world beyond its sand-colored stone walls.

I also thought of the Palestinians I met who lived under an Israeli occupation. My visits to Pakistan with cousins who politely pointed out that America had caused plenty of problems for their sovereign nation. My girlfriends in Saudi who resented the non-Muslim world for telling them they were backward because they covered their hair—but who were raising sons to ship off to military academies abroad. I thought of my father's sisters in the subcontinent who had never left. I thought of the life he would have lived if he had gone back to marry the woman to whom he was promised. I thought of what might have happened if my mother had studied in the Philippines instead of accepting a Fulbright to Philadelphia. I thought of the Muslim refugees I met in Macedonia who made it home because of the intervention of the united Western world. I remembered the women I'd met not long ago in Iraq, patient but frustrated, who asked when the war would end.

Was America the problem or the solution? Countries blamed us for their troubles but also seemed to think America alone could arbitrate any internal or regional disputes. Instilled in me were the values I learned from childhood. That, despite its imperfections, there was still no country in the world that could compete with the values of the American ideal. A country weighted with an ethical and financial responsibility to lift partners up where it could, to answer as best it could the call for moral leadership. I had seen so much of that effort up close that I knew progress was possible. Now I would be joining HRC to do this work from the State Department.

Some things hadn't changed in the decade since I had worked in the White House. Osama bin Laden was still at large, now presumed to be in hiding somewhere between Pakistan and Afghanistan. India and Pakistan were still in conflict. The Middle East was still convulsing. The war in Iraq had been almost universally recognized as a mistake but was still in progress.

On January 21, 2009, HRC was sworn in as secretary of state.

From here on in, her moniker would simply be S, as secretaries of state are known within the department. When she walked into State for her first official day at work, she was met with thunderous applause from a thousand foreign and civil service officers crowded into the cavernous atrium.

"The building," as the imposing main State headquarters is known (its official name is the Harry S. Truman Building), is large enough to house only a fraction of the seventy thousand people who make up State's fully functioning bureaucracy. The key to a successful term as secretary of state, we had been advised, was understanding and respecting the building, and the lifelong public servants who ran it. When the elevator door opened onto the seventh floor, we arrived at Mahogany Row, where the offices for the secretary and other senior officials were located. With plush carpet underfoot and dim reading lamps, the hushed, low-key ambience reminded me of a university library. I ended up in what veterans call the fishbowl, the small office adjacent to HRC's personal assistant, who sat in the main reception area. With glass windows on three sides, two facing the inner office and the third with a view of the Lincoln Memorial, it was indeed a fishbowl.

Cheryl Mills ran the transition process for the State Department on behalf of HRC. When I was working in the White House, Cheryl worked in the counsel's office and had become a legend after her defense of the President during the Senate impeachment trial. She spoke in brilliant, clear, fast sentences, her mouth somehow able to keep up with the rapid-fire workings of her brain. Each word landed with impact, and she held eye contact through every conversation. She rarely wore makeup or had her nails done, was rail-thin even though she mostly survived on potato chips and soda, and was always the most striking woman in any room. Cheryl's only weaknesses were her love of the *Daily Mail*, a British tabloid, and her habit of sending emails at 3 a.m. with articles that were often outright fake news. It was baffling, but at least she was always on top of what the other side was saying! When she offered me the job of deputy chief of staff for operations, I asked if she was coming too. She said she was going to be counselor and chief of staff, which only made saying yes easier.

Jake Sullivan, who had been on HRC's policy team during the campaign, would be deputy chief of staff for policy. From the minute he walked into Hillaryland in 2007, Jake had been universally embraced as the golden boy he was. He would go on to become one of the youngest national security advisors in American history. Absolutely no one who knew him was surprised when that happened. He listened to everyone else's ideas respectfully, even when his own were far superior, and had the ability to bring consensus to any meeting he joined. Jake and I had complementary but separate portfolios. I oversaw all of HRC's domestic and foreign travel, and Jake would be her primary policy advisor. Philippe was coming too, as a deputy assistant secretary for communications. He was a perpetual source of entertainment and was already concocting a myriad of creative new ideas for HRC's first one hundred days. Lona Valmoro, who had overseen HRC's schedule in the Senate, was also joining. Endlessly patient, Lona would listen to everyone drone on about fantastical plans, and then, being the ultimate organizing maven, she actually made them happen. The learning curve for our new roles was steep, but the passion and commitment were equally high.

We integrated our small personal squad into the existing infrastructure, a team of highly professional foreign service officers long accustomed to working on operations where a single misstatement or slighted leader could cause a foreign policy disaster. Joe Macmanus, the executive assistant, was the most senior diplomat in the office and sat on the other side of the only actual wall in my office. Joe was responsible for all material that went in and out of HRC's office, and he served as the primary counsel and guide to HRC and the rest of us on just about every State Department–related matter. Joe became my primary go-to from day one. All strategic, big-picture planning related to HRC's international travel agenda was guided by formal consultations Jake, Philippe, and I would have with our deputy secretary of state, Jim Steinberg, a foreign policy expert whom I knew from the Clinton White House years, and Bill Burns, the soft-spoken career diplomat who was a legend in the foreign service.

To build out all the foreign travel we worked with Dan Smith, the executive secretary, and his deputies; each oversaw the work of the foreign service in different regions of the world. Lew Lukens, the executive director of Dan's office, was responsible for all the logistics that went into planning a trip. Moving HRC would be like moving a small army. All of my main points of contact on a daily basis were seasoned diplomats. Their next posts, after they'd completed these jobs, would send them around the world as deputy chiefs of mission and ambassadors.

I felt lucky to have these partners. They all seemed eager to help make HRC a successful S. My first day on the job I stared at a tall stack of paper enumerating requests for action on what seemed to be dozens of matters, all of them apparently equally urgent. It remained to be seen how we would reengage with the world, set a new agenda, and reestablish relationships with our international partners, alliances that had cracked under the strain of the past eight years and the accumulated post-9/11 pressure.

HRC had already been using the term smart power, the idea that being an effective global leader didn't just mean having a massive military force, strong power if you will. It was about how to use all available resources—including diplomatic, economic, cultural—to forge relationships with other countries, while also using those relationships to advance our values of democracy, prosperity, human rights, and women's rights, and accepting the inevitable compromises that have to be made. When she was First Lady, HRC's trips were part of pushing forward a broader agenda set by the White House. In the Senate, her international travels were occasional fact-finding or oversight missions. In this role, the trips *were* the job.

It had been decided that her first trip as secretary of state would include Japan, then Indonesia and South Korea, and end in China. Our own economy had taken a beating during the Great Recession, so we thought it strategically important for her to visit the region with the second-largest economy, which also happened to be one of our biggest trading partners, and as important as any other place she could go.

When it came to actually planning out her days, I approached every trip by analyzing what the foremost message goal was for each stop, then trying to ensure that all the working parts of the trip complemented and reinforced that message, and that the trip ended with a "deliverable," a news-making announcement, usually of financial assistance or a new partnership. Also included in most of these trips were meetings with women leaders or activist groups that HRC considered sacrosanct. This was not typical fare for an American secretary of state. Even at her testimony before the Senate Foreign Relations Committee, she had called women's rights not just a moral issue but also a foreign policy and economic imperative. Elevating women, giving them an audience with her, remained a priority. So much so that at one point in our planning meetings, Philippe, one of only two men in the room, lifted his hands defensively. "Hey, when are we going to start doing meetings on these trips with men? I am beginning to feel really insecure here."

Even though I spent my entire career working for an icon of women's rights the world over, and pushing that agenda in meeting after meeting, in many ways I had a blind spot about standing up for myself. After the very first trip-planning debrief, when our team reviewed the schedule for our inaugural trip, Cheryl, who rarely nitpicked on any trip details, asked me to stay behind. Once everyone had left, she said she noticed that I had not added my name to the list of participants in any of the meetings on the trip, something that in my role I had full discretion to do. That, she told me, was a mistake.

"You need to recognize that you are deputy chief of staff to the secretary of state. You are no longer the person waiting outside for the meeting to end. You have a seat at the table. You have had one on the inside for a long time. Now it is time for you to occupy it in the outside world. Listening to and understanding the policy issues that are driving decisions made by the secretary of state on behalf of this administration will make it much easier for you to do your job as you weigh where she goes and how she spends her time. Do not forget, you work for someone who has spent decades lifting other women up. We are not sending her into rooms to be surrounded just by white men."

If it hadn't been for Cheryl, it wouldn't have occurred to me, but after that conversation, I did notice how heavily male our meetings often were.

Once, during a meeting in Asia, the host foreign minister opened his remarks by saying, "Madam Secretary, I want you to take note that we have more women on our delegation than men. It is inspired by your leadership. We thought you might appreciate that." HRC smiled widely and said, "Yes, yes I do, indeed, Minister. That's wonderful." She then quickly jumped into her points, because on our side of the table sat mostly white men, with the exception of two women: HRC and me.

* * * *

In the White House, I had first been one advance person among hundreds building out a single event often on long trips with many stops, each to drive forward a narrative the administration wanted to promote. Then I graduated to directing those events, then to helping to conceive and plan them, and now I was part of the strategy deciding what that story would be each time we landed in a new country. Something else had changed over those years too. When I first stepped foot on foreign soil on behalf of my country in 1997, America was arguably the sole superpower of the world. Since then, our country and the world had been rocked first by terrorism on a sustained international scale, then a war that opened with shock and awe but quickly descended into loss and devastation, and then a global economic crisis. Reframing the story of American power in the world was central to the new mission: We were no longer focused on sending boots on the ground. No, this time we were sending Hillary Clinton in kitten heels.

Loading up for the first trip felt like old home week for me. Back at Andrews Air Force Base, at the same terminal, the same familiar coffee and warm chocolate chip cookies, the exact same planes we had used during the Clinton administration, a little grayer and creakier but still featuring the blue-and-white official seal of the United States. HRC had a cabin with two captain's chairs, a sofa bed, a coffee table, a closet, and a bathroom. When I opened the closet door, I found a large black chest that took up most of the space, leaving little room for luggage. "What is that?" I asked the chief flight attendant as I stepped out into the main cabin. That, he explained, was the video monitor for secure video conferences, to be used to join meetings with the NSC while HRC was in flight. Okay, so some things had changed.

I sat in the section after HRC's cabin, in a window seat among a quartet of business-class chairs. Jake sat across from me, and Philippe next to him. We saved the empty seat next to me for HRC since she had expressed a preference for sitting with us, which put most everyone a little on edge except for Philippe, who announced that he planned to sleep no matter what. On the other side of the aisle sat two line officers and the speechwriter. The line team was comprised of talented young foreign service officers responsible for writing, compiling, organizing, editing, clearing, and collating the briefing books and all the paper, memos, and talking points for each meeting and event. They worked hand in hand with Joe Macmanus, and now with Jake and the rest of us. Basically, nothing would happen without the line team.

Our first stop was Tokyo, where I joined HRC at the official lunch hosted by the Japanese foreign minister. The exquisite array of sushi we were served was a far cry from the McDonald's meals my siblings and I had insisted on during our childhood trip to Japan. HRC paid her respects at the historic Meiji Shrine, and had the honor of being invited to tea at the Imperial Palace by the Empress Michiko (a tribute to her former status as First Lady), while I sat for tea with the empress's lady-in-waiting.

Our second stop was Jakarta, Indonesia. I had fond memories from a summer I'd spent there with my family, running down the banyan tree–lined neighborhood streets with the children of my father's colleagues while he went to meetings at the university. With the largest Muslim population in the world, Indonesia was trying to balance democracy and women's rights in exactly the way HRC wanted to encourage. Next stop was Korea, to discuss the challenge posed to both our countries by the unpredictable regime of North Korea, and then on to China for discussions with the leaders of the soon to be second-largest economy in the world.

In each country we went to on that first trip, we managed to achieve a balance between the official schedule of high-level talks, interviews with the local media, civic engagement through appearances in public forums, and visits to cultural touchstones. We had many, many trips to go, and the hope was that we could continue to meld all those priorities.

After inaugural trips to Asia, then the Middle East and Europe, and then Mexico, we headed to Europe in April for G-20 and NATO meetings in London, France, and Germany, our first trip with President Obama. We made sure HRC's schedule was in lockstep with the President's. We flew on Air Force One with President Obama from the G-20 in London to Strasbourg, where he and HRC would meet with President Nicolas Sarkozy of France, and then traveled on to Baden-Baden in Germany for a NATO reception and meetings that German chancellor Angela Merkel was hosting.

For almost a year HRC and I had been talking about her taking a proper vacation, so when I saw ninety minutes free on her schedule during our time in Baden-Baden, I thought it might be a good chance for her to relax. I suggested she get a massage at a famed spa that was located in the hotel where she would be waiting, or "holding" as we called it, until it was time for the next series of meetings with the President. She rarely, if ever, got a massage, and she was reluctant, but after some pushing, I managed to convince her.

"It will be great. You never take the time," I insisted. "What's one little hour?"

When we arrived at the Brenners hotel, I walked with HRC to the spa as our line advance, a young, courteous foreign service officer, led the way. Once HRC was in the spa room, I went back upstairs to catch up on work alongside Jake and Philippe, who had spread out in HRC's comfortable suite. A few minutes in, the line officer walked in with HRC's assistant looking on nervously, and politely said to me, "I just want to let you know we have to leave the hotel in fifteen minutes."

What? I shot up, looked at my phone, then the schedule, then my phone, then Obama's schedule to see how this had happened. A typo somewhere had showed a free hour and a half when in reality we only had thirty minutes.

I ran back down to the spa room as fast as I could, and gently knocked on the door to say we needed to wrap up.

"Wow, that time went by very quickly," she said as she stepped out into the hallway, hair mussed, mascara leaking.

"Yes, it did," I mumbled as we raced back to the room and kicked the boys out while she changed for the formal dinner that was next on the schedule.

In minutes, she stepped out in a black-and-gold striped formal coat and black pants, hair and makeup fixed, ready to go. For purposes of protocol, it was imperative for us to arrive before Obama. Missing his arrival or walking on camera late, especially on their very first trip abroad together, would be misinterpreted as an intentional slight. Trying to be helpful, the lead line officer suggested a shortcut we could take if we walked.

"Okay, let's do it!" HRC called out, and we all marched rapidly to the back of the hotel, poking our way through a meadow in heels. It seemed like the perfect solution, except that once we got close to the edge of the property, we came across a wooden gate that was locked. HRC was now visibly annoyed. Getting pulled off the massage table after just fifteen minutes she took in stride, but now I was pushing my luck. Still, it was ridiculously funny to imagine all of us climbing over the gate in our formalwear. Minutes later, hotel security came running out with a magic little key. Gate opened, we ran and arrived in time. Just barely. I wondered if either Chancellor Merkel or President Obama picked up the lingering scent of massage oil as they all air-kissed hello. I had not intended for HRC's "vacation" to be so brief, but we managed to laugh about it later that night. The only person who might still be confused about what happened is the German masseuse.

* * * *

Many of our trips brought me back to countries I'd visited with my parents during my childhood, or landed me near friends from my Saudi days who had spread out all over the world. I was now seeing those locales from a new perspective—as a representative of the U.S. government, and also as an adult.

The trip most personally meaningful to me was President Obama's in June 2009 to Cairo, where he was set to deliver a speech calling for a "new beginning" in our relations with the Muslim world. After we landed in Egypt and made our way in to the Sultan Hassan Mosque for a visit, the President called me over to congratulate me. He had been told, I assume by Reggie, that I was recently engaged.

"Let's see that ring," he said after a quick hug.

There he stood in Cairo, at the steps of a centuries-old mosque, the Christian president of the United States, with a mixed Muslim and Christian heritage, acknowledging the engagement of his Muslim staffer to a Jewish man from New York. I felt a rush of emotions. I was on a high both because of my engagement and from being on this trip, with the added excitement of the momentous speech I knew he was to give the following day.

When a Muslim talks about her religion, my father often said, she is not necessarily talking about specific beliefs or practices, but a total way of life. In one of his articles, my father wrote that the *ummah* live "in varied climes, speak in myriad tongues, dress and eat in different ways, and represent a wide spectrum of social traits and habits. Nevertheless, undergirding these differences of race, color, language, and national origin is a spiritual unity that is unique to this community of Islam." Obama intended to speak to this *ummah*. Not through the fraught prism of terrorism or war or the forever stalled Middle East peace process. He was going to talk about education, entrepreneurship, new networks, collaboration, exchanges, and the power and potential of youth.

I had been included along with Jake in a meeting in the White House situation room as the NSC team worked on the speech, and I knew Obama was not going to disappoint. I was working for a president who, like me, had lived between two worlds. Other presidents had tried to engage with the Muslim world. I had seen that firsthand in President Clinton's White House. President Bush engaged in his own way too. But I had the distinct impression that Barack Obama really understood us.

"I've come here to Cairo to seek a new beginning between the United States and Muslims around the world, one based on mutual interest and mutual respect, and one based upon the truth that America and Islam are not exclusive and need not be in competition. Instead, they overlap, and share common principles—principles of justice and progress; tolerance and the dignity of all human beings." Listening to Obama's words at Cairo University, I heard an echo of all the ideas my father had written and spoken about and advocated for decades earlier. Obama was positing that the Western and Eastern worlds had to know and understand each other better. That there was little universal benefit to religious absolutism and that any system that elevates one group over the other is destined for failure. Obama acknowledged that modernity posed serious challenges—triggering fears of lost identity that fed "mindless violence" and glorified materialism. Abbu had written, "People all over the world [have] experienced a surfeit of materialism" but that Muslims mustn't forget our identity as we adjusted to today's world. Abbu would have been so gratified to know that the President of the United States shared his beliefs and expounded them on the world stage.

Later, as probably was to be expected, the speech would be criticized for being either too rosy or for making promises that simply could not be kept. Still, to make the effort, to elevate basic principles and values for the whole world to hear—*that* mattered.

MOVING ALONG
THE SEAMS

The greatest threat to freedom is the absence of criticism.
—Wole Soyinka

In August 2009, we were scheduled to make an official visit to South Africa, which was to include a private meeting between HRC and Nelson Mandela. There was perhaps no greater exemplar of personal sacrifice for the good of his people than Mandela, or Madiba as he was popularly known in his own country. Madiba will remain one of history's most inspiring figures. His struggle for freedom and equality for all Black South Africans, which kept him imprisoned for twenty-seven years, spotlighted the cruelty of apartheid.

I had had the privilege of meeting Madiba a number of times, starting with a handshake during the Clinton administration. On a visit to South Africa a number of years before this trip, I told him that my mother had been included for tea at his home after she delivered a speech to a woman's conference in Durban. He smiled and said he remembered her. After that, whenever I saw him, he would ask, "How is your mother? Give her my regards."

Up close, Madiba was not the rabble-rousing, hotheaded young lawyer my mind had envisioned, though I know he had been that too. He had patience, tolerance, and an unwavering belief that he was doing the right thing, and in the end he prevailed. He had a gentle manner and a soft voice; a warm smile, hands that didn't betray his decades of hard prison labor, and bright eyes.

During the moments I was privileged to share with Madiba I

would often recall the debates we'd had in a college seminar about him and another Black leader: Malcolm X. My curiosity about Malcolm X, who had first joined the Nation of Islam, then embraced Sunni Islam, was inspired in part by the recognition that we shared a faith. I researched his life, his speeches, his interviews, was stunned by some of his fiery rhetoric. "If we are extremists," he said in one interview, "we're not ashamed of it. In fact the conditions that our people suffer are extreme and extreme illness cannot be cured with moderate medicine." He spoke out against the hypocrisy of the powerful and called for the people to rise up. Our seminar professor had asked: How would history judge leaders like Madiba and Malcolm X? Madiba ultimately embraced nonviolence to transform the social, economic, and political structure of South Africa. Malcolm X was killed just as he began to turn away from some of the militancy of his earlier years. In the end though, his struggle was like that of other civil rights leaders, including Madiba—for racial and social justice.

When we arrived for the private tea for HRC and Madiba, his longtime advisor Zelda la Grange explained that, at ninety-one, Madiba's memory was hazy, so they limited his meetings just to people familiar to him, meaning only HRC and I would be allowed to enter the room. As HRC approached, Madiba made a motion to stand, but both Zelda and HRC insisted he remain seated. HRC bent down to embrace him, then sat down in the chair next to him, and they began catching up like any old friends would. I hung back and stood in the entrance to the room along with Zelda. After a few minutes of chatting, Madiba turned his head and noticed Zelda and me in the archway.

"Why are you standing?" he said to us. "Come inside. Take a rest."

I was startled to be acknowledged and instinctively started moving backward, but Zelda put her hand on my back and whispered, "Go," while HRC motioned with her head for me to sit on the love seat next to her. Though I was self-conscious about intruding on this very intimate conversation between two people who had such a long history, Madiba made a point of asking me a few questions before returning his attention to HRC and asking after Chelsea, who was particularly close to him. An hour later, after posing for some farewell photos, I watched HRC hug him gently goodbye. The man we were leaving was undeniably slower and frailer than we had expected. It was the last time I would see him.

On that same trip to Africa we made a stop in Nigeria, where I had made plans to see Fatima, one of my best friends from Jeddah, who had returned to live there, in Abuja, after high school. HRC was no longer surprised when I had a friend or relative I was escaping to see on a trip, whether it was in London, Delhi, Ankara, Toronto, or here in Abuja.

When Fatima pulled up to the front door of the hotel to pick me up, so many good memories came flooding back. She looked exactly the same as she had in high school, though she was now married with several children. Even more reminiscent of the past, she was sitting in the backseat, with an expressionless driver at the wheel, just like back in Jeddah.

"You can take a girl out of Saudi . . . ," I said teasingly as I climbed in the backseat.

"Hey! I do this out of necessity, not luxury!" she insisted.

We quickly moved on; there was too much to catch up on. Over dinner we talked and laughed about a less complicated time in our lives. Before jobs and partners and kids and having to pay bills. It was very late when we headed back to the hotel, still transported to a world of our memories, so that when we slowed down to stop, I assumed it was for a traffic light. Suddenly, Fatima shushed me, then tossed me one of her head scarves, instructing me to put it on as she adjusted her own. It appeared to be an informal checkpoint. It was then that I realized I did not have any identification on me. My diplomatic passport was sitting in a safe in Lew Lukens's room at the hotel.

"Fatima, I don't have my passport," I said, guilty that I had neglected to bring it.

"Good, you don't want to be an American right now."

I was sitting in the seat behind the driver and saw a young man in a dark green uniform, a machine gun slung over his shoulder, his hands resting on top casually. On the other side of the Jeep, there was another similarly dressed young man with a handkerchief tied just below his mouth, the lamppost backlighting his young face. He looked no older than a teenager. He eyed the driver, then Fatima, then me. Fatima was whispering instructions in Hausa to the driver as he lowered the window. The driver and the policeman exchanged words. When the officer jutted his chin out toward me, I tightened the scarf around my face. That's when Fatima leaned forward in her seat and began to speak loudly. After a minute of back-and-forth, the volume escalated, culminating in a tense silence. The boys made eye contact with each other, then nodded and the driver slowly pulled away.

"What was that all about?" I asked.

"Bribing and sometimes even kidnapping is a problem here," she said.

We were two women out very late at night, she came from a prominent local family, which already put her at risk, and that's why she always had a driver with her. Of course, I theoretically knew that this was a problem. I had read the travel advisory in our briefing book on the flight over. I was with a secretary of state who was in this country in part to address issues like good governance and corruption, and yet I hadn't anticipated seeing it so up close.

"Wait, what did you say about me?" I asked.

"I told him you were my friend from Saudi." Technically, that was true.

* * * *

The grab bag of my identity served me well in Abuja. This had always been the case, ever since childhood, except for one critical aspect of my background, the weight of which I would not appreciate until I was older: being of *both* Indian and Pakistani heritage. As we planned an official visit in October to Pakistan, the perpetual hostility with India along its borders and between the countries hadn't abated.

The security situation in Pakistan was tense. After the Taliban had been defeated in Afghanistan by U.S. forces following 9/11, its leaders had fled to tribal areas across the border in Pakistan, and there was a burgeoning terrorist network operating and potentially threatening the democratic government there. This was part of the reason HRC had recommended the appointment of Richard Holbrooke, the charismatic, peripatetic diplomat, as special representative for Afghanistan and Pakistan, or, in diplo speak, S/RAP. She pressed me to stay in touch with the White House scheduling office to ensure that President

Obama would attend the announcement of Holbrooke's new role, to signal to Afghanistan and Pakistan, or what we called the "AfPak" region, how seriously this new administration would take our relationship with both countries.

As we mapped out the trip to Pakistan, we agreed to include stops at both the capital, Islamabad, for government meetings, and Lahore, one of its largest cities. HRC would be doing all the required official bilateral meetings: with the president, the prime minister, the foreign minister, and because the military was always a power center in Pakistan, with the chief of the army.

"Let's present an alternative to radicalism. I want to make it clear that we are encouraging democracy when I announce the aid package," she said, referring to the money to fund social and economic reforms—the "deliverable." "Also," as though she even needed to reinforce the point, "I don't just want to do government meetings, I want to talk directly to people. I want to do public events, and I want to do as many local press interviews as you can fit in."

It's going to be ugly, we all warned her.

"If we are too scared to hear them out, I shouldn't be going."

I was nervous as we put this stop together. Like all trips, I wanted it to run smoothly and accomplish all the imperatives that an HRC trip required, but this one was going to be testing a lot of our resources, particularly on the security side. On the public diplomacy front, we knew we were not going to particularly friendly territory. The average Pakistani's opinion of the United States was extremely low; we were often blamed for showing preferential treatment to India and for bringing the war on terror to their homeland.

There were serious concerns for HRC's safety in Pakistan. It was one thing to go in and out of heavily guarded government complexes, but we needed to find venues for public events too. Working with our embassy officials, we started to put together ideas for a town hall meeting and visits to cultural and religious sites. But I knew events anywhere outside of a secure government compound were not going to be an easy sell to Diplomatic Security.

As we started building out the schedule, I met with Fred Ketchem, the head of HRC's Department of State Diplomatic Security detail.

He was concerned about several of the public events we were propos-ing. He had served in Iraq and was an expert at operating in challeng-ing environments. Fred was only doing his job, but there was no way to execute this trip without adding these elements. This was the deli-cate balance we would have to strike for years: between HRC's security leadership, whose responsibility it was to ensure her safety, and those of us on her staff, who were helping her to tell the story she thought was important at each of these destinations, which always required events where she could engage with the public.

I figured this was one of those countries when our own security didn't entirely trust host country security, and vice versa, but I pushed Fred to see if his team could figure it out. To his credit, Fred talked to the team on the ground, then came back with his conditions. They weren't ideal, but I agreed and made a mental note to not schedule any events at religious sites during prayer times. He had one or two other red lines, but basically we had a deal.

I certainly understood his concerns. Part of the anger I knew we would encounter was due to the feeling of being beholden to America for so much financial aid. This was a country that had faced gale-force winds from day one: Partition, the conflict in Kashmir, the splitting off of East Pakistan to become Bangladesh, the death of Pakistan's inspiring founder Muhammad Ali Jinnah a year after its founding, assassinations of leaders, a struggling economy, the devastatingly frag-ile institutions of democracy that left military commanders in charge for more than half the country's existence. Now the United States was fighting a war with terrorists on Pakistani soil. I couldn't say I knew how it felt to be in their shoes, but I got it. This was, after all, my mother's home country.

Growing up, whenever I was asked where I was from originally, I always said I was half-Indian, half-Pakistani, feeling equal allegiance to both my parents' homelands. In college, I was equally committed to Indian and Pakistani students' associations. In 1997, however, soon after I started working at the White House, I had an experience at the Pakistani embassy in Washington that showed me that having an equal allegiance and love for both countries was not so simple.

When I tried to help Heba get the necessary documentation for a personal visit she planned to take to Pakistan, a stern-looking consular official started grilling us about our family background, focusing in particular on questions about my father. Was he Indian? Was he Muslim? Where was he? When I interjected that he wasn't alive, the man responded by summoning a supervisor who went through the exact same round of questions. When we were asked for a second time *where* exactly our father was, something inside of me snapped. "Why does any of that matter?" At which point the papers were shoved back into the envelope, and I was told they needed to examine the case further, with no guarantee that the situation could be resolved in a timely manner. I was irate that a person who wasn't even alive but was from a country viewed with suspicion was enough to warrant "further examination." The next day, I did exactly the thing I didn't want to do—the thing I hate to do: ask for a personal favor. I emailed a contact in the ambassador's office I had known since college. The document was ready within hours. When I returned to the embassy, the same man was there, standing behind the same counter without a smile or a greeting. He wordlessly handed me an envelope. I wordlessly accepted it and walked out.

All those years before, when our parents told us to identify simply as Americans, not as Indian *or* Pakistani, although we were to love and respect both aspects of our heritage equally, they were trying to spare us this deep divide, and in this moment I viscerally understood why. Whenever I have had to get a visa to visit India, I have had the same challenge with similar questions about my mother. Over time, I have just learned to live with it.

That single negative association aside, I have an unequivocally positive picture of the Pakistan I saw on many visits with family members there. It is where strong, sugary tea is exquisite, where mango *lassi* tastes like manna from heaven, where the vegetable seller pulls up to your home on a horse cart, having just left the farm, where the bazaars are so overcrowded and cacophonous they make Balad seem calm and orderly. It is where I ate and ate, and still weight fell off of me, which convinced my mother that I had ingested a tapeworm.

In Pakistan every visit unearthed a new discovery, whether visiting the tree-lined, wide avenues at one aunt's house in Islamabad, manicured and quiet, or the hustle and bustle of Karachi at another aunt's house, which was filled with pictures of my great-uncle in his naval uniform. Uncle Ahsan was a figure of great pride in my mother's family. As an enlisted officer in what was then India, he had served his country—that would be Britain, when India was still under the British Raj—with distinction in World War II. He was later appointed aide-de-camp to the last Viceroy of India, Lord Mountbatten. When the English were leaving the subcontinent in 1947, officers had the option to stay in India or move to Pakistan. He chose Pakistan. According to family lore, at their last meeting, Mountbatten asked Pakistan's founder, Muhammad Ali Jinnah, to retain the counsel of his aide by saying, "Jinnah, I leave you Pakistan and I leave you Lieutenant Ahsan." Uncle Ahsan went on to help establish the naval intelligence services and later became commander in chief of the Pakistani Navy. Each trip held a revelation such as this one. A new relative or cousin or story, each fantastical and exciting in its own way.

All these memories and people flooded my head as we flew on a State trip to Pakistan. Knowing everyone was on heightened alert, I did not make plans to see family as I normally would have. Since our time on the ground would be short, we had jammed the schedule, and if something were to go awry, I wanted to be on hand.

After a day of meetings, HRC was being hosted for dinner by President Asif Ali Zardari at the presidential residence in Islamabad, and the entire traveling party was invited. She always introduced our ambassador, our assistant secretary, and the National Security Council representative to heads of state or foreign dignitaries when she walked into meetings. For the rest of the team—Jake, Philippe, me—it kind of depended on the day, the meeting, the mood. Over time, as his value as a key advisor became more and more obvious to everyone, Jake joined the senior group, and Philippe and I would hang back and make funny faces at him. Philippe would find other "meetings" to attend instead, which usually meant he could be found napping in the staff van or under a table in the holding room.

In Pakistan, however, given my background, I suspected HRC would pull me to the front.

"Mr. President, I'd like you to meet my deputy chief of staff. Her mother is from Pakistan and she has many relatives here."

I don't know if it was true or if he was just a very good politician, but he said that his late wife, Benazir Bhutto, whom I had met on a few occasions before she was killed in a terrorist attack, had mentioned to him that Hillary had a Pakistani aide. After we talked a little about my extended family and where they now lived, HRC then told him that I had recently become engaged. The President turned back to me and said, "Congratulations! I hope it is to a nice Pakistani boy?" I couldn't help but say, "Imagine exactly the opposite, sir," which caused him to stop for a minute to consider, and then laugh out loud.

Later, at the democracy town hall we had organized at the Government College in Lahore, no one pulled their punches. When one woman said, "You talk about 9/11, we have daily 9/11s in this country," it was the first time I heard firsthand such a public confrontation about the American military drones operating against suspected militants and also harming innocent civilians. HRC couldn't discuss this topic, even though drone strikes were covered in the press in both Pakistan and the U.S. As I had read through her briefing points beforehand, I turned to Jake.

"Is this the best she can do? We are accidently killing Pakistani civilians and she is going to say no comment?"

Jake was doing his own verbal gymnastics. He had to finalize language the best he could to be sympathetic to civilians while not betraying any classified information. When HRC was confronted, she said she couldn't really address the question aside from saying that any targeting was meant for Al-Qaeda and any innocent loss of life was a tragedy. At the end of the event, a few of us talked to the students who lingered. It was unclear whether they were satisfied by what they had heard, but at least they were able to get their points across, and on an international media platform, which is exactly what HRC had intended—to show that the secretary of state of the world's most powerful democracy was here to listen.

* * * *

By the end of the year, HRC was in her groove as secretary of state. In our trip debrief meetings, Philippe cited articles that reported on her skills as a diplomat, her displays of authenticity, humor, and candor in various foreign capitals. These contrasted with the coverage she had received during the 2008 campaign, when she was panned for her stiffness on the stump, especially in comparison to the easy charisma of Obama.

"The press loves the new you," Philippe teased.

"Philippe! I am the *same* person!" she protested.

Of course she was, but she couldn't detect the switch that flipped on when she stepped onto a stage and morphed before our eyes into a formal, highly skilled policy wonk, and then flipped off in smaller, more intimate settings, in roundtables, in town halls (or townterviews, a term Philippe coined for them), and on late-night TV shows. That was where people saw the HRC we saw every day: irreverent, funny, gracious, warm.

That was the Hillary Clinton I had gotten to know well over a decade and a half. We had clocked so many hours together, weathered deep disappointments and celebrated profound joys together, and had never run out of things to discuss. And always I saw the side of her that put others before herself.

HRC hadn't even been at State for a year when she slipped on the wet surface in the basement garage as she was heading out for a meeting with President Obama. When she walked back into the office, she was holding her right elbow with her left hand cupped over it. Then I noticed her security agent carrying her things. This was officially not good. I had never seen her hand her purse and briefing binder to an agent.

"I'm fine," she insisted to her assistant Claire Coleman, a civil servant who had had a long, distinguished career in the building and was close to indispensable. She knew everything about the building, how it worked, where things were located, who had answers to any and every question.

"Just call the White House and let them know I'll be a little late," HRC said.

Claire did, but only after she called the medical unit to send someone to examine HRC, who then walked into her office, sat on one of the formal stiff-backed sofas, and winced when the medic tried to extend her arm. I was already texting her family doctor who was based at George Washington University. With no change in tone, she volunteered, "I think I need to get an X-ray and see what's going on."

At the hospital, HRC was taken straight into an examination room. She carefully eased off her jacket and winced again as the technician started adjusting her swollen arm—which was not at a natural angle—for the X-ray.

Suddenly, she did something odd. She started pointing in my direction. I was shivering and soon felt a warm blanket thrown over me. I looked down and noticed that I was no longer standing but sitting in the black chair that the technician had occupied only moments before.

"What is going on?" I looked up to find HRC's doctor before me, rubbing my hand and reassuring me, "It's okay." HRC, still sitting in the chair with her grotesque-looking arm laid out in front of her, said, "Please get her some juice. She probably hasn't had anything besides coffee today." The *her* being *me*. Then it dawned on me that I had just come to. As soon as I saw the arm at a distorted angle, I had passed out. Oh, and as if that wasn't bad enough, I had also wet myself—the mortifyingly first and thankfully last time that has ever happened to me. In the very moment that everyone should have focused on the secretary of state's elbow, she was instructing people to care for her queasy, hospital-averse staffer.

A few juice boxes and crackers later, I felt as good as new, and I refused to leave the hospital until we knew more about HRC's condition. She didn't force me to leave. We are both stubborn in the same ways. The news wasn't great. Her right elbow was fractured and she would need surgery. I kept her family updated until they could arrive, and I stayed connected with the State Department team.

By the end of the night, despite her protests, we were working on a press release saying she would be adjusting her schedule. Over the next few days, before and after surgery, the smell of the hospital seemed to have no effect on her. She just powered through.

"Are we setting up the secure call for Saturday afternoon with Jim Jones and Bob Gates?" she asked, referring to the national security advisor and the secretary of defense, who she had missed an in-person meeting with.

"Yes, it's set."

A few minutes later: "Did we get Biden the Mitchell memo?" referring to the latest memo from Special Representative to the Middle East George Mitchell on the Middle East peace proposal, which she had promised to send to the vice president for review. That was the last instruction she had given me before she slipped and fell. And she had not forgotten.

"Done."

Another time: "What about the statement about the problems with the Iranian elections? Did it go out?" She just couldn't help herself.

"Yes, yes, that too."

On the first night she returned to Whitehaven, I helped her get settled and she thanked me for everything, especially for dealing with the dozens of concerned calls from her family, friends, supporters, and colleagues. Then, as though it was a huge favor, she asked if I could help with the little clasp on her necklace since she couldn't raise her arm to reach it.

"You will be a good mom someday," she said as I removed the necklace.

I didn't really know how to process that since I couldn't quite envision having a baby at that point in my life, even though I was engaged to be married. Some things could just wait, I thought. Especially babies.

She never told anyone I had fainted at the hospital. She had become the primary person I confided in, the one I vented to when I was frustrated, turned to for advice before making any big decisions like buying my apartment in DC ("Do it!") or small ones like getting bangs ("Maybe just a trim"), and with whom I shared all my anxieties about getting married to a public person. It helps to have someone in your life you can turn to for solid advice, candid insights, and discretion. In my case, it just happened to be Hillary Clinton.

WHAT WOULD
PEOPLE SAY?

*Love is our essential nutrient. Without it, life has little
meaning. It's the best thing we have to give and the most
valuable thing we receive. It's worthy of all the hullabaloo.*

—Cheryl Strayed

In the six months we had been engaged, Anthony and I had had no
concrete conversations about planning our wedding. We were both
consumed with work. Anthony was no longer a young man in a hurry
but a seasoned politician who was carving out a leadership role in the
healthcare debate that was unfolding in Washington, and using his
position in Congress to advocate for affordable universal healthcare
through policies even more progressive than the White House was
expected to unveil.

So the procrastinating continued until Thanksgiving. This year, it
wasn't going to be a huge, unwieldy affair like Thanksgivings I typically spent in New Jersey with dozens of my aunts, uncles, and cousins.
Anthony and I borrowed a friend's weekend house in Long Island so
we could host his parents, Mort and Fran, his father's partner Linda,
and his brother Jason and sister-in-law Almond, who were parents of a
nineteen-month-old and lived nearby. The house was warm and comfortable, with floor-to-ceiling windows along the entire back side of
the kitchen, living, and dining rooms, which looked out onto a small
manicured lawn, a pool, and the narrow Sagaponack Pond beyond.

Jason, a chef with popular restaurants in Manhattan and the east
end of Long Island, brought all the food with him, so I had been left

with little more to do except unpack my store-bought fruit pie and lay out empty white serving platters. Mort, a retired lawyer, was clearly used to being the family patriarch, commanding attention with every story or joke. Fran, a retired high school math teacher, always seemed to be busy between book clubs, ski trips, and working her shifts at the Park Slope Food Coop. Though Mort and Fran had divorced when Anthony was in his twenties, they still came together for family holidays. Linda, a retired elementary school teacher who lived with Mort in the house where Anthony grew up, brought a smile, a hug, and lightheartedness to any room she walked into. Almond, an artist whose bold and vibrant work hung in Anthony's Forest Hills apartment, arrived carrying their daughter Rive, the only grandchild, who captured everyone's attention for most of the evening.

Our holiday meal was filled with easy banter. Anthony's family mercilessly ribbed one another over everything from healthcare policy to the best way to grill meat. They were funny and irreverent, a little rougher with one another than my family was, but it was refreshing. No one was off-limits to be teased, no topic too sacred to be challenged. I felt comfortable here, fully welcomed into their midst.

* * * *

As the year came to a close, I prepared to join the Clintons on their annual trip to Punta Cana, the island town in the Dominican Republic with cerulean-blue Caribbean water, powder-like sand beaches, and pale limestone homes that blended into the seascape perfectly, allowing the forests of deep green palm trees to dominate. We would be spending New Year's at the home of Oscar and Annette de la Renta.

Oscar had called shortly after my engagement and offered to make my wedding dress, which was one aspect of wedding planning I was really excited about. On one of my regular calls with Oscar he asked, "Are you bringing Anthony with you?" Even though I had spent many New Years with the de la Rentas, I traveled to Punta Cana as HRC's staff. Oscar had never seen me with a romantic partner, but like HRC, from the moment Anthony walked into my life, he was welcoming. So, I brought Anthony.

For a few precious days our biggest decisions were whether to take a nap or go for a swim after lunch. Invariably, we ended up back on our computers or phones because that's how we were wired. Neither of us really knew how to relax. Sitting on the lounge chairs of the two-bedroom casita we were sharing, BlackBerries in hand, I felt like we were truant students waiting for the principal to discover us and send us back to class.

"Should we elope?" I asked on one of those lazy afternoons at the beach. Anthony said, "Sure," his eyes half-closed, *New York Times Magazine* open before him, phone resting on his chest.

On Thanksgiving weekend, I had received an email from Chelsea addressed to family and friends. It was an official announcement—she had just gotten engaged to her longtime boyfriend, and I called to congratulate her. As we chatted, she told me to let her know when we were setting a date for our wedding. Since I got engaged first, she didn't want to interfere with my planning. I replied, "Oh, sure," even though I was thinking, *She had been America's first daughter, her wedding would be national news.* We would have some overlap with our guest lists, but I just work for her mother, who cares about my wedding? I couldn't imagine where I would find the time to actually plan a wedding, but Chelsea's question about timing had pushed the issue to the forefront for me.

"Maybe we should get married at City Hall and then have a party so our family and friends can come." Without opening his eyes, Anthony murmured, "Sounds good."

"Well, maybe we should have a proper wedding. You only do it once in your life, we should do it right." "Fine," he said.

We spent the rest of the afternoon in blissful calm, lulled by the sound of waves crashing on the beach steps from our feet and the seabirds swooping overhead.

Soon it was time to get ready for dinner at the de la Rentas' house. It was New Year's Eve, and embracing my role as fiancée, I suggested Anthony and I call our families to wish them a Happy New Year. As I stood up to go back inside, Anthony took both my hands in his.

"I don't care if you want to run away together or if you want to have a wedding with a thousand people." His tone was uncharacteristically emotional. "I just want to be married to you and be with you the rest of my life.

"Besides, I'm broken," he said, "and you need to fix me. You should call my parents. They will be happy to hear from you." I laughed out loud as he stood up. If there was anybody who didn't need fixing, it was the man walking away from me, the relentless problem solver, the perfect companion. I didn't linger much on those words then. They were said in jest and received as such. Looking back now, however, I suspect they might have betrayed something Anthony sensed about himself but hadn't yet acknowledged.

On his way to take a shower, he dropped his magazine, BlackBerry, and laptop on the coffee table in the little sitting area between the two bedrooms. I threw a pillow after him, still laughing as I grabbed his BlackBerry to dial first his father, then his mother.

The BlackBerry was open to his email inbox, and I noticed an unread email from a woman whose name I did not recognize. In that split second, I didn't even think twice. I opened it and read the message. I felt a hot rush of blood from my head down to my fingertips. The message was fawning, flirtatious, and very familiar, as though this was a woman Anthony knew. Without hesitating, I called out to Anthony, the phone in my outstretched hand. "What is this?" He was pulling dress pants out of his closet. When he looked at the Black-Berry, he said in an entirely composed manner, "Oh, that's nothing. Just a fan."

"A fan? How does she have your email?"

Now he looked surprised. "Are you upset about this? It's nothing, she started sending me messages and I've never responded. The whole world knows how to reach me."

He didn't seem concerned, wasn't defensive, didn't raise his voice to match my pitch. He was treating the message like it was nothing. I searched for the name in his inbox and, sure enough, there were two other messages, both unopened, the second one expressing her frustration that he wasn't responding to her. Seeing that I was still troubled, Anthony wrapped me in his arms.

"I am so sorry," he said. "I would never want to upset you and I swear to you now that I will always be faithful to you."

It was inconceivable to me that there was anything more to this exchange, because Anthony lived in a world of straight talk. He didn't have a filter and didn't even bother with little white lies. If we were late meeting friends for dinner, rather than say we were stuck in traffic, he'd breezily offer that he had taken a quick nap before we had to leave or that I had decided at the last minute to get my hair blown out. If I tried to slip out of the office early, feeling guilty about not working, when Anthony came to pick me up, he would announce that we were going to a movie. If I was in a disagreement with my sister at a family dinner, everyone politely tiptoeing around the issue, Anthony would joke about it—"I hope you guys can settle the cold war so we can at least enjoy dessert"—and everyone at the table would laugh, any tension immediately subsiding. At formal dinners with chairmen of Fortune 500 companies, Anthony would broach the issue of pay discrepancy between the executives he was seated next to and their employees.

One night on this trip in Punta Cana we'd had dinner with an array of New York luminaries, including veteran journalist Andrea Mitchell and her husband, former Federal Reserve chairman Alan Greenspan. Greenspan had just published a memoir about his five terms helming the Federal Reserve. He believed in the benefits of a "bipartisan free market ideology," which had yielded some impressive returns for democratic capitalism following the Cold War, but at this moment the global financial collapse was a year old and inflicting severe hardship on many Americans and Anthony wouldn't let it slide.

In the midst of the conversation, Anthony pressed, "Don't you feel responsible for any of this?"

I put my hand on his thigh to settle him a notch, and the conversation shifted back to people's tennis matches the next morning. At the end of dinner, I apologized to Andrea and she was gracious. She had been in her business for a long time and wasn't easily flustered. Anthony had been in his business for a while too, and didn't feel he needed to moderate what he said in this privileged setting, or any other.

Anthony believed that powerful people deserved to feel a little uncomfortable, and this exchange had been no exception. In Congress he was known as a pugnacious and feisty progressive. When we were out in the city, people often stopped him to thank him for fighting for them. He was gaining prominence nationally in large part because of his outspoken advocacy for people who'd been cheated or ignored or not given a fair deal. If being confrontational with other powerful people came off as plain rude, he didn't care.

The Anthony I knew and fell in love with called it as he saw it. There were no dark secrets, nothing hidden, nothing too small or embarrassing to talk about. He was an open book. That's what I believed.

The email I had discovered was a warning sign; but that's something I would understand only in hindsight. The fantasy world into which Anthony was just beginning to stumble was beyond anything known to me. I didn't know a seed was being planted in his psyche that would grow into something much darker and uncontrollable, something that would ruin us. I was in the midst of what I believed was a deep, true love affair. Nothing in my experience could possibly have prepared me for what was to come.

* * * *

We returned to New York the next day, to a new year and to our usual frenetic lives, dictated by events outside of our control: his by the voting schedule in the House of Representatives, mine by the calendar of our secretary of state. Anthony left immediately for a planned CODEL to Egypt, Turkey, and Israel. I was preparing to leave for Hawaii for a speech HRC was to deliver on the future of America's relationship with Asia. I was also in the midst of planning for a fairly last-minute trip to London, where the British government was hosting a meeting with representatives of nineteen other nations regarding Yemen, a growing hot spot in the Middle East for terrorist activities, which had an abysmal record on women's rights.

Most of the time, Anthony and I led lives independent of each other. Our work kept us physically apart. I lived in DC and he lived in New York. His apartment was his and mine was mine. When Anthony suggested I stay at his place while he was in Egypt and I needed to work in New York, it was a first, a sign of the increased intimacy in our relationship.

He lived in a pleasant, tidy two-bedroom, third-floor apartment in Forest Hills Gardens, Queens, a leafy and quiet neighborhood with convenience stores and mom-and-pop shops. He had two cats, a Persian and a Maine coon, both old, one sick.

On my first night alone at Anthony's, as I worked on my laptop at the desk in the second bedroom, which functioned as an office, Anthony's home computer sat behind mine. When I bumped the mouse, his screen lit up and our New Year's Eve conversation came flooding back. On the large monitor, it was all just sitting there, daring me. Email, Twitter, Facebook open in various windows.

For the first time in my life, I did something totally out of character: I looked through them. All of them. For what? I was not entirely sure. Did I find something, anything damning? Nothing, though I was struck by the endless number of doting messages. People telling Anthony he was their hero, that they loved him, that he was amazing. On and on. Hundreds of people. Yes, there were a handful of flirtatious women asking to meet him and sending pictures of themselves. I couldn't imagine how people publicly posted messages so brazen. There were also horrible hateful messages, the flipside of the adulation. In January 2010, Twitter was still relatively new. Anthony had told me about "trolls" who populated the site, often from fake accounts that spewed all kinds of vile messages. One day, he told me about a man named Andrew Breitbart, a conservative right-wing media personality who had threatened to hurt him. *Who has the time for this?* I wondered, scrolling through this electronic universe of Anthony's groupies and adversaries, before concluding that it was pointless for me to be looking at this stuff.

He called early the next morning from Egypt, standing outside the pyramids. I was silent, feeling guilty from searching through his emails, and also somewhat unnerved that I had felt the need to do so.

"Huma? Hello?"

I told him I was having cold feet.

"What?"

In the hours I'd had to think, I was certain about one thing. That though this was the only man I had ever loved, I was nervous about what I was getting into. The religious complications seemed overwhelming, but that wasn't all. In my workplace I was on the periphery, watching another person live her entire life in public. I was scared to get further swallowed up in Anthony's universe. It was so much bigger than just us. I had to deal with that circus in my professional life. I didn't need it at home. Occasionally being pursued by photographers and tabloid gossip columnists was one thing. The electronic intrusion I had glimpsed on Anthony's devices was another level.

"Please don't do this," he said.

There was a numbness in my chest and my head was throbbing. The apartment was overheated and I felt suffocated, trapped by windows blurred with frost, the dust on the bookshelf driving me crazy. There were also new and uncomfortable emotions, feelings of jealousy and insecurity, and I wanted to shed them immediately. I had even stooped to snooping. All I said was that I was unsure, that I didn't know if I could move forward.

"Is this about that email?" he asked. I remained silent.

These are the kinds of moments when Anthony is at his best: when he has something to prove. He challenged me to go to his computer and find a single inappropriate message that he himself had sent. Anything. Why was I blaming him for being the recipient? It was true, I never found anything from him. But I didn't know how to navigate this domain and didn't have anyone to confide in.

I closed the door to Anthony's apartment the next morning not knowing when or if I would return. I flew back to Washington. Back to work, to a life I understood. As soon as I connected with HRC at the airport, a switch flipped. I snapped back to my professional self, my confidence returned, and I felt whole and stable again. They call it compartmentalizing. I started getting very good at it. Maybe I always had been.

*   *   *   *

After a few days, I was back in my usual work rhythm. Before the holidays, I had met with each of the deputy executive secretaries to get priority requests for the upcoming year, then the assistant secretaries from relevant bureaus for the Middle East, Africa, East Asia and the Pacific, and Europe. Everyone wanted HRC to visit their region, and we had to determine what fit into the message priorities we had laid out for the year. My role was to initiate, manage, and run interference for the complex chain of events that would result from these decisions: a core team consulted, the relevant State leadership notified, visas procured, staff assigned to travel, a plane requested, security informed, stacks of paper generated, a speech written, a schedule drafted, a team sent ahead to walk through each tiny detail.

On top of all of this, foreign travel had to be done in consultation with the White House. I had a good working relationship with my counterparts at the National Security Council. I kept them informed of our goals because I figured that if they understood them, they would be more likely to say yes to our requests, and they were always good partners. Internally, our team worked well together too.

Sometimes there were communication breakdowns. I awoke early one morning to a press alert that Jake had been promoted from my co-deputy chief of staff to director of policy planning, one of the more senior positions at State. I was shocked, not because he didn't deserve it, but because I'd had no idea. I shot a note around to the core group saying I couldn't believe no one told me. Jake had thought HRC would tell me and HRC had thought Jake would tell me. This was the irony about being in a role where everyone thinks you know everything; sometimes I really was the last to know. Occasional communication lapses aside, I always felt respected by my colleagues and very much part of the core team: Cheryl, Philippe, Jake, Lona. I will trust them, have their backs, cheer them on, support them, mourn and celebrate with them for the rest of my life. And I don't even need to ask if they would do the same for me.

* * * *

My work was a constant balancing act between long-term planning and rapid response to last-minute world events. In January 2010 a devastating earthquake struck Haiti while we were in Hawaii for her long-planned speech, and HRC told us she wanted to head there as soon as possible to survey the damage and offer American assistance.

As soon as we boarded the plane to Haiti on January 16, I saw Philippe's gaze drop to my left hand, which was bare. We looked at each other. He said nothing. Neither did I.

After we landed, HRC went into a small white makeshift tent that had been set up on the tarmac for a briefing with Haitian President Préval, a few Haitian officials, Cheryl, and the team on the ground leading the rescue and recovery efforts for the U.S. government. There was little room or need for anyone else in our delegation, so Philippe and I took a walk on the tarmac.

"What's wrong?" he asked as soon as we were out of earshot of the others. I stared at the asphalt. "You are not exactly yourself and you aren't wearing your ring."

I didn't tell him much as we made our way past the secretary of state's large 737 air force jet and other international planes, each of which had landed with humanitarian supplies for the hundreds of thousands of people who had lost their homes, who'd lost everything. When I tried to form the words, they sounded silly, frivolous even. I told Philippe that I wasn't sure how things were going with Anthony. He didn't make any judgments and offered to be helpful if he could.

"Anyway," I said offhandedly as we headed back to meet the delegation, "how can I even think about calling off this wedding now? What would people say?" As the words were leaving my mouth, I knew just how superficial they sounded.

"Why do you care what anyone else says? It's your life," Philippe said in his characteristically direct manner.

Deep down inside, I did care a lot about what people might say. To live in the shadow of parents I admired so much and who were so highly esteemed by others, and siblings who were so accomplished and such pillars of their communities, made me even more sensitive.

When Anthony returned from his Middle East trip, we met for coffee and discussed what I'd seen on his BlackBerry. Realizing that it still troubled me and taking my concern more seriously than he had before, he encouraged me to pick up his BlackBerry anytime if I had any lingering doubts. It was then that I decided just to accept that I was in a relationship with someone who led a very public life, who was charming and charismatic and clearly attractive to other women. I had been to events where women flirted openly with him while I looked on, apparently invisible to them. He would gamely pose for a picture and move on. Next event, next group of people, and he didn't seem to discriminate between men and women; he flirted with the world.

The incident began to fade. We resumed our normal lives, which still meant we didn't see each other that much. I was abroad most of the time. Often I would land at Andrews Air Force Base in the evening, make it home to my DC apartment with just enough energy to roll my suitcase into my front hallway, throw my laundry in the wash, and rummage for comfort food before collapsing on my bed, too exhausted for long calls with Anthony, who spent his own days and nights running between votes in DC and the multiple events he attended in New York.

* * * *

I turned to planning an important trip to the Middle East, which would include an official visit to my hometown in February. My mother was there and took frequent trips to the United States to visit Heba and me, to England to visit Hassan and Hadeel and their growing families, and to other far-flung places for academic conferences. My annual vacations to Jeddah had long since ceased, so I was excited to be able to make plans to spend a night with my mother in my childhood home.

In the past decade, I had been invited on a couple of former President Clinton's trips to Saudi Arabia. With each visit, I saw signs of restrictions beginning to relax. There were more women on the streets not covering their faces and more women operating retail stores. There was even talk of lifting restrictions on women's driving. In 2002, when WJC was invited to address the Jeddah Economic Forum, his office had conveyed to the hosts that it was important to him that women be invited, and the organizers confirmed that they would be—in the same room, separated by a partial screen. This would have been unheard of in years past.

As we pulled up to the event, the President shook hands with the greeters, all businessmen dressed in *thobes*. I exited last.

"Come on, Huma," the President called as he walked through the "men only" entrance. I saw the alarm on one of the host's faces as I marched past them. To make his point clear, the President handed me his speech box. I could feel the men's discomfort, furtively looking away or simply ignoring me. I stood there, rigid and immobile as the

President ascended to the stage, until a minute later when I was shown somewhere I would be "more comfortable." Baby steps, I guess.

After the speeches, a frantic man beckoned me back over to the men's section. "The *raees* is looking for you!" he said, using the Arabic word for leader. When I went to rejoin the group, the President was shaking hands with men in the audience but could clearly hear and see the women cheering in his periphery. He whispered, "Should I go over there?" I looked over to the women's section. They seemed thrilled that there was a woman in this very forbidden part of the room. "Absolutely, sir." He asked, "Should I shake hands?" This was delicate. "Only if they extend theirs first. Otherwise, no." So he walked over, the crowd roaring, the men's section a little more muted than the women's, and shook many extended hands.

Progress was slow coming to Saudi Arabia, and when we headed back to the U.S. from these trips, I would climb up the metal staircase from the Saudi tarmac with a palpable sense of freedom returning as I took each step. As soon as we got into the cabin, I'd tear the scarf off my head and throw my *abaya* into a pile on one of the seats, glad that I had visited my beloved childhood city but always ready to go home.

The visit I was now planning had come about after an action memo from the Bureau of Near Eastern Affairs recommended that HRC travel to Saudi Arabia on a regional trip that would include a speech to the U.S.-Islamic World Forum in Doha in January 2010. The forum had been organized by a group of think tanks after 9/11 to bridge the divide between the United States and Muslim communities, a core priority of the Obama administration.

HRC thought bigger than anyone who had been in her position before about the importance of engaging with Muslims living as minorities around the world, so she created a State Department position of special representative to Muslim communities. She appointed Farah Pandith as the first ever representative; under President George W. Bush Farah had successfully launched workshops and youth programs in Europe that sought a greater understanding of the challenges young Muslims faced there. Ultimately, the goal of the program was to deter young Muslims in Europe from following the path of radicalization—many of them felt isolated and alienated in environments where they were expected to assimilate to local customs and shed their own heritage. It was real and concrete programming that made an impact when done properly. HRC wanted Farah to build out those initiatives elsewhere in the world. The substance of the work was important, as was the symbolism of the U.S. government appointing Muslim public servants at high levels. It was also personally close to my heart because this program was doing the work that my parents had been saying was so critical for decades.

After HRC's stop in Doha, we would head to Jeddah for a community outreach event. When I asked the embassy for recommendations for where HRC should go in Jeddah, they came back with two women's colleges: Dar Al-Hekma and Effat University. *Did I have a preference?* they asked. Dar Al-Hekma was the college my mother had been involved in creating, and I didn't want to appear to favor something that was associated with my family, even though I was incredibly proud of it.

A decade or so earlier, a group of prominent Saudi families had approached my mother with the idea of building a world-class college for women in Jeddah. Women tended to go to the local public university unless their families had the means and were permissive enough to send them abroad for higher education. This group wanted to give young women in Saudi Arabia the option of an excellent education without leaving home. My mother was invited to a presentation of the proposed building's blueprints.

"What about what happens on the inside?" she asked. She was shown more renderings of the building.

"No, I mean the content," she said. "What is your plan for the curriculum?" She was given a list of core courses to be offered and saw that they were planning a two-year program. She pushed harder. "Don't you want to give women more options?" They hadn't even considered her question, so they asked if she would come on board to build the curriculum, and she agreed. From the U.S. consulate, she learned about a group in Austin, Texas, called the Texas International Education Consortium or TIEC, which specialized in academic institution building. A few days later, she called me in Washington. Could I take a few days off work and go with her to Texas?

"We are creating a new college in Saudi Arabia, the first of its kind to be based on a fully American university curriculum" she said.

"Okay, Mom, sure." It was so hard to get anything done in Saudi, and creating a college from scratch seemed daunting, but nothing discouraged my mom.

Fast-forward to January of 2010, when I had to decide which college HRC should visit. I knew the work at Dar Al-Hekma would speak for itself, that it was exceptional, that HRC would be interested and impressed, but I did two things to check myself. I called my friend Dina Powell, who had traveled to Jeddah as deputy undersecretary during the Bush administration. She said hands down that Dar Al-Hekma was the right choice, and she herself had chosen to visit it on her official trip. Then I asked our ambassador in Riyadh what he thought. He confirmed that Dar Al-Hekma would be ideal. Their programs were impressive and were only getting stronger, and the embassy had a close working relationship with them. It was decided. The two most important women in my life were doing an event together, and we were going to give young Saudi women an opportunity to have a direct exchange with HRC and ask whatever they wanted.

EVERY WEDDING IS
A WONDER . . . OR
A MIRACLE

Nothing is so good as it seems beforehand.
—George Eliot (Mary Ann Evans)

A year into HRC's term as secretary of state, she had traveled to scores of countries, some multiple times, logging hundreds of hours in the air, in cars, in armored SUVs, in conference rooms and hotel rooms and banquet halls. While the message she needed to deliver at each stop shifted depending on the specific circumstances, the purpose was always the same: to build relationships around the world, in meetings tense and friendly, formal and informal. When we traveled to Saudi Arabia for her first trip there as secretary, both of us were walking into territory that was both familiar and uncharted.

In mid-February, as we flew to the capital Riyadh, our first stop, I heard from our line officer who served as advance lead: Prince Saud Al Faisal, the foreign minister, wanted to ride with HRC to the meeting with the king at his desert camp Rawdat Khurayim, about forty-five minutes away from the airport. It wasn't typical for ministers to ride together, but because she had long relationships with many foreign leaders, this was a sign of their respect for her and a gesture of friendship.

"Um, there is just one thing," our line officer added. "He will be coming in a recreational vehicle. Like a camper." I thought I had misheard. "A what?" In all the years I had seen any motorcades anywhere, they were always made up of sleek limousines or large Suburbans. What the heck, it was always an adventure.

I stepped off the airplane in Riyadh and into the dry, acrid desert air. I was representing my country, and landing in the country of my childhood without wearing an *abaya* and *tarha* for the first time in my life. Among the many social norms that had shifted informally over the years, non-Saudi women were no longer expected to cover. At the end of a long red carpet stood a large gold-and-tan RV, glinting in the sun, followed by the usual cavalcade of Suburbans, sedans, and press buses, everyone slowing as they eyed the unusual "limousine." The prince offered HRC one of the captain's chairs and then sat in one across the aisle from her. I grabbed a seat in front of them, feeling like I was going cross-country with Mom and Dad, except they were the oddest couple ever.

HRC and the prince chatted informally during the drive, and at one point, she began to ask questions about one thing Saudi Arabia had a lot of: camels. The small talk of diplomacy.

"I cannot stand camels," the Prince volunteered immediately.

"Does His Majesty like them?" HRC asked, referring to the prince's half brother, King Abdullah. I quickly turned my back to them so they wouldn't see me struggling to keep a straight face.

When we arrived at the campsite, we saw that the "tent" was actually a proper structure with a roof angled to look like a tent, just as the RV had not been a typical American Winnebago.

Protocol required a quick formal greeting and photo op first in a room where the king and HRC would sit in two oversized armchairs as our delegations lined the sides. Almost always, these were a few minutes of silence or minimal small talk as cameras got what they needed. It was more stilted when there was a language barrier as there was with King Abdullah, but HRC dove right in.

"Your Majesty," she began as the cameras clicked away and the rest of us began to enjoy cardamom coffee and dates, "His Highness thinks camels are ugly." Diplomacy is a lot more than big-picture geopolitical strategy. It's also about meeting the world with open eyes, attuned listening, and small gestures of social outreach. It was second nature to Hillary Clinton.

What was not second nature to her was how to eat with a Saudi king. After the photo-op, we entered a large dining room, which had a long, narrow table and a buffet lined with platters of food. The king went first, accompanied by a server who carried two round silver trays. One was empty; the other had large tablespoons neatly arrayed on it. HRC followed behind with her own server. This was the "tasting" session. They would try a dish with a fresh spoon then discard the spoon on the empty tray. The king had distinct tastes. He nodded if there was something that interested him, and a third server would then place a small amount of that item on a large dinner plate. We went past a variety of salads, cheeses, olives, bread, assorted *mezze*, then meat and chicken and fish dishes, rice and pasta, and a long dessert buffet with baklava, parfaits, and chocolate mousse. HRC was enthusiastic, sampling dishes, nodding often, commenting on how delicious everything was.

The king and HRC were escorted to the two chairs at the head of the table. Promptly, the empty place settings were removed and servers brought plates with their respective lunches to them. HRC was brought one plate, then another, and another. She motioned me over, trying not to laugh because it was dawning on her what she had done.

"I am full!" she whispered. She had eaten her way down the entire buffet.

"Sorry, you are going to have to be a glutton for your country," I said as I handed her cards with talking points to raise over lunch.

She knew she couldn't leave her plate untouched, lest it insult her hosts, so I did take some pity on her and asked the waiter not to bring her any more plates.

"But there are two more on the way," he said, slightly panicked.

"Bring them to me instead," I said. I sat a few seats down from HRC, next to a young man who kept referencing his uncle as he nodded in the general direction of the king. It occurred to me that I had no idea who he even was; that the line of succession past the generation of aging Al Saud brothers like the king and Prince Faisal, who had been foreign minister since I was born, was entirely opaque to me. I was the staff member presumed to know the most about the Saudi royal family members, yet I knew little about my generation of royalty, the thousands of young princes and princesses, a handful of whom I

271

had met and known when I lived there. Once the older generation of brothers passed the crown as planned among themselves, what next? In what direction might Saudi Arabia head? What did this uncertainty mean for the future of the country, for its relationship with the wider Middle East and the rest of the world?

A minute later, HRC pulled out briefing cards to start a conversation with the king about their substantive agenda. As she was checking her cards, he grabbed a remote control, pressed a button, and a large TV screen came up from within the table with a soccer match on full volume. I thought I had been given a good seat until I realized that the television speaker was right in front of me.

"Is this part of your usual lunch routine?" I asked my seatmate.

"This is the time to eat," he responded. "Talking is for later."

After our lunch and soccer match, we were each handed a towel doused in perfumed water to clean our hands, then escorted toward a more intimate room for the formal bilateral meeting. HRC excused herself to use the restroom. As the rest of us waited awkwardly in the hallway, the Saudi ambassador to Washington, Adel al-Jubeir, beckoned me over and formally introduced me to the king as a "daughter of the country," "*bint al balad*." We talked for a minute about where I grew up, and he was interested to hear about my mother's work at her college.

When HRC rejoined us, she was directed to the seat next to the king, on the left side of the room. The Saudi delegation took their seats on overstuffed blue satin damask sofas and chairs on the right side. The rest of us were to fill the remaining seats on the left. The protocol chief looked at me standing at the end of our delegation, his expression a little befuddled, before pointing me to a seat on the Saudi side. Not wanting to embarrass him, I made a motion to sit where he directed me, and the minute he turned his back, this daughter of the country moved to the left.

* * * *

On the short flight to Jeddah, after we all turned down dinner—we were still digesting lunch after all—HRC came out of her cabin, papers in hand, and sat next to me.

"I think it's going to be really impactful for these young women to see you doing your job," she said referring to the students at Dar Al-Hekma. "I want to reinforce that I am here to listen but also to push how important it is for women to have choices, how growing educational partnerships and encouraging civil society give them more opportunities. It might not be the most popular thing to talk about here but I need to do it."

"You are not going to face unfriendly questions here," I said, thinking back to my many conversations with Saudi friends. "But there is still a general sense that the West doesn't understand this part of the world and that the media characterization has been only negative. These are students who won't be afraid to speak their minds."

"Good, I want them to," she said. "That's why I am here."

The year I spent at King Abdulaziz University after high school, I had bristled at the stifling limitations for women in Jeddah, but simultaneously found myself defending my experience to my American cousins. I knew there were going to be young women in that audience at Dar Al-Hekma who wanted more liberties, to travel freely, to have the same choices as their brothers had. I also knew there would be women who were happy with their lives, who enjoyed the sense of security that comes from living in a communal, homogeneous society. Who resented outsiders telling them how to live. They believed they could pursue worthy professions and not give up their cultural heritage. Many, if not most, wouldn't be able to travel overseas on their own even if they wanted to. Part of the reason for the rise of institutions like Dar Al-Hekma that imported a distinctly American education was that many Saudi students couldn't get visas to study in the U.S. post-9/11; and if they could, their parents were worried that they would face hardships once there. I largely supported the approach of HRC and her State Department advisors, but we agreed that it required cultural awareness and sensitivity; that she should champion their freedom to choose rather than tell them what they should want. I wasn't sure anyone who hadn't lived there would ever truly understand this dichotomy.

HRC was looking out the window as we approached the sprawling urban landscape that was my hometown. The dark of night was scattered by the thousands of yellow lights dotting the city's buildings and streets. Our line officer had thoughtfully arranged for my mother to meet the plane when it landed at King Abdulaziz International Airport. Mom had just hosted British prime minister David Cameron at the college, but she was far more nervous and excited about this visit. After rushed hellos, protocol dictating formality, I departed with her for one night in my childhood home.

Early the next morning, I wandered around the ground floor of my house savoring this brief escape to a time in my life that was less complicated, lingering the longest in my father's office, which my mother had left untouched since his death. *Would he be proud of me?* I wondered as I ran my fingers along the volumes in his bookcase. *Would he bless this marriage I was about to enter?* I peered out the window from his desk, to look at what he might have seen when he lifted his head during a break while writing. I opened the side door into the backyard yearning for the intense aroma of jasmine from his beloved plant box but finding only withered plants. If I had come here for clear answers, there were none. I found no comfort or guidance, just a hollow silence. What would he have said? *I raised you to make your own choices. Only you can decide.*

As I made my way upstairs to pack my things, I was walking past our formal dining room, when something caught my eye. Was that *the* china set laid out immaculately on the table?

One of my mom's prized possessions, normally displayed in a china cabinet, was a formal dinner set that she had bought during our trip to Tokyo. The plates had a delicate white base with hand-painted red, white, and black Asian motifs and gold filigree throughout. For years afterward, anytime her back or shoulder ached, she would say, "I carried that Noritake set around the world for you children." One afternoon when I was maybe eight, my siblings and I were chasing one another when one of us banged against the cabinet. Immediately we heard crashing and tinkling, then dead silence until my baby sister marched down the hall to my parents' room proclaiming "Nothing brooooooke!" I think it was the closest we came to really testing my mother. Hadeel, in her meticulous manner, quietly collected the broken teacups and plates, sat at our dining table with Super Glue, and reconstructed the pieces until they were good as new. We only used that china (the dishes spared the Super Glue) on very special occasions, and even though we hosted a lot of parties, I didn't remember ever eating off of them.

"Mom," I called from downstairs, "What is going on in the dining room?"

"Oh, that was just in case Hillary decided to come over for tea," Mom said nonchalantly. "I wanted to be prepared." I laughed. Hillary Clinton definitely merited the paper-thin, continent-spanning china set. She never made it for tea, but I had learned how high the bar was for the china.

* * * *

That afternoon, we arrived at the newly constructed Dar Al-Hekma building complex. The president, Dr. Suhair Al Qurashi, my mother's boss, had given Mom the honor of introducing HRC. I stood at the back of the room. As she listed all the pioneering programming that had been instituted in the last decade, I knew I was hearing many of the details she had shared with me during our weekly calls, but when I heard them in the aggregate I was astonished by their breadth. Exchange programs with Tufts University for a course in Diplomacy and International Relations. An Architecture program and an affordable housing project with the University of Colorado. A graduate Business program with the University of California at Berkeley. A collaboration with students from Harvard University on a Habitat for Humanity project to build homes for Palestinian families in Amman, Jordan—one of many such projects because community service was mandatory for all students at Dar Al-Hekma. Plus, just as my mother had promised, the school was on its way to becoming an accredited university. There was my mom, operating within a rigid, fixed system, persistently nudging people to embrace greater opportunities for the next generation of women leaders. We had left the Texas International Education Consortium offices all those years ago, Mom's head full of ideas and plans, and she had made all of them a reality. When HRC acknowledged me, there was loud applause, but all the credit for whatever I represented to these young women belonged to the Abedin sitting with her on stage.

Ultimately, the message that HRC conveyed was exactly what my mother, and her mother, and her mother's mother lived: the value of an education for girls. Noting that the majority of Saudi Arabia's population was under twenty-five, she cautioned that many young people were not being educated, or offered adequate healthcare, or generally given the basic tools needed for a productive future. She went on to commend efforts to strengthen civil society "as well as local indigenous efforts to expand opportunities, so that more girls and women everywhere can participate fully . . . if they choose to do so."

The questions she was asked ranged from the curious to the pointed. As I watched HRC answer each question with ease and candor, I remembered what she'd said on the plane the day before, "That is why I am here."

Unbeknownst to either of us, her visit would serve another purpose. When the program closed and she was done taking photos and shaking hands, my mother guided her into the reception room, asking if she had a few minutes to talk.

"No, Mom. There is no time." I was caught off guard, and so I instinctively tried to stop them from walking into the room together. HRC had television interviews lined up, but they weren't my main concern.

"I have plenty of time, I want to talk to your mother," HRC said as Mom linked her arm with hers and led her to the windows. They sat facing each other on a sofa, their knees almost touching. I hadn't intended to leave, but when I saw my mother hesitate, and HRC take her hand in her own to put her at ease, I backed out of the room. Just as I'd feared, this was going to be a serious conversation.

I left the door ajar and stood in the archway to eavesdrop. After they each praised the other for a successful program, Mom said, "Hillary, I am jealous of you. My daughter has spent more of her life with you than she has with me." HRC laughed her big, full-throated laugh, lightening the mood. I imagined my mother clasping her hand tighter and HRC holding on. HRC was rarely the one to pull away first, whether it was a handshake on a rope line or a friend who kept holding it after a greeting.

"This is such a difficult, confusing time for our family. I know so little about Anthony, and while he seems very impressive, I am worried for my daughter." HRC couldn't have been entirely surprised because I had shared much of this with her already. "Normally, our families would have met and spent more time together, but that has not been possible with me here and my son and daughter in England. It is so difficult to know if this is the right choice for her." Then Mom went there. "If my husband were alive, he would have known what to do. In the end, the most important thing is my daughter's happiness. Is *this* the man to make her happy? Can you please advise me?" In the hush of the room, I heard her voice catch, a rare occurrence. My heart jumped to my throat. Mom must have adjusted her eyeglasses, wiping her eyes with the corner of her scarf. HRC must have nodded sympathetically and given my mom's hand another squeeze or a pat. HRC had just given her own blessing for her only child's marriage, and she had had the benefit of having known her future son-in-law for many years.

"Saleha, I understand how hard this must be for you. What I can share is that he seems very committed to her and I have never seen her so happy. I know this is uniquely challenging given how far away you are. I know too how it feels to just want your child to find a good partner in life. Maybe the best thing we can both do is to trust our children to make the right decision."

The room was silent. HRC had welcomed Anthony from day one. Talking to my mother, she vouched for the many hours she had seen us together on the campaign trail, the trip to Punta Cana, the countless lunches and dinners the Clintons had hosted and included Anthony in. She saw what I felt we were: a happy couple. I couldn't take it any longer. I swung the door open and said, "We *have* to go!"

When I gave my mother a long goodbye hug, she seemed somewhat less burdened, as if the conversation had eased her anxiety. Though she had spent time with Anthony in Washington, she had been overwhelmed by his big personality. Anthony charmed her with his easy manner, entertained her with his jokes, impressed her with his intellect, but within thirty minutes of meeting her he had, of course, mentioned his conviction that all Saudi textbooks were anti-Semitic, which was certain to start an uncomfortable debate. I just put my head in my hands.

Still, Anthony quickly endeared himself to her, as he had to me. Over the entire length of her visit that previous summer he made himself of service in small ways. Driving her to appointments, grabbing her favorite groceries, offering to pick up her prescriptions at the pharmacy. Despite cultural and religious differences that appeared so vast, and his engulfing personality, I think she was surprised that she liked him so much.

* * * *

In May, Anthony and I flew to England to spend a long weekend with my family, who would join us for a private Islamic ceremony. Our first stop was Hadeel and her husband Saeed's house. This was the first time for either of them to meet Anthony. Saeed shook Anthony's hand, showed us into the living room, and they seemed to hit it off immediately. Hadeel, as always, was serene, beatific even, despite the chaos of raising three boys. She had a comfortable house with a large garden. Leaving the men to chat, I followed Hadeel into the kitchen. While she cooked, I gazed at the greenery through the kitchen window.

Hadeel was bent over the open oven door, prodding her baked chicken with a fork, when suddenly I felt an unfamiliar shudder and heard a strange sound. She must have heard it too, because she looked up at me, then past me to where we could hear the low din of Saeed and Anthony talking in the living room. She pulled me through the door to the garden. The sound was me, crying. Quiet at first but now exploding into loud sobs. I fell into my sister's arms. I was so disconnected from my emotions that I didn't even recognize what was happening to me.

"I miss Abbu," I finally said, still mid-embrace. She held me tighter.

The emotional weight of being on my own all these years, losing my father just when I was going out into the world, had buried my mourning in some deep cavern in my chest, from which it rarely escaped. Now I was embarking on this big change in my life without him, and after so many years of exercising such tight control over myself, I was finding the courage and strength he had inculcated in me hard to muster. Maybe my outburst was prompted by Hadeel's beautiful, perfect family. Maybe I had always been jealous that all my siblings had found their life and love partners so early. What I had been waiting for all this time had finally arrived, but in a package that was so unexpected, so impossible to have ever imagined, that I couldn't help doubting it. Maybe I was just scared. After my father died, I was left with the feeling that anything good, beautiful, promising could vanish in an instant, as he had; that the very experience of love was inviting the terror of loss. I was finally in a place—the house of my sister—where I could be sad and not have to explain why.

As I pulled away to compose myself, she said, "Of course you miss Abbu, but he is here with us, in you, in me. If you go into anything with good intentions, that is the best you can do."

We stayed out there until after the heaving had subsided and I caught my youngest nephew staring at me from the kitchen window, wide-eyed and curious. We walked back into the house and ate with Anthony, Saeed, and my three nephews, no one commenting on my red eyes or sniffles, except for my little nephew, who just kept staring at me. When he said, "Huma *khala*, why are you . . . ," his mother asked him if he wanted more rice.

Hadeel and Saeed had rented a lovely cottage in the Cotswolds, where our family was gathering for the first full family reunion in years. Mom was coming, as was Hassan, his wife Sara, and their three children. Heba, her husband Sohail, and their three boys were joining too, flying in from New York.

It was spring in England, and for once, mercifully, it was not raining, though I wouldn't have minded if it had. Overcast mornings transformed gloriously when the sun burned off the dew as we walked through nearby meadows. Evenings were cool as we gathered at the long wooden dining table for meals that Hadeel and Sara prepared. Anthony seemed comfortable in this world of Abedins, particularly happy to play with my nieces and nephews. Watching him, I was reminded of a visit we'd made to see his baby niece, Rive, in fall 2008, when Mayor Michael Bloomberg had just succeeded in changing the law in New York City to run for a third term, leaving Anthony with the tough decision of whether or not to challenge him the following year. Running for mayor had been his dream his entire adult life, but now he faced daunting prospects against a formidable incumbent.

"What are you going to do?" I had asked him.

"I don't know," he responded as he held his niece. "I think I'd rather have this."

This, he had said, staring intently at Rive. At the time, we were still defining our own relationship, and I definitely did not feel ready for motherhood, with Anthony or anyone. Here in the Cotswolds, even if I still wasn't ready to think about parenthood, I felt confident that Anthony would be an amazing father someday.

Saturday morning, we had a small ceremony sitting under a pergola in the yard. An Islamic wedding, similar to Ketubah ceremonies in Jewish tradition, is essentially a business contract. It is designed to protect the interests of the bride. Whatever assets the woman brings into the marriage, she maintains control over during marriage and takes with her should there be a divorce. The husband is required to gift the bride a *mehr*—a sum of money, a piece of property or jewelry, whatever he can afford. Sometimes the bride can forgive it entirely. We agreed to come to the marriage equally and leave equally, and I forgave any dowry from Anthony.

As we sat down for lunch afterward, I realized how serene and settled I felt. Something I had never felt before. Surrounded by the people I loved most and who loved me. There was no agenda, no one was pulling out briefing cards or talking about the goals of the gathering. We were just there to be there. In fact, we were there for me. The two parts of my family, old and new, were coming together, and we fit. I looked at the empty seat at the end of the table that no one had occupied, as though waiting for an additional guest to join the feast. I closed my eyes, imagined my father in it, and knew he was still with me.

* * * *

Our May escape to Europe was brief, just a long weekend. The work juggernaut continued when I returned to DC, preparing for another trip, this one to Costa Rica, Brazil, Chile, and Uruguay. Our wedding date was set for July 10, and any empty windows of time were filled with all the decisions you have to make when you are getting married. My wedding advisor, aka Hillary Rodham Clinton, was on hand whenever I needed her. At the end of our daily 8:45 a.m. meeting with the small group of senior staff, when we received reports on any number of hot-button issues around the world, we often walked out together to her small private office and she would ask me for the latest on my dress, the flowers, and the venue we had chosen, a hotel on Long Island. It was a fun distraction. One morning, as we walked back to her office, she asked, "Who is going to perform the ceremony?"

I explained that we hadn't figured it out, but that I really wanted my brother to do it. He was gentle and eloquent and had inherited my father's ability to hold any audience captive. I hoped he could speak to the coming together of our two communities and the evolution of our relationship.

"Hassan was very quiet when I asked him," I told her. "Like he didn't want to say no to me. So he just said 'I'll do whatever you want.' Mom, on the other hand, seems upset. He is supposed to be filling the role of my father at the wedding. That is really important to her. 'Your father is not meant to be the one who performs the ceremony, he is meant to give you away.'" HRC was nodding and I stopped. I always tried to catch myself when I was rambling, remembering that I was talking to one of the busiest humans on the planet.

"In any case, I'm sure we will figure it out. I'll keep you posted." She nodded a thanks, then started pulling out files and grabbing her reading glasses and a pen to get back to work.

The next day, Lona and I met with HRC in the inner office for a quick review of her schedule. Lona went through the minutiae of each meeting, and I was on hand in case HRC questioned why she was doing something. As we stood to leave, she said, "Huma, can you stay a minute. I want to talk to you about something."

As soon as Lona left HRC asked, "What do you think about Bill performing your wedding ceremony?"

Huh? This was territory I dared not tread. When I was first engaged, I promised myself I would ask nothing of the Clintons. People asked them for things all the time. I was not going to do that. I wanted them to be guests and enjoy themselves. They were already giving us an extraordinary wedding present by hosting our reception at their home in Washington and inviting more than two hundred of our family, friends, and colleagues. Since I had said nothing in the last few seconds besides the "Huh . . . ," which was still hanging in the air, she continued. "All the things you said were important to you are all things he can speak to. He knows you both, he can speak to your communities coming together, and I think your mother would approve. So, unless you don't want him to, I think you should call Bill."

I hesitated, still unsure, but also incredibly touched.

"If you really think he would, I think it would be amazing."

"I think he would," she said, smiling.

I walked out, feeling both a sense of relief and excitement, made a quick call to check in with Anthony who was equally humbled and excited, before making the call. I dialed the house phone a little nervously because in all the years I had spent with him—the countless official and unofficial trips, the late dinners, brief vacations, the long walks, miniature golf and shopping excursions, simultaneous nodding off on planes, exchanging of dog-eared books, the long, long, long conversations about the most arcane and frivolous topics—I had never asked WJC for anything for myself.

He picked up right away, not even waiting for me to formally ask, and said, "Well, Huma, I couldn't manage peace in the Middle East, but the fact that I can do this is pretty darn close!" It was news when others learned he would be marrying us. The brash Jewish congressman with the bright future, the mysterious Muslim aide whom everyone saw but never heard, the former president with epic oratorical skills. No one knew this was Hillary Clinton essentially doing what she did best: problem solving.

* * * *

I visited Oscar de la Renta's atelier, where he showed me a sketch he'd made of a wedding gown for me—a slinky, strapless, fitted column. Sexy, and decidedly not me. "Well I had to try!" he smiled, eyes twinkling. I wanted what I wore to give some kind of nod to my heritage, so I had brought the necklace my mother had worn for her own wedding. It was a Hyderabadi-style choker with uncut diamonds in irregular shapes embedded in gold, and large semiprecious green stones dangling along the bottom. The design he later suggested to me, which I loved, would have embroidery created by Oscar's design team, inspired by this family heirloom.

A few weeks later, I got a call from his atelier. Could I come in at 7 p.m. that very night? They had a gown they had just completed and Oscar wanted to see if I liked the silhouette. I was in New York, so I ran over in between events and slipped on the embroidered gown. It was strapless and cream-colored, made up of many layers of a light, gauzy fabric.

"Why was this so urgent?" I asked, as I fumbled to get all the layers over my clothes, careful not to touch or snag this clearly very special dress.

"This is going to Cameron Diaz for the Academy Awards. We need to send it out tomorrow morning, but Oscar thinks this color and style is you."

He was right. I stared at myself in the mirror, an impostor standing in a gown belonging to a celebrity, but I loved it. Oscar left me a voicemail a little while later, "Don't worry, I am putting sleeves on your dress!"

As July approached, the urgency at work didn't abate. The State Department put out a statement of support for democracy in Pakistan following a terrorist attack in Lahore at a Sufi shrine. The Iraqis decided to call off a session of parliament that would have established coalition rule, and instead Prime Minister Maliki instituted a caretaker government.

Even on the day of my wedding I was on and off work calls, responding to unending email chains because HRC was leaving shortly for a weeklong trip to Pakistan, Afghanistan, South Korea, and Vietnam, each destination involving a different imperative and a different set of scheduling priorities. A honeymoon would have to come later. Sitting in my hotel room before the ceremony, I looked up from my phone every few minutes to hug a new relative or friend as they showed up to say hello. Once I was fully made up and ready to put on my dress, Isabelle Goetz, who was used to dealing with a constantly moving head from her many years doing HRC's hair, realized my bun was off-center. "This is because you don't know how to sit still!" Isabelle scolded, forcing me to sit back down so she could pull out the pins and adjust the bun.

With the help of a master event planner, Bryan Rafanelli, I had selected a beautiful hotel on Long Island called Oheka Castle. It had formal gardens that reminded me of the European gardens I had visited on childhood travels, with geometric reflecting pools and a center fountain, surrounded by stone pathways, dotted with neatly trimmed boxwoods and lined with tall London plane trees. It had rained all day but miraculously stopped an hour before the ceremony. I watched from the window as people filled the outdoor seats tiptoeing through the still wet, squishy grass. When I walked out and down the aisle, I was all nerves. I did not enjoy being the center of attention. It was only when I locked eyes with Anthony that my unease subsided. A friend later said I looked like a zombie bride.

WJC opened the ceremony. "We welcome you all to the union of Anthony and Huma. If every wedding is a wonder, this one is a miracle." He continued, "This is a remarkable day as we all know in part because these two people have come together across two great traditions, two different faiths, two different backgrounds, that today too many people in the world believe can't be reconciled. They have reminded us that the only way to reconcile them is through the enduring power of love. To Anthony's family and friends, I would tell you that for Hillary and me we've never loved a human being outside our family as we love Huma."

For my part, I never felt more surrounded by love, starting with the man in whose hand I had just placed my own. The grass and trees glistened with raindrops, my dress sparkled with its intricate gold embroidery, and semiprecious stones shone from my neck, but nothing compared to the light I felt coming from within.

I had found the perfect partner for what seemed like a perfect life. From the outside, it looked like I was living a fairy tale. That's because I was.

SHAME, SHAME,
GO AWAY

What I want back is what I was.
—Sylvia Plath

When I awoke in Buckingham Palace, it was as if I were still in a dream. I turned my head to the tall, narrow windows, where sunlight was just beginning to peek through the gray clouds. I had drawn open the heavy drapes the night before so that I would rise with the first light and see the view of the Queen Victoria Memorial and gardens. At the palace gates, the Queen's Guards stood erect in their red-and-black uniforms. The balcony where the Queen stood annually to inspect the Trooping of the Colour Parade and where Prince William and Kate Middleton had waved to fans on their wedding day three weeks earlier was just down the hall from the bedroom where I lay. It was early, but the fatigue I had been experiencing over the last few weeks felt like a distant memory. I pulled the sheets down to stare at my belly. My long fitted gown for the evening's white-tie dinner hung on the bathroom door, and I hoped I would be able to get the zipper all the way up.

At the foot of the bed was an elegant chestnut-brown writing desk where I had left the briefing book I had started reading the night before. On top of that was the secretary of state's private schedule, which noted the evening's dinner hosted by Queen Elizabeth in honor of President Obama's state visit to the United Kingdom. Among the many staff members on this trip, I was one of a fortunate few invited to stay at the palace and attend the dinner, courtesy of the White House. Next to my formal invitation to the dinner was a stack of pale blue palace stationery. I climbed out of bed, wearing one of the delicate white nightgowns I had been given at my bridal shower, impractical until this trip, and I sat down at the desk to begin my day.

When I had caught up on emails, I pulled out a single piece of stationery and wrote a letter to my husband.

"Dear Anthony—Is it possible for any two people to be happier or more blessed? Some days, I cannot believe it. We must remember to be grateful to God that He has given us so much. I love you. Huma Weiner, May 24, 2011."

I hadn't legally taken Anthony's name when we were married and never used it except for this one single time. He had never asked me if I wanted to or would. And since in both Islamic and Middle Eastern custom, a woman retains her maiden name when she marries, the question had never occurred to me until we were applying for our marriage license and the official asked if I planned to take my husband-to-be's name. I declined without even considering it. In this moment, though, I felt more connected to Anthony than ever before. I placed the note in the matching envelope, got dressed, and went into the adjoining sitting room that connected our two bedrooms to meet up with my boss, who was seated in a wingback chair reading some papers as the palace staff wheeled in scrambled eggs and properly brewed tea. For a moment, I thought I would tell her but I stopped myself. It was too early to share the news.

I first got my period when I was eleven and, in a panic, ran to my father for help. He calmed me down, patiently explaining that it was a natural process in a woman's body. He then gently passed me off to my mother to show me how to use what he referred to as the "necessary napkins." From that day on, I have been down-to-the-day regular. So when, four weeks earlier, I had to struggle to zip up my skirt—feeling bloated, but not menstruating—I knew.

I didn't share my suspicion with Anthony, but stopped at a pharmacy to pick up two pregnancy tests, both of which almost instantly developed a faint pink line. I handed Anthony an old black jewelry box with one of the sticks in it, and he looked down at the box, then at me, thunderstruck.

"What is this?" and then "Are you sure?" as he lowered himself onto our white sofa in Washington, his eyes instantly beginning to water. Anthony, never at a loss for words, was, for a brief moment, speechless. He kept staring at the stick, then at me, stuttering, "I can't believe it." As the news began to sink in, he went right back to being himself. "Are you okay? How do you feel? Have you been sick? How long have you known? What can I do? Oh my God, I can't wait! I am going to be a father! We are going to be parents! Are you craving anything?"

No, I wasn't craving anything in particular, and I felt fine. Those were the cursory answers to his questions. On a deeper level, I was uncertain about what this meant for my life. I had gone from dating a man—my first serious relationship—to engagement to marriage and now to pregnancy in the blink of an eye. Whenever I visited friends and family who had small kids, I was comfortable holding, playing with, feeding, and babysitting them, but I was always happy to return them to their parents at the end of the day. I also couldn't quite register how quickly I had gotten pregnant, since I had been so often warned about the challenges, especially since Anthony and I were "old" to be new parents—I was thirty-five and Anthony was forty-six. Some part of my mixed emotions was sheer disbelief. But the obstetrician later pointed out that I was healthy, had no family history of difficult pregnancies, wasn't a smoker, didn't consume alcohol. She was not at all surprised that it was so easy for me to conceive. I could finally allow for the possibility that God really was granting us this gift. Walking out of the doctor's office that afternoon, reassured that all was and would be okay, I was so excited that it seemed almost impossible to contain this new secret.

By the time I got to Buckingham Palace, I was about eight weeks along. We had told our parents and siblings but no one else, and now I sat at the very end of the long formal banquet table in my orange gown, which had thankfully zipped but was definitely snug. While the palace staff reviewed with us all the dos and don'ts of royal protocol— *Wait till Her Majesty extends her hand before you attempt to shake it. If you run into the Queen in the hallway, only speak to her if she speaks to you first. Otherwise, simply carry on. This is her home after all. Wait for Her Majesty to stand for the toast before you stand. No one will leave dinner before the Queen and the President*—I was fixated on only one thing. What if I felt sick? I worried that getting up mid-meal would be a breach of protocol. At the end of the briefing, I asked if it would be acceptable to use the restroom during the multicourse meal. Yes, they assured me, it was perfectly okay.

This was a working visit, but staying at Buckingham Palace made it singularly special. That afternoon, HRC and I had explored the Queen's private gardens with one of her gracious ladies-in-waiting. Over the course of my career with the Clintons, I had been privileged to sip tea and eat meals at royal palaces, to attend elaborate functions at grand hotels and mansions, to tour monuments and cultural attractions few other people had ever seen, all around the world, from the Middle East to Southeast Asia to Europe. Nothing, however, quite compared to this visit to Buckingham Palace, which was particularly welcome after an intense month.

Before we left for the trip, a woman had been arrested and jailed for driving in Saudi Arabia. The rules banning women from driving were premised on guardianship laws instituted in 1917 that required women be granted permission from their male guardian to marry, or to study or travel abroad. Driving fell under the travel category. The arrest seemed like a warning to all Saudi women. This was an internal matter involving a sovereign ally and the way HRC generally dealt with situations like this was through a private conversation with her foreign counterpart, which in past instances had proven successful. The young woman driver, whose name we learned was Manal al-Sharif, had been arrested in the midst of launching the Women2Drive movement to challenge the guardianship laws, and was jailed for nine days. As the movement began to gain steam, HRC wanted to do more than make a private call so she made a public statement commending the woman's bravery. Eventually al-Sharif had to leave her family in Saudi Arabia and move abroad for her safety. Only later did we find out that her release had been conditional on her promise never to drive on Saudi land again.

The most consequential of the month's developments was the death of Osama bin Laden. The raid was authorized to take place the night of the annual White House Correspondents' Dinner, which the media and most of Washington's political and social elite attended each year. It had been a big night for me because it was the first time I was going to an event after learning I was pregnant, and I worried that people would notice my belly.

When President Obama nodded hello casually at me from the stage, I carried my little secret, not knowing that he was carrying a far bigger secret: the mission to get bin Laden was to begin in a matter of hours. I had gleaned that something was up when HRC started attending meetings in the White House Situation Room about which I was told nothing. That was unusual. For Principal Committee White House meetings, the secure phone on my desk would ring and I would be told the agenda so I could inform the NSC who on her team would accompany HRC. For these recent meetings, the NSC had offered no topic and I wasn't asked who would join HRC. I didn't press her for more details. If there was anything more I needed to know, she would have told me.

HRC called me as she left the White House after President Obama announced the death of bin Laden. I could hear the note of vindication in her voice and my mind was transported back to Ground Zero, the many trips we had made there since the day of the attack, watching the rubble removed, then the slow rebuilding. How right this moment felt, how completely right.

*　*　*　*

Two days after the state dinner with the Queen of England, we flew to Islamabad. The U.S. had carried out the raid on bin Laden's compound without giving any notice to the Pakistanis. Under any normal circumstances, our country would not send Black Hawk helicopters into another sovereign nation that also happened to be an ally. The purpose of these meetings with the civilian and military leadership was to smooth over any ruffled feathers. President Zardari had lost his own wife in a terrorist attack and was supportive of the U.S. action. When I looked at the faces of the military leaders as we walked in for meetings, however, I sensed tension. Even the tea they served us was lukewarm. On our last trip to Pakistan, HRC had said publicly that she believed bin Laden was hiding out there, possibly with at least tacit protection of some of the leaders, but the government and the military always denied it.

After a long, full trip, we returned home, and I dragged myself into my DC apartment at a little after 1 a.m. and climbed straight into bed.

As was my norm, I woke up in the middle of the night to scroll through my BlackBerry, groggy from jet lag but driven by the nagging compulsion to check on any emerging world crisis. I was one of the main points of contact for the secretary of state on any news, information, or messages coming from or going to her, which left me essentially on call all the time. In this job, I couldn't afford to wait until 7 a.m. to check in, too much might already have happened by then. As I scrolled through my new emails, a text appeared from Anthony, who was in New York.

"You there?"

"Yes," I replied. It took a few minutes for the next message to come through.

"My Twitter was hacked and someone posted a photo. There might be a story, but I am working on fixing the problem. Nothing for you to worry about. See you soon."

He told me not to worry, so even though the concept of being hacked was unsettling, I didn't. I just saw this as yet another item on the unending stream of incoming. Anthony was the problem solver in our relationship, and since he said he was handling this one, I was sure he would. Besides, there was nothing I could do about it, so I moved on to the next ten issues in my inbox. In the past year, we had visited 53 countries, spending 481 hours traveling. Now we were almost halfway through a year where we would plan and execute visits to 46 countries and spend 570 hours traveling. There was so much work, it always felt like I was just scratching the surface.

I put the BlackBerry down and tried to catch a few more hours of sleep before boarding the noon shuttle to LaGuardia the next day.

When I walked through the US Air shuttle arrivals area after landing in New York, something was amiss. For nearly two years, without fail, anytime I landed, Anthony would be in baggage claim waiting, chatting up the airport staff or taking a picture with a constituent or pacing back and forth on a conference call. I'd walk out, he would envelope me in a hug, and grab my bags to carry them out to the car. Anthony had never been late until today. Puzzled, I called him and he said he was outside. I walked out, and sure enough, our gray Ford Escape was idling in the taxi lane, Anthony at the wheel, slightly slumped over. He was wearing an old gray T-shirt that I always thought was too short, like it had shrunk in the wash, and a pair of mustard shorts I had bought him. He looked exhausted and gaunt and like he hadn't showered. He gave me a weak hug.

He had predicted correctly that there might be news. That morning a right-wing blog had reported that an indecent image of a man wearing gray boxer briefs had popped up on Anthony's Twitter feed before being quickly deleted. Just as Anthony had said in his message to me, his spokesman was claiming the photo was the work of a hacker. But Andrew Breitbart, the right-wing provocateur who had threatened to come after Anthony, was sharing details about the deleted tweet on his site, demanding a "full-scale investigation," and later saying that he had even more photos.

Anthony would sometimes tell me about the combat he engaged in online, and he seemed to enjoy the virtual version of it just as much as he did the in-person bouts. Still, I never felt like he was on it too much. I was on my phone as much as he was, if not more, rarely putting it down for more than ten minutes during waking hours. Sometimes we talked about the comments he was getting on his feed—lies, vitriol, threats directed at him, President Obama, our party. I couldn't understand why he would wade through that garbage voluntarily. "They're just cyber trolls," he'd remind me. "But I'm not going to let them bully me." If anything, they seemed to egg him on.

"Why don't you just quit Twitter?" I asked one day as we were sitting on the couch in the living room sharing the paper.

"What, and let them win?" he said. "Never."

As we drove home to Forest Hills from LaGuardia, his right hand resting on my belly for the ten-minute ride, I went into consoling mode. "Are you okay? Have you guys made any progress figuring out who did this? What is the plan?" He gave me short answers. He told me he was on it and that he might need to hire a firm to get to the bottom of it.

I felt violated, angry for him, but also confident that he would get past it. HRC had been falsely accused of all kinds of nefarious acts, so scandal based on even the wildest of fabrications wasn't exactly new territory for me.

After the weekend, we left the city as planned, to spend a night with friends on Long Island. It was Memorial Day weekend, the two-year anniversary of our engagement. The city was unseasonably hot and I was glad to have a break from it. On the drive we chatted about how we would tell people I was pregnant once I passed the twelve-week mark, though that was still nearly a month away. As the weekend progressed, and the story moved beyond the tabloids and exploded onto cable news, Anthony began to seem distracted. Still, I was sure he would be able to figure out how to battle his way out of this; the Anthony I knew always did.

Over dinner, the conversation turned to children; our friends' beautiful son was running around, charming us all, and the couple was expecting their second in a matter of weeks. Naturally, they started teasing us about when we were going to have children. Perhaps because I was bursting just being surrounded by this happy family, perhaps because I wanted to lift Anthony's spirits, I volunteered that I was pregnant. It felt good to share my secret, to make the abstract idea feel real in the world.

The next morning, we both flew to Washington. Anthony was quickly engulfed by press gaggles everywhere he went on the Hill, proof, as if we needed more, that the story wasn't going away. Anthony called to tell me he'd decided to do a round of interviews to clear things up, and I wished him luck. Meanwhile, I buried myself in work back at State.

When I walked into HRC's office for my first meeting of the day, she got right to the point.

"What is going on?" she asked.

I assured her that it was nothing and that Anthony's team hoped to discover the perpetrator soon. From there we shifted to discussing plans for the next trip. That whole week had the quality of a cold coming on, when you feel achy and drained and never know if you'll be better tomorrow, or worse. On Wednesday, Anthony sat down for four hours of back-to-back TV interviews, once again denying that he had sent the message or any others like it. Everything he said, or didn't, seemed only to add gasoline to the fire.

The next weekend we went to the same friend's house where we had hosted our first Thanksgiving as an engaged couple with Anthony's family. Our little apartment had begun to feel very claustrophobic. We didn't talk much on the two-hour drive. Once we got to the house, there were flashes of the usual Anthony but also stretches of unusual silence. Gone was the lighthearted mood of celebration and anticipation about becoming parents. When I woke up the morning of our departure, alone in bed, I realized that Anthony had never joined me in the bedroom. I walked past the small guest room at the end of the hall and noticed that the bed there had been slept in. I walked down the stairs and found Anthony standing in the door frame with his head down, bags laid at his feet. Not in. Not out.

"What's wrong?" I asked.

And then, just like that, life as I'd known it was officially over.

"It's true," he said. "I sent the picture."

I still remember everything about where we were in that moment— the white shaggy rug, the wooden staircase, the front door ajar, the sofa to my left. Anthony opened his mouth to speak, and as though a dam wall had burst, words came flooding out. He said that he couldn't stand lying anymore. His body shook as he tried to choke back tears.

Over the next few minutes, he admitted he had intended to send the picture as a direct message with someone he had befriended over Twitter, but accidently posted it publicly and then deleted it, that it had been a tawdry joke, a dare, it didn't mean anything and he was ashamed and embarrassed and sorry that he had brought this upon us. I felt something explode inside my chest, and suddenly it was hard to breathe. I was simultaneously filled with rage and stunned to my core. It felt like a bolt of lightning had struck me and run straight through my body. That bolt was the only thing keeping me standing upright.

Whatever personal pain and betrayal I felt, I instinctively set aside. I didn't break down in tears or collapse on the sofa. The first thing out of my mouth wasn't *How could you do this to me?* or *I thought that you loved me.* The first thing I said was, "You mean you've been lying to the whole world for a week? Anthony, you have people counting on you. You owe them the truth!"

"I know," he said. "I have to go back and deal with the consequences."

His first impulse was to drive back to Manhattan right away, but I stopped him. There was no point waiting a single minute longer. He needed to get on the phone with his senior team, tell them the facts, and start arranging for a press conference where he would tell the truth. We both stood in the living room as his advisors got on the phone, and then we endured the silence on the line as they digested the news, followed by the quick pivot to arrange a press conference so that he could come clean to the world. I left Anthony to deal with the details and walked out to the deck overlooking the pond. I breathed in the warm air as I looked out at the placid water, every fiber in my body screaming: *What is happening to my life?*

Perhaps if he had told me that he was secretly seeing someone, I would have been so hurt and angry that I would have walked out on him then and there. But at that moment it seemed to me that my husband had done something infuriating, deeply inappropriate, juvenile, crass, and stupid, but not something that fundamentally altered our relationship. The shock, the fury traveling through each cell of my body, was more for my child than for myself. Or for the joy that was slipping away when we had just begun to feel it. These were supposed to be the days when we reveled in the arrival of this miracle, days of bliss and blessings. And they had been for me. What had they been for him?

The drive back to the city was stony, silent. Him remorseful, me armored with mute anger. What was eating at me more than the betrayal was the full week of lies. He repeated how sorry and ashamed he was, how much he loathed himself for what he had done.

"I just want our baby to be proud of their daddy," he said. *Then why did you do what you did?* The words raged in my head.

As he did another conference call with his press team, I stared out the window, tuning out most of what they discussed because I needed to focus on something else—preparing myself for the gathering press I suspected we would find outside our apartment. Since our engagement, I had gotten used to posing for photos at red carpets and all kinds of political and cultural events. Once inside whatever ballroom or auditorium or private fundraiser, I usually had a great time. Our social life was fun, glittery even, and I accepted the obligatory photo ops as part of his job. But now the attention was going to be on my doorstep, and I knew it would be hostile and invasive.

There wasn't much I could do about any of it, but I did want to try to control the possibility that my baby bump might be visible enough to make my pregnancy apparent in a photo. An hour away from the city, I called Heba and asked her if she could meet me a few blocks from our apartment with a loose blazer or jacket, anything that would cover my belly.

"What in God's name is going on?" she asked.

At that moment I didn't have the heart to tell her, so I just said, "Please, just do this for me." She did then what she would do over and over in the coming years, showing that she unquestioningly always had my back. Heba drove to Queens with a gray blazer, met me on a street corner, gave me a quick hug, reminded me she was there if I needed her for anything, and barely looked at Anthony, who sat at the wheel.

We parked the car a couple of blocks from our home. I put on my borrowed blazer and steeled myself. As we approached our building on Ascan Avenue, I stared straight ahead and rushed past the cameras. I climbed the three flights of stairs to our apartment, and felt trapped the moment I walked in. I opened all the windows and sat seething at the dining table, not sure whether to unpack my bags or break something. Suddenly, there was a knock on our apartment door. We ignored it. Then, we heard a woman's voice outside the hall repeating Anthony's name over and over. We ignored that too.

I don't know why I went with Anthony for his press conference. Maybe it was to be sure he did it, maybe because we were now so used to being a unit, any other possibility seemed unnatural. But as I sat in the conference room of his campaign attorneys' office in Manhattan and listened to him read his statement aloud to his team, I understood for the first time that he had exchanged inappropriate messages with more than one woman. Risa Heller, Anthony's savvy, tell-it-like-it-is communications advisor and a good friend to both of us, looked at him as he said those words, and then at me. When someone asked if I would be going out to the press conference with him, I shook my head, and there was at the same time a unanimous "no way" around the room, with Risa's voice the loudest: "no *fucking* way." As they all walked out of the room and toward the cameras, I slipped out to the lobby and onto the streets of Manhattan. Free. Anonymous. This was Anthony's mess. He needed to clean it up.

I jumped into a cab and headed toward the midtown hotel where a friend had booked a room so that I wouldn't have to spend another night in our apartment, staked out by photographers and surprised by random knocks at the door and voices in the hallway. A few family members and friends joined me, mostly because I didn't want to be alone with Anthony and my anger. I ordered comfort food for everyone. As people congregated in the sitting area outside the bedroom, there were lots of hugs and expressions of sympathy. When Anthony arrived after his press conference, casually loosening his tie as though he'd just gotten through some random work event, there was a marked shift in the mood of the room. I tried to relieve the tension by directing people toward the trolleys of food, but one by one they excused themselves: checking their watches, remembering somewhere they had to be, thanking me for offering, but they just weren't hungry. The night was brief and awkward, the conversation stilted, the food untouched, departures early and en masse. *None of those people wanted to be here*, I thought as I climbed under the crisply starched hotel bedsheets and mercifully found some peace and sleep.

*　*　*　*

I didn't read or watch the news coverage then or in the days thereafter. I had been in politics long enough to have a healthy skepticism about the gossip that appeared in the press, especially in the tabloids. From my White House years on, I had gotten used to reading stories about my boss that were riddled with inaccuracies. Our approach had always been to avoid responding to the crazier accusations, especially the salacious gossip, so as not to elevate the stories. Now that it was my husband who was in the headlines, I decided that for my own mental health I would avoid all the news about Anthony. If there were any important developments I needed to know about, I could rely on others to tell me, even if Anthony didn't. Still, I was well aware that a media storm was swirling around us. The coming-clean statement hadn't settled anything, it just raised more questions. What was the nature of these relationships? Who were the women? Was he using government devices for these exchanges? Some House colleagues and other political leaders swiftly called for a House investigation, others for his resignation.

On top of everything, it turned out I was wasting my time trying to think up creative ways to tell my extended family, colleagues, and friends that I was pregnant. That was another unintended casualty of the week.

The day after Anthony's press conference, I was standing in our galley kitchen washing dishes when Philippe called.

"Well, I have never had to make a call like this and it is really awkward but I just got a message from the *New York Times* saying that they intend to report that you are pregnant."

This second bolt of lightning was more visceral, more vivid, more enraging, and I felt the heat rise in me as I struggled to keep calm. *No, no, no.* This was my body, my special secret. Isn't this what women get to do? Isn't this a rite of passage that people are entitled to? Find the space and way to tell the people they love that they are bringing a child into the world when the doctors tell them it is safe to do so. This is not something a reporter shares with the world amid tawdry headlines and indecent images.

"Philippe! *No*, they cannot do that. I am not even twelve weeks and I can't tell anyone until then. You have to explain that to them. There have to be mothers at the *Times*. They have to understand."

"Well, first of all, congratulations. I am really happy for you. Second of all, they have two sources, so they don't really need my official confirmation. They are going to run with it. They're just giving me a courtesy heads-up. Is there anyone you want to tell personally before it becomes public?"

"*No!*" I shouted as I sank to the floor, "This is wrong." *Two sources. Who could have told them?* My mind immediately went to the friends I had seen the weekend before. *Could I no longer trust my close friends?* I felt guilty the instant my mind went there.

"It may be wrong but it's also news. It's big news. Do you want to at least call Hillary and tell her?"

"*No!* This is *not* how I am telling her, over the phone, sitting on my kitchen floor, screaming. I dare them to run this story. They just won't do it. I know they won't."

Philippe sat on the other end of the phone listening patiently while Anthony stood in the door frame, head bowed.

I reaffirmed I had no intention of telling anyone until I was safely past my first trimester. We hung up. I had let all the rage and anger blaze out of me, and still no tears had come. I was on the linoleum floor, back against the wall under the small kitchen window. On a low, recessed shelf next to me was a wedding present, a blown glass decanter in the shape of a U. A few days later, it tipped forward and broke neatly in half. Maybe a gentle breeze had blown it over, or maybe the cats had wagged their tails and knocked it. Whatever the cause, it seemed a perfect metaphor for my broken heart.

Over those painful hours, I was just existing, trying to make it through each day. When I wasn't strangled by fury, I did manage to ask Anthony the only question that rang incessantly in my head: *Why?* "Why would you do this? You have someone who loves you, who is carrying your child. You have a job that is challenging, fulfilling, exciting, and purposeful. You have family and friends who love you, a future that any casual observer would say is full of possibility." *Why? Why? Why?*

Anthony's answers were never long and never satisfactory. He didn't know. It was all a virtual game, he said, he would tune in, play with other avatars, and then return to reality. Many of the women used fake names, posted fake pictures of themselves, so their true identities were often a mystery even to him. It was maddening to hear that.

"I know. I promise. I won't do it again," he said over and over again.

It is not as though political sex scandals hadn't already rocked the Democratic Party in recent years. I had been in the car when New York's then governor, Eliot Spitzer, called to tell HRC he was about to resign effective immediately and then admitted to soliciting prostitutes. I connected Dina McGreevey's call to HRC when her husband, Jim McGreevey, had resigned as governor of New Jersey after admitting he was unfaithful, and come out as gay. And of course, I had been working in the First Lady's office during President Clinton's impeachment trial. There was a very long list of examples of what might be viewed as "traditional" marital infidelity. Cases where there was a spate of stories, an epic fall from grace, a shocked set of constituents. In Anthony's case, it was a scandal that had all the same elements. Except, it seemed, the sex. This behavior was in an entirely digital arena that no one really understood yet. Which led back to the question of *why?*

Anthony's staff was inundated with calls as the pressure to resign increased. Other senior Democrats were now on the spot in every press conference, being asked to comment on Anthony. Even the White House was asked, and mercifully, they said the President would not be weighing in; but the mere fact that the question had been posed was humiliating. That Obama didn't call on Anthony to resign gave us some breathing room. If our president had called for his immediate resignation, the pressure—as bad as it was—would only have been worse.

There were unrelenting questions from colleagues, reporters, concerned family and friends, all demanding answers about what the "plan" was. We needed time and space to think, and privacy, but all were in short supply. Anthony needed professional help, and we had to figure out where to get it. Having no idea where to turn, and with no time to research therapy programs, we sought crisis psychiatric care. The therapist we were introduced to in New York suggested Anthony go to a center in Texas, which specialized in psychiatric evaluations. When we spoke with the director of the center, he recommended that Anthony come alone for two days of interviews as soon as possible. Then we would return together for two additional days of couples therapy and evaluation, after which they would write a report with their assessment. It sounded like a plan.

We signed up not even knowing if we could afford it. Part of me thought it was a little overkill, but if Anthony was willing, and they could talk to him about this "game," and help him get past it, I would embrace the process, whatever my doubts. I still was certain that Anthony could just stop if he wanted to, so did he really need a long-term therapy plan? After all, everything about Anthony's way of life was moderation. He never overate, or overshopped, or overspent on anything. He was disciplined about working out, about focusing on his job, about reading the *New York Times* front to back every weekend.

This behavior seemed so outside of Anthony's DNA that I was sure it was just a weird blip, something I didn't understand but that he had put behind him. And despite everything, the rage, the shame, the ache in my heart, I knew I still loved him.

*   *   *   *

I turned my full attention back to what I could understand: my job. The day after Anthony's press conference, I was scheduled to leave for the United Arab Emirates. I returned to Washington and walked into HRC's office on the afternoon of June 7.

For two and a half years, I'd been in and out of her private office several times a day. I would walk through an outer reception area where Claire sat, past the formal sitting room, then enter the little sanctum. Her office was elegant, small, with wood paneling, a cream-and-gold embroidered damask sofa, colorful paintings on the wall, from both her own and the State Department's extensive collection. The Lincoln Memorial was visible from the recessed windows, which had yellow cushioned benches. Several sculptures adorned the built-in cabinets behind the desk: one of a pregnant African woman, a reminder of who does the world's labor, and another of Eleanor Roosevelt, watching over HRC as she worked.

When I walked in, HRC looked worried, and I hated that her evident concern was because of me. Philippe had clearly told her about my pregnancy, because she stood, came around her desk, and offered me a careful congratulations.

"I wanted to tell you myself" was all I could get out before I burst into tears. She walked me over to the window seat, sat with me, rubbing my back, trying to reassure me, telling me over and over again that it was going to be okay. I was crying so loudly that Claire closed the door to the outer office. A full three days after receiving Anthony's earth-shattering revelation, the tears were finally flowing. The fact that I could not share my pregnancy news the way I had wanted, with the people I loved, is a trauma that stays with me even now. Everything else was awful, but this was something else—my once-in-a-lifetime gift. A full decade later there are many days when I am in the shower or cooking dinner or browsing in a shop, and I hear the words "I am pregnant" emerge from my lips, without any conscious intention, as though my brain is reminding me I never got to say them when it mattered most to me.

After I don't know how long before I caught my breath, HRC asked, "Do you still want to go on this trip?"

"I think it's important for me to do my work," I said, blowing my nose.

"I think it would be good for you to go too," she said.

I walked into her private restroom and looked at myself in the mirror. My eyes were puffy and red. I splashed cold water over my face, blotted it gently with a hand towel, and took a deep breath. Then I returned to work.

That night, we boarded the secretary of state's aircraft, and hours later, when we were crossing from Europe to the Middle East, Lew Lukens mentioned we would have to switch planes in the next few days, which happened from time to time. He had already placed the request through State, but asked if I would call the White House for approval, to make sure we weren't stranded on one of the Africa stops.

I picked up the phone by my seat and called the State Department Operations Center to be connected to White House deputy chief of staff Alyssa Mastromonaco. I asked whether she had received our request for the plane, and she assured me she had. Then there was a moment of silence.

"Everyone here is thinking of you," she said. Then she added that the President had wanted to reach out. She hadn't known what to suggest. A phone call or perhaps a note? A phone call with the President of the United States to talk about my personal humiliation? It was more than I could bear.

"Please just tell him I am so sorry for embarrassing the administration."

I hung up and stared out into the blackness through the window. *Who was this man who sent the tweet?* I did not know that Anthony. The Anthony I knew was so many things, but not that. I was snapped out of my daze when HRC appeared from her cabin to join Philippe, Jake, and me at the table that anchored our quartet of seats. It was only a few minutes into this briefing that I realized that I had tears rolling down my cheeks again. I hoped no one would say anything. The one thing that was worse than what I was feeling was the idea that people would take pity on me. Everyone acted as though nothing was amiss.

A few hours later, before we landed in the Emirates, Philippe looked up from across the table.

"It's out," he said.

On June 8, at 5:11 p.m. eastern, a day after Philippe's warning call, the *New York Times*, followed almost immediately by several other media outlets, announced I was pregnant. Cheryl, Jake, Lona, and Philippe had all given me big hugs congratulating me when I walked into work the previous day. They chose to focus on the happy news, as I'd expected they would. But most of the dozens of people on this large airplane had not known until they got breaking news alerts on their laptops that the woman a few seats away from them was pregnant. Under any normal circumstance, it shouldn't have been national news. It wouldn't have been national news. But it was now.

* * * *

It was close to midnight when we arrived at Emirates Palace Hotel in Abu Dhabi and, operationally, it was business as usual. Except, I was no longer anyone usual. I was now the thing in the room that everyone avoided talking about. HRC had a meeting at our hotel the next morning with the crown prince Mohammed bin Zayed, or MBZ as many of us called him. He would be accompanied by his ambassador to the United States, Yousef Al Otaiba, a longtime good friend of mine. The cameras had already assembled to capture their greeting with HRC.

I half wondered if I should join her or if I should avoid being a distraction, but no one told me not to do my job so I just kept doing it, though I hung back a little as we filed into the room. HRC easily could have avoided the official introductions of her team, but she beckoned me forward and made a point to introduce me. At a moment when any other politician might have disappeared her embarrassing staffer, HRC signaled to the entire world that she wasn't ashamed of me. Then Yousef gave me a reassuring hug. His wife Abeer had just had a baby and we had marveled about their experience as new parents when I'd had dinner at their house recently. He smiled, said congratulations, and whispered, "You okay?"

That night Yousef organized an informal dinner for a few of us at the hotel. I had just begun to eat when I got a message that Cheryl wanted me in HRC's room. When I arrived in her suite, HRC and Cheryl told me I should go to my own room, that there were some people waiting to see me. I assumed this would be about some kind of crisis awaiting us at our next stop but usually I was the one informing her, not the other way around.

My room was big and comfortable, with high ceilings, plush carpeting, a neutral-toned bedspread and curtains. As I entered, I saw a large coffee table, laid out with an elaborate tray of fresh fruit, dates, and chocolates, and beyond that, on a low L-shaped sofa in the sitting area, was my mother; my brother Hassan paced nearby.

"How did you know to come here?" I blurted out.

"Hillary," my mom said, and I didn't need to know anything more. I hugged them both tight, and my mother, my brother, and I sat together, holding one another's hands, soothing one another, my mother asking over and over, "Are you okay?"

"I am so sorry I've brought this on the family," I said quietly. I waited for them to say, *We warned you, we were never certain about this marriage*. Instead Hassan said, "We are here to support you. Whatever you choose to do, we are with you." With concern for me etching deep lines into her face, Mom added, "I have been so worried. You need to focus on being healthy for the baby. I cannot wait for this grandchild, it is a blessing. We are always here for you and love you." We three just sat together, silent for some time, a little pod of gloom and love.

HRC and Cheryl joined us after a while, and the conversation turned toward the baby, my maternal health, and plans for the future. One where Anthony's place was uncertain.

* * * *

We weren't even halfway through a trip that included Zambia, Tanzania, and Ethiopia. By day, I was executing a schedule we had spent months planning, by night I was on the phone with Anthony, discussing the mounting drumbeat. Would he resign? From the beginning,

Anthony resisted going down that path. He thought that if he hung in there and got treatment, that his constituents would forgive him and allow him to continue serving. His office had put out an official statement saying he would be seeking professional help to "focus on becoming a better husband and a healthier person" and that he had requested a short leave of absence from Congress.

Public polls suggested a majority of Anthony's constituents wanted him to stay in office, but the pressure from congressional leadership was unyielding. The chair of the Democratic Party, Congresswoman Debbie Wasserman Schultz, called for his resignation early on. She phoned me a few days later to tell me how hard it had been for her to do it. She had known and served with Anthony for years, he was a friend to her family, and she was shocked and saddened to have to make the statement, but she thought it was important for him to step aside. Anthony's campaign attorney warned that a House investigation into his conduct would be costly. Then President Obama was asked directly about it in a televised interview, and he said, "If it was me, I would resign." Anthony's behavior had become a distraction the Democrats did not need or want.

In Africa, Cheryl, Philippe, and Jake encouraged me to come out with them each night, to wind down from our hectic days on those evenings when we ended early enough for restaurants to still be open. One night, our team had planned drinks with our traveling press, something we tried to schedule regularly, where journalists could have off-the-record sessions with HRC. We traveled with a group of smart foreign policy journalists we all really liked, among others veterans like Kim Ghattas, then with BBC, and Matt Lee from the Associated Press. That night they all gave me the greatest gift. They asked no questions about Anthony; they congratulated me on my happy news, but otherwise they treated me like every other staff member. Like I was normal. None of them wrote stories about my situation or even hinted that they were curious for gossip. I have never forgotten their professionalism, their kindness, their decency, and their respect.

On our way back to the U.S., we stopped in Abu Dhabi to refuel, but our plane blew out a tire, and by the time it could be fixed, the

BOTH/AND

pilots would be going into the obligatory fifteen hours of crew rest, so Lew had to scrounge up some local hotel rooms for us.

HRC texted me shortly after we settled into our rooms, "If you are awake, come see me." I was on the phone with Anthony, who was now in Texas, waiting for the therapy sessions that were scheduled to start the next morning. Just before we took off from Ethiopia, stories had appeared that Anthony had told reporters he would consult with me before deciding whether to resign or not. But we didn't discuss it that night, and when I hung up with him to go see HRC it was still unsettled.

I went to her suite, and found her dressed and sitting by the window.

"Why is he putting this on you? What are you going to do?" she asked.

I told her I was still finding my way, that I was overwhelmed with the pressure and so tired I could barely think. We had been on six flights in the last six days, spending a total of thirty-four hours in the air. I didn't know what Anthony was going to do. I didn't know what I was going to do—whether I would stay or go. But I wanted to see if the doctors in Texas could help him.

"Yes, but you have to recognize what *you* are going through. It is immensely painful, it's also a process. I know what shock and trauma can do and the pressures you are facing."

Then she gave me what I thought was the best advice anyone could have possibly given me.

"Take the time that you need to fix yourself and your family."

She said I could plan and oversee the next few trips, but I shouldn't feel pressure to travel. I should remember that I now had a baby to think about and that should be my priority. Left unsaid was her own experience, and the impossible position she had faced. She didn't say anything about it, but she didn't have to; I had lived through that with her in 1998. In the end, whatever decision I made, she said, "You will always have my support."

Grateful, but still drowning, I told her what was in my heart.

"The one thing I know with conviction is that I want to give my baby a chance to grow up in a household with two parents just like I had. I didn't have a choice when my father was taken from me." She nodded. I stood up and returned to my room to gather my things. When our friend Tom Freedman emailed that morning to check in on me, I responded, "I have good moments and then times it is so unbearable I don't think I can get through the day. But I'll be okay, I have to focus on staying healthy for this baby. And Anthony needs to get healthy for himself. And the rest is the rest."

* * * *

We landed in Washington at 3:30 a.m. on June 15 and I drove home in the dark. I was not expecting cameras outside my apartment, but I guess I should have been. I had to lower my car window to punch in the underground garage key code, and as I did, a video camera appeared over my left shoulder with a voice calling out, "Are you going to tell him to resign?" The minute it took for the steel door to creak open was excruciating. Thankfully, no one followed the car down the ramp. It was still early days.

Outside my door, there were two plants left by neighbors with "thinking of you" notes, and a stack of mail. I only had a few hours to unpack, rest, and then pack again for my flight to New York the next morning. By the time I got there, Anthony would have flown back to New York from Texas.

Sleep still came easily those days, but so did the nightmares. In one of the nightmares I had that night, there were many women hovering outside my apartment window saying they had come to take Anthony away, that he belonged to them, not to me. One woman was holding a spear, another an empty baby sling. In another, I was in labor and rushing from hospital to hospital, turned away each time because no doctor was willing to deliver my baby. And then came the worst of all: In it, Anthony and I were driving through the countryside with our baby safely buckled in the backseat, but when I turned around, the baby had disappeared and Anthony and I were running through the forest in a desperate search. These were vivid visions, interrupted only when I awoke covered in sweat.

Once I gave up on the hope of sleep, I got out of bed and turned to the pile of mail left by the door. There was a letter from the White House. I opened that first. President Obama had written that he was rooting for me and encouraged me to "hang in there." The vast majority of the letters were like this—supportive and kind. One single letter, however, stood apart—not that it was unkind, just that it said something so beyond my comprehension.

It was from an old friend with whom I had lost touch. The first line startled me: "My husband was also a sex addict." It went on to say that she knew that I would come out of this experience a changed person, that I would grieve not only for my marriage but for the person I used to be before all this sadness was heaped on me. She urged me not to blame myself but to focus solely on the baby and my own health. I had had many shocks to my system by then, and you might think this was yet another, but it was not. To my mind it was only an oddity, a surprisingly definitive diagnosis at a time when my own understanding of what Anthony had done was so murky. I had so many more questions than answers. How then could someone who did not know my husband, did not live inside our marriage, make such an unequivocal statement?

As daylight arrived, I heard a sound by my front door and found a note from a neighbor. He wanted me to know that he had seen a lot of reporters outside, so if I needed help getting groceries, he was available. I didn't need groceries, but I was grateful for the tip-off about the press. I needed to quickly figure out how to get to the airport without being trailed.

Three weeks earlier I had drifted along in a dream. Waking up at Buckingham Palace, writing in longhand to my husband on powder-blue stationery, filled with love and pride and above all, gratitude, for our life together. Now my immediate concern was hiding from the entire world, not wondering whether the evening gown I planned to wear at a state banquet would still fit—that felt like many eons ago.

ELEPHANT IN THE ROOM

The earthquake of Anthony's revelation caused a massive fracture: between the past and the present, appearances and reality, whom I could trust and whom I had to be wary of. It was so unsteadying, so upending, that I had to feel my way, never sure if the thing I grabbed on to for stability would hold. It rewrote the stories I had told myself about my life and rewired my relationships with family, friends, colleagues, and even strangers in ways I never could have imagined.

I got to the airport without being spotted that day by repeating something I had done before, but hadn't expected to be doing again. I called my colleague Monica Hanley, who had reached out early that morning and asked if she could help. She met me in my basement garage, and I tossed her my car keys and folded myself into the trunk. The last time I had done this, it had had a clandestine, cloak-and-dagger feel to it. This time it just felt creepy, sordid, pathetic. When the car finally stopped after what seemed like forever, the trunk popped open, and it took my eyes a few moments to adjust to the sunlight. Monica had thought a reporter was trailing her so she'd kept going, until she knew she was in the clear.

There on the outskirts of Washington, Monica got into a cab to go home and I drove to BWI airport in Baltimore, Maryland. I had intentionally not booked a flight from nearby National Airport because it felt too risky. After checking in, I stopped in the bathroom before the flight boarded. As I was washing my hands, the woman next to me made eye contact in the mirror, then looked back down. She dried her hands and then came over to me and gently put her hand on my arm as I stood at the sink. .

"I know what you're going through," she said. "Hang in there."

I was used to being recognized when I was with HRC or Anthony, but not often on my own. I didn't know how to respond so I just said, "Thank you," and made my way to my gate. After boarding, I found my seat, and noticed a man a few rows behind watching me. As I began to lift my carry-on to put it in the overhead bin, he leapt up, took the bag, and shoved it in place for me. Again, I said, "Thank you," and he nodded wordlessly. Throughout the hour flight, whenever I looked back he seemed to be staring at me. It made me uncomfortable, so when we landed, I sped off the plane as fast as I could. "Excuse me!" I heard from behind as I raced through the terminal. I stopped and turned. It was the man from the plane.

"Our prayer group has been praying for you and your family," he said. "If you ever want to pray with us, just reach out."

"Thank you, sir. We need your prayers," I said, and I meant it.

He pressed his business card into my hand, along with a small medallion with a simple cross on it, and went on his way. This man, and the woman who had spoken to me in the restroom, were the first of many strangers who approached me in the days that followed, usually with good wishes or stories of their own to share. The attention surprised me at first, but after a while I got used to it and was simply grateful for their words.

I headed home in a taxi, since I had asked Anthony not to pick me up. As I gazed out the window barely registering all the landmarks I drove past once or twice every week, the words of the kind stranger turned over and over in my mind. *Family.* I looked down at my belly. My fairy tale had taken such an unexpectedly dark turn that I didn't know if Anthony and I could ever go back to what we had. All I knew was that I now had my own family unit, one that was only just beginning to form, one I had to figure out how to fix.

When I got to the apartment and saw Anthony, I didn't hug him and he didn't try to hug me. He seemed both deflated and relieved. We were finally alone together—he back from Texas and I from halfway around the world—and we forced ourselves to discuss the thing that had eluded us for over three weeks: us. Our first conversation was long and painful. Mostly, I repeated how shocked, angered, and confused

I was by his behavior. He said he was confused too. He said he hated keeping secrets and being deceptive. He had found his trip to Texas helpful and was eager to go back with me. He had already decided he was going to resign when he asked me what I thought. I agreed it was the right decision.

When Anthony called Risa to tell her, she asked, "Well what are you going to say the reason is?"

Knowing she was completely trustworthy, and that Anthony had some preliminary feedback from the therapists, I took the phone from him and said, "We are going to find out for sure, but apparently he has some narcissist issues."

"Seriously?" Risa asked. "Doesn't that describe every politician on the planet?"

The next day, on June 16, Anthony went to a senior center in Brooklyn and announced he was resigning after serving seven terms in Congress.

* * * *

Back at the State Department, I had to navigate doing my job with colleagues who were caught between acknowledging what was happening in my life and remaining professional and just ignoring it. Some people congratulated me on my pregnancy, others pretended nothing had changed, and still others would stop talking when I entered the room, giving me solemn looks that I read as expressions of how sorry they felt for me. I decided to take HRC's advice and skip the upcoming trip to Guatemala and Jamaica, but I showed up at the office every day to prepare for her next trip, to Budapest, Vilnius, and Madrid the following week and then to Turkey, Greece, India, Indonesia, Hong Kong, and China scheduled for mid-July.

My family checked in by email or phone, asking if I was "okay," but aside from Heba, who was in New York, everyone else was so far away that it was difficult to have in-depth conversations. Even when we did talk, what more could any of us say? Everyone was shocked, confused, and embarrassed. They were there for me, they always would be, but there was nothing anyone could actually do for me.

The situation took a toll on my friendships too. Many, many

friends reached out and said they were rooting for us to see our way through this, all harkening back to our recent wedding, the vows, the feeling of promise in the air that day. Then there were a few people who made clear they were there for me, but not for us. They were furious with Anthony and could not forgive him.

At lunch later that month, a friend said, "You can walk away from all of this and go back to your old life. You are young, you could easily get remarried and start a family when you are ready." It took me a few seconds to grasp the full import of what was being suggested. When I did, I had to excuse myself and go to the ladies' room so I could throw up, the only time I did during my entire pregnancy. A young woman was there at the same time. When I stepped out of the stall, she asked if I was okay, and I could tell that she recognized me. I begged her not to tell anyone she had just heard me flushing my lunch down the toilet. I dreaded giving the tabloids yet another pregnancy-related nugget to feast on, and she assured me she wouldn't; a generous stranger who kept my secret.

I ricocheted between thinking this was all just some stupid game Anthony had played, which wasn't fundamentally about our relationship, and feeling deeply hurt by his behavior. The only thing I was certain about amid the upheaval of those weeks was how eager I was to welcome our child into the world.

I don't remember anyone who told me directly that I should leave Anthony. I was shocked by his behavior, hurt that he had betrayed our marriage vows, livid that he had lied for days, but mostly, I was confused and incapable of reconciling the man who had done this with the Anthony I knew. By so many measures, Anthony wasn't just a good husband, he was an excellent one. We were equal partners in life and love, and if anything, he was the one constantly lifting me up, encouraging me to pursue my professional dreams, letting me make all the decisions in our life, from where we lived to social plans. From the first day we met, he had always put my wishes and desires first. Still, I needed answers.

* * * *

In another circumstance, the shock might have led me to paralysis, to climb into bed and stay there for days, but that was simply not possible. For the first time in his adult life, Anthony was unemployed, at least for now, and there was never even a question that I would continue working after the baby was born. What we didn't discuss was how I would manage a newborn while commuting between Washington and New York every week. He assured me he would figure something out, and not to worry.

We turned our entire focus to getting ready for the baby. Since we were "older" parents, a Washington obstetrician suggested we undergo genetic testing to ascertain any possible abnormalities with the fetus. On June 24, we went in for an ultrasound, and when we sat down with the doctor, she looked at the scan and asked, "Do you want to know?"

"Yes!" we both said in unison.

"I'm pretty confident you are going to have a boy," she said. "And he's progressing beautifully."

From the beginning, neither of us had a preference for a boy or a girl, but knowing the gender drove home to us for the first time that we were bringing an actual human being into the world.

We didn't walk out of the office, we floated. Anthony's BlackBerry pinged as we left the doctor's office, and he pulled it out of his waist holster to check it. "The House clerk officially accepted my letter of resignation," he said. We let the news hang in the air for a minute and continued quietly to our car. Anthony came around to open my door as he had done since the first day I rode in his car, a huge smile breaking out as he said, "This is the happiest day of my life."

* * * *

On his first trip to Texas Anthony had registered at a nondescript Hilton hotel under an alias, worn a baseball cap and sunglasses, and managed to remain undetected. For our joint trip, I was bracing for what the therapy sessions would entail. I came only with questions. Therapy itself was a foreign concept. No one in my family had ever gone to a therapist. When my father was undergoing his kidney transplant and the hospital administrator handed my mom a pamphlet listing the support services they offered partners and children to talk through the stress, she was appalled. Talk to a stranger about our personal problems or feelings? Never! So she didn't and we didn't, and in the years that followed Abbu's death, each of us carried the pain of it by ourselves, in our own way. In the early years, our family couldn't talk about my father without upsetting my mother, but over time we all began to speak of him often—mostly laughing at his antics and remarking about how thoroughly ahead of his time he had been. We never divulged to one another the depth of our feelings of pain, sorrow, anger, abandonment.

Anthony and I flew to Texas on June 30 and checked into the same Hilton hotel using the same alias Anthony had used previously. We closed the blinds, asked that no calls be put through to the room, and ordered off the room service menu. At 9 a.m. the next morning, we walked into the clinic, and I immediately felt reassured by the warm, competent, and focused professionals with whom we would spend the next two days, as a couple and individually. Anthony was back for round two of conversations he had started on his first trip and was already seeing a therapist in New York twice a week. My work was to confront the private betrayal, and the fact that he had lied for days, compounding the betrayal.

As soon as we sat down with the psychiatrist, Anthony launched right in. He had three questions he wanted answers to. Why did he do it? How could he ensure it never happened again? How could he help me process and try to resolve the crisis in our marriage? The doctor nodded, then asked me if I agreed with these goals, and I said I did. In that very first session Anthony asserted that he did not believe that these "chats with groupies" were all that egregious. To be clear, he would never want to do it again, but he likened it to watching porn or playing a game. He argued that he never met anyone or "did" anything. He was confident that he could chat when he wanted to and stop whenever he wanted to. Maybe it was easier for Anthony to finally say this to me in the presence of a professional, for these were certainly not sentiments he had expressed to me before.

He repeated what he had told me, that he couldn't remember how many women—a handful, he said—he had had these exchanges with, nor could he remember many names. It wasn't the specific individuals he was attracted to so much as the adoration; the more he got, the more he sought out. When I pressed him on who these women were, he said they were people he had been sure would never betray him or go public. There was a reckless naïveté in the way he put his trust in these strangers. As for how long this had been going on—when I had seen the message from the woman back in Punta Cana eighteen months earlier, but hadn't been able to find any responses from him, it was not because he was hiding them from me, but because his surreptitious online activities were just beginning then. As these new communications portals—Twitter and Facebook—became more ubiquitous, the ease with which he could dip into and out of them and all they offered, any moment of the day, proved irresistible. Their lure overpowered his good sense, his capacity to measure the risk. He could satisfy his craving for this attention, and then switch back to reality. Or so he thought.

I was mostly silent in these couples sessions because my question was so simple and I waited with every answer to hear it. *Why?* Anthony didn't seem to see things from my perspective. Could he not understand how hurt, devastated, and shamed I was? That he didn't was almost more upsetting than what he'd done, because it left me feeling so utterly alone, abandoned, in my pain. From his perspective, he had a problem, and was confident he could fix it. From mine, I had been betrayed, and I had to figure out whether I could forgive him. He seemed determined and optimistic about the possibility of change, and the therapists seemed encouraging about it too, if he was willing to stay committed to working on it.

In my own session with the family therapist, I told her I was having a hard time understanding Anthony's "game." I told her I didn't know if I could ever trust Anthony again. I told her I had no experience in relationships, that Anthony was my first and only. I told her about my nightmares. I told her I felt like I was always being watched, that I had lost all semblance of privacy and that my inner life had been badly shaken after the news of my pregnancy had leaked. I told her that I was insecure about my place in the world, that I no longer knew whom I could trust.

Toward the end, I tentatively raised the issue my friend had written me about. In 2011, the term sex addiction was not widely known, certainly not part of the everyday lexicon. I had heard about celebrities taking time off and seeking treatment for alcohol or drug addictions but not for sex addictions. "Is this even a thing?" I asked. The therapist jotted something down and said the team would address this in their report. The sessions ended that afternoon at five. Emotionally drained, we made it back to our hotel and ordered room service again, before falling into a fitful night of sleep.

On day two, Anthony was less defensive and spoke about himself in a way that made me understand more about his inner life, and I learned much that I hadn't known about him. He rarely allowed himself to appear vulnerable, to express insecurity. He confessed that when David Remnick from the *New Yorker*, whom we both admired, had reached out to do a profile of him, he didn't think he was worthy enough to be a subject. That if anyone looked too closely, he feared they would find that there was nothing really there. It began to feel like this recent behavior was less about women, and more about fulfilling the need for validation. What I heard made me more sympathetic toward him.

By the end of the day, I felt better just having gotten everything off my chest, as well as more hopeful that we could overcome together whatever this was. At the end of the sessions, we decided to venture out for an early dinner at a restaurant.

It was still daylight, and we were grateful to be liberated from the stale air of hotel and conference rooms, when it happened for the first time.

"Oh my God, is that Weiner? Hey! Weeiner. Weeiner." The catcalling, the laughing, the whistling, the foul-mouthed references to his tweeted image, all followed. Anthony stared straight ahead, ignoring the group of young men sitting at the outdoor table. My right hand clasped his and my left went to my belly. I defiantly stared right back at the faces with their twisted mouths, their eyes hungrily reveling in our shame. I suddenly felt protective of Anthony. It felt like an assault on *my family*.

About two weeks later, we received the ten-page report in the mail. The professionals we'd seen had done an evaluation of Anthony's life and how his transgressions fit into it, based on all the things they had learned from the days with him alone and the days with us jointly.

Since this is Anthony's story to tell in full, or not, as he chooses, I will share only the broad overview, insofar as it related to me. I was married to a narcissist. Specifically, what they determined was that there was "disturbance in the self-structure that affects his sense of self-esteem and personal identity." What I wanted to know was how to fix it, and the report addressed that too.

The clinic's report recommended therapists in New York who specialized in treatment and stressed that the most important steps were that Anthony be in regular therapy and that the two of us go to couples therapy and find ways to spend dedicated time together. I was diagnosed as suffering from a form of PTSD due to this seismic event, which was why I was having nightmares, and they suggested that I too talk to someone, to get some help with the trauma I was experiencing.

The report also answered the question I had asked in my private session. "Our evaluation does not show any evidence that Mr. Weiner is a true sex addict. He lacks the history or the intense drive to have sex with strangers that is so characteristic of sex addiction."

* * * *

Our first meeting with the couples therapist in New York began with Anthony asking the same simple questions: how to explain the compulsion, how to stop it, and how to regain my trust. At home, our conversations always circled back to stopping the behavior, and he repeated how important that was to him. Deep down, I began to feel more confident.

Still, life as I'd known it, or parts of life anyway, had become unrecognizable. Work was much the same. It called me away for long periods and was a relief. But a tectonic shift in our social life had been set in motion, so that it was never to return to what it had been. From the moment the scandal broke, our presence at social functions seemed to make people uncomfortable; conversations sometimes halted when we entered a room, smiles became strained.

Earlier in the spring, an old friend had invited us to a large summer destination party. Many of my friends would be there and I looked forward to this escape. Knowing that our presence might cause a spectacle, I sent the hostess a note asking if it was still okay to attend. Her note back was full of love and support, saying how much she looked forward to welcoming us.

The trip was an extravagance for us but one we felt would be well worth the expense because we would be surrounded by people who loved us. It was to some extent following doctors' orders too. They had recommended that we find ways and places to spend quality time together. We bought the tickets and booked the hotel. A day before we were to leave, I received a second, apologetic email from the hostess saying that another couple had asked her to tell me that they would not attend if we did. The couple could not in good conscience appear as though they were condoning "immoral behavior."

I read the words over and over, until they started to blur, until they were just loops and lines on a screen. Then I heard from the couple directly. As much as they wanted to be supportive of me, they just couldn't be in a room with Anthony. That single email represented the rupture between the friendships I had counted on before and what they have become since. It was also a moment where I had to choose. I could certainly have gone alone. But I didn't. I chose my family.

In hindsight, I realized a few things. First, that the party would probably have been a miserable experience for everyone, including us; our presence would have taken the attention away from the host couple, whom we would have put in a really uncomfortable situation, and we would have regretted going. Second, I fully respect and in a way am grateful to the couple who objected to our presence. I learned later they weren't the only ones who felt as they did, just the only ones forthright enough to tell me directly rather than whispering behind my back.

That July, for our first wedding anniversary, we spent the weekend in Miami Beach. Anthony rented a small boat for a surprise sunset cruise, and we spent a couple of hours under a sticky, windy, cloudy sky. Exactly one year before, we had been surrounded by all our friends and family celebrating our new life together. Now it was just the two and a half of us floating on Biscayne Bay.

THE BEST YEAR

The first time the baby kicked Anthony and I were in Italy. We had never managed to take a proper honeymoon after our wedding, so it felt like a babymoon was well warranted. Plus, with my BlackBerry and my body long accustomed to working in different time zones, I justified that it would be a working vacation anyway. Anthony felt so badly about my missing my friend's party, he asked one day, "Where did your parents never take you that you have always wanted to visit?" Without hesitating, I replied, "The Amalfi coast."

Until our plane touched down, I hadn't realized how much I needed to flee New York, where I was beginning to feel like a zoo animal, stared at, pointed at, photographed. Now we were in a place where no one knew who we were, where we could just be: a newly married couple, expecting their first child, adventuring together, searching for hotels online, trying out new foods. He wasn't a disgraced former congressman; I wasn't an aide to one of the most influential women in the world, or the wronged wife. We wandered through Capri, Ravello, and wound our way up and down Positano, just regular tourists eating pasta and two gelatos a day. I took frequent breaks to check my BlackBerry or join a conference call. When my feet got too swollen to comfortably fit into my shoes, we stopped at a sandal-making stall to buy a pair, and my feet felt liberated. When my jeans felt too snug on my belly, Anthony walked down to the market by the water and bought me a white cotton dress that was light and loose, and I felt even less constricted.

Over long lunches and dinners we began to talk about how to communicate better with each other. How he needed to be more honest about his insecurities, and to try to look at the betrayal from my

319

perspective. How I needed to be more aware of what was going on in his life and not take him so much for granted. We were blissfully anonymous—until Philippe emailed news stories about us, noting where we ate, where we walked, and where we shopped. These days, it seemed, someone was always watching.

When we returned after Labor Day, I was certain enough of our path forward that I told Anthony I would move to New York full-time after the baby was born. Also, that I wanted to leave Queens and live in Manhattan. In the report, the therapists had supported the idea of a fresh start and moving to a new home, which was fine with me. I wanted to be closer to Heba when I had the baby anyway. I knew Anthony loved Forest Hills and preferred to stay there, but he said, "Whatever you want," and immediately began looking for a place in Manhattan. We listed our Queens apartment for sale, and a tabloid newspaper outed it as our home. I only found out about that when a woman I knew stopped by my table at a restaurant in Manhattan to make small talk. "By the way," she said, "I am sure you are glad to be out of that little place. It must have been so hard to manage there." Scanning her Balenciaga purse, her perfectly frosted blonde hair, her Manolo heels, I bit my tongue. What I wanted to say was that it was actually a very comfortable middle-class home and that I had spent some of my happiest days there. "Thank you," I said and let her walk away.

In the Gramercy Park neighborhood Anthony found an apartment that I fell in love with. It was big enough that we could have a home office and a guest room for my mom, who I knew would stay with us a lot once the baby arrived. It was on a floor too high for anyone to peer in. It was also well beyond our means: I was on a government salary, and had emptied my checking and savings accounts to pay for the wedding. So Anthony would have to bear the burden of paying for it with whatever consulting work he could get. When I asked him if we could afford the apartment, he should have said *no!* with a bright flashing neon sign. Instead he said, "If this is what you want, of course we can." We were repeating a common pattern in our relationship: Anthony always taking care of the details, always accommodating me, always making my life easy—in every way except one.

* * * *

Back at the State Department, ignoring what was happening to me became much harder now that my six-month baby bump was quite pronounced. Most people congratulated me, others still couldn't bring themselves to acknowledge it. Our team was preparing for the two weeks HRC would be spending in New York for the annual United Nations General Assembly meeting. The President and other senior cabinet and administration officials would be in attendance as well, and it would be the first time I would see many of them for a sustained period of time.

When President Obama was in New York for leader-level meetings, HRC's schedule was dictated by his; as secretary of state, she joined many of his gatherings with foreign leaders. On the first day of this trip, I walked with her to a meeting with the President at the Waldorf Astoria. I hadn't been in close proximity to the President since the story broke. Over the summer, at meetings in the White House, I had studiously avoided being in his sight line. Now, when he saw me, he walked over, gave me a hug, asked how I was doing, and reminded me to take care of myself. Over the coming years, during other trips, on the sidelines of meetings, at long dinners, anytime his and HRC's schedules crossed paths, the President would check in on me, ask a question or just chat briefly. In his own way, he always made me feel less like the elephant in the room and more like a valued and respected member of his team. I never conveyed to him how much his kindness and his generosity helped get me through those sometimes impossible days.

* * * *

In October, HRC was scheduled for a long trip to Malta, Libya, Oman, Afghanistan, Pakistan, Tajikistan, and Uzbekistan. It would be another beast to plan, and though I considered proposing dropping one or two of the stops, each felt urgent and in line with the State Department's strategic mission for the year, so we pressed forward. In Libya, opposition forces seeking to oust longtime dictator Muammar Gaddafi had taken control of Tripoli with the help of coalition forces, and Gaddafi had fled the city. In Oman, HRC would be meeting with the sultan to begin the dialogue leading to the secret back-channel talks that would eventually result in the Iran nuclear deal. Afghanistan had long been on our list for a visit because of an impending American troop withdrawal. The Central Asia stops were places we had committed to visiting much earlier in the year when we had decided that human rights would be a core part of HRC's message in that region. In each of the countries we visited, she pushed the leadership on lifting restrictions on civil society. All these trips were building toward a big end-of-the-year speech to the Human Rights Council in Geneva, where she would state that "gay rights are human rights and human rights are gay rights" in an echo of her 1995 Beijing speech about women's rights.

I was knee-deep in planning when Claire popped into my office to say that the State Department medical unit had asked to speak with me urgently. They recommended I not travel. This seemed preposterous to me. In my second trimester, my energy had come back and my pregnancy was easy and symptom-free. "Are you telling me or advising me?" I asked when I called the medical unit. They said it was their strong advice, so after consulting with HRC, I decided to call my obstetrician.

I love Dr. Sassoon. He is a tall, dashing, worldly man, with a gentle and reassuring manner. When I called him and listed the countries and dates, he laughed, "Do they think you are a porcelain doll? You are healthy and it's a low-risk pregnancy. I am totally comfortable with your going." So I did.

A few days later, my rather large belly made a cameo appearance as I handed my phone to HRC in between interviews with the news that Muammar Gaddafi was dead.

*　*　*　*

The baby was due on New Year's Eve. By mid-December, there was more to do than there was time to do it. Work had not gotten less busy, and on top of that I had just sold my apartment in Washington, which meant I was organizing and packing the last sixteen years of my life. Since there is no paid maternity leave policy for federal government employees, I submitted forms to the Human Resources office to take vacation and sick leave to add up to three months. I didn't want to be away that long, but everyone I talked to said *you won't know how you feel until you have the baby*, so it seemed best to set aside the time.

My friend Rory Tahari threw me a small baby shower in New York with a few friends. I didn't want anything bigger, but HRC and a lot of my Washington friends decided to organize a second shower at the home of Rima Al-Sabah, one of the most gracious and generous hostesses in Washington. What was even more special than the beautiful and elegant surroundings was how many people came. After six months of feeling insecure, here I was surrounded by a hundred women all of whom I loved and admired. Had I been wrong to think I was an outcast? Had my own feelings of shame given me a distorted lens through which I assumed other people viewed me too? After the toasts, I told everyone that 2011 would end up being the best year of my life.

Rima's baby shower took place on Saturday, December 17. I had awakened that morning to find that I had bled a little bit. Dr. Sassoon told me it was something called a bloody show, a common sign of prelabor. "Call me if you need to, but it's nothing to worry about now and I will see you on Tuesday. It just means the little guy is getting ready. He might be here very soon."

"That just isn't going to work for me," I joked, listing off all the things I needed to get done in the next two weeks. I hung up with him, and then patted my belly and said, "Stay in there, little one."

At my Tuesday checkup, Dr. Sassoon seemed even more confident that the birth was imminent. "I hope your bag is packed. You're already three centimeters dilated. I'll be seeing you at the hospital tomorrow." Anthony was ecstatic. I was still in denial. The due date, December 31, was eleven days away. Both men laughed at my continued insistence that I was not ready.

When we got home, I pulled out my little notebook and looked at the unchecked boxes on the list of things to do before the baby. They were too numerous to do much about now but I decided to chip away at what I could. I tidied the apartment, did some laundry, reluctantly packed my go bag, and cooked a large pot of penne pasta with spicy chickpeas and spinach. I texted Heba to let her know what the doctor had said. I had been in the delivery room when she had two of her children, and I wanted her with me when I had mine. "Call me, even if it's the middle of the night," she said, and reminded me that when she went into labor with her first child, it had been a full day and night before my nephew came into the world. I used that as my benchmark, and was sure that Dr. Sassoon was wrong, that nothing would happen for at least another couple of days. So I told no one else in my family or at work.

Anthony and I ate the pasta and started a movie. Midway through I left Anthony in the bedroom and got up to return to my laptop. At some point, I woke up, having nodded off in front of my computer. I popped my head into the bedroom to find that Anthony had fallen asleep in front of the television. I felt pressure in my belly and headed into the kitchen, suddenly feeling very hungry. Standing at the stove, I ate the rest of the pasta straight out of the pot, adding extra red pepper flakes. I looked at the clock: 12:42 a.m. I decided the responsible thing to do would be to try to get some sleep. I went to lie down, but I was up every thirty minutes or so, the pressure in my belly coming and going. Was this labor? Wasn't it supposed to hurt?

Around 2:30 a.m., I shook Anthony. "I think I am having contractions." He was immediately alert, grabbed the pencil and paper, and started timing them. There was no steady rhythm. It was long periods then shorter, then long again.

"Why don't we call Sassoon?" he said at around 4 a.m.

"I am not bothering him in the middle of the night!"

Anthony was incredulous. "Honey, that is his job!"

I was insistent. I was still not even sure I was really in active labor. *Isn't labor supposed to hurt?* I kept thinking. I waited until 7 a.m., which seemed like a decent hour to bother a doctor, and his call service patched him through immediately. When he got on the phone, I listed the span between each contraction, now pretty consistently at two minutes or less, and he told us to head to the hospital as soon as we could and that he would meet us there. I took a hot shower, relaxing as the water fell over my shoulders and belly. Reluctantly, I turned off the water. I'd had a few contractions standing there. They still didn't hurt. The pressure was intense, but mostly I marveled at the power I felt within my body.

When we got in the car to drive to the hospital, I called my mom. She had been planning to take leave from her job at Dar Al-Hekma so she could be with me for the delivery and in the weeks after, and I knew missing the baby's birth would upset her. When I told her I was on my way to the hospital, she exclaimed, "Huma, why didn't you wait for me?!"

Mom started rattling off her plans to get on the next flight, and I felt a sharp, searing pain in my side. It took my breath away. I handed the phone to Anthony while I lowered the window to breathe some fresh air.

When we got to the hospital, I resisted being put in a wheelchair, because I felt much better standing, but I did what I was told and braved the few minutes of questions as we checked in at the nurses station. In the birthing room, a nurse examined me and then said, "Girl, where have you been?" She looked at the clock: 8:45 a.m. "You will be out of here by noon."

Sassoon sailed in, calm and cheerful, broke my water and told me I was 7 centimeters dilated, pretty far along. "Do you still want the epidural?" So far, the pain hadn't been too bad, but I opted to get one since that had been the plan we settled on during our last doctor's visit. The birthing team encouraged me to rest so that I would have energy to push when the time came. Then they shut off the lights and left.

Heba arrived bearing my favorite decaf coffee and a comfy set of black pajamas. She and Anthony sat with me, each admonishing me to rest as I continued to respond to emails. From time to time, a nurse would check on me, see how frequent my contractions were and how far dilated I was, to determine when I would be ready to actively start pushing. Then I dialed into my trip call. Václav Havel, the famed human rights activist, playwright, and leader of the Velvet Revolution who had gone on to become president of a democratic Czechoslovakia, had died a few days earlier, and HRC was scheduled to leave for his funeral in less than twenty-four hours. Soon after the call I started to doze off, and then thirty minutes later, the lights flicked on bright and the nurses were back in my room. It was time, they said. Heba was on my left, Anthony was on my right as I began to push. A few minutes later, I noticed the nurse and doctor whispering to each other. "What's wrong?" I asked. I looked at Heba, who was rubbing my back, and then at Anthony, who was holding my right arm and ankle. The room silent.

"Dr. Sassoon, is everything okay?"

My panic came on fast. I could survive anything but was terrified that the baby might be hurt. The doctor turned to me and spoke very deliberately.

"Just listen to me. When I tell you to, I need you to push as hard as you can. Can you do that for me? Everything you've got. But not till I tell you."

When he told me to push, I did what he said. And then again. That was it. It was so fast it felt like a sudden explosion when this little being burst into the world, heart beating, mouth open, eyes scrunched, a little alien-looking but all mine. Ours. A human being we had brought into the world.

Anthony and I both started crying, overwhelmed. I managed to remember to whisper the *adhan* in our baby's ear quickly, an Islamic tradition to ensure that the first words an infant hears are an allegiance to one God. The words are usually spoken by the father, and though Anthony had gamely offered to do it, I wanted to say them myself.

There were many things related to this baby that I had been unprepared for, but what I was least prepared for was the feeling of love so overpowering, so satisfying, so necessary to my existence. Already, I couldn't remember what life was like before him. Someone called out the time of birth: 11:45 a.m. Only three hours earlier, I had walked into the hospital, and just as the nurse had said, this little being was in my arms before noon. It was as though God had decided I'd had enough challenges this year. He couldn't just hand me this child, but the birth would be as easy as any woman could possibly hope for. That moment of high alert while I was pushing had been something minor that Sassoon had easily managed but since my mind was always so tuned to the possibility of bad news, I had immediately jumped to worst-case scenarios. Now life felt as close to perfect as it could ever be.

Heba and Anthony emailed family, friends, and colleagues with the news. Jake responded immediately, "I don't understand. I was on a conference call with her an hour ago." HRC was on a shuttle to New York, and when she landed at noon, she drove straight to the hospital from the airport, and Chelsea joined her. They were the first people to meet the baby and I hoped no one would tell my mom.

The first few days were a blur, with dozens of people coming by to see us. When we had to file the paperwork for the birth certificate, Anthony sat in the chair by me and asked, "What do you want to name him?" Over the summer, we had discussed options. Anthony wanted to name him after his grandfather, Wolf. I had always wanted my child to have a name that was universal. Having spent my entire life saying my name, then repeating it, then spelling it, I wanted to spare him that. We settled on Jordan Zain, after the Jordan River, which connected the two peoples our baby descended from, and of course, my father. My mother arrived from Jeddah a day after Jordan Zain was born, much to my relief. From the minute she walked into the hospital room, I felt at ease. She had been on hand for the arrivals of many of her ten other grandchildren and she took over like a pro.

The hospital had a protocol in place where they buzzed the room before allowing anyone to come through. On the first day, they made people wait at the desk until Anthony or another relative retrieved them. After the first twenty-four hours, the influx of visitors was so overwhelming, they shifted to announcing the names through an old speaker on the wall behind my bed, so we had a heads-up but nobody had to run down the hall. Crackle, "Bari is on her way in." Crackle, "Monica is coming down." On the second day, as I was nursing Jordan, I heard the crackle, "Krrrtt is on the way in." I perked up. "Who?" Anthony sat up in his chair. He couldn't make out the name either. Maybe just another relative from New Jersey, so I rested my head back and continued nursing. Then, after a nagging second or two, we both said, "Maybe we should check." My brother-in-law stepped into the hallway, and sure enough, the person he intercepted was a reporter from one of the New York tabloid papers. It was a near miss.

We brought Jordan home the next day. Our new apartment was still sparsely furnished. We had given away Anthony's bachelor furniture from the apartment in Forest Hills, which had seen better days, brought what we easily could from my place in Washington, but we were still waiting for the chairs for the dining table and seating for our living room. The nursery, on the other hand, I had lavished attention on, and it was complete.

We were operating in a newborn haze scented by baby laundry detergent, fresh flowers, and good food simmering on the stove courtesy of my mother, who now occupied our guest room. Visitors were steady and plentiful, and baby gifts overwhelmed first the nursery and then our living room. I ate everything I craved. I followed a careful schedule of nursing and kept meticulous account of each diaper change to report to the pediatrician. We went out for daily walks through Christmas and New Year's, being sure to cover the stroller with a blanket in case a photographer was waiting outside the apartment building. The photographers were always friendly and chatty, trying to get a reaction, anything, to make a more interesting picture. While Anthony had always seemed unfazed by photographers following, I was still irked by this new reality.

For my mother, who especially wasn't used to them, the reporters were a constant reminder of the reason we were of public interest in the first place, and they made her anxious. So she remained holed up in the apartment. One day, I persuaded her to join us for lunch a few blocks away. She bundled up, and tried her best to ignore the camera flashes and questions as we walked down the street. Anthony and I had a habit of walking fast once we saw the reporters were going to trail us, and my mother had a hard time keeping up with us. We didn't make it very far before she suddenly stopped walking, put her hand on her chest, and seemed to be struggling to breathe. What was happening? Was it a heart attack? I helped her sit on the sidewalk while we called a doctor friend who suggested we take her straight to the hospital. Since I was still nursing around the clock, Anthony spent the night at the hospital with Mom. It hurt not to be with her when I was so worried about her, but it turned out she'd had nothing more serious than a panic attack. Once I heard that, I stopped worrying—about anything. The new little human in our lives made everything else, all the things that had seemed so enormous and overwhelming and hurtful before, seem petty, small, unimportant.

One day I bundled Jordan up in a baby carrier to take a walk. The same photographer who was there most days appeared from a hidden corner to take pictures, then asked how I was doing, how the baby was doing, where Anthony was. I gave him a faint smile but looked down and kept walking. He ran up ahead of me.

"Just a few more! Can you look this way, Huma? Can you turn the baby to the front? Huma please?"

I was desperate to say, *just leave me alone*, after six months of photographers constantly following me down streets, into coffee shops. Still cheerful and not missing a beat he said, "I am sorry. So sorry. But you have to understand. I gotta make a living. " In that moment, my frustration with him subsided. This was not ill will toward Anthony or me or even HRC. This was a story to sell—about us, but not ours. Shame was not going away. Not for a long time.

PATRIOT OR SPY

Fools multiply when wise men are silent.
—Nelson Mandela

All day each day, I felt tied to this new being, as he was to me, and while I was often tired and definitely sleep-deprived, I never felt dragged down. I just took Jordan with us wherever we went, and he began to feel like a natural extension of my body, just as he had been when he was in my belly. I nursed him at friends' apartments, in restaurants, in the park. During night feeds, I would sit in the white rocker in the nursery, reading *Catherine the Great* by Robert Massie until one or both of us had nodded off, only to stir when Anthony picked Jordan up from my lap and walked me back to our bed. Every morning, Anthony would bundle him up for their daily father-son adventures while I tried to catch a little more sleep.

After a blissful two weeks at home over the holiday season, as we ushered in a new year, I was ready to get back into work. I didn't want one world or the other. I wanted both, and having both seemed entirely possible. Maybe if Jordan had been colicky or fussy or more demanding, I wouldn't have felt I had the bandwidth to do more. Maybe if Anthony had not always been available, eager to take Jordan off my hands, I would have been too overwhelmed to think about doing anything else. Maybe if I had had a particular expectation of motherhood, I would have done it differently, but I didn't. I would do the best I could in both realms, and not punish myself for falling short.

My leave technically lasted through March 2012, although I began to call into meetings at the beginning of January, two weeks after Jordan was born. There were many hours during the day when Jordan would just lie in his bouncer on the floor by my desk sleeping quietly or staring around the room, eyes alert, drooling or cooing every so often but otherwise not interrupting my work. I had conceived him easily, carried him easily, birthed him easily, so it was no surprise that as a little human, he was just that. Easy.

In Hillaryland, it was easy too. I was in an environment where colleagues allowed me plenty of leeway as I figured out how to rebalance after such a life-altering event. Neither HRC nor Cheryl nor anyone else I spoke with suggested I couldn't do my job and do it well. They had both been working mothers to young children and had long advocated for policies that supported families. We all just figured that together we'd make it work.

When Jordan was two months old, HRC's senior team was overdue for our core team strategic planning meetings to map out our travel planning priorities for 2012. These were my primary responsibility to organize, so I was scheduled to be in Washington for a long, full day in early March and little Jordan made his DC debut. When I walked into the State Department, embraced by enthusiastic colleagues who came by to meet him while he sat curious and alert, I thought, *Okay I can swing this. I can do both.* That is, until it was time for his feeding and I realized I had left the bottles of pumped milk at the hotel we had just checked out of.

Panicked, I called the concierge, only to be told that housekeeping had tossed them out.

Now I was due in Cheryl's office for our two-hour planning meeting. With no other option, I told Cheryl I would need to nurse Jordan during the meeting. She looked up from her computer screen and said, "Okay great!" Then I lifted a now fussy and hungry Jordan out of his stroller, covered him lightly in a blanket, and proceeded to nurse him. HRC, Cheryl, and Lona were completely unfazed, though I couldn't say the same for Jake and Philippe; they fidgeted in their seats until they had their backs to me.

* * * *

I was starting to adjust to my new normal, living in New York full-time and commuting to Washington for meetings. It was no longer feasible or appropriate for me to be a full-time State Department employee after my leave was over at the end of March. So, after another round of meetings with the personnel management office, I signed paperwork to have my status switched to special government employee, or what was called an SGE, which is basically like a consultant to the federal government, a fairly common designation for those who have employment outside the agency they are advising. At State, there were many others who functioned as SGEs. I would no longer make my full government salary and would need to begin to keep a time sheet with hours I spent on State Department work.

Since HRC had announced it would be her last year at the department, and since I would be leading her transition to life post-State, we agreed that it would be more appropriate for me to be paid separately, both by HRC personally and by the Clinton Foundation. Then I took on another role, mostly to keep up with the additional expenses of our new life with a baby in Manhattan. Doug Band, President Clinton's advisor, hired me as a consultant with Doug's new corporate advisory firm, Teneo. At the foundation I strategized with colleagues on the three initiatives that HRC might undertake when she left State— programs focused on women, on early childhood education, and on wildlife preservation. At Teneo, I mostly helped advise on an event they were organizing in the fall and attended internal brainstorming meetings.

Anthony had taken on consulting work with a few private clients. We were able to pay our bills and to settle into a comfortable routine. This new life we had cobbled together was better than any we would have had if he'd stayed in Congress, a job that would have forced him to sprint back and forth between Washington and New York, sometimes daily. I probably would not have been able to keep my job, or to take on my additional roles, if we hadn't had the flexibility his work afforded us. He would take a few meetings a day, hold conference calls while bouncing Jordan on his knee, and that would be it. If HRC needed me I could always agree to last-minute changes to my schedule and Anthony would adjust his own accordingly.

From time to time, an old advisor would pop by for a visit, suggesting that Anthony could resurrect his political career. With the

2013 mayor's race coming up, there was almost universal acknowledgment among people we knew that he had the right mix of smarts, straight talk, and charisma that New Yorkers appreciated. Before he had resigned from Congress, he had said in public several times that he had a "passing interest in the management of New York." But we never talked about it after Jordan was born. Anthony was so besotted with fatherhood that little else competed for his time or attention.

Anthony and I worked on our relationship as best we could, but since I hadn't realized we had a problem before his texting scandal, it was difficult to pin down what exactly needed repair. It's hard to fix something when you don't see where it is broken. We were diligent about date night once a week. Anthony encouraged me to indulge in self-care—manicures or blow-outs—and to sleep in on weekend mornings while he played with Jordan in the living room. I don't recall a single argument from that time in our lives together, though there was plenty of new-parent worry to occupy our conversations: Did Jordan have a fever? Had he slept enough? Should we try rice cereal or oat cereal first? Do I need to make homemade purees or was jarred fruit okay?

I fully believed that Anthony had stopped his online activities after his and our whole world collapsed—that the shame and the guilt and the sheer stupidity of it had scarred him as deeply and searingly as it had me. In part because I had never really understood the benefits of therapy, I felt like I wasn't the person in the relationship who actually needed it, so our weekly sessions together became less frequent, and when I found my solo sessions unenlightening and pointless, I stopped going. When Anthony returned from his solo sessions, he would share a story about an issue he'd debated with his therapist, like healthcare or taxes. "Aren't you supposed to be talking about you?" I'd ask, and he would always respond, "Yeah yeah, we did that too."

Sometimes, I suggested that family or friends meet with him and help get him refocused on his career. In most cases, when I followed up with them, they would say that Anthony had given them a great idea for their business or that he was solving some other problem for them. Oh, and that he seemed to be "doing great!" His public persona was always upbeat and confident. He was totally reliable in every way—a considerate caretaker, a family provider, a good father, a loyal friend. Always the person who was fixing everyone else's problems. So who, in the end, could fix him? Certainly not me, though he had outright asked me to on that last magical New Year's Eve in Punta Cana. Back when I was inexperienced, untouched, and unprepared in so many ways.

I never probed deeply. I didn't have the tools to understand that Anthony's inner life might be much more complicated than it seemed, that his easy confidence that he could quit his online activities was not warranted. It seemed that we were back on track.

The only out-of-character thing I agreed to do that spring was appear in an article in *People* magazine and pose for a family photo when Jordan was six months old. I didn't make the decision lightly. After the scandal had first broken and it was revealed I was pregnant, interview offers came in from everywhere. Reporters and talk show hosts who normally emailed interview requests for my boss now wanted to talk to me. I said no to them all. Doing *People* went against my initial instincts. Then I made a discovery.

The day Jordan was born, I had asked Anthony to keep a copy of the New York newspapers as a birthday keepsake for Jordan. A few weeks after we got home, I found the saved papers buried in a drawer. I unfolded them and was horrified. It had been front-page news in New York and its characterization made me sick. What child gets welcomed into the world with "Pop Goes the Weiner" or "Baby boy for Huma and louse"? So we posed for *People* and talked a little about our post-scandal life with Sandra Sobieraj, whom I had known and respected since she was a White House correspondent during the Clinton administration. It was a short, sweet piece, one I could actually save for Jordan, with a picture of the three of us and an interview with Anthony and me in which we talked about nothing more newsworthy than laundry and diapers. I was glad to have something out in the world connected to my family that didn't feel smarmy or sleazy.

*   *   *   *

The year before Jordan's birth had featured some extreme highs and lows in my personal life, but it was an even more tumultuous year on the international front, marked by a surge of populist uprisings coursing throughout the Middle East, demanding rapid change in real time.

On December 17, 2010, a Tunisian fruit seller, shamed by a female police officer for selling goods without a permit, set himself on fire. He had been working without the proper documents because their cost in bribes was out of his reach, and he was forced to choose between starving or making a living the only way he knew how. His public self-immolation was a searing cry of hopelessness, helplessness, frustration, and degradation, an indictment of conditions that were common, widespread, and unacceptable. It unleashed pent-up frustration with the status quo in Tunisia, lit a fuse in other countries in the region, and sparked the Arab Spring.

A few weeks later HRC and our team were bound for the United Arab Emirates, Yemen, Oman, and Qatar. HRC wanted to use the trip to express her concern about the current state of affairs in the region: that political and economic conditions were, at best, stagnant; that most Middle Eastern countries didn't have political parties or campaigns or truly democratic election cycles; that unemployment was high, particularly for youth and women; and that corruption in some places was rampant. I had watched HRC raise many of these issues privately in her meetings with leaders over the years. Most, if not all of them, acknowledged that change should come and would come—but in due course.

Before leaving for the trip, we had stopped in New York for a hastily arranged meeting between HRC and the Lebanese president Saad Hariri, who was struggling to hold on to power. Days after they met, his government collapsed. After our New York stop we went to Yemen, where we were hosted by strongman Ali Abdullah Saleh, who had ruled for decades. Saleh exemplified a dilemma Western leaders faced when dealing with partners in the Middle East. On the one hand he was a staunch opponent of Al-Qaeda forces, a defender of Sunni Muslim factions and thus a close ally of Yemen's neighbor and our ally Saudi Arabia, and a reliable partner in the ongoing cold war with Iran. On the other, he ran an autocratic regime, overseeing a fractured nation that had made no economic or social progress, where women and girls had few rights.

Over lunch at the presidential palace, I sat a few seats away as Saleh told HRC how secure Yemen was under his leadership. As if to prove the point, he invited her to take a last-minute unplanned driving tour of the old city.

"You are under my protection. *Wallahi* nothing will happen to her," he assured me when I tried to protest. The tour was fascinating, wending through twisting narrow one-way streets, but it was not lost on me that it would have been quite a feat to escape had there been any hostility directed against us.

Two days later, in Doha, Qatar, at a conference with leaders from the Middle East and North Africa, HRC delivered one of her most pointed speeches. She said, "In too many places, in too many ways, the region's foundations are sinking into the sand. The new and dynamic Middle East that I have seen needs firmer ground if it is to take root and grow everywhere . . . Those who cling to the status quo may be able to hold back the full impact of their countries' problems for a little while, but not forever. If leaders don't offer a positive vision and give young people meaningful ways to contribute, others will fill the vacuum. Extremist elements, terrorist groups, and others who would prey on desperation and poverty are already out there, appealing for allegiance and competing for influence."

The applause that greeted that speech was polite and muted. But change was coming whether these leaders chose to accept it or not—and it was coming fast.

A day after her Doha speech, January 14, President Zine el-Abidine Ben Ali fled Tunisia, seeking asylum in Saudi Arabia, and several months later he and his wife—the woman who told me to be silent back in 1999—were convicted in absentia of embezzlement charges. Within weeks, Yemen's President Saleh, who had been so confident, so certain of his popularity, faced calls for his ouster.

Within days, protests in Tahrir Square in Egypt had swelled to hundreds of thousands as people, connected and united by social media, saw that change could happen, the powerful could fall. By February 11, President Hosni Mubarak, who'd been in power for almost thirty years, had been forced to cede control to the military, and left the capital for his seaside retreat.

Shortly after Mubarak fled Cairo, our plane was headed there. HRC would be the first senior U.S. official on the ground in Egypt to meet with the military leadership, and with the activist leaders who had helped bring about this rapid change.

Like many growing up in the Middle East in the eighties and nineties, I found it difficult to envision an Egypt without Mubarak, who had been in power for most of my life. By design, Mubarak had appointed no successor. Outside of the military, there was only one political party organized enough to fill the void: the conservative Muslim Brotherhood, which in Egypt had a history of violence and extremism. It was not only a political movement but an Islamic social movement providing much-needed services like schools and hospitals, which gave it a constituency long underserved by Mubarak's government. The organization was founded in Egypt, had offshoots in other parts of the Middle East, and had disavowed violence in the 1970s but was still viewed warily in certain quarters.

How would my generation, one that had never known any other leaders or another way, cope with rapid change now that it was suddenly upon them? After we landed in Cairo, HRC met with the activists who had formed a loose alliance of Tahrir Square protestors. HRC asked whether they had begun to form coalitions with one another, and whether any of them might put themselves forward for elective office. Several said they didn't want to engage in the world of politics. They seemed focused only on the purity of their cause, refusing to accept that the only way to hold on to the gains of their movement was to build parties that could govern. I took notes, looking over at HRC and Jake from time to time, feeling increasingly deflated as the meeting proceeded.

The next morning, as HRC waded into the crowd at Tahrir Square herself, a few people came forward to shake her hand. "*Marhaba.*" "Welcome." Arab hospitality at its most basic. No matter what, when guests arrive in your home, you treat them with respect. "Welcome to the new Egypt," someone called out in English.

Six months later, in November 2011, the Muslim Brotherhood

won nearly half the seats in the first parliamentary elections since Mubarak's departure. In the months following, the Brotherhood would continue to consolidate power. Its elevation would present challenges to U.S. policy in the Middle East. And as I would find out the following year, to me too.

* * * *

I was sitting at my desk at State during that first summer after Jordan was born when my desk phone rang. "Before you say anything, hear me out," Philippe said. I assumed he was calling from his office a few floors below with another one of his crazy ideas for an event for HRC, and I was preparing to say, *Whatever it is, Philippe, the answer is no.* But he was not calling about a trip or an interview. He was calling about me.

A congresswoman from Minnesota, Michele Bachmann, along with four other Republican House members, had sent a letter to the inspector generals of the State Department, the Department of Homeland Security, the Department of Justice, the Department of Defense, and the Office of the Director of National Intelligence asking that I be investigated for possible terrorist "infiltration" of the State Department. The "evidence" cited in her letter was a video series on YouTube created by a man identified by the Southern Poverty Law Center as a notorious Islamophobe. The videos served up a slew of wild and totally unsubstantiated allegations against a handful of Obama administration officials who happened to be Muslims. They also slandered my father, my mother, and my brother.

In all my years in the United States, I had never fit neatly into any clear category, and it hadn't mattered one bit. On my U.S. college applications, none of the boxes described me; I wasn't Caucasian, Hispanic, African American, Native American, or Asian American/ Pacific Islander. Without intending to be ironic, it was clear that I was "other," so I marked that box, writing in "South Asian."

My Muslim identity had never adversely impacted my ability to do my job. For the most part—from joining the talks at Camp David to being cleared for Iraq CODELs—my identity had always, *always*, been a plus. The one exception was during HRC's first campaign for the Senate in 2000, when she was visiting a community of Hasidic Jews in New York and a campaign advisor politely suggested that perhaps it would be best for me to wait in the car. In 2007, when our team was deliberating over the fact that HRC's small traveling campaign team needed more diversity, I asked, "What about me?"— only to be laughingly told by a colleague, "You don't count." That was basically right. In 2007, nothing about being South Asian or Muslim made any difference in a presidential election. Not yet, anyway. A year later, Barack Obama, then the Democratic party nominee, would be branded a foreigner, a Muslim, and an Arab—with all the fever-pitch insinuations those associations conjured. Perhaps I should have seen it as a canary in the coal mine, but the then Republican nominee, John McCain, repudiated the attacks, Obama sailed to victory, and the Islamophobic fringe seemed exactly that: fringe.

But now a member of Congress, someone who sat on the House Intelligence Committee, a one-time presidential candidate, had taken the opportunity, and had been joined by four others, to target not just me but also my family. In Bachmann's letter, she wrote, "the Department's Deputy Chief of Staff, Huma Abedin, has three family members—her late father, her mother and her brother—connected to Muslim Brotherhood operatives and/or organizations. Her position affords her routine access to the Secretary and to policy-making." It was preposterous. Philippe assured me he was going to monitor the story and he had a few ideas up his sleeve in case it started to take off.

Although several Muslim government employees were mentioned in Bachmann's letter, I became the focus of the news stories because I had the misfortune of being the most visible: frequently photographed alongside HRC or Anthony. I tried to keep things in perspective. Bachmann was known for her incendiary rhetoric and promotion of fringe-y conspiracy theories. Maybe no one would take her seriously. When I never heard from the Inspector General's Office at State or any other agency, suggesting they were investigating me, I concluded that they did not see merit in the accusations.

I was offended by the accusations, but I was also no stranger to political slander. That was not so for my family. Far more traumatizing than the impact on me was the guilt I felt about the impact on them.

In one single letter, Michele Bachmann spat on my father's sterling academic professional reputation, his respected social standing, and his pious nature. My mother's and brother's good names and reputations, built up over a lifetime of hard work, had been questioned, in a culture where integrity is so valued. Over long-distance calls with my mom in Saudi Arabia and Hassan in England, they assured me they were fine, that they had been shocked by the attacks, yet were far more concerned about me. "Don't make me feel worse than I already do," I told my mom. "I have brought this on all of us *again* and I am so sorry." There was nothing I could do or say to fix this, to correct the record. If I tried, it would add fuel to a story that was so absurd it didn't deserve the attention. Most reasonable people would just dismiss it, but would some believe it?

I began to worry about my family's physical safety too. The Muslim Brotherhood was viewed with suspicion in parts of the Middle East. With all this churning in my head, I turned back to my job, where, as it happened, we were planning a July 2012 trip to Egypt, where a government run by the Muslim Brotherhood political party had won the country's first free presidential election in decades—less than a year after having dominated parliamentary elections.

This time when we got to Cairo, protestors were gathered outside the Four Seasons hotel where we were staying, aiming their frustration at the U.S. secretary of state, this very public symbol of American power. Diplomatic Security briefed me that if protestors made it into the lobby or breached the stairwell or an elevator, they would have to evacuate HRC. They recommended we sleep in our clothes and be prepared to move in the middle of the night. Jake, Philippe, HRC, and I spent the evening talking in HRC's suite about the state of the region. I looked out the window from time to time.

"What are they shouting now?" HRC asked at one point. I couldn't hear their words but their message was clear.

"They are telling us to get lost."

The country was still in a state of upheaval, and sectarian tensions were high. Just weeks before our arrival, there had been an attack on a Coptic Christian teacher by an extremist Muslim. The attack was reciprocated, and now the Christian community, which had been protected under Mubarak, was worried that this was just the beginning of their persecution. After her official meeting with the new president, Mohamed Morsi, HRC was to meet with a group of Christian leaders at the American embassy.

As the discussion at the embassy was beginning, I had to step outside to attend to some minor crisis, but was quickly summoned back to the meeting room. Jake passed me a note that read, "She wants you to stay behind after the meeting—your Brotherhood issue just came up."

A few eyes darted toward me and then looked away when I met their gazes. I had grown accustomed to being in places like Afghanistan, where I could help HRC make a human connection with her fellow dignitaries with comments like "Mr. President, my aide grew up in Saudi Arabia, and she can tell you they ate many pomegranates there just as you do here." No doubt, the Bachmann letter, outlandish as its claims were, had landed as fact at some official meeting thousands of miles away in Egypt. It had sown distrust of the U.S. secretary of state and the U.S. government—all because of me?

As the meeting drew to a close, HRC motioned toward me. "As you can see, Huma has rejoined us, and I think you should talk to her directly and ask her any questions you might have. I can assure you that what you have seen on social media is fabricated and I think spending a few minutes with Huma and staying in touch with her directly would be a good idea." With that, HRC pushed her chair back and stood to leave, breaking up the formality of the setting, forcing others to follow. She had no intention of putting me in front of a firing squad in the presence of the entire Egyptian delegation. Jake leaned over and asked if I wanted him to stay. I told him I would be fine, but I was happy to see Philippe linger in the room, keeping watch.

My accuser, the leader of the group, was tall with short brown hair. We met at the far end of the room, where I offered my hand and formally introduced myself. He shook it limply. He seemed baffled that I had even been at the same table with him. "We have been very concerned reading about you and your background," he opened. "Mrs. Secretary, she told us that these stories about your membership in the Brotherhood have been exaggerated, but as I said, our community is

Cracking the glass ceiling, 2008.

With Nelson Mandela in 2009 at his foundation office in South Africa. It would be the last time I saw him.

27

HRC being greeted by the Saudi foreign minister after landing in Riyadh, Saudi Arabia. I am in the background disembarking unveiled there for the first time in my adult life.

Jake Sullivan and me, the two deputies, briefing the Secretary of State before a meeting.

It rained all day on our
wedding day, but nothing
could compete with the light
I felt coming from within.

July 10, 2010. Surrounded by the people we loved most, we were so happy. And Heba,
as always, had my back.

Oscar de la Renta created my dream wedding dress with embroidery inspired by a family heirloom choker. The world always seemed more perfect when he was in it.

Two-month-old Jordan laughing with First Lady Michelle Obama and HRC on his first trip to Washington, DC.

HRC, Jake Sullivan, Cheryl Mills, Philippe Reines, Lona Valmoro, and me giving our farewell speeches at the State Department. I'm in my preferred location: the background.

34

HRC's daily check-in meeting at State with Lona. This is the room where HRC and I first talked about my pregnancy.

Visiting Senator John McCain and his wife, Cindy, at their ranch in Sedona, Arizona. In his hand is the letter I had just given him thanking him for defending my family's name.

36

When I found campaign offices with the cross streets "Tillary" and "Clinton," it felt meant to be. Taking our first walk in our Brooklyn neighborhood after the 2016 campaign launch.

37

Team Vice Chair: This was a team of rock stars! I was lucky to work with them.

Being silly on the road in Nashville, Tennessee, with Nick Merrill and Marlon Marshall while campaign surrogate Tony Goldwyn and policy advisor Maya Harris prebrief before an event.

39

I turned forty-one on the day HRC accepted the nomination for president at the Democratic National Convention. It was starting out as a pretty extraordinary decade.

At the Met Gala with Katy Perry and
Dasha Zhukova, May 2016.

42

Anna Wintour makes the impossible seem
effortless.

President Obama always
made me feel like a valued
and respected member of
his team.

44

4

Jordan and Mommy.

very concerned about the advice you are giving the U.S. government."
His expression was clear. He totally believed it.

"I am not a member of the Muslim Brotherhood and neither are any members of my family."

"But, but, *they* say you are Brotherhood, that you want to convert everyone to Islam, that you have supported terrorist activities."

"I don't believe in terrorism or violence and have nothing but respect for other people's faiths." I was still calm, still matter-of-fact, and that seemed to rankle him further.

"Your own congresspeople are investigating you. You are saying that this is all lies?"

"Yes, all lies."

This back-and-forth went on for a little while. I kept smiling, and when it was over, he must have been slightly reassured that I wasn't the enemy because he now shook my hand warmly and asked for my email address so he could send me updates or ask me more questions.

While I was glad that I'd had an opportunity to correct the record with this one man, it felt like trying to empty the ocean with a teaspoon. One conversation in the face of thousands of clicks on social media. These stories not only traveled with the speed of light, they also arrived with no cultural context, no understanding of the domestic politics that propelled Michele Bachmann to impugn my family, my fellow Muslim colleagues, and me. The right wing of the Republican Party was increasingly using race and ethnicity as a rallying cry for their base. In the coming years, that fringe would take over the reins of the GOP, but we weren't quite there yet.

I appreciated that this was all much bigger than me. I also knew as I stood in that room with the Coptic Christian man, that my life story had tumbled out of my hands. When the *New York Observer* had labeled me "Hillary's Mystery Woman" in 2007, it was meant in a playful way, a nod to what was viewed as my exotic background and how little was known about me. But now, after Michele Bachmann's letter, in some corners at least, *mysterious* took on a darker implication. Exotic now meant sinister too.

When we got on the plane, I said to Philippe, "Maybe I do need to do something. If he is saying there are thousands of people reading this crap and believing it, I can't just ignore it."

All Philippe said was, "Leave it to me."

* * * *

A day after we returned from our trip, a day before Ramadan was set to begin, Philippe called. "Turn on CNN." I flipped on the TV, and there on the Senate floor stood Senator John McCain, delivering a speech. He said, "Huma represents what is best about America: the daughter of immigrants, who has risen to the highest levels of our government on the basis of her substantial personal merit and her abiding commitment to the American ideals that she embodies so fully," McCain continued and ended, saying, "I am proud to know Huma and to call her my friend." I almost fell back in my chair.

Philippe had called McCain's office and asked if they had seen the letter from Bachmann and the social media explosion that followed. They told Philippe that the senator was outraged and would be making a statement. But none of us had expected this.

In that one speech, John McCain had given me an invaluable gift: a defense of my family's name that would be heard around the world. For weeks, I had felt so frustrated, so completely impotent, screaming into the wind, "This is not true!" I called my mom to tell her about the speech, but it had been breaking news in Saudi too. She had already seen it.

"Abbu would be so proud to have someone like John McCain say those things about you, acknowledging all your efforts, your sacrifices for your country."

What Senator McCain did was more meaningful than simply the restoration of my family's honor. He was standing up to the worst impulses in our politics, and affirming the basic rights and freedoms of all Americans to worship as they wish, to not be considered suspect based on their race or ethnicity or religion. When I called the senator to thank him and told him how much it meant, he gruffly mumbled that anyone would have done what he did. "Hang in there, kid." Vintage McCain.

Other Republicans and Democrats came out in support too.

344

Republican senator Lindsey Graham criticized the attack, as did Republican House speaker John Boehner, following Democratic leader Nancy Pelosi. Even Ed Rollins, who had run Bachmann's presidential campaign, said that Bachmann had a "challenging relationship" with the truth.

Bachmann's fabrications epitomized the phrase "a lie can travel halfway around the world while the truth is still putting on its shoes," especially for people who want to believe the lie. Not even a week had gone by after McCain's statement when an article ran in a New York paper about a man in New Jersey threatening to kill me for being a member of the Brotherhood. I had just landed in New York from DC and was in a cab headed home when HRC's head of Diplomatic Security called to check in on me; so did the Secret Service. I thanked them for reaching out. For the first time in my life, I was nervous about my physical safety.

When I walked into my apartment that evening, Anthony was on the phone in the kitchen leaning against the counter, his head bent. I picked up Jordan, now seven months old, and then had a sudden panic. Had I locked the door? Could someone have followed me? Our photo had been taken so many times walking in and out of the building, could the address have been visible? Was the Duane Reade pharmacy or the nail salon on the ground floor easily identifiable? I went back to double bolt the door and lower the shades, even though we were twelve floors up, where no one could possibly see in. Anthony hung up after saying, "She just walked in. I will let her know."

"Who was that?" I asked. He said it was NYC Police commissioner Ray Kelly, that the police intended to locate and interview the man who had made the threat. In the meantime, he suggested we stay alert. They would be sending a patrol car to drive by our building from time to time. The press stories mentioned that my security detail was going to be augmented, given the death threat. I almost called Philippe to say we should correct the piece—I did not have a security detail—but stopped myself. If someone was considering hurting me, let him believe I had protection.

We sat down to break the day's fast, and in my prayers that night I asked God to not let anything bad happen to me in front of my son.

* * * *

President Obama's annual iftar dinner was always a highlight, and this year was no exception. When I received the invitation, I immediately RSVP'd yes. I got a follow-up call a few days later from Rumana Ahmed, the National Security Council aide at the White House who organized the dinner, asking me if I was sure I was coming. I confirmed I was. "Did you not get my RSVP?" I asked. Yes she had, she said, she was just checking.

On the evening of August 10, I entered the White House through the east arrivals gate, and walked through the East Wing, up the familiar staircase that landed at the marble-columned foyer of the State Floor, and mingled with friends and colleagues on the gold-bordered red carpet outside of the grand rooms.

"I am *so* glad you made it," Rumana said as she hugged me. I was too. I was with my people. The tables in the State Dining Room sparkled with crystal and candles, the centerpiece blooms burst with color, and the tables were set with the Clinton china. I remembered when HRC had created a gold-bordered charger plate that easily matched all other White House china, and there it was adorning each setting. The only significant difference between this event and most other White House meals: no alcohol was served. We all mingled until sunset, then broke our fasts with dates passed around on silver platters.

It was only when I walked to my seat and saw my place card, not in the middle or the back of the room as I was used to, but right up front, next to the podium, in a seat beside the President of the United States, that I understood why Rumana had been so diligent. I looked up and she smiled and nodded from across the room. My *ummah*, this community of Muslims in government, was showing me they were standing with me. They were acknowledging that I was publicly bearing the brunt of the nasty, negative stories, the hate and discrimination online and off, that had been aimed at them too.

When President Obama walked in and sat down next to me after greeting other tables, I stayed quiet so he could talk to the other guests. Then we made small talk.

"How is your mother?" he asked, remembering that she had attended the dinner the year before.

"She's still recovering from the fact that you knew what *keema* is," I said of the traditional minced beef dish that is a staple in Pakistani homes.

Once the speaking part of the program began, Obama acknowledged many of the other Muslims in government, and thanked the two Muslim members of congress, Keith Ellison and André Carson, for their service. Having planned many of these events during the Clinton Administration, it was familiar territory to me. Each year I worked at the White House, I was among the staff who suggested which Muslims to honor.

I applauded along with everyone else, and then the President turned to look at me and continued speaking. "They are entrepreneurs and lawyers, community leaders, members of our military, and Muslim American women serving with distinction in government. And that includes a good friend, Huma Abedin, who has worked tirelessly in the White House, in the U.S. Senate, and most exhaustingly, at the State Department, where she has been nothing less than extraordinary in representing our country and the democratic values that we hold dear. Senator Clinton has relied on her expertise, and so have I. The American people owe her a debt of gratitude—because Huma is an American patriot, and an example of what we need in this country— more public servants with her sense of decency, her grace, and her generosity of spirit. So, on behalf of all Americans, we thank you so much."

The moment he said my name, I had an out-of-body experience. His words rang in my ears, but it didn't really click that it was me he was talking about. This was, among other things, about confronting the Islamophobia that had sprung out into the open following the September 11 attacks, more than a decade earlier. Obama was calling it out, proclaiming that the hate crimes, the suspicious looks, the harsh treatment that my community had had to endure, mostly without complaint or recognition, was not okay. He continued. "These are the faces of Islam in America. These are just a few of the Muslim Americans who strengthen our country every single day. This is the diversity that makes us Americans; the pluralism that we will never lose."

GETTING UGLY

At the end of Ramadan, our little family celebrated Jordan's first Eid with a big meal. I cooked brisket for Anthony and me even though it was August and hot. For Jordan, I pureed carrots and mashed potatoes. On a weekend afternoon shortly after, Anthony and I took Jordan for a walk, a welcome break from chasing after him as he crawled all over the apartment, pulling himself up and sweeping things off the coffee table. The death threat was still fresh so I was generally more vigilant and on edge. Anthony was pushing Jordan in his stroller and we stopped at the Union Square farmers market to pick up some fruits and flowers. I had to jostle and weave my way through the sea of bodies to get to my favorite farm stand, while Anthony and Jordan waited a short distance away. I grabbed an apple from the pile, glad to see they had my favorite Pink Ladies in stock, and turned to glance over at Jordan. A man was talking to Anthony. Even from where I stood, I could hear that the man's voice was loud and agitated. He had a single bulging vein in the center of his forehead as he leaned in close to Anthony. When he raised his hand and jabbed Anthony in the chest, pushing Anthony back ever so slightly, away from the stroller, I dropped the apple from my hand and ran toward them.

Anthony was clearly trying not to escalate the situation, both hands gripped on the stroller. As I got closer, I heard the words, spat out through the man's clenched teeth: "I see you. I know you. I am going to destroy you. I am going to hunt you down and destroy you. You hear me, Anthony?" Anthony began to raise his hand to calm him down or put some distance between them, but his calm seemed to enrage the man more. The terror in my heart was directly correlated to his proximity to my eight-month-old baby. I pushed the hood of the stroller down to conceal Jordan, and thrust my right hand straight out between the man's chest and Anthony.

"Hi!" I said in the loudest, cheeriest voice I could muster. "I'm Huma!"

My interruption transferred the man's blind rage. He grabbed my hand, and squeezed so hard it felt like my bones were being crushed. His skin felt like sandpaper, dry and cracked and unpleasant in every way. He pulled me in toward him, his breath all menthol and menace.

"Hi Huma. Good luck to you because I am going to destroy you too."

My instinct was not the same as Anthony's, who tried not to engage. "Can you please show some restraint? We are with our baby." It was as if he hadn't noticed that Jordan was there. He looked down, and in that moment of distraction, Anthony steered me away and we headed home as fast as we could. I turned around once to get a last look at the man's hateful twisted face, to commit it to memory. When we got to our apartment, Anthony brought Jordan into the nursery to play as though it had been a walk like any other. I went straight into a hot shower to wash the man's smell and touch off me and only then could I breathe freely again.

Increasingly, the only place I felt I could let my guard down was home. I had been angry with my husband, incensed, but the foundation of my love for him had not been broken. We had talked, both in therapy and at home, about his behavior, and had many painful, raw discussions. When I turned the key each night to open our front door after a long day of work, I walked into an apartment in good order, the fridge always stocked with the items from the list I'd left on the counter in the morning. Home was a safe space where I was always met with an open ear and open heart—and a baby who had been cuddled and coddled by a doting father all day long.

The outside world was another story. I still rarely read the tabloids or gossip columns, not wanting to come upon an item about the state of our marriage or what I was overheard saying in a restaurant. I read only the State Department press clips with articles relevant to work. The friendly "gotta make a living" photographer still seemed to delight in surprising me. He would smile and wave, ask a question or two, and then go on with his day. I mostly operated as if under surveillance from the moment I walked out of my apartment building. Privacy existed only in the home I shared with my husband and son.

In solitary moments, I sought answers from my faith. Occasionally, I would sit in my favorite fuchsia armchair in the corner of our bedroom and pick up my copy of the Qur'an, looking for guidance on grief, betrayal, parenthood. Sometimes I would read the verses out loud in Arabic. The sound is so melodic, just hearing it calmed me. When I was feeding Jordan in the middle of the night, I would close my eyes and recite the verses from memory. What I found on every occasion was that when I stepped back from the world, stopped thinking about what others were saying about me, tried to let go of the residual anger that I still sometimes felt toward Anthony, I was less burdened. It was impossible to look at my life and not feel grateful for it.

At the office, nothing was even close to slowing down. Obama's reelection campaign was moving into the final stretch. It was HRC's last year at State, and it would be just as full as any other. The difference for me was that I would be on the road much less, planning and executing the myriad trip details remotely. As always, the work required a balance between putting out geopolitical fires as they arose and devising a proactive agenda that year focused on, among other things, human rights, climate change, and strengthening ties with our allies. I traveled to DC one or two days each week for meetings and got on conference calls or responded to texts early in the morning or in the middle of the night while HRC and my colleagues were on the road.

I thought I would mind not traveling, and there were moments I did, but what I missed most was being part of a team. I had a new life with far more autonomy, where I could schedule meetings around my time at home with Jordan, but I missed physically being with my colleagues.

*   *   *   *

While Anthony and I worked to build a sense of normalcy in our marriage, we had one incident that set us back for a period. It couldn't have come at a worse time. It was in the aftermath of the Bachmann accusations, in the months following the death threat. The man who had made the threat was questioned and then released after promising to stay a certain distance from me, which wasn't exactly reassuring. And now I was preparing for a trip to Washington that dwarfed the awfulness of everything that had come before.

Two days earlier our consulate in Benghazi, Libya, had been attacked. I had been in New York the night of the siege, September 11. I had received the first alarming operations alerts on my BlackBerry and read with increasing agitation as the crisis unfolded. I wanted so badly to be with my colleagues in Mahogany Row as they waited for further news. I went to bed knowing little about the fate of the Americans who worked at the consulate, but awoke in the middle of the night to another ops alert, with the news that our ambassador Chris Stevens's whereabouts were unknown. I learned the next morning that the ambassador, former Navy SEALs Tyrone Woods and Glen Doherty, and air force veteran Sean Smith were all dead, the attack having ended in the most horrific and tragic way imaginable.

On September 13, while I was making plans to join President Obama, HRC, and the rest of my colleagues to receive the bodies of the four Americans at Andrews Air Force Base, Anthony and I were working together at the round table in our home office; he at his computer on one side and me with my laptop on the other. I swung my chair next to Anthony to use the printer near him and noticed a chat window open with a small image of a blonde woman smiling out. I scanned the message quickly. She was complimenting Anthony on how good he had looked at a recent event. I took the mouse out of his hand and scrolled up. Her messages were what some might consider innocent flirtations. But they raised my eyebrows. Anthony mentioned she was someone with whom he was working on a project.

"Who writes this way to a married man? And, who in their right mind writes this way to *you*?"

He said that I was reading way too much into it. She was just being "playful." What I mainly felt then was anger at *her*, at this stranger flirting with someone who had lost his entire career for having inappropriate online relationships with strangers. I left the room. There was no space for "playful" language after what Anthony had put me through—the lurid chats published in newspapers and on websites for the whole world to see, the strangers who stared at us on the street, in restaurants, on subways.

I took a breath and walked back into our shared office a few minutes later. Anthony apologized, saying he should have known better.

I made my way to my laptop and stared at its blinking screen.

"Maybe we can talk about this in therapy?"

"We'll talk about this later," I finally said.

Maybe it should have been a warning that he couldn't simply stop falling into certain behavior, but I was overwhelmed with work and worry, devastated by what had happened in Libya. Our team was in shock and then in mourning. Should that single flirtatious text that night have been higher on my list of what to deal with in that moment? In my mind, then and now, the answer is an unequivocal no. The next day I went, as planned, to DC, and the grief I felt for the terrible loss of four Americans superseded any and all other thoughts that might have occupied my mind the night before.

*　*　*　*

A week later, Anthony and I were back at therapy. We had allowed regular couples therapy to taper off since Jordan's birth, but now we had a clear setback to address. When Anthony raised this latest episode, our therapist did not express surprise, she just nodded sympathetically. She said he had to remain vigilant, that there was always a chance that someone "like Anthony" could slip again. He just needed to build his own walls, and with continued therapy, he would be able to control the impulse and the bad judgment.

Who exactly was someone "like Anthony"? Why was his judgment so bad? Why did these things that seemed so wrong to me seem so insignificant to him? She explained, among other things, that his isolation from society in the last year was exacerbating the problem. The people who wrote him off, the friends who no longer returned his calls. So he searched for connection in a space where he probably felt safe and validated. Our case was not unique, she explained. Many couples were struggling with issues around online relationships. Most people were able to work through it privately and most people didn't lose their jobs or reputations over it. She also posited that our unique circumstances had deprived Anthony of the arena in which he felt he could be productive and make contributions to society, which had been the focus of his work life, and that this had put even more pressure on him.

Our New York therapist, like the team in Texas, probed our family histories, exploring Anthony's early life to get to the root of what she referred to as his "acting out." My own story was not so complicated to explain. She knew I had family trauma related to the death of my father. I shared with her my mother's inability to let go of any physical reminder of him and the years it took all of us to process the grief. She knew the house I grew up in was filled with both verbal and physical affection, with parental praise and encouragement expressed openly and regularly. There were plenty of hugs and kisses and "love yous" from childhood through adulthood. Every night when I was a little girl my mother would gently rub my back until I fell asleep, and my father would poke his head in, just as my sisters and I were dozing off, for a book reading or a good-night kiss. When we visited my dad's sisters each summer, they cried when we arrived and they cried when we left. I grew up feeling special because I was treated as special.

Anthony had a different upbringing. When we met and he had told me he was raised by wolves, it was hard to reconcile that with the man I would marry, or the family I met. He was always physically affectionate, always telling me how much he cherished and loved me, marveling aloud how lucky he felt to be with me. He did not keep his feelings bottled up. They were out in the open just like every opinion he had about anything going on in the world. When we visited with his family in the early days of our courtship, his characterizations didn't quite compute. I was struck by how smart, funny, and all-around great company they seemed to be.

Over time, though, I noticed a certain tension in Anthony's relationship with his parents. His father called him every day, sometimes multiple times a day. Anthony patiently lingered on the phone until his dad ran out of things to say. He was always a dutiful son, on hand if there was a problem at the townhouse in Park Slope where he grew up and where his dad still lived. His mother was a regular presence in our lives. After Jordan was born, she asked if there could be a dedicated day each week when she could take care of him. Having had a close relationship with my own grandmother, and since my mother mostly lived in Jeddah, I was glad Jordan was lucky enough to have a grandmother nearby, and they quickly developed a very close bond. To this day, whatever she asks him to do, he does without complaint. Whatever food she puts in front of him Jordan eats and enjoys.

There were times early in our marriage when I bristled at the way Anthony spoke to his parents. I felt it was not the way one should address one's elders. Once I reprimanded him for being too harsh with his mother, even though she immediately laughed it off and said it was not a big deal. I chalked up my reaction to the occasional culture clash I could expect, having married into a Western family. But one thing that struck me as foreign, even apart from any cultural differences, which Anthony spoke of during our earliest meetings with therapists, was that hugs in his family were merely polite and perfunctory, not the long, lingering greetings I was accustomed to. I never once heard him say to his parents or they to him the words that punctuated every phone call and every hug goodbye in my family: "I love you." And there was the tragic loss of Anthony's older brother, Seth, who had battled with drug and alcohol addiction, and died in 2000 at age thirty-nine when he was hit by a car. I never knew how they all managed to get through that trauma.

I could certainly relate to Anthony's sense of isolation because I too felt it in my day-to-day life. I had an office full of extraordinarily supportive colleagues along with friends and acquaintances I saw at social functions, but I rarely confided anything too personal to anyone. When gossip columns quoted what I'd allegedly said to friends, I withdrew even more, wondering if my confidences had been betrayed. I didn't have a best friend who lived in New York or a close group of girlfriends I saw on a regular basis. What I had was what was allowed for in a life where there was time for work and my child and little else.

Feeling less welcome in the social universe we had once inhabited so comfortably, and not wanting to allow ourselves to be turned into shut-ins, Anthony and I had tried other ways of being out in the world, seeking out opportunities to be of service. Anthony found a food bank where we started volunteering on weekends, and it was the thing we most looked forward to each week. I would drop Jordan off with my friend Bari for a few hours and we would head to the facility. Shortly after we attended the group's annual fundraiser, they told Anthony we should stop coming to the food bank. I never asked why, but I guessed we were an unwelcome distraction for too many people.

In October 2012, Hurricane Sandy devastated parts of New York and caused severe damage in Anthony's former district. He immediately reached out to community leaders to see how he could help and drove out each day to volunteer, to advise small-business owners about how to submit their insurance claims, to help remove debris from the streets and sidewalks and from people's homes. He came back each night wiped out, with a story to share about someone he knew who had lost everything or someone else whose business had been ruined. He would take a hot shower, eat quickly, and get ready to go back out the next day.

One of those nights, he came home exhausted and confided that he wished he were still in Congress so he could do more. With his consulting business going well, he was now making more money than he had ever made in government, but after the hurricane he seemed much more focused, more invested, more interested in what was going on in his district. It was well over a year since he had left office, and this was the first time I'd heard him say he missed his old job. Seeing in his reaction to the hurricane a flicker of the old Anthony—the doer, the problem solver, the activist—I began to wonder if he was ever going to be professionally fulfilled in the private sector.

* * * *

On HRC's last day, her State Department colleagues gathered for an emotional farewell. The crowd who filled the lobby looked even larger than the one who had greeted her when she walked in four years earlier. This time felt different. Teary, bittersweet, and incredibly gratifying.

Along with an amazing team at the State Department and in good partnership with the White House and other cabinet agencies, HRC had done what she had promised she would do. She had succeeded in elevating both diplomacy and development as the pillars of United

States foreign policy. She had worked to strengthen old alliances and forged a whole new set of global partnerships. She had traveled nearly a million miles, visiting 112 countries, spending more than 400 days on the road over the course of her four years at State. Most significantly, HRC had completed the foremost task that President-elect Obama had given her when he chose her to be his secretary of state. She was a full partner in leading the way to restoring America's standing in the world.

When HRC stepped off the world stage and into the private sector for the first time in decades—and for the first time since I had begun working for her while still in college—she set up a personal office and asked me to run it. Although I was no longer a federal government employee, I was still incredibly busy, and work remained fulfilling, challenging, and exciting. I found office space in the Times Square neighborhood in Manhattan. HRC was planning to write a book about her life at the State Department, and work on Clinton Foundation initiatives, launching the programs I had helped research during her last six months at State.

She was also still dealing with the aftermath of Benghazi. After the attack, the Republicans launched multiple investigations, ostensibly to find out what went wrong. They asserted that she had left her colleagues in Benghazi to die. The many hearings were political cover for attacking several members of the Obama administration, with a particular target on HRC. She had already testified at congressional hearings on Benghazi, and would have to go through more. Republicans had not waited until she was out the door. In case there was even the slightest chance she'd run for president, they were going to take every opportunity they could to derail her.

* * * *

As HRC was exiting public service, Anthony was feeling his way back to it. Over dinner one night in early 2013, he told me that he was talking to a few old advisors and asked me how I felt about him running for mayor. I was uncertain. He was too.

Many among Anthony's small group of advisors had been with him throughout his decade serving in Congress. All of them saw his talent and his promise. All of them had been lied to and burned when he was forced to resign in 2011, so while they were loyal, a few were tentative about committing to another campaign. As a first step, they decided to run some focus groups to get a sense of the public appetite for Anthony's potential return to politics. The groups would meet over a few days. After the first night, Anthony came home, sat at our dining table a little dazed, and asked if I would come to the next session.

In a neat and sparse office in Manhattan, I stood in a small room watching and listening through one-way glass as people gathered at a long conference table. Most participants were already familiar with Anthony. I squirmed when they said what they knew about me: that I worked for Hillary Clinton (*fine*); that I was Muslim or an Arab as they called it, and that I was connected to the Muslim Brotherhood (*not good*). About Anthony, what several people said was that they disapproved of the personal conduct but would be open to giving him a second chance. Hadn't his punishment been too harsh given the crime? Doesn't everyone deserve a second chance? Did some media outlets make this a witch hunt? Would he fight for the middle class? Doesn't everyone have secrets? Weren't politicians who have done far worse still in office? For each of these questions, both men and women answered in the affirmative. Like voters anywhere, they mainly cared about how Anthony would run the city, how he would do his job for them. People who were resistant to his running at the beginning of a session were nodding in agreement by the end. An hour after saying he would never vote for Anthony again, one man leaned back, crossed his arms, and concluded, "I think he would be the best candidate of the lot."

Risa Heller and Glen Caplin, both former communications advisors to Anthony who had gone on to successful careers of their own, came over one night after the focus groups were over. They had been supportive throughout the ups and downs in Anthony's life, and I also trusted their judgment and their no-holds-barred advice. We were sitting at our dining table, picking over a takeout dinner. Anthony made it clear that he had come around, that he was prepared to jump in, but ultimately it was my decision whether he ran. Over the next hour, both Risa and Glen warned that it was not going to be easy for our family. That the scrutiny would be intense, Anthony's hours would be long, the coverage unforgiving, with no guarantee of victory. "You sure you want to go through this? It will get ugly," Risa cautioned.

I wanted to laugh. I didn't think she could tell me anything about ugly I didn't already know. I thought of the last year and a half. Of the sneering on the street, of the friends disavowing us, of feeling like a pariah whenever I walked into a room. For the rest of the evening, I listened and asked questions. Part of Anthony and the team's calculus had been that the current roster of candidates was weak and that this was probably his time. He had already been working on a policy platform with sixty-four ideas for how to keep New York the "Capital of the Middle Class." Transportation, hunger, tax reform. He had an idea and suggestion for everything.

I was not delusional. I knew we would once again be in the public eye, and that would come with the expected media scrutiny. They weren't the ones who'd brought all this on us. Anthony did that. So I knew the press would probably be tough on us and I was okay with that. I was encouraged by the sense of promise from the focus groups. People believed he had been good at his job. They recognized and valued his contributions. Anthony was young, he had a lot more to give.

As they stood to leave, I finally answered Risa's question from earlier in the evening. "Risa, I just want our life back." A life where we both had jobs we loved. Purposeful, fulfilling lives. For both of us public service had been a passion, a bond that we shared, a thing that connected us. Did I think his personal indiscretions were disqualifying? At the time, no, I did not. It seemed most other people didn't either.

In the end, the reasons I joined the chorus encouraging Anthony to run were simple. He had been a popular congressman who won every election with at least 60 percent of the vote. Even in the midst of the 2011 scandal, most of his constituents hadn't wanted him to resign. I thought he would be a good mayor, that he was full of ideas and would be hardworking and obsessive about problem solving for the city the way he was about everything else. His personal failing, to me, didn't seem to preclude his ability to be professionally impactful. A job with immense responsibility would keep him focused on something good and important, which would be helpful, as our therapist had said, in getting him to manage his impulses. There was no reason in my mind that he couldn't try to have a second chance at a job he had always said was his dream. This was a path forward for him, for me, and for our family. More than anything, misguided though it was in hindsight, I thought and hoped and prayed that we could simply go back to the way we were.

I agreed to appear in Anthony's campaign announcement video in May because I was aware that a big question would be *Where is his wife?* I did it on the condition that I not be expected to participate in the campaign any further. Anthony interviewed and hired a group of talented, mostly young, rising stars to run the campaign, and it took off really fast. The team included a videographer, as most modern politicians collect the footage for ads and archives. While initially I was not happy about the idea of having a camera in our home, which would sometimes be filming Jordan and me, after a few weeks I got comfortable with the videographer. I went back to focusing on my own work and got updates from Anthony on his when we regrouped at the end of each day. Anthony rose quickly in the polls, and after a few weeks of campaigning, it felt like a rebirth of our normal, with him returning home from work at the end of each long day animated and energized.

I kept my distance from the campaign until one day when one of Anthony's aides who was at the apartment described the energy on the road. He said it was incredible and thought I should come see for myself. I decided to accompany Anthony on a few campaign stops: to visit churches and walk in a street festival one Sunday. It felt odd at first to go from staff to principal, being pushed to the front, asked to pose for a photo, when I was used to stepping back to make sure HRC was posing for the right shot. But what I still remember from the few days I spent with Anthony on the road was the enthusiastic reception he got everywhere. He moved easily into crowds, leaning in, touching hands, dancing to street music. There was an almost palpable charge of electricity that ran between him and the people he engaged. I loved seeing him in what seemed like his natural habitat.

Feeling encouraged by the reception and getting caught up in the excitement myself, I agreed to do a fundraiser for the campaign, and one of HRC's close friends, Jill Iscol, agreed to host it at her home.

Many of my friends showed up and I delivered a short speech expressing my gratitude for their generosity. "Those of you who know me are probably surprised to see me standing up here. I'm usually in the back of the room, as far away from the microphone as possible. I'm doing it because I love my city and I love my husband. Launching this campaign was not an easy decision for my family. People say a lot of things about my husband, some nice, some not so nice. Putting yourself out there is hard. But the challenges that we went through are nothing compared to what so many families in this city face every day. No one fights harder on behalf of people. And no one will make New York safer, stronger, and more secure than my husband, Anthony."

It strikes me now how certain I was that what "we went through" was all in our past. We had both endured the awfulness of what it meant to lose so much in 2011, I couldn't imagine Anthony would do anything to risk it again.

RUNNING FROM GHOSTS

It isn't what we say or think that defines us, but what we do.
—Jane Austen, *Sense and Sensibility*

My phone would not stop ringing. First it was Mom calling. I didn't answer. Then it was HRC. I didn't answer. Then again and again. Finally, I threw the phone into my bag and turned back to read the statement I had just drafted.

I was sitting in the front passenger seat of our car. Anthony was at the wheel staring straight ahead, his eyes fixed on the afternoon rush of midtown traffic. He was composed, as though we were driving to a weekend with friends, though this was anything but.

It was July 23, 2013, and it been a few hours since Anthony had texted, "You there? Can you talk?" He then called to tell me that there was a story about to break about another woman who had just leaked their past exchanges. For the last two years, I had known that there were more women with whom he had had inappropriate exchanges before his resignation from Congress in 2011 and that they could come forward at any time. I also knew about the woman with whom he'd exchanged the flirtatious text I found the night during the Benghazi tragedy. But that was all I knew. He now told me this relationship was someone new. How new did not sink in fully in the panic of that morning, however. We were now on our way to a hastily organized press conference in an empty office space that the campaign had found at the last minute.

I called Philippe to tell him the plan. He said, "This will be the first time most Americans will hear your voice. You sure you want to do this?" I was sure. I had fully supported Anthony's decision to run for mayor, participated in the campaign, and felt that having done so I could not remain on the sidelines now. So I was steeling myself for the next thirty minutes. Anthony didn't plan to say very much. I didn't either. We would be in and out quickly. Anthony would speak first.

Maybe if I thought too much, I would decide against it. But there was no time to think. I made decisions for a living. I could do this. I had made a choice I believed was right and I would deal with the consequences.

When we pulled up to a nondescript building, I stepped out of the car, quickly buffered on all sides by Anthony's campaign aides, and marched through the unremarkable lobby, onto a crowded elevator, then into a huge empty room filled with prefab cubicles. We moved fast, zigzagging our way through the maze of a floor plan like we were in a Pacman game running away from our own ghosts.

I turned the final corner and the camera flashes blinded me. I braced myself for this singularly gut-wrenching moment in the spotlight. Anthony stepped up to a black stand with multiple microphones. I waited for my turn to speak. I was wearing a sleeveless dress, one size too large, which I had purchased after Jordan was born. It had a bright floral print and a forgiving waistband that expanded to accommodate my still larger than normal post-pregnancy frame. Though it was the middle of summer, I was wearing a black knit sweater to cover my shoulders. That morning, I had washed my hair and gathered it into a loose bun while it was still wet, pinning it haphazardly without looking in the mirror. There were strands falling messily behind that I had not noticed and had not fixed. Though I could have changed into something more flattering, or had my hair blown out or taken extra care to apply makeup to cover up, at the very least, the dark circles under my eyes, I hadn't bothered to do any of those things.

When I looked up to make eye contact with the people before me, I felt something visceral across the chasm that separated us. I saw it in their eyes, in their postures, even in their hands as they held up tape recorders and microphones. I sensed that even they, especially the women, did not want to be here, recording my shame, exposing each and every wart in my marriage. We were all so far down into the minute details of my personal life, I no longer knew what belonged to me and what did not. Yet here I was fighting to retain what little privacy I thought I was entitled to.

I had attended hundreds of press conferences, but always on the sidelines. Standing next to my husband before a throng of reporters, TV cameras, and photographers, over the rapid-fire camera shutter clicks, I spoke.

> As many of you who have followed this campaign know I have spent a good deal out on the campaign trail at churches, and street fairs, parades. But this is the first time I've spoken at a press conference, and you'll have to bear with me because I'm very nervous and I wrote down what I wanted to say.
>
> When we faced this publicly two years ago it was the beginning of a time in our marriage that was very difficult and it took us a very long time to get through it. Our marriage, like many others, has had its ups and its downs. It took a lot of work and a whole lot of therapy to get to a place where I could forgive Anthony. It was not an easy choice in any way, but I made the decision that it was worth staying in this marriage. That was a decision I made for me, for our son, and for our family. I didn't know how it would work out, but I did know that I wanted to give it a try.
>
> Anthony has made some horrible mistakes, both before he resigned from Congress and after. But I do very strongly believe that that is between us and in our marriage.
>
> We discussed all of this before Anthony decided to run for mayor. So really what I want to say is I love him. I have forgiven him. I believe in him. And as we have said from the beginning, we are moving forward. Thank you very much. Thank you for your time.

The reaction was swift and some of it was brutal. The headlines blared: "Is Huma Abedin Doing the Right Thing?," "The Public Humiliation of Huma Abedin," "The Overrated Huma Abedin." It felt like everyone—the talking heads, the whispering friends, the man on the street—was puzzling over a different version of *What was she thinking?*

On the day I joined Anthony before the cameras, I stood exposed to the world, judged for my actions, for my choices. But I'd made the decision to be there. I was no longer a bystander caught up in the wreckage of someone else's life. The phone calls I had ignored in the car were from women who cared for me, worried about me, wanted to protect me. Yet I no longer felt I could hide behind them. I had to do whatever explaining I could in my two-minute statement. Now I accepted whatever fate lay before me.

As awful as stepping up to the microphone was, I mostly felt relief. Anthony was asking the public to trust him with a job that touched on every aspect of their lives. People had a right to hear from him—and also from me. We owed them that.

Once it was over, my email inbox was deluged. Many messages from friends and acquaintances read "we are here for you unconditionally" or "you are very brave." Still, there was something lingering in the air, a stony silence from others, leaving me to conclude that, for some, I had crossed over ever so slightly from victim to accomplice.

My mom and HRC were disappointed, and I didn't need a conversation or email from them to know that they believed it was a mistake for me to have made a public statement. When I told them I planned to step off the campaign trail, they each agreed it was the "right decision" and offered little more. With Mom, I shifted the conversation to Jordan. With Hillary, to work. I asked Heba to take Jordan for a few days because I knew there would be even more reporters outside, and she was over in minutes to collect him and assure me that she would keep him for as long as I needed. She kept her judgments about Anthony to herself, showered her nephew with affection, and brought adoring cousins to play with him.

I knew my press conference statement would not be the end of the questions for me. If anything, it suggested, for the first time, a willingness to engage. So journalists just did their jobs. Reporters began following me as soon as I walked out of our apartment building, asking for a comment. Photographers trailed me as I went to work. The tabloids had new tactics. One day, a man bumped into me then dropped his bag on the subway platform. When I bent down to help pick up his things, he pulled out a small video camera, and asked me to respond to something someone had said that day. Another day, a woman sitting next to me on the subway complimented my shoes, and when I said "thank you," she identified herself as a reporter and asked if I regretted encouraging Anthony to run. When I went to get a haircut, a tape recorder suddenly appeared in front of my face with a reporter asking me about Anthony's latest campaign event and whether I would be rejoining the trail. After a few days of this fresh onslaught of attention, Jordan and I went to stay with a friend on Long Island. I needed to be in a place where I could find some peace, where I could think rationally about our next steps during the day and sleep at night.

It was only when I was ninety miles away from Anthony and we were on the phone together that I was able to have a proper conversation with him. His standing in the race had nosedived. I raised the possibility of dropping out. He sounded tired but said he felt he needed to carry it through to the end, that there were people counting on him and he thought he could manage the pressure.

That night, as we talked about where things stood—in the mayoral race and between us—I finally learned that the relationship that had prompted the press conference had taken place soon *after* the chat I had discovered in the wake of the Benghazi attacks, *after* we'd gone back into therapy together, *after* I thought he had ceased his online betrayals. I suppose I had wanted so much to put this in the past that I willed myself to believe that's where it lived. I wanted to think I knew all there was to know, that I had made informed choices that were rational and right. Now the bottom dropped out and I was tumbling down into an abyss.

Angry and beyond frustrated, I tracked down his therapist.

"Did you know what he was doing?" I asked her. She did not confirm or deny but from the look on her face, I felt she did not.

"So, after all this, you are saying it is possible that he was in therapy, and he still did this?" She hesitated before she said yes. What would it take for Anthony to understand this was immoral, destructive behavior, and that he now had a nineteen-month-old child who was the biggest victim of all? She told me to be patient, that we just needed to take more time exploring the root causes of the behavior. In all the sessions, we'd spent so much time delving into the why that we'd had little to no concrete discussion on what to do about it, how to stop it, at least not in a way that I could understand. Obviously just being "in therapy" was not enough. I was fed up. Plus, my own new reality began sinking in immediately. The next morning, I awoke to an email from HRC suggesting that I skip a trip out west for an event the following day. I responded, "Okay," not questioning or pushing back.

* * * *

By the time primary election day arrived in September, even I, who had completely unplugged from the campaign, knew things would be bad. I didn't go with Anthony and Jordan in the morning to our polling place to vote, but I joined him later at the campaign head-quarters to thank the tireless group of campaign staff who had given up so much of their lives to the effort, working even harder when the end was bleak. Anthony's campaign manager had resigned a day after the story broke, and two incredible women had stepped up to steer the ship with class and tenacity. They had been dogged and upbeat and put aside whatever their personal feelings might be, because they believed in Anthony as a candidate.

Anthony's next stop was to be the election-night party, though nothing about it would be celebratory. I had been noncommittal about going. Then I learned that the woman who had leaked her text chats with Anthony six weeks before, thus precipitating the disastrous outcome of the race, planned to be there, and I decided against attend-ing. I cringed at the idea of being confronted by someone who seemed to be enjoying the attention. As we prepared to leave the campaign headquarters building, Anthony, however, pressed me to go. I tried to restrain my shock.

He looked at me intently, as though he was challenging me, maybe secretly begging me. Behind the rigidity of his posture, the intensity of his gaze, I couldn't see that he was crumbling within. I glared at him. *How could you subject me to that, something no sane, loving spouse would ever ask?*

All this time, I had stood with him, supported him, tried to help him, loved him, encouraged him, but none of it had been enough and now he was asking for more. This time though, he was asking for too much. At that moment, I felt a seismic shift in our relationship.

When we stepped out of the campaign headquarters building, we were not the same couple who had entered it. We had crossed a line, and from the other side it didn't appear there would be any turning back. I knew I was more on my own than ever before.

Anthony conceded that night, and there was no more talk of a future in public service or really any future at all. Each day was painful just to get through. I had given up trying to understand or decode Anthony's mental health. If he needed any clearer indication that he had to stop these reckless chats, two epic downfalls in two years should have been enough of a wake-up call. I decided I was not going to be traipsing around to various therapists' offices to be told again that he needed to be in therapy to solve this problem. We confined our terse conversations to the narrow corridors of survival: our baby and his needs and how to pay our bills. I could not conceive of how Anthony would resurrect his consulting business and started to fear for my own job security.

I had been hearing rumors from colleagues over the last few weeks that "some people" were unhappy with me, though no one confronted me with their feelings directly. Most people who reached out with words of support were polite and encouraging. Well, except for Oscar de la Renta, who minced no words at all. A few days after my press conference, he called and left me a voicemail in his trademark teasing tone. "Huma, my love, I am very angry with you! Come for lunch." This was something I did from time to time. Pop into his office to say hello, have a quick visit, look at the designs for the next collection pinned on whiteboards, as he stood, always perfectly dressed in a formal suit, fabric in hand, in discussion with his team.

That is how I found him the next week when I went to see him. After receiving me with a big smile and hug, he took me into to the glass conference room adjacent to his office for a light lunch. Emotions did not seem to be complicated to Oscar. He either loved something or hated something and rarely had no opinion. As soon as we sat down, he launched right in.

"Do you know why I am angry with you? If you had called me one night and told me you had murdered your husband, I would have come to help you hide the body! That is how much I love you. Why did you not get help from your friends when you needed it? Why do we have to read about everything in the newspaper?"

He was asking me something I could not quite answer. I told him I'd thought I could handle it on my own, thought I had it under control. I had no intention of excluding my friends from anything. And besides, I would have been too ashamed to ask any friend for help with something like this. We sat in that conference room for a long while as he reassured me that I could always come to him when I needed help.

When I left his office, I had another realization. What I had gone through in the last two years had been clouded by such overwhelming shame, and grief, and uncertainty, that I simply didn't have it in me to just say to someone, to anyone: "Please help me." I had tried to navigate the mess I was in with the man who had created it, who was at least as confused and overwhelmed as I, and with a therapist who seemed—to me anyway—to not be helping. In my professional life, I had always been the doer, the fixer, the one who confronted any problems head-on and resolved them. In my personal life, I did not know how to ask for help. I had tried to do it on my own and I had failed spectacularly.

* * * *

A few days after Anthony's loss in the primary election, having heard from enough colleagues about the "rumors" that I needed to be fired, I reached out to Cheryl. I needed some clarity and advice. I flew down to Washington, and we met at Whitehaven, knowing it would be the most private place to talk. I had emailed Philippe to join, partly because I suspected I might need cheering up afterward, and we three gathered in the Clintons' third-floor home office.

I asked Cheryl if I needed to worry about my job.

Cheryl paused. Always direct, always one to go straight to the heart of a matter, she said that each of us makes choices in our lives that we think are right for ourselves and our families, and those choices can have consequences we simply cannot control. While this was not her opinion, she confirmed that there were a number of people—staff, friends, and important supporters of the Clintons—who disapproved of my decision to defend my husband.

"What are they suggesting?" I asked, not really wanting to know but needing to. "That I be let go?"

Cheryl did not say yes, she did not say no. Instead, she said, "Given your relationship with Hillary, I think it's most appropriate you talk to her directly. This has been a difficult few weeks for her too. What I will say is that it is hard to see a scenario where your role remains unchanged. It seems untenable given what has transpired." I nodded. She added that she would be there for me to help me move forward in whichever way I chose. There was little else I needed to know from her. I had expected bad news, I had received it, and now I could mentally prepare to act on it.

Philippe and Cheryl changed the subject and talked about other things, but I have no memory of what they were. My body may have been present but my mind was elsewhere. The last seventeen years of my life were unraveling before me. All the effort, focus, intensity, adventure. Just like that.

I heard from HRC the same night. I knew she would not drag this out. She had waited to get past primary election day before talking to me. She asked if I would come see her in Chappaqua. They had just brought home a new puppy, a mini Labradoodle named Maisie, and she thought Jordan might like to play with her.

We went on a beautiful fall Saturday morning. I didn't know how long I would be there so I packed extra snacks, extra diapers, a second outfit for Jordan, and some milk.

Jordan and I drove the fifty minutes it took to get to downtown Chappaqua. As we headed to the Clintons' house, I saw the Starbucks we went to occasionally, the Britches where I bought clothes for Anthony during the holiday sales, the French restaurant where HRC and I had eaten our first meal when they moved to Chappaqua, the Lange's deli where many campaign days had started with an egg sandwich and a cup of coffee—all reminders of the life I was about to be cut off from. I slowed down as I approached the white gate at the end of the cul-de-sac on Old House Lane, and lowered my window to wave to the Secret Service agent, who waved back as he opened the gate for us.

HRC was exuberant when she saw Jordan, now twenty-one months old. That was always her mood when little people were around. Oscar Flores, the devoted, tenderhearted property manager in Chappaqua whom I had known since our White House days, who had generously taken care of all of us for years, and who loved children, reached out to pick up Jordan. "Jordan, come with Uncle Oscar. Let's go meet Maisie!" Jordan shrieked in delight at the sight of the blonde puppy prancing around on the beautifully manicured lawn.

I didn't need to be told where to go. It was all routine. I followed HRC into her kitchen. I remembered the days when she was going through color samples and trying to explain the precise shade she wanted for her kitchen cabinets, leaving the rest of us scratching our heads. Not red, not orange, not quite brick, but she knew exactly what she had in mind and it had turned out beautifully. She asked me if I wanted coffee. I said I did and instinctively went to the top right cabinet and grabbed my cup while she took out the cream she knew I would want from the fridge.

I thought I heard a marked shift in tone, a certain coolness coming from her when she said nothing more consequential than "we have a new flavored cream too if you want to try it?" I didn't, but I took it and poured some into my cup. We walked past the kitchen island to sit in the sunroom. On the table sat the house phone where the President usually made his calls. There were a few papers and a stack of books probably being read by either or both of them. As I lowered myself into the cane chair across from hers, I looked at the scene out the window. Oscar, Jordan, and Maisie were playing in the yard. Jordan had just been knocked over by Maisie and he was squealing with excitement. Oscar helped Jordan back onto his feet, and Jordan lifted his arms up in the air as if to say, *again, again*. He was thrilled to be there, his wide smile carefree. *At least his last visit to Chappaqua will be a happy one*, I thought.

I had planned to start the conversation with an apology but then decided I would let HRC speak first. It was clear neither of us was relishing this talk. I had no idea how exactly she would let me go. She asked after my mother and my siblings and then asked about Jordan's progress and how he was faring over the last few intense weeks. She did not ask about Anthony. I told her my mother sent her best, because she had, and that my siblings were all thriving, as they all always seemed to be. I told her Jordan seemed to be unaffected by the mayhem around him, that he remained unfazed by the cameras, with the exception of primary day, which had been overwhelming even for a normally oblivious toddler. Then she said what I'd expected to hear.

"You know I have been hearing from people who are upset about your press conference appearance?" I nodded. I had prepared for this and now that it was here, I wanted it to be over.

"I do and I am so sorry for all of this. I did what I thought was right for me and my family. I know people are upset about it, but they don't live in my home or know what happens in it. I take responsibility for encouraging Anthony to run, thinking all this madness was behind us. I did not think after what happened two years ago that things could ever possibly be worse, but here we are. I so badly wanted to move on. I was prepared to move on, but it was a mistake to try. I still think he would have been a better mayor than anyone else. But he was wrong and I was wrong and I have to take responsibility for it. Having said all that, I can imagine how angry people are at me and that there are consequences, and I understand."

This is when it got hard to keep talking but I wasn't going to allow myself to get emotional. "Mostly, I just want to thank you for all your support and guidance and friendship and want you to know that it has been an honor to work for you."

Her expression remained unchanged as I spoke. She looked at me directly and I continued rambling for a bit. She let me finish. Suddenly, she changed the script I thought we were both meant to follow. Her response was crisp and clear. She did nothing Cheryl had prepared me for. She didn't say I told you so, she didn't tell me I was fired or that she would help me find a new job. In fact, she gave no hint that anything about my role was to be altered.

What she wanted to tell me was that though people were pressuring her to let me go, she did not believe it was the right thing to do and had no plan whatsoever to listen to my critics. Then she proceeded to list all the reasons why. That I was valued in our organization. That she had confidence in my work. That she believed I was a good manager, an effective problem solver. That she knew the number of people who supported me far exceeded the number who wanted me out. That she did not intend to be bullied into doing something just because that's what other people wanted. That she knew that I had a son to think of, and she wanted to be sure I was able to support him. She didn't say this, but we both knew that if she fired me I might be completely ostracized from Democratic politics and largely unemployable, something I couldn't even fathom. And last, she said that she did not believe I should pay a professional price for what was ultimately my husband's mistake, not mine. I think I started breathing again only when she finished talking.

This morning had not turned out how I'd expected. Thirty minutes into the conversation, after I thanked her for having faith in me and apologized for causing so much embarrassment, we were already onto a regular discussion about work, as though all the trauma and the stress that still awaited me on the street, and now even at home, was not going to interfere with my job. I stood up to leave after seeing through the glass that Jordan and Maisie had had enough playtime and both looked like they needed a nap.

"Are you going to be okay?" she asked as I gathered my things. I told her then what I had known in my heart since the moment Anthony and I walked out of the campaign office on primary election day: "We share a son, we will be connected forever, but this campaign broke many things, and the biggest break was in my marriage."

She nodded. She didn't press. She knew me well. I always told her the truth, even the ugly, messy, not sugarcoated stuff. And she did the same for me, which was probably why I had not answered her calls on the day of the press conference. I hadn't wanted to hear it in that moment.

I had been walking a tightrope for so long and had finally slipped. I was in free fall when she set out a much-needed net. Now I had to get up, dust myself off, and wrap my head around how I was going to move forward.

* * * *

The people who had told HRC that I should be fired never revealed themselves to me, although I picked up on whispered clues here and there. As for my colleagues, while one or two made clear they thought it was a mistake for me to retain my job, I didn't blame anyone for how they felt and knew it must not have been easy on any of them. They had to deal with calls from friends and supporters and the media about me and my problems, and they had enough work on their plates already. I ached to go back to normal professionally, so I made a conscious decision to keep my head down and not make waves, to do everything I could to stay out of the gossip columns. That wasn't always possible. But on some occasions it actually proved useful.

A few weeks after my Chappaqua visit, I received an invitation for Michael Kors's annual God's Love We Deliver Golden Heart Awards charity benefit, where HRC was going to be honored. Unsure if I should go, I asked HRC if I should sit out the event. "You should go," she said, and so I did, nervously following her into the room and being sure to avoid the slew of cameras that met her as she walked in with Michael Kors and Anna Wintour.

The advance lead escorted HRC to the head table, and I found my assigned place at the far end of the room. I was in the middle of small talk when the woman sitting across from me suddenly sat up straight, her eyes widening as she said, "It looks like Anna Wintour is coming to our table." Sure enough, there was Anna, heading my way. Slight and elegant in a navy lace dress, her hair perfectly blown out into her trademark bob, her makeup subtle, her smile even more so—her presence, iconic in its instantly recognizable style, always commanded attention.

Over the years, we had had brief interactions at social functions or at Democratic fundraisers. Some people found her intimidating, but I treated her like all other public people I met; respectfully but still like a human being. I stood as she approached my seat. "I was wondering if you might like to have lunch sometime?" she asked. I didn't have to think twice before I said I would love to. She did not linger long, just spent enough time with me for guests to notice that Anna Wintour was at a table in no-man's-land talking to the woman with the Scarlet Letter on her chest.

I was nervous enough that I spent a few extra minutes deciding what to wear before our date at the Lambs Club in midtown Manhattan the next week, a short walk from both of our offices. Over lunch, we talked about everything from Jordan to the challenge of living out one's life and marriage in public. Though we did not know each other well, our conversation was easy and free-flowing. Unlike my colleagues at work, my family, and my friends, she had not been personally affected or publicly embarrassed by the scandal. She had not had to field reporters' calls about it as my colleagues had. She did not have to see her son-in-law or brother-in-law or uncle or dear friend's husband's embarrassing texts in the newspaper.

The conversation that began that day at lunch, which would continue over more lunches, then dinners, then weekends at her house over the coming years, was the foundation of a much-cherished friendship. We talk about our lives, our families, our mutual friends, but also about fashion and politics, news of the day and occasionally even gossip too. When asked, she gives me advice that is always simple, direct, and practical. She has always encouraged me to stand up for myself, to speak up and use my own voice. Once I told her of my uncertainty about where I was welcome and where I was not, she simply brought an entire new circle of friends into my universe, all of whom remain in my life today.

My first outing with Anna made news in the gossip columns. A few weeks earlier, another prominent woman in New York, the author and editor Tina Brown, had taken me to lunch and that was reported on too. If those women and HRC were willing to be seen with me in public, acting as though it was business as usual, it seemed to be good enough for everyone else, and whispers of my removal eventually died down.

From the very beginning, I refused to apologize for my decision to stand with Anthony at the press conference. I held my head high even as I heard things like "You know, Gloria Steinem thinks you have Stockholm syndrome?" I always took a breath, absorbed the gut punch, and tried to be gracious, especially when it was someone I knew and admired like Gloria, which hurt tremendously. Only years later, when she took me out to dinner, did I learn that her words had been taken out of context, but I did not know that then. Then, I was just relieved that the many years of my life that I had committed myself to doing the best job I could had counted for something.

PART FOUR

HERE WE GO AGAIN

We honor the dream by doing the work.
—Cleo Wade

I wasn't surprised when HRC told me she wanted to enter the 2016 presidential race. Well, she didn't exactly tell me she was running. There was no single conversation that began with her speaking those words. Rather, there were occasional chats in 2014, on the phone or a long flight, where she weighed the pros and cons. They were more a call-and-response of her own internal debate. This is how they went. HRC: "I have a good life." Me: "Yes, you do." HRC: "I think I would be a good president." Me: "Yes, you would be." HRC: "I have so many ideas." Me: "I know." HRC: "This might be an insane undertaking." Me: "Most definitely."

Plenty of people were sharing their views and she wouldn't lack for support, including from a range of top Democratic political advisors. In mid 2013, a few months after HRC left State, I had run into David Plouffe, Obama's 2008 campaign manager, in Washington. When he asked after HRC, I told him that she was well and working on several projects. Then I added, "If you have time, it would be great if you could meet with her." I said it off the cuff, without thinking. Our team hadn't been talking about HRC running for president in the next election, but in the back of my mind I sensed that it wasn't a closed door. He said he would happily meet with her, which I hadn't really expected him to say. Though teams Obama and Clinton had worked well together for the last four years, we had had little interaction with Plouffe because he did not work at the White House in the first term. It was unclear that he would want to help her in any way should she decide to throw her hat in the ring, especially because there was the obvious possibility that Obama's vice president, Joe Biden, might choose to run.

When I told HRC about my conversation with Plouffe, she was surprised too. "Why not meet with him?" I suggested. "It doesn't mean you have to decide to run, but what do you have to lose?"

After thinking it over for a few hours, she gave me the green light, so I set about arranging the no-particular-agenda meeting. Later on, there would be breathless speculation about how all this came about: that it had been a calculated move on the part of Obama's team or that she had plotted to get Plouffe to meet with her early, before others made a decision about whether to run. The truth was much less exciting: it happened on a whim at a time when HRC was not actively talking about running for president. It initiated a relationship and developed into something more only later, as she was closer to making a decision.

That "something more" started to take on a new life as 2014 wore on, and so did the reality of what HRC was about to embark on. Like everyone who worked for HRC in 2008, I knew what loss at that level felt like. I was worried about the physical, emotional, and psychological impact another run at the presidency would have on my boss. I knew she would be the best leader for our country, but was this best for her? I also had to think about whether working on a presidential campaign would be best for me. I had a two-and-a-half-year-old, a rocky marriage, and I had also become the target of two investigations that would become a major headache for me and a potential distraction for HRC.

The first was an investigation that had opened a year earlier, just before Anthony's campaign fell apart. Iowa Senator Chuck Grassley sent a letter to the State Department requesting an investigation into my status as a special government employee and the consultancy positions I had taken with Teneo and the Clinton Foundation for the last six months I worked at State. I had kept a time sheet of my work hours, as required of all SGEs. The hours might be late at night or on weekends because that was the nature of my job. If the secretary of state called me at nine o'clock at night with a question about her trip to Russia, was I supposed to say, "Sorry, Madam Secretary, my State

Department hours are over"? Grassley concluded that I had earned too much money from State, neglecting to acknowledge that I was paid by the hour, and I worked a lot of them! He also alleged that I was providing "political intelligence" to Teneo.

The congressional inquiry did not outright accuse me of doing anything wrong, just implied that it *looked* like I was doing something wrong, so I *must* be doing something wrong. As with the Muslim Brotherhood videos, if the goal was to taint me, I knew it was successful when my SGE position became a front-page story in the *New York Times*. Simply being "under investigation" was enough to imply that I was corrupt, or at the very least in the wrong.

Some months after Grassley's public letter, I learned of a second investigation, and this one was more serious. The State Department inspector general was examining whether I had inappropriately taken time off for my maternity leave and it was especially unsettling because it was coming from the Department. From the place I owed so much gratitude to. The place I had so loved to work at and was so honored to be associated with. I had submitted the appropriate paperwork just before Jordan was born so that I could use my accumulated vacation time and sick days as maternity leave, given the lack of paid maternity leave for federal employees. Regardless, I was working again two weeks after I gave birth. I couldn't understand why these questions were being raised.

I went through my files but could not find a copy of the form I'd submitted. I did find a printout of a note I had sent a few colleagues saying I had submitted the paperwork, but not the actual form. Remembering those frenzied last days before Jordan's early arrival, I was not all that surprised that I had turned the form in without making a copy for myself. But I was puzzled by the fact that the Human Resources Department could not find the form either. I called a former Senate colleague and friend, Miguel Rodriguez, now an attorney in private practice, with a calm, reassuring manner to help guide me through what I thought would be cleared up quickly but wound up lasting years.

As the investigation dragged on, I learned that the source of the complaint was an internal whistleblower. Even before I started at State, a friend had warned me that there was internal wariness of our new team, and of me in particular. One criticism was that most of us did not have foreign policy experience, which seemed odd since our immediate predecessors also hadn't had foreign policy experience before they started at State. At the time I simply filed it away in the back of my mind and saw little evidence of the hostility my friend had anticipated.

However, it didn't help that a fairly large part of my portfolio was to say no. There were many occasions when a colleague would stop by my fishbowl office with a proposal for a great trip or event or initiative for HRC; but the reality was that there wasn't enough time, and it wouldn't have been practical to try to put every idea into action, even good ideas. By the end of HRC's term, I suspect I had become the office where dreams sometimes went to die. I accepted it as part of my job responsibility. This way no one would blame HRC for rejecting a proposal they thought was brilliant.

Whatever the origins of this particular investigation, I had to deal with the consequences, and they were severe. Without any physical record of my request, it looked as though I had taken paid leave without prior permission. They added up the hours for which I would need to repay the government and came up with a large sum for the three months I was "away" after Jordan was born.

It felt like I was in a maze; every turn, a wrong one. Get designated a special government employee to avoid conflicts of interest? Nope, that's a conflict. Keep a time sheet of your working hours? You worked too much. Take maternity leave the only way possible in the government? Sorry, we lost your file. Work during maternity leave anyway? You shouldn't have been paid, pay up. There seemed to be no way to do my job without rubbing someone somewhere the wrong way.

* * * *

Over the course of 2014, I was also trying to figure out my marriage. As I had known from the night of Anthony's primary election, something was irretrievably broken in our union, but I didn't yet understand what that meant practically. On the surface, there was plenty about our life that was normal. We still talked about Jordan, about politics, about plans for the weekend, about health issues that concerned our parents. We still took weekend walks all over the city and shopped at the farmers market a few blocks away. I still went to the office each day to work on projects with HRC. Jordan and his dad still took their regular adventures, which began with Anthony laying out the NYC subway map on the dining table and Jordan pointing to a stop, which was how they'd decide on their destination. We always maintained civility in front of Jordan, gathering to eat with him, to bathe him, to take him on excursions.

At night, however, once Jordan was in bed, we generally stayed apart, afraid of what might come up in another conversation about us. I buried my head in my own work, and Anthony in his consulting business. On the nights when we did spend time together, the pain and anger I hid from Jordan and bottled up in public had to go somewhere and I unleashed it all on Anthony. Our fights tended to follow a similar Sisyphean script.

"If it were not for you . . ." I would seethe at him.

"I know, I know . . . ," he'd say, in his generally unaffected manner.

"No, you don't know. You have no idea how selfish and arrogant and destructive your behavior was. How do you expect me to trust anything you say?"

That was when he'd switch gears, softening, pleading. He'd tell me that he loved me, that he believed I still loved him. He would beg me to go back to therapy with him so that we could both find a deeper understanding of his actions and resurrect our marriage. But we had been through therapy, lots of therapy, and he had ended up in inappropriate chats with women despite it. How would more therapy help? On nights I was particularly angry, I would ask him if he was still communicating with other women and his answer would always be a loud "of course not!" which left me furious because I didn't believe him, which in turn put him on the defensive.

"Have you thought about seeing someone yourself?" he'd offer almost too casually. "You clearly need help dealing with all this anger."

And that is when I would end the conversation. Rather than clarifying anything and helping us move forward, we were left where we'd started—me furious, Anthony defensive. The next morning we'd have breakfast with Jordan, I'd go to work at HRC's Times Square office and get home late, just in time to read Jordan a bedtime story. Nothing would change.

How did we get here? How did we get from those moments of pure joy and love we both seemed to feel in the beginning, to this cold and dizzying downward spiral we were now in? It was heartbreaking and maddening. But still we carried on. If nothing else, for Jordan.

Ever resourceful, Anthony got clients quickly and began to take meetings and travel for occasional business trips, including one a few months after his election loss. The first night he was gone, I awoke in the middle of the night to hear "Daddy, Daddy" coming from Jordan's room. I opened the door to find my toddler standing in his crib. "I don't feel good, Mommy," he said. The minute I picked him up, I felt his body convulse, and he threw up in my hair, down my back, and onto the floor. I took him into the bathroom so I could clean us both up. I asked him if he felt better, he nodded, then I tucked him into my bed with me. A few minutes after we settled in, he sat up and vomited again, then in his little two-and-a-half-year-old voice, through tears, he said, "Mommy, I am sorry for messing up the sheets." It was so comical I would have laughed if I hadn't felt so sorry for him.

"Oh, it's okay, little one," I said. I scooped him up and stripped him down to his diaper, laid some towels on the bathroom floor and sat with him as he threw up a third time, this time in the toilet bowl. As he whimpered and shivered, I ran a wet washcloth over his face, wrapped him in a towel, and leaned back against the bathroom wall, cradling him close. This was the first time he had thrown up so much, and I wasn't sure what I should be doing or giving him.

I pulled out my phone to text his doctor, then began googling. In a low voice, half-awake, half-asleep, he started calling out for his daddy again. No word back from the doctor. I said, "Okay, let's call Daddy. He will know what to do," and I tried to FaceTime Anthony. There was no answer. I tried calling and then I emailed and texted. He must have been in his meeting. Jordan's body slowly relaxed into mine until he nodded off again. Anthony got in touch several hours later, after Jordan and I had both managed to fall back to sleep. Early the next morning, as I was pouring the rehydrating Pedialyte into his bottle with one hand, holding the phone while waiting to speak to his doctor in the other, and half listening to a work conference call on speakerphone, I was reminded of how much easier it was to share parenthood with a partner. Perhaps I even harbored a tiny bit of hope that one day Anthony would come home and tell me they figured out what was wrong with him and we could be what we had been before.

On New Year's Eve 2014, Anthony and I went out for dinner at a French restaurant. Jordan had just turned three, and HRC was having her final conversations about officially jumping into the presidential race. In the dim light of the room, at a table illuminated by candles, before an obscene amount of food, my long dress gathered beneath the table, I suddenly saw my reality with clarity. To an outsider, we must have appeared like any other couple fortunate enough to be ringing in the new year at an elegant restaurant, but what we looked like on the outside was so different from what I felt inside that it was like a slap in the face. I was deeply unhappy in my marriage; and my spouse didn't seem particularly happy either, although he put up a much sunnier, braver front most of the time. I told Anthony I wanted to separate.

I hadn't walked into the dinner planning to say it, nor had I thought about what an actual divorce would entail. If anything, my words were just an acknowledgment that my heart was beginning to yearn for so much more than what we had.

Growing up, I knew no one with divorced parents. My own parents raised the bar so high that a marriage as happy as theirs might have seemed impossible to match—except that all three of my siblings seemed to have found life partners and marriages that were equally happy. To this day I have never once seen any of my siblings argue with their spouses, or even seen them and their partners annoyed with each other. How had my brother and sisters managed to pull off something that seemed so out of reach for me? Why had I been the outlier?

So, though I had said the word, and meant it when I said it, I did nothing to follow up on that New Year's Eve statement, and our daily lives remained unchanged. I didn't tell Anthony to move out and I didn't leave either. The idea of splitting custody and having my son with me only part-time was totally incomprehensible. Jordan was always surrounded by those he loved—not just Anthony and me but our family—and I wanted to keep it that way. My mother would visit for long periods of time, and my mother-in-law still came every week, occasionally moving in to help out if both Anthony and I were traveling. We had a reliable, regular babysitter and Heba took Jordan whenever I asked her to. Still, none of this was the kind of round-the-clock, day in, day out care our son would need now that I was about to get back into campaign mode. After all we had put our family through, I dared not ask for anything more.

The life I had built for myself in New York was very different from the *ummah* of Jeddah, where the moment my dad had to have his kidney surgery my parents' friends had swooped in and taken care of my sisters and me as if we were their own children. Even though I had a large extended family in New Jersey, I saw them only if I went out to visit them. An open door always, but I had run off on my own adventures nearly two decades before, and on the occasions I sought them out, I couldn't help noticing that the family I left behind had moved on without me. In their minds, I was always doing something more important for someone more important—a president of the United States or a would-be president—and they never wanted to impose. What inadvertently grew in the place of that unspoken mutual support system that family members share when they are intimately involved in one another's lives? Distance. I felt this acutely years later, after a beloved uncle died. The family gathered to say goodbye to him as he was dying, but it occurred to no one to tell me. I only learned he had passed when a friend from Saudi Arabia sent a condolence text. I was devastated, but rationally I also knew it was a natural consequence of the life I had chosen.

In 2011, I had stayed with Anthony because I was still very much in love with my husband and because I thought he had a problem that could be fixed. In 2013, I didn't take our baby and walk out although I could have and perhaps the women who thought I had Stockholm syndrome would have cheered if I had. As 2015 dawned, I threatened divorce but did not follow up. Why? Mainly because Anthony was a good dad and had a strong bond with Jordan, and I felt we needed to do all we could to make our son feel as secure as possible at a time when HRC's campaign was ramping up and I would be away from home a lot. I was certain that Anthony and I could keep it together—with safety pins and glue stick if necessary—and deal with our personal mess down the road.

And admittedly, Anthony still made my life easy in so many ways. Jordan adored his daddy, who was loving, attentive, playful, and more present than I was. And when I wasn't overwhelmed by the fury that I sometimes felt, I appreciated the fact that Anthony still seemed to be the same person I had met a decade and a half before on Martha's Vineyard. He was still one of the smartest people I knew, and always had a suggestion to make or a solution to offer or an interesting nugget of information to share. Anthony still took care of all the bills, the household, Jordan's school and social life, his doctor's appointments. On the nights we fought, he would say I treated him like the house manager, and it always shut me up because I had to concede it was true.

Despite my feelings of personal devastation, I resolved to stay, and to set my sights on something much bigger than myself. Every time I walked out the door with my suitcase, Jordan asked me, "Mommy, why are you leaving? When are you coming back?" On other days Anthony would send videos from home with Jordan saying to the camera, "Come back home now!" There were so many moments I was plagued with guilt, but I was also tugged in the other direction by the value of the work I was doing. To be a mother fighting for the kind of world I wanted my son to grow up in was just as important as being a mother who was there to tuck him in every night. Wasn't it?

* * * *

By January 2015, HRC was starting to put together her senior team for her presidential run. John Podesta, Cheryl, and Robby Mook were already laying groundwork for the campaign. Podesta would be campaign chair. I first met Podesta at the White House in 1998 when he became President Clinton's chief of staff. He invited me and a few other junior staff to his office to probe us on our thoughts about how the complex operated and for any suggestions we had for improvement. He listened and took notes as he fed us lunch from the White

House Mess. He treated the most junior of us with just as much respect as he did his peers.

Robby was to be campaign manager and carried the burdensome label of "wunderkind." In 2008, every state that he had run resulted in victory. Cheryl would have no formal campaign role, but nothing big happened in HRC's life without her, and she would operate as consigliere to HRC as she had in the past.

HRC asked me, as she asked the other three, for suggestions on senior team hires. She had me join her as she interviewed candidates and then asked what I thought after each one walked out. She made her decisions swiftly. Podesta recommended Jennifer Palmieri, currently Obama's communications director, for the same position with the campaign. She was a seasoned strategist with just the right temperament for a really tough job. For pollster and ad team, HRC chose Joel Benenson and Jim Margolis, also part of Obama's team and the top of their fields. I knew them well because they had previously been Anthony's political advisors. HRC also brought back Mandy Grunwald for strategic communications. Mandy had worked on every campaign with the Clintons since Bill Clinton's 1992 run. Tough, direct, she pulled no punches and was in a league of her own professionally. Marlon Marshall and Brynne Craig, two seasoned political mavens who had worked with Robby on other campaigns were on board to run the national political operation. Minyon Moore, who had guided HRC through the tensions of the 2008 convention, agreed to come on as senior advisor. There were many more positions to be filled in the political, digital, and analytics departments, but rather rapidly it felt like HRC had assembled a dream team with a perfect mix of old and new blood.

Maybe in one of those sessions I was being interviewed for a job myself, although I did not know it. When Robby called and told me he and Podesta had an idea for a role for me, he asked if I had any strong feelings about what I wanted to do before he pitched it. In a throwback to the White House days when I told Kelly my commitment was simply to support HRC in whatever way would help her succeed, I said, "I'll do whatever Hillary and you want me to do."

Less than an hour later, an email appeared in my inbox from Robby.

The role HRC was offering was campaign vice chair. This involved overseeing the scheduling and advance operation, the road team, the correspondence office, the friends and family outreach program; managing incoming calls and issues from longtime political friends and supporters; building advisory groups to accommodate the immense outside interest in supporting the campaign; and coordinating with President Clinton's and Chelsea's offices as they got involved in the campaign. I would be based at campaign headquarters managing a department of fifty people. They also wanted me to help raise money. It felt like a big job and it was. I called Robby back and said I didn't need such a fancy title, but he said Podesta, Cheryl, and he had decided this was the right title and HRC had agreed.

When I found space for headquarters in Brooklyn Heights, at the cross streets of "Tillary" and "Clinton," it was as though it was meant to be. The two-story, vast office began filling up with staff as we all built out our teams, and I felt that familiar excitement each day I got on the 4/5 train from Union Square to Brooklyn Heights.

For my team I hired many people whose work I had long admired. I asked Connolly Keigher to be trip director. She had done advance in 2008 and was capable and tough when she needed to be. For scheduling director, I hired Alex Hornbrook away from the White House, where he had run Vice President Biden's scheduling operation and earned an impeccable reputation for astuteness about the priorities of political scheduling. For advance director, Alex recommended Jason Chung, who brought calm and competence to each meeting. They became the no-drama team, essential to making everything work.

For my own sanity, I brought my amazing, resourceful assistant Sawsan Bay to help manage my schedule, and she was the only reason I got anywhere on time. Rob Russo, who handled HRC's correspondence and briefing book and had become our walking institutional archive, joined up too. To run our friends and family outreach, I hired De'Ara Balenger, an attorney who brought creative ideas about how to expand our outreach universe to a broader, more diverse group of people who were not typically involved in politics.

Greg Hale would be our production director, the person tasked with creating the right shot, and building the sites for our large events.

Greg was deservedly known as the best "picture person" in Democratic politics. He had been such a believer in HRC that in 2008 I don't think anyone cried harder than Greg when she lost the nomination to Obama. Calling him was a technicality since I knew he would say yes. Before we hung up, realizing he and his recently grown bushy beard might occasionally wind up on camera with Hillary, he asked, "Um, do I need to shave my beard?" I never would have judged a female colleague for the length of her hair, so I just asked "Does Mica like it?" referring to his wife.

"Yeah, she does" came the reply.

"Then no. See you in Iowa!"

I had been operating from a defensive crouch for so long, professionally and personally, that I had not expected to be elevated. Even as I had joined HRC for those interviews for her senior team, I hadn't known what kind of place there would be for me on the campaign. I saw the job offer from Robby, John, Cheryl, and ultimately HRC, as a clear sign of the trust and confidence my boss and colleagues had in me. I had been asked to serve by a woman who had always been there for me, and I would be there for her no matter what.

DECLARATION
OF SENTIMENTS

To get HRC to Iowa the way she wanted to go—incognito—meant it had to be something of a stealth mission. It's hard to slip into places unrecognized when yours is one of the most famous faces on the planet and you are traveling in a van straight out of the cartoons, along with a phalanx of security. Nonetheless, that was the plan, because she wanted to meet people in as low-key a way as possible, without big crowds and cameras making every outing an event. She didn't want it to be a big barnstorming tour, but something quieter, which would allow her to take the pulse of the country—similar to the listening tour she had done in New York in 1999 to launch her run for the U.S. Senate. "I want to know what's on people's minds!" she kept saying. The road trip we mapped out for her was designed to take her to people's homes and schools, the corner stores and diners where they congregated for breakfast or afternoon coffee, the town halls where they convened to discuss community concerns, places where she could listen and talk face-to-face.

On April 12, 2015, HRC and I hopped into Scooby to drive the thousand-mile trip to Monticello, Iowa, where she would meet with caucus-goers. Early that morning in Chappaqua, she had taped an official campaign announcement video to be released later in the afternoon. It featured a diverse montage of people from around the country talking about their plans for the near future: a mother and daughter moving to a neighborhood with a better school, another mom heading back to work after five years at home raising her kids, a man and his brother on the verge of launching their new business, a college student looking for a job. Toward the end, HRC appeared and said, "I'm getting ready to do something too. I'm getting ready to run for president." She believed that the deck was still stacked against everyday Americans, she explained, and she wanted to be their champion.

In the first hours of our road trip, we filled the time reading the event briefings, chatting about how the campaign was coming together, making phone calls, and occasionally paging through *People* and the home décor magazines that lay on the floor between us. We stopped to refuel for gas and HRC jumped out eagerly, happy to just blend in. As we went into a convenience store to buy snacks, no one seemed to know who she was. I leafed through the rack of newspapers, the cover stories speculating when the woman behind me eyeing the candy bars would announce for president.

By the time we stopped in Pittsburgh for the night, she had still managed to remain undetected. Then on day two she decided she wanted fast food for lunch, and we pulled off the highway for Chipotle in Maumee, Ohio. HRC didn't usually wear her sunglasses indoors, but that day she did because they were prescription lenses and she couldn't see well without them. She joked that maybe I should keep my sunglasses on too, so she wouldn't look so out of place. I played along and we managed to stay unrecognized. After we left, the security video of our little escapade found its way into the press and the rest of the team teased us for looking like "masked bandits."

The first of the events HRC attended when we arrived in Iowa was an informal afternoon coffee. Next was a small roundtable at a community college with students and educators, listening to them describe their innovative career development strategies, then explaining why she was getting in the race. "I've been fighting for children and families my entire adult life," HRC said. "I want to stand up and fight for people so they don't just get by, but they can get ahead and stay ahead." After the roundtable, she walked down the street to chat with people and explore retail stores. In those early days of the campaign, these small gatherings, with time built into them for more than just handshakes and selfies, felt like opportunities for a genuine exchange of ideas.

After that inaugural trip, I joined her in hundreds of intimate gatherings where people shared their problems, their fears, their hopes and aspirations. A woman who feared losing her health coverage because of her partner's pre-existing condition. A grandmother lamenting the toll of the opioid epidemic on her community, another who was raising her grandchildren but was barely able to put food on the table and pay her rent. An unemployed young woman who had $189,000 in student loans and no ability to repay them. A small-business owner strapped by rising commercial rents. A mother who worried about her daughter's mental health after a friend's suicide. All these stories informed the campaign's policy process. Along with infrastructure, healthcare, and plans for the economy, HRC added issues like mental health and substance abuse to her agenda. These topics were not typical fare in a presidential campaign.

HRC saw more than just problems, however; she also saw promise. Students who had become activists in civil rights and social justice movements, people of color who were mobilizing their communities to vote because they understood what was at stake, raising their voices so that long needed policy changes could be added to the list of national priorities. Black Lives Matter went from a handful of protestors at events here and there to a powerful, impactful, and important national movement. Dads carrying their daughters on their shoulders to watch this blonde woman in her royal-blue pantsuit clearing the way forward so that their path would be that much easier. To see people visualizing the kind of leadership they wanted for their children was the clearest reminder that for most Americans, our political process, while not always smooth, can be fundamentally optimistic.

These were the stories that mattered to HRC. But the story reporters seemed to care the most about was: emails.

* * * *

On March 2, 2015, a month before HRC hit the road to Iowa, the *New York Times* published a front-page story titled: "Hillary Clinton Used Personal Email Account at State Dept., Possibly Breaking Rules." The article noted that her use of a private email account had come to light because of emails she turned over to the committee investigating the Benghazi attack. A few days later, our newly formed senior campaign team gathered with HRC to map out a response. She was getting ready to do a press conference, and we all knew that many of the questions would focus on this. HRC's response didn't seem complicated. She said she had nothing to hide and had asked the State Department to make her work-related emails public.

As I was sitting in the conference room that day, leafing through the pile of briefing materials stacked in front of me, another *New York Times* article related to HRC's personal email account caught my eye. This one said that senior aides, including me, had been asked to turn over documents and emails in response to various Freedom of Information Act requests. But no one had asked me to do any such thing.

When I got back to my desk, I texted the article to Heather King, now an attorney, asking her for advice. She suggested we loop in Karen Dunn, who had been HRC's communications director in the Senate and was now a partner at Heather's firm and one of the top attorneys in the country. Her petite frame, wire-rim glasses, and forever smile belie her talents. She excels not just in a particular realm of expertise but in many—politics, communications, policy, the law—on top of being a terrific writer too. Like Heather, she is one of those Hillaryland women I can call after months or even years of not being in touch, and when we connect, it is like we spoke yesterday. In the months that followed, Karen reached out to the State Department on my behalf to let them know that I would be complying with the request and I met many times with Karen and her team to review my emails and to prepare for interviews with investigators—which ended up not taking place until more than a year later.

In the meantime, I still had a presidential candidate's road trip to plan! Shortly after my exchange with Heather, my phone rang. It was Alex, HRC's new campaign scheduling director. He had seen the news about the email investigation. "Are we changing anything about the trip?"

"Nope," I replied. "Let's get a draft schedule ready for HRC soon."

"Yes, ma'am," he said.

Ugh. I was already bracing for turning forty in a few months. Having always been the youngest on the team, now I was having some trouble letting go of that status.

"Alex?" I said back into the headset.

"Yes?"

"Don't call me ma'am."

* * * *

During those early weeks on the road in Iowa, New Hampshire, and California, we were building toward June, when HRC would host a large rally to officially launch her candidacy. It was up to me and my new team to propose options for the event. We had to find a place that would distill the essence of what HRC stood for, a place that had a lot of symbolism and would also provide a beautiful picture both for the moment and for history. I proposed Four Freedoms Park on Roosevelt Island, between Manhattan and Queens, on the East River, named for President Franklin Delano Roosevelt. HRC loved the idea. There's a stunning outdoor memorial to FDR on the island, one of the last buildings designed by the renowned Modernist architect Louis Kahn. The lines engraved on one of its granite walls, from the "Four Freedoms" speech FDR delivered shortly after our entrance into World War II, invoke a future in which everyone, everywhere in the world, will be able to enjoy freedom of speech, freedom of worship, freedom from want, and freedom from fear. These ideals were a perfect match for HRC's own.

On a beautiful sunny afternoon in mid-June, HRC gave a stirring speech about all the reasons she had decided to run, and was met by cheers from the thousands of supporters there. The event turned out just as I had hoped and set the tone for all the speeches she made in the many months that followed.

Three days after HRC's rally, Donald Trump launched his candidacy before a small crowd of supporters in Trump Tower in Manhattan, some of whom, according to what we later read, had been paid to be there. As he made his bizarre descent down the escalator to a marble lobby to announce his bid for the Republican nomination, spewing racist comments and hurling a series of jabs at the other Republican candidates, he gave a great preview of his own campaign rhetoric.

We paid little attention to him, until one day in August, when HRC and I were backstage at the annual Democratic Wing Ding Dinner, held in the Surf Ballroom in Clear Lake, Iowa, a must-stop event for any political candidate, when we happened to catch part of one of his speeches—if you could call it that. We were sitting in the trailer that served as her holding room, a plate of untouched fried chicken on the table in front of us, watching the television mounted on the wall. "I just don't get it," HRC said as she listened to him ramble incoherently about himself, never mentioning anyone else except to demean them. Inexplicably, his grandiosity and bigotry seemed to be met with genuine enthusiasm from the audience. He was still battling more than a dozen Republicans at this point and we had no idea who GOP voters would pick as their nominee. But his words were so alarming that we quickly hit the mute button. It was hard to imagine being in a general election contest with someone like him. In any case, before we could think about which Republican HRC would be running against in the election, we had to focus on defeating her main opponent in the upcoming Democratic primaries—Independent senator Bernie Sanders from Vermont, who had entered the race a few weeks after HRC, proclaiming his presidential campaign a "revolution."

As a campaign team, our mission from day one was to work hard and smart. President Obama had instructed HRC directly, then Podesta and me for good measure, soon after she had announced her candidacy, telling us not to "run her ragged" this time. I did not need reminding of the 2008 days when we would pull into a hotel after other candidates and then leave before them the next morning. Now, in 2016, as our campaign manager Robby emphasized at each briefing, we would make data-driven, informed decisions on where our candidate went and what she did. For primary season, that meant knowing precisely where she needed to go to achieve the delegate count she needed to win the nomination.

HRC had entered as the front-runner, but knew that history rarely rewarded the candidate following a two-term president from the same party, which made the climb steeper than it might appear. She was prepared for a constant barrage of attacks both from the outside and from within our party. Those attacks had come and they would continue. Complacency was a problem too. Some people downplayed the urgency of this election, and that made us nervous. How do you tell people this is the most important election of their lifetime when they hear that every four years? Still, she did tell them. And whenever I was called on to speak for the campaign, so did I.

* * * *

For months I had been on the campaign trail with HRC, working to ensure that our messaging was aligned with what was happening on the ground. I was managing a talented, dedicated team at headquarters and on the road, making use of the experiences I had accumulated over two decades of working for Hillary Clinton. Now my position included a new role: fundraising, which was how I found myself in the foyer of a stately house in London's Grosvenor Square on a cool rainy night in October, chilled—and very nervous.

I was here as a campaign surrogate, the person meant to attest to the character of the candidate, a role typically assigned to far more seasoned people, or what my mind conjured as "more seasoned" without realizing I had already become that person. One day early in the campaign, with many events left to go, HRC's voice was getting hoarse and she wondered aloud about how she was going to be able to get through all the speeches on her schedule for that day. Casually, she turned to me in the car and said, "You may have to do one of these for me." I sat physically paralyzed, my mind racing to come up with things I could say if I had to appear before an audience. I had memorized *her* stump speech but didn't think that's what I could or would say when advocating for her.

London would be the first time I represented the campaign alone and I didn't want to get anything wrong. More than that, I hoped that the Americans abroad I was speaking to wouldn't feel that spending an evening with me was a waste of their money. I was still not sure why I had been the one chosen for the London trip. The guest list would include foreign policy experts, and it seemed that Jake, now the campaign's policy director, would have been much more suitable. But Dennis Cheng, the campaign's national finance director, had requested, or rather instructed, that I go, and we all generally did whatever Dennis told us to do!

The host greeted me with a hug as if we had known each other in a previous life, even though we had never met. Elegantly dressed, with a touch of makeup and minimal jewelry, she could have been a member of a Middle Eastern royal family. She told me how pleased she was that I had come, then led me into her living room to introduce me to her guests. We mingled for a while, before sitting down to dinner.

When it was time, with hands clammy and legs shaking, I told the guests about the Hillary I knew. I made eye contact with one person at the table, then another, and noticed a head nodding in approval. Soon, it began to feel less like a speech and more like a conversation as I talked about why she had decided to run, and our experiences on the road.

"And now, we are here," I said. "She is doing it *again*." This line brought jittery laughter from the audience. People were not sure whether it was a stroke of brilliance or sheer insanity that she was back for round two.

I talked about HRC's tenacity, her empathy, her curiosity, her generosity, her humanity. I told them what she meant to me as a role model, a colleague, a friend. I shared specific stories about what I had recently seen or witnessed or known about her.

At the end, one of the audience members pulled me aside and said, "How come she doesn't talk this way about herself? I am blown away by these personal stories."

"Because she doesn't think this is about her," I said.

As guests were mingling over coffee and dessert in the dining area, the hostess asked me to join her in the living room. I told her how much I had enjoyed the evening.

"You might be wondering why I asked you to come?" she asked with a smile.

"Yes," I responded, eager to hear.

She told me that years before she had been battling cancer. While in the hospital for treatment, she picked up a copy of *Vogue* magazine and came upon a profile of me. She was intrigued both by my background and the work I was doing—it wasn't every day that a Muslim South Asian woman who grew up in the Middle East and worked in high-stakes American politics was featured in a prominent magazine. She felt a certain pride reading it, and she told herself that if she ever got well enough to be able to support me in some way, she would. She was now keeping that promise to herself. This elegant, sophisticated woman, in her impeccable clothes and her beautiful home, a woman who seemed so safe and secure, felt a connection to me from thousands of miles away. To me this moment was a reminder that everything, even in the tumultuous juggernaut of a campaign for president of the United States, is ultimately about human connections.

Both honored and reenergized by this unexpected encounter, I headed back over the Atlantic to face a less welcoming invitation: to testify before the House Committee investigating the Benghazi attack.

* * * *

In spring 2014, House Republicans had announced an eighth Benghazi investigation—though I was beginning to lose count of how many times they would accuse HRC of leaving her colleagues for dead before ultimately exonerating her in their final reports. For this investigation they intended to interview HRC's senior staff from the State Department, including me.

Now, over a year after the announcement of the investigation, I was finally being called to testify in a closed-door hearing—one of the last witnesses to do so prior to HRC, who would come before the committee, in a very public appearance, toward the end of October.

The hearing took place in a small, frigid conference room on Capitol Hill and lasted approximately six hours, during which I made frequent trips to the restroom, mostly to defrost. None of the questions turned out to be surprises. Republican Congressman Trey Gowdy of South Carolina, who chaired the House Committee hearings on Benghazi, would lead the hearing at which HRC appeared the following week. But he wouldn't be at mine, a clear indication that even they knew it was a waste of time to bring me in. There was nothing I could tell them that was new, that was of relevance, that could have helped the investigation. In Gowdy's place the Republicans sent a congressman from Kansas named Mike Pompeo.

The ranking Democrat on the committee, Elijah Cummings, dropped by, which I had not expected. Cummings was a giant in the House. I had been on trips with him when I was in the Clinton White

House. Then a relatively new member of congress, he was known as an affable, smart legislator on the rise. Now he was in the senior leadership, widely respected, and when he spoke he commanded attention. He had long called the investigation a waste of taxpayer money since the attack had already been thoroughly examined with no indication that there was any negligence on the part of the secretary's office. He did not stay long that day, but he was clearly intending to use his time to set a few things straight for the record.

"Your title, Ms. Abedin, deputy chief of staff, operations, might lead some to believe that you did have an operational role in overseeing security for overseas posts. Was that the case?"

"That is not the case, sir."

"So you had no role with regard to operations?"

"None at all."

"So you were never personally reviewing or responsible for assessing and managing security needs and assets for the temporary mission facility in Benghazi?"

"That's correct, sir."

With each question, the volume of his voice rose a notch; with each, he was establishing how absurd it was that I was even being questioned.

"One thing that is often overlooked is the fact that Secretary Clinton, like others in the department, lost members of her team, individuals who were a part of the State Department family, and I understand it's a very close family. Can you share with us on a personal level what that meant to her and what it meant to you and others?"

"I wasn't even aware that we'd lost Chris Stevens until I got the department-wide email when I woke up to it the next morning. And I was stunned. I'd never experienced anything like that in all of my years in government service, and I just never had—I never dealt with anything like that before, and you know—I'm really sorry."

I was apologizing because my voice had suddenly cracked, and my eyes had welled up. I simply had no more words for how awful that day had been.

Cummings reassured me and gave me a moment to collect myself. Once he was done with his questions, I thanked him. "I'm honored by your presence," I said, because I was. After he left, I made eye contact with Pompeo and then looked at the line of Republican House staff seated in a row of chairs behind him. They all looked away. Cummings, in a matter of minutes, had summarized the gist of the investigation, that it was a sham, and they must have known it.

Pompeo had overlapped with Anthony only briefly in Congress so there was none of the awkward "this is the wife of my colleague" vibe from him that I had experienced with other House members. He was all business. I could tell from the beginning of his interrogation that he knew I had no information about the Benghazi attacks. He had another mission in mind: emails. He asked me question after question about the Clinton email server, about what email accounts I used, my email communication with a friend of HRC who had not worked at State.

When it was over and I walked outside, I read a short statement to the assembled press saying that I had done my best to answer all the questions asked of me. HRC appeared the next week for the public hearing, answered questions for eleven hours, and, in the end, even Trey Gowdy had to admit they had learned nothing new from this latest round of the investigation.

The press reported her appearance as a "triumph." The Benghazi hearings were now behind us. Except they were never really behind us because, despite her having been exonerated, as the campaign wore on, "Benghazi" became shorthand among much of the public for incompetence, corruption, emails, you name it. For the Republicans Benghazi had become nothing more than a tool to chip away at HRC's approval ratings, as House Republican leader Kevin McCarthy had inadvertently admitted in an appearance on Fox News in September: "Everybody thought Hillary Clinton was unbeatable, right? But we put together a Benghazi special committee, a select committee. What are her numbers today? Her numbers are dropping."

* * * *

In December 2015, Donald Trump made a major announcement: calling for "a total and complete shutdown of Muslims entering the United States until our country's representatives can figure out what is going on." Ostensibly, it was a response to a mass shooting a few weeks earlier in California by suspected sympathizers of ISIS, a terrorist organization spreading through Syria and Iraq. In reality, he was just leapfrogging off the news to do what he had been doing since he launched his campaign: sowing division and stoking hatred against any racial or ethnic minority. Muslims were one of several targets. A month earlier he had called for surveilling mosques and keeping a database of Syrian refugees.

No votes had been cast yet, but Trump was leading every poll to become the Republican nominee for president. Through cunning and vitriol, he managed to set the agenda on the right, and because his statements were at once so ludicrous and so cruel, they prompted us to respond, to delineate a contrast with him, but also to draw a line at simple common decency. Our campaign printed up posters with the slogan "Love Trumps Hate," which we handed out at rallies and made into stickers and buttons.

To call out the ignorance and the hate Trump was stoking, I was asked to step into another role—this time representing the campaign to the Muslim community. I wrote an op-ed about being an American Muslim and began attending events around the country with Muslim supporters. I thought often of my dad during these trips. Watching the way race, xenophobia, and Islamophobia were playing out in real time, I wondered whether the American ideal my father believed in was actually true: Is "Americanness" big enough to include people of different faiths and ethnicities? What is an American? Who gets to define Americanness?

Nothing got to me more than the story of the Khan family. Khizr Khan was the father of Humayun Khan, an American Muslim soldier who gave his life to protect his comrades. When a suspicious-looking vehicle approached Humayun's unit, he walked toward it as he warned everyone else to take cover, and when the suicide bomber blew up the car, the blast killed him. Mr. Khan spoke out forcefully against Trump's proposed ban in an interview in *Vocativ* in which he recalled his son's heroism and his patriotism. "We still wonder what made him take those 10 steps. . . . Maybe that's the point where all the values, all the service to country, all the things he learned in this country kicked in. It was those values that made him take those 10 steps. Those 10 steps told us we did not make [a] mistake in moving to this country. These were the values we wanted to adopt. Not religious values, human values," he said.

Many people found his story to be a profound rebuke to Trump. HRC was moved by it too, and talked about the Khans on the trail. To me, Humayun Khan's story had significance far beyond whatever it meant politically, and the fact that it had become a campaign issue bothered me. Why did his Gold Star family have to justify themselves as patriots? Had they not sacrificed and suffered enough? Muslims needing to defend their Americanness reminded me of my mother's family being forced to prove their "Indianness" in the days of Partition. It's true that by sharing stories like those of the Khan family, we were seeking to counter the hateful narrative that Trump was constructing about Muslims. But it was deeply disturbing that Trump's racist views had the power to frame the conversation of the election, and not just on the right. The grounds were constantly shifting based on the ravings of someone who was intentionally unleashing an Islamophobia even more intense than what we had seen after 9/11.

Across the country, we met Arabs and Muslims who were fearful about what a Donald Trump presidency could mean for them. Because Trump's statements were so harsh while at the same time lacking in any specifics, making them hard to refute, even those who had lived in the country all their lives were worried. At a Dallas fundraiser, I talked to a man of Middle Eastern descent who told me, "I have been a lifelong Republican, but I am now supporting Hillary. My parents came here as immigrants. I want to make money. I want to be successful. I want my kids to be successful. But you know what I realized when I started listening to Trump? I figured it doesn't matter how much money I have in my bank account if I am living in a concentration camp."

I also met American Muslims who gave Trump the benefit of the doubt. At one event in Los Angeles, I gave my stump speech, describing the work HRC had done on behalf of the causes Muslims cared about: everything from efforts at the global level to foster Middle East peace to plans for supporting local Muslim-owned businesses in this country. I ended as I always did, with a warning about the dangers Trump posed to Muslims. An older man raised his hand during the Q&A session that followed. "That was a lovely speech and very passionately delivered, but I think perhaps you are taking it a little too seriously. I don't believe Trump is going to do any of these things he says he will do. He is just saying it for attention. I am an American. He cannot keep me out of this country." Trying to convey the seriousness of the risk I said, "What about your brother from Pakistan? Or your in-laws from India? What if they won't be allowed to visit you?" He shrugged.

Then there were those who were thrilling to Senator Sanders, who believed that Bernie would be the one to give them free college, to solve climate change, and even to bring peace to the Middle East, though that was not an issue most people associated with him. On a trip to Michigan, I met with a group of young Muslims, most of them college students, for whom this was the first election in which they planned to participate. I was excited that they had come to hear more about HRC's campaign. One young woman, speaking for her peers, said she really *wanted* to be excited about the first woman president, but she had to support Bernie because she believed he would be more effective at finally brokering a peace treaty in the Middle East. Everyone around her nodded. I asked the group why they doubted Hillary Clinton's ability to do the same.

"Well, she has done nothing to help the Palestinians."

Taking a deep breath, I asked them if they knew that she was the first U.S. official to ever call the territories "Palestine" in the nineties, that she advocated for Palestinian sovereignty back when no other official would. They did not. I then asked them if they were aware that she brought together the last round of direct talks between the Israelis and Palestinians? That she personally negotiated a cease-fire to stop the latest war in Gaza when she was secretary of state? They shook their heads. Had they known that she announced $600 million in assistance to the Palestinian Authority and $300 million in humanitarian aid to Gaza in her first year at State? They began to steal glances at one another. Did they know that she pushed Israel to invest in the West Bank and announced an education program to make college more affordable for Palestinian students? More head shaking. They simply had no idea.

"So," I continued, "respectfully, what is it about Senator Sanders's twenty-seven-year record in Congress that suggests to you that the Middle East is a priority for him?"

The young woman's response encapsulated some of what we were up against.

"I don't know," she replied. "I just *feel* it."

* * * *

During the months on the road, I encountered lots and lots of these sorts of *feelings* and heard all kinds of feedback. It could be roughly divided into a few buckets. There was the glowing adulation, the army of supporters we could count on to volunteer and cheer and persevere with us, and we were grateful to have them. That was one bucket. Then there was the bucket of tsk-tskers, the moral high-grounders— like the young woman who came to take a picture with me at a millennial event and told me, "I'm a feminist but I am not sure Hillary is my kind of feminist." Ah, okay, got it. And who exactly was her kind of feminist? No clue. It must be that fantasy woman, the one who was never actually running. Then, somewhere in the middle was the *yes, but* crowd. Friends and strangers and everyone in between who could support her but were sure she could be doing better if she just did this or that differently.

As we moved through the primary season, HRC faced a never-ending stream of ridiculous, almost comical advice on navigating the double standards of the campaign trail. Yet I welcomed much of it because it clarified for me the caricatures of HRC that were still shaping the world's perception of her, and forced the issue of what we needed to do about the apparent problems—one of them being whether she was "likeable." Who doesn't want to appear "likeable"? And why was HRC *not* likeable? This was particularly difficult to understand for those of us who knew her, since as far as we were concerned that was a quality she had in abundance.

But the question of likability could not be ignored. Her communications director, Jen, her deputy, and I met from time to time discuss how to help HRC increase her likability quotient. We noted that whenever she appeared on lighthearted talk shows, like *The View* or *The Tonight Show*, our phones would blow up with encouraging messages from friends. So, one day, we showed HRC interview clips and Jen offered suggestions for rephrasing certain answers or expressing her emotions differently. HRC should find the right balance between warmth and toughness. She had to exude competence but not display anger or frustration. She had to stop nodding her head when listening to people. She needed to keep her voice steady and a little deeper. On and on it went.

One day, I received a set of detailed notes from a prominent filmmaker, whose thoughts had been solicited by a mutual friend. I didn't know him but I respected his work. He offered to give HRC voice coaching, speech training, and general ideas about presentation if she had a few days to spare. He would put her in front of his camera and help mold her into the right kind of female presidential candidate. The notes were designed to address our conundrum: research showing that the more successful a woman is, the less she is liked. So in one of his first notes his advice was that she not "try" to be likeable because that will read as insincere, just "be likeable." In another he advised her not to raise her voice when she made a speech, to speak to the people watching on TV not the cheering people in the room. He also said that because she was so focused on the nitty-gritty of policy she made people feel lectured at, and that people wouldn't remember what she said, only how she made them feel. When I had asked if he had a model politician in mind, to give HRC a sense of who she might emulate, his answer was:

"Her husband."

When I asked for another option, he responded, "Obama." The obvious fact that neither was a woman seemed not to have occurred to him. Clearly there was no model to follow and no magic key that would unlock her success, because no woman had ever been here before. Don't *try* to be likeable, just *be* likeable. Be authentic so long as you keep your voice down.

Another media strategist told me that she always looked angry when she gave her stump speech, and he had an idea for how to make her facial expression more appealing. What was the idea? I asked. He suggested we place a photo of her grandchild on the podium so that when she looked down at the notes for her speech, she would see something that made her happy and therefore she would look happy.

Other women in politics sometimes consult with stylists for their wardrobe, but not HRC. She just didn't care that much about fashion. In past years, she would call her friend Oscar de la Renta, say she needed something new, and he and his team would send suggestions, then make something beautiful for her, a gown for a special event, a bespoke suit for major appearances like a convention speech. But sadly Oscar had died the year before she launched her campaign, and while she still wore many of his old staples, she could use a few new things. So, when a few fashion designers reached out to the campaign offering to dress her, I decided to follow up, in part because it would be an opportunity to lift up other American designers.

Knowing she would have little patience for design meetings and fittings (although I loved them), we set aside a day to go to three studios. The first meeting was with a respected designer who declared that her jackets needed to be cut off in the middle of the hip, not longer. Though Oscar had always given her a slightly longer jacket, she said okay. The design team also suggested she stick to neutral tones. She nodded along and bought a few pieces. The second stop took her to a dynamic young designer. There, it was pointed out that her jackets were way too short, that they should be below the knee to elongate her. She nodded again and bought a handful of pieces there too. The final visit was with Michael Kors, whom Anna Wintour had recommended. He had a totally different attitude. "I will make you whatever you feel beautiful in," he said, and she proceeded to buy quite a few items from him.

Set with a dozen new outfits, we went back to the real world, but the endless fashion commentary continued to stream in. Jim Margolis told me that based on their research, people in Iowa responded well to an image of her in a black-and-white striped T-shirt that she had worn to a backyard event. I thanked Jim for the feedback. Weeks later, in Northern California, a supporter pulled me aside and urged me not to make her look like a soccer mom. "She needs to look presidential and wear business suits, not these flimsy T-shirts you have been putting her in." I nodded again. *Wear color! But not pastels. Only wear black and navy with button-down shirts. Don't wear big jewelry. I like her hair short. No, long is better. Is her makeup person with you today? She looks tired.* I could talk to eight different people and get eight different opinions about her appearance. In fact, I had!

Everyone on the campaign, not just me, got pointers about her appearance, and all the while we were running against someone who didn't have to deal with any "helpful" advice about his hair or style. By the end of the campaign, HRC had spent six hundred hours on her hair and makeup—six hundred hours, the equivalent of almost a full month that her male opponents could spend shaking hands with voters, thinking about new ideas, or just resting up for the slog ahead.

Comments on her clothes mostly came from other women. Men were focused on her voice, a nagging manner that reminded them of their wives or mothers or, heaven forbid, their mothers-in-law. Ambition at a certain age, an age when women are expected to disappear, was unacceptable. And forget trying to become commander in chief.

* * * *

As the primaries wore on, I was on the road at least three or four days a week doing fundraisers or accompanying HRC to the early primary states—Iowa, New Hampshire, South Carolina, and Nevada. So there were many nights when I didn't make it home, or arrived so late that Jordan had already gone to sleep. I missed him so much that when I got home after his bedtime, I would crawl into his little bed fully dressed, snuggle up next to him, and fall asleep. Thanks to Anthony, Jordan was comfortably ensconced in his routines while I was gone. He managed Jordan's daily drop-off and pickup from nursery school, prepared all his meals, organized babysitters when he had meetings or played hockey, connected me to Jordan for FaceTime calls every night I was on the road, and sent daily videos of Jordan's visits to local museums or zoos. If I had clothes that needed dry cleaning or shoes that needed fixing, I just left them by the front door and they would be taken care of. I didn't even see a bill, or worry about a single thing at home because I had Anthony. But there was one issue that Anthony, who handled everything, couldn't fix.

At a fundraising dinner around the holidays, my seatmate leaned over and whispered conspiratorially that she had just watched an early screener of what she referred to as "your" movie. She wanted me to know that she thought it didn't reflect "too badly" on me and mostly that she felt extremely sorry for Jordan. "My *movie*?" I had no idea what she was talking about. She seemed surprised I was not aware. "It is a film about the mayoral campaign." Then, it clicked. The videographer from Anthony's campaign had made a movie out of the footage he had captured during the campaign.

When I'd gotten wind of what he was doing, some time before, I had asked Anthony to make sure that neither Jordan nor I would appear in it. Anthony said he had no power to stop the videographer; he didn't control the material and he had granted access. Frustrated, I considered suing the videographer, because he didn't have my consent to use footage of Jordan and me, but in the end I didn't, figuring a lawsuit would be a lost cause. I resorted to hoping and praying that the videographer would have the decency to keep us out of the film.

The film was accepted to the Sundance Film Festival, and I heard about it constantly—from supporters, friends, strangers, Fortune 500 CEOs. Everyone had an opinion about it. Most people who watched it told me it appeared as though I had actively participated, that I had contributed to this further exploitation of my son's privacy. When they described the scenes I was in, the words I said during moments of extreme stress, I wanted to throw up. It felt like I had been physically violated.

My friends who appeared in the film were upset too, and rightly so. They had given money, attended events at my behest, and they felt I had betrayed their trust or abused their friendship now that their faces appeared on the big screen without their knowledge or permission. When the videographer had filmed these events, the hosts had assumed he was making something for use only by the campaign.

I had trusted the videographer during Anthony's race. I had been vulnerable and honest in front of him, and it was a mistake I was now paying for. What I should have recognized was that he was no different from the "gotta make a living" photographer on the street, just someone who thought he might have a good story to sell.

* * * *

Iowa Caucus night was February 1, 2016. It began with a discomfiting reminder of the awful night in 2008 when HRC had come in third behind Obama and Senator John Edwards. Early results were showing a neck-and-neck race between HRC and Bernie Sanders, and the fear—while unspoken—that we would lose Iowa again was palpable as we waited out the vote count. As the evening progressed, as more precinct results came in, Robby predicted it would be a squeaker, but he was confident HRC would win. That was enough for most of us, especially HRC, to decide to declare victory. In 2008, we had approached every primary contest with caution, never claiming a win until it was ironclad. In 2016 we were bolder. I called Connolly and Greg Hale as we drove to the event site.

"Just get her out there as fast as you can," I told them.

She leapt onto the stage and claimed the night. It was a page out of the Obama 2008 playbook, and those of us who carried the ghosts of that past urged her on. Generating momentum was key and no one wanted to let a second slip by. It didn't matter how narrow the victory—in this case her 49.84 percent to Sanders's 49.59 percent—a win was a win and we needed it. We hopped on a plane for New Hampshire that very night, to prepare for the next debate and to campaign for the primary the following week.

On the flight to New Hampshire, one of our consultants pulled me aside to pick up a conversation we had had many days before. Why did Hillary insist on campaigning in New Hampshire? In early strategy meetings, advisors had suggested skipping aggressive campaigning there, given Sanders's advantages as the senator from a neighboring state. HRC was firm; no matter what, she was campaigning and competing in New Hampshire. Now on the plane, talking to someone who had been on the Obama team in 2008, I simply said, "If you'd been with us in 2008, you would understand." In 2008, New Hampshire voters had picked HRC over Obama even when polls showed her down by double digits. These people were there for her when no one else thought she had a shot, and she was going to show them the respect they deserved whether she had a chance of winning or not.

A week later, Sanders beat her in New Hampshire by twenty points, and she did not have a single regret about her decision to stump there. She just continued to roll out her policy proposals, deliver solid debate performances, and focus on upcoming states. She won Nevada, then South Carolina, then most of the Super Tuesday states in March, then on to other caucuses and primaries where she won some and lost some. With each contest, she methodically racked up the number of delegates she needed to secure the nomination. When she finally made it, it was weirdly anticlimactic.

We were in Los Angeles preparing to head to Long Beach for a final primary campaign rally when Jen called from Brooklyn. The Associated Press was about to report that HRC had secured the Democratic Party's nomination. By public count, she had 1,812 pledged delegates and 572 superdelegates, which meant she had cleared the bar. It was over, even though six states were voting the next day, including California, where we were campaigning at that very moment. I put Jen and a few other senior staff members from HQ on speakerphone to deliver the good news to HRC directly so we could discuss how she should claim this historic victory. But HRC was not happy.

"They announce this the day *before* the final six states?"

"Uh, well, it just happens to be mathematically correct," Nick Merrill explained. Nick had been her primary press advisor since she had left the State Department and was an expert at handling high-stakes moments like these. Always smiling, always reassuring, always coming up with good solutions to big problems, he had a mild manner that belied a steely resolve, especially when he knew he was right, which was often.

"I am not declaring anything until people get a chance to vote tomorrow. I am not going to say to thousands of people your vote doesn't matter because I've already won. Why would I do that? I am not doing that!"

It seemed an oddly principled stand. Just about any other candidate would have said, "I won! Great!"—and moved on from there. We stood around awkwardly. Nick needed to tell the traveling press something, and HRC needed to figure out what to say about it in the speech she was about to deliver.

"Let's just get in the cars," I offered, in order to give us all some breathing room. As HRC and I jumped into the Suburban, I stayed quiet. Once or twice, she said out loud, irritated, "No announcements should be made until everyone gets a chance to vote," and I just nodded. Have I mentioned she is stubborn? Over the thirty-minute drive to the rally site, messages of congratulations came pouring in by email and text. The calls that came in, I just silenced.

When we pulled up to the site, she asked for a copy of her speech. We had language from HQ which was pretty forward-leaning claiming victory. Nick and I formulated a slightly less robust version that we handwrote into the speech. Then she took the pen and the speech and wrote over some of it. Most of the time I can read her handwriting, but this was true chicken scratch. She wasn't about to have Nick or me review it so that we could offer changes or report in to HQ. We got to the event, and as she walked to the auditorium, none of us knew if she would jump on stage and proclaim "we did it!" or begin with her usual stump speech. She ended up landing somewhere in the middle. She acknowledged that there had been some promising news but that she was in this until the end and that she hoped everyone would vote. Her reaction was summed up in her tweet that evening: "We're flattered, @AP, but we've got primaries to win. CA, MT, NM, ND, NJ, SD, vote tomorrow!"

Those two experiences, the refusal both to give up on New Hampshire and to declare victory prematurely, showed exactly who HRC was at her core. That despite all the accusations about her ruthless ambition or questions about her integrity, Hillary Clinton always tried to do the right thing.

As 2016 progressed, she mostly ignored the false stories that dogged her. That she was dying. That she was cold and uncaring. That she had left her team to die in Benghazi. The email story, so confusing and complex to most people that it created a lot of skepticism about her, kept metastasizing. By now, she was labeled "crooked" by Trump on a daily basis. While she was surprised by each new malicious story, she never let them fester for long, she just moved on. There was always something more important to do. And now it was to defeat Donald Trump in the general election.

*   *   *   *

The night after the California primary, June 8, she would formally accept the nomination for president before supporters at the Duggal Greenhouse, a modern glass cube of a building built out of an old factory on the waterfront at the Brooklyn Navy Yard. We had decided on that as the venue for her victory speech because in 2008, HRC had marked the 18 million cracks she and her supporters had visited on the highest, hardest glass ceiling. Now, celebrating her historic nomination in a room with an actual glass ceiling seemed perfect.

"There's just one thing," Greg said tentatively when I checked in about the event status on our daily team countdown call. "There is a glass ceiling but you can't see it. It's blocked by steel and iron support beams on the interior so if you look up, you can't actually see the glass part. But it's there. Trust me."

"Greg!" I laughed. "I just hope this is not a bad omen!" I called HRC's head speechwriter and Jake, and told them we needed to tweak her speech just a tiny little bit.

That night was in some ways just like any other campaign night— a large rally in a packed room, people standing on bleachers, a rope line populated by enthusiastic and emotional supporters, music filling the hall. But the "fighting for us" placards that we had used most of the year were now replaced by little American flags which the advance team handed out as people waited. On this one evening, unlike every other evening on the campaign trail, we were not in campaign mode. This night was about making history.

I had to read the draft speech a few times for it to sink in that this was it. I had spent the last few years constantly bracing for bad news, prepared for disappointment—and yet I signed up every time, always hoping, ready to believe. And now something incredible was about to happen. As we were heading to the stage, buoyed by the electricity in the cavernous space crowded with three thousand bodies, it was hard not to be overcome by the moment.

HRC would always insist that the campaign was about the voters, about the American people, those she met in city after city and town after town starting with that quiet first trip to Iowa a little over a year ago. By emphasizing those points, she was laying out her belief in the virtues of our democratic system. She was also doing what women do a lot: being self-effacing, both because she believed it was her job to serve others and because it had the side benefit of mitigating her potential threat as a powerful, ambitious woman.

In this moment though, I wanted her to take it all in. To see that all of these people, along with the millions who had come out in the primary, were there for *her*. They supported and admired her, volunteered and cheered for her. Yes this was about the country, this was about the "we" and "us" that she always talked about, but as she stood in the wings waiting to be announced on stage, to claim the moment for the millions of American women and girls on whose behalf she had made history, I whispered, "When you go out there, just pause a minute. Take it all in. Allow these people to celebrate *you*." She strained to hear over the roar of the crowd, but she nodded that she understood.

When she took those five steps up to that stage, bathed in Greg's Hollywood lighting, surrounded by the deafening cheers, the music of Sara Bareilles blaring over the loudspeakers, she put both her hands on her heart and then opened her arms wide, as though she were bringing the world in for a hug. Then she began her speech: "It may be hard to see tonight, but we are all standing under a glass ceiling right now. But don't worry, we're not smashing this one. Thanks to you, we've reached a milestone—the first time in our nation's history that a woman will be a major party's nominee for president of the United States. Tonight's victory is not about one person. It belongs to generations of women and men who struggled and sacrificed and made this moment possible. In our country, it started right here in New York, a place called Seneca Falls, in 1848. When a small but determined group of women, and men, came together with the idea that women deserved equal rights, and they set it forth in something called the Declaration of Sentiments, and it was the first time in human history that that kind of declaration occurred. So we all owe so much to those who came before, and tonight belongs to all of you."

BRACING

If everything on earth were rational, nothing would happen.
                                        —Fyodor Dostoevsky

In April 2016, it was reported that I was on ISIS's hit list, along with other American Muslims, including Minnesota Congressman Keith Ellison. ISIS was a new terrorist network forged out of extremist groups in Iraq. They had made an international name for themselves by kidnapping hostages and videotaping their gruesome beheadings. In one instance, they burned alive a captured Jordanian air force pilot as he stood trapped in a metal cage. So when they published their target list, the authorities in New York did not take it lightly. Unlike in 2012, when they were able to identify and interview the man who made the threat against me, no one knew where they might be able to find these ISIS operatives. Whereas my own location was quite easy to pin down since so much of my boss's schedule was published far in advance, and where she went I was likely to be found too.

When I returned home the day the story broke, I overheard Anthony on the phone with a reporter. "Writing a follow-up to a front-page story will only give more fuel to this nonsense," I heard him say. I shook my head. When Anthony hung up, I told him that, as a precaution, I wanted to be careful about not being out alone with Jordan. I was grateful that my son had a fully present parent who had the ability to be the primary caretaker.

My phone then rang from an unknown number. It was Mayor Bill de Blasio calling to tell me he recommended a protective detail while intelligence services did a threat assessment. I balked. "What would people say if they knew taxpayer dollars were being spent to protect me?" Anthony was wildly gesturing at me and mouthing, "Just say yes!" Had he already talked to de Blasio? I could never tell with him. In any case, the mayor was not taking no for an answer.

"What would people say if something happened to you? We can keep it to a limited time frame and reassess, but let us first investigate the threat."

I said I would think about it, and hung up with de Blasio. Then I got a call from the NYPD intelligence chief, John Miller, a respected expert on counterterrorism whom HRC had known for many years. While he believed the real threat to be quite low, taking appropriate precautions and investigating was the responsible thing to do, he offered. Miller said he would have a police cruiser drive by our apartment at regular intervals. I would have a very light security detail while they did their investigative work, and Miller said he would see to it that the investigation was conducted as expeditiously as possible.

After thinking about it and discussing with Anthony, I realized that Miller and de Blasio were probably more concerned for another reason. Even if ISIS itself was not an imminent danger to me, the threat might give copycats some ideas. I was a familiar face around New York City, stopped on the street daily for chats, selfies, questions about the campaign. It had become such a normal part of our everyday existence that one night at dinner, Jordan asked, "Mommy, why do people on the street talk to you and Daddy?" Before either of us could say anything, Jordan continued, "Is it because you work for them?" "Yes it is!" Anthony and I both said in unison.

So I decided to accept the offer of the security detail. Miller told me that the team who would be with me were all seasoned men and women who had worked with the Secret Service in the past and knew how to blend into the background. Which they did. And they would remain with me until I boarded the train to Philadelphia from New York's Penn Station on my way to the Democratic Convention three months later.

The fact that I needed security was hard for me to wrap my mind around. I couldn't help feeling that my life had become a grotesque comedy. In 2012, American members of Congress were calling me a traitor and their followers were sending me messages telling me to "go home," which presumably meant back to Saudi Arabia. Now extremist forces in the Middle East were saying I should be killed because I was supporting a Western, therefore apostate, government.

Where did I belong exactly?

* * * *

The run-up to the day when HRC's delegate count assured her the nomination had been demanding. And the run-up to the Democratic Convention at the end of July, when HRC would formally accept that nomination, would prove rocky too. We weren't going to be able to just coast our way to triumph once she achieved a delegate victory. Chief among our problems were emails—investigations into, and leaks thereof. Emails were going to plague us right up to the very day of the convention.

In April I was finally called in for an interview at the FBI about HRC's use of private email when she was secretary of state. I had been preparing for this interview ever since I'd first reached out to Karen Dunn more than a year earlier. The investigators presented me with printouts of my emails. I was then asked for an explanation of each one, specifically whether I believed anything was classified or not. Over and over I explained that it was not my responsibility in my job at State to determine classification of material, that the emails they were showing me had all been sent to me on my unclassified account. By the time I left, after several hours of testifying, I had no idea what they had made of what I told them. Their faces remained unreadable throughout.

Then at the beginning of July, without giving the campaign any notice, and in a break with how directors had operated in the past, FBI director Jim Comey held a press conference about the email investigation. He announced that although the FBI had found that HRC's email practices had been "extremely careless" because she was sending emails from a private server instead of through the State Department system, they were not recommending any charges.

The FBI's objection to her use of her personal email was because this supposedly made the communications more vulnerable to a security breach than the State email system. Ironically, this ignored the fact that the State system was disrupted from time to time, and we would get notices from the administrative offices instructing us to use personal emails until the situation was resolved. Even though former officials had used private emails before, and Trump officials would do it after, blame for this practice landed on HRC alone.

To most of the world, the endless email investigations were so confusing and hard to understand that all people seemed to take away from them was that Hillary Clinton had done *something* she wasn't supposed to—they really weren't sure what exactly. But that was damning enough.

After Comey's unprecedented announcement, just in case we hoped we could now put the subject of emails behind us, we had an email issue of an entirely different kind to contend with. In late July, on the day HRC announced Tim Kaine as her running mate, at an event in Florida, Wikileaks released thousands of emails hacked from the Democratic National Committee server. Our proactive message that day, about her choice of Tim Kaine, was being drowned out by a more salacious story of leaked emails.

More problematic were the now public emails among DNC staff, some of whom were personally more supportive of HRC than Bernie Sanders, which made it appear that the DNC as a whole favored HRC. During the GOP convention a few days before, Trump had hammered on the theme of disunity in our party and suggested that the system had been rigged against Sanders. The Wikileaks emails seemed to confirm Trump's accusations.

We'd already had enough trouble with the Sanders camp. Sanders endorsed HRC about a month after the AP reported that HRC had won the nomination by close to 4 million votes and had enough delegates to be the nominee. But even after Sanders suspended his campaign, his supporters, the self-identified "Bernie Bros"—a loyal contingent consisting mostly of men—often disrupted our campaign events and sometimes harassed and bullied Hillary supporters online. They weren't violent, just consistently disruptive. Meanwhile, all through the interim weeks between HRC's speech at the Duggal

Greenhouse and Sanders's official endorsement, Robby was negotiating behind the scenes with the Sanders team to be sure the two sides could come together as smoothly as possible at the Democratic Convention. Now the emails from Wikileaks were sure to aggravate tensions.

The GOP convention had featured high-profile speakers who led chants of "lock her up!"—the catchy rallying cry Trump had come up with to drive home his contention that HRC's email use had been a crime. The Wikileaks emails made it all the easier for Trump to exploit the public's vague suspicions.

Of course the real wrongdoing, the real crime, was the Wikileaks hacking itself. Hacking is theft, clear and simple, and anyone trading in hacked information is relying on material that has been stolen to damage its victims. Unfortunately and infuriatingly, much of the reporting focused on the gossipy email exchanges between DNC staff, instead of on the crime that had brought them to public view.

Robby went on the offensive immediately. In interviews the day before we rang in our convention, he told reporters that our campaign believed that Russian state actors had stolen the emails from the DNC and timed their release expressly to interfere with the beginning of our convention. "I don't think it's coincidental that these emails were released on the eve of our convention here, and I think that's disturbing," Robby said in an interview with CNN's Jake Tapper, who seemed skeptical of Robby's assertions.

"How did it go?" I asked him.

"Good! I am trying!" he said, ever upbeat.

His assistant stood next to him shaking her head.

"They think he's crazy, don't they?" I said. She nodded. For most of the world, it might have seemed far-fetched, a plot out of a spy novel. It sounded that way to me too when I first heard it. But time would show that our campaign's conclusions, wild as they might have seemed, were well warranted.

* * * *

On July 25, we opened the week that would officially mark HRC's ascent as the Democratic nominee for president. In planning the

Democratic Convention, we had been determined to build out a program that would showcase the America we all believed in. Our creative team included HRC's media advisor Jim Margolis, convention CEO Leah Daughtry, and the Emmy Award–winning producer Ricky Kirshner. The America we wanted to see reflected in the convention was the America my parents believed in, its ideals so compelling that half a century before they had each abandoned everything they knew for them—their countries, their homes, their families, their friends. Leaving the familiar for the unknown, they had believed that America's promise of freedom, equality, diversity, liberty, would outweigh the risks they took. And it did. But this was not a perfect country, and they knew that too. They had seen the turmoil of the civil rights and the antiwar and the women's rights movements, the assassinations of Malcolm X, of Martin Luther King, Jr., of Robert Kennedy, the shootings at Kent State, the killing of Fred Hampton. They'd witnessed riots in the streets, demonstrations that turned violent, and violence from the police too, in a country sometimes convulsing under the stress of its internal divisions.

Yet still they believed that America's founding principles made it the place where anything was possible. Their faith in America had informed mine. And sure enough, here I was in Philadelphia, preparing for the first woman to accept the nomination of a major political party for president, a testament to those very ideals.

Our team set out to build a series of nights that reflected the values of our candidate and our party, and that repeatedly made a direct call for unity. One night of the convention was themed "United Together," another "Working Together," the final was "Stronger Together." We wanted to make sure every American watching could see themselves in our party and on that stage. Another reason we came back to the theme of unity night after night? Because we badly needed it. After the Wikileaks hacks, the intra-party vitriol, Jim Comey's unexpected press conference, and the tableau of fear and division the country had witnessed during the GOP convention, we wanted to put on a show that would bring people together, not drive them further apart.

We invited our party leaders, elected officials, and a contingent of celebrities to speak. Because HRC wanted us to broaden our coalition to bring in moderate Republicans, we also invited former NYC mayor Michael Bloomberg, who happened to be a legitimately successful New York businessman. In a deeply effective way his speech exposed Trump for what he was.

Then there were the Americans who raised their voices to share their personal stories: disability rights activist Anastasia Somoza, whom HRC had worked with for twenty years; an eleven-year-old Dreamer she had just met in Nevada, who worried about her parents being deported; the African American Mothers of the Movement, each of whom had lost a child killed by the police or by gun violence; survivors of the horrific mass shooting at the Bible study class at Mother Emanuel AME Church in Charleston; a home healthcare worker advocating for raising the national minimum wage to $15 an hour; an LGBTQ activist; a sex trafficking survivor. One of the most dramatic moments was when Khizr and Ghazala Khan, the parents of the slain Muslim soldier Humayun Khan, took the stage, and Mr. Khan pulled out his well-thumbed copy of the U.S. Constitution and challenged Donald Trump to read it. The audience erupted in a roar of applause.

On the first night of the convention, about two hours in, we heard consistent booing from the California section. HRC had won the California primary, but the loudest voices in the delegation were carrying Bernie signs. A few of us walked over to explore the cause of the commotion and realized that there was an open bar behind the stand and what seemed to be a party going on. Michelle Obama, the most popular person in our party, would be taking the stage soon.

I recalled the convention in 2008, when HRC descended into the stands to graciously release her delegates to Obama, a critical step toward creating the party unity he would need going forward. Tonight, she was being afforded no such respect.

"Shut the bar down," I told the advance lead. I was not going to allow this ill will to tarnish our unity message.

On the second night, when the votes were tallied and the party officially declared Hillary Clinton the nominee, Podesta, Jake, Jen, and I stood on the corner of the stage as the chair of the convention, Congresswoman Marcia Fudge, made the official announcement. The pounding on the floor was so intense, it felt like we were all going to fall through.

The third night concluded with a speech from President Obama, who described the America he saw—"Black, white, Latino, Asian, Native American; young and old; gay, straight, men, women, folks with disabilities"—and told the audience that the only candidate in the race who saw the same America he believed in was a woman "who has devoted her life to it; a mother and grandmother who'd do anything to help our children thrive; a leader with real plans to break down glass ceilings, and widen the circle of opportunity to every single American. . . ." We couldn't have asked for a more full-throated endorsement—or a more resounding affirmation of our message of unity—and of progress. Here was the first African American president looking to pass the baton to the first woman president. HRC joined Obama on stage after his speech, and their embrace was such a moment of hope that it felt like America would never turn back again.

The frenzy climaxed the next night, July 28, when HRC took to the floor in her white Ralph Lauren suit to formally accept the nomination. If there was a single night I truly believed Hillary Clinton would become president it was that night, as a blizzard of confetti and a hundred thousand red, white, and blue balloons descended from the cavernous ceiling. The song "Stronger Together," written and recorded for that evening, echoed through the hall, competing with the deafening sounds of fifty thousand supporters clapping and cheering for the woman in white on stage. Once HRC accepted the nomination, she began tossing giant blue balloons emblazoned with white stars out to the audience; to Tim Kaine, her running mate; to Chelsea, who had spoken so eloquently to introduce her mother; to her husband, who had given his own moving tribute to her on the second night of the convention and now looked exuberant as he waded through the waist-high drift of balloons that rained down.

Afterward our delegation of about twenty Clinton/Kaine family members, campaign staff, and officials made its way through the balloons to the small backstage hold area, and Tim Kaine surprised me by leading the rest of our group in an impromptu singing of "Happy

Birthday." It was my forty-first birthday. This new decade was turning out to be pretty extraordinary. Or so it seemed.

*   *   *   *

It was the end of August. After a long day in the midst of a week of fundraising events on the east end of Long Island, I joined Anthony and Jordan in a home that had been lent to us so that I could stay close to the Clintons in nearby Amagansett. The house we were in was a pristine construction of glass and wood. It was lovely, surrounded by manicured lawns, with a tennis court and rectangular gunite pool in the back. It was this scene of unblemished perfection that would soon be the setting for the collapse of my entire house of cards.

When I walked through the front door that evening, Anthony was in the middle of his end-of-day routines with Jordan, and I joined my nightly conference calls. He played games with Jordan while bathing him, then dressed him in pajamas and handed him to me so I could read him a bedtime story. Anthony had been checking his phone regularly, but no more than I.

Jordan fell asleep beside me, and I continued to sit with him, my dress crumpled around me, the lamp still on, his picture book open in my lap, my iPhone in my hand as I began responding to the messages that had come in over the past thirty minutes.

"Can you talk?"

Anthony had quietly walked into the room. From the tone, I knew it was bad.

"The *New York Post* called."

Really bad.

It was late. There was simply too much going on in my world for Anthony's problems to surface at this moment. The DNC server being hacked; the turmoil at the convention; Trump publicly calling on Russia to find Hillary's emails; Trump speculating that perhaps "Second Amendment people" would take action against Hillary; Robby's warnings about Russian election interference; death threats from ISIS. I was also planning the final two months of the campaign. On the home front, Jordan's first day of school was the following week and I was worried I wouldn't even be in town for it. I didn't have the bandwidth to take in any more information or contend with any more problems.

Distracted and overwhelmed, I halfheartedly asked, not wanting to know, "What is this about?"

He opened with an apology, the admission that he didn't entirely know what was in the story. He simply said the *Post* had a picture of him and that Jordan might be in it but he had no idea what picture the reporter was referring to, couldn't remember what it could be. I envisioned a photo of Anthony and Jordan out somewhere. One of the many pictures he sent me while I was on the road. On the ferry. On the subway. On a park bench. I inferred that he had sent some such picture to another woman. I had given up on expecting him to respect the vows of our marriage, but our child's image being shared felt more violent than any humiliation I had faced in the past.

The stakes were already so high, almost unbearably so, and I needed help navigating how to handle the story. Around midnight, I emailed Philippe all I knew, which was essentially nothing. "Philippe, I think I have a problem," I typed before falling into a night of fitful sleep. I knew only one thing: It wouldn't be as bad as Anthony said. It would be worse.

And it was.

A response from Philippe appeared in my inbox in the early hours, "Yes, you do. You need to look at this picture yourself." And so I clicked on the link Philippe sent. I wish I could take back the image that appeared but I can never erase it. There was Jordan, sleeping peacefully next to an indecent Anthony, an image shared with a stranger, or a "friend" in Anthony's view, and now for the entire world to see. This crossed into another level of degradation, a violation of the innocence of our child. There were no more "what were you thinking?" questions left in me. It was over.

If there was anything unforgiveable in a marriage, a partnership in raising a child, this was it. It was not rage that motivated me that morning because the word rage would not do justice to what I was feeling. I think God had put me in this perfect glass and wood–framed house for a reason, because I would have destroyed everything around me if I had been in my own home. I simmered until I thought I would explode. After checking to make sure Jordan was still asleep and closing the door to his room, I marched out to the living room, where Anthony was lying on the sofa, still fully dressed from the previous night, his eyes bloodshot, phone in his hand, no doubt having seen the article as soon as it posted. I informed him I was putting out a statement announcing our separation, to which he responded quietly and simply, "Okay." I then told him that he needed to find another place to live when we returned to Manhattan. He would not be welcome to sleep in the apartment or spend any nights alone with our son ever again. He nodded, looking down while I screamed at him. The yelling didn't make anyone feel better but I did it anyway.

I went outside and got on the phone with Cheryl and Philippe a little after 7 a.m. and asked them to help me with a statement. Cheryl suggested some language over the line that I didn't really hear but I said it sounded fine. Philippe said he would get it out. I couldn't close my eyes without seeing the image pop into my head. I felt my insides coming apart, hot blood drowning what was left of my heart. I paced by the long pool to gather myself, repeating a familiar prayer over and over again, asking for some solace, some sanity, some peace, some escape. *"La hawla wa la quwatti illa billahi."* A prayer that is simply an acceptance that no human being has the power over anything except through God's grace. I needed that grace now more than ever.

I steeled myself, took a few deep breaths, then dialed HRC. She did not need this. Our campaign did not need this. She counted on me, had faith in me, and I was bringing more scandal, more shame to what should have been a laser-focused effort to close out the campaign. I don't remember what I said. She said that she was glad I was finally moving on with my life. I then dialed Bari, now Chelsea's chief of staff, and emailed President Clinton's team too, apologizing to them all. I knew they would face questions about this on the campaign trail.

I thought the image might kill my mother, so I sent her an email, told her I was leaving Anthony and assured her I was fine and that Jordan would be okay. I was glad she was close by, visiting family in New Jersey, because I knew she would come to help me; but I couldn't have her hear my voice in that moment because then she would know just how bad it was. The overall silence from the rest of my family was a gift. I had brought shame on the family before. This was violence.

Everyone has a limit and I had finally reached mine, ages after everyone else had gotten there. The next day, my mom, my sister, my nephews would all descend on us.

I received all sorts of messages that began with "I don't know what to say" because "I'm sorry" didn't seem quite enough this time. Most people congratulated me for finally freeing myself from Anthony. Among the many texts was one from the parent of a child Jordan was supposed to have a playdate with the next day. It came to me from the mother, someone who usually communicated with Anthony directly. In light of "everything," she thought it best "for everyone" that our children not interact. I didn't respond. That evening, I received an email from one of the mothers in Jordan's school, whose son was Jordan's closest playmate. I held my breath before I opened it. "We all stand in support of you and want to help with Jordan however we can. If you need to leave him with me after school, we would love to have him. I can even keep him for sleepovers." I was so grateful to this mom, to my friends, and my family; I needed this village now more than ever before.

Twenty-four hours later, my family was on their way to join us, and the fundraisers were in full swing. But I had something else on my plate. New York State Administration for Children's Services (ACS) was making their first visit to interview Anthony and me, to ensure that Jordan was "safe." Children's Services investigations can be triggered by calls to the agency from members of the public concerned about the well-being of a child. Enough people had called in to report us that Children's Services said they had no choice but to open a case. It was a tense and uncomfortable visit. A young woman and two or three men in suits filled the chairs at the dining table and asked questions. Anthony couldn't remember enough details to answer. When was the photo taken? Who was it sent to? Were there others? What was happening in the image? Was the child awake? I felt like I was in a bad movie where the acting was subpar and the plot made no sense.

After a few minutes, they shifted their attention to me. Did I have any prior knowledge of Anthony taking suggestive pictures in which

Jordan was present? I tried not to let the anger within me distort my voice when I said of course I did not. They had to ask and I had to answer. Then they asked me if I had had any concerns about the level of care being provided to Jordan by his father. I said categorically that I had not. Never, for one second, did I think Anthony would do anything to harm or expose our child. Ever. Until now. The barrage of questions continued, and in the brief silences during their note-taking, my mind could escape back to the old world I had lived in, the world of reason. I wondered why Anthony would do this now, just when we both had so much at stake in our lives. I was on the campaign of a lifetime, which, if successful, would be historic. His life was finally back on track. He was in talks to anchor a television news show, write a book, launch a podcast. None of these opportunities could possibly survive the scandal. And they didn't.

The only person who seemed oblivious to it all was Jordan, who was sitting on a bed in an upstairs bedroom playing with his cars without a care in the world. Strangers engaging in grown-up conversations around him was nothing new for him, and he didn't know that this time he was the subject of the commotion. But when the investigators said they needed to interview Jordan, I became protective of him and tried to resist. The young woman, who had identified herself as the primary investigator, assured me she would only ask him a few general questions about how he was doing, and there would be nothing that would make him uncomfortable.

It took a few excruciating minutes. I brought her upstairs and introduced her to Jordan as Mommy's friend who wanted to say hello. Jordan was eager to tell her how much he loved to play chess, and liked watching *PAW Patrol*. Then she asked him what form of punishment his parents gave him if he misbehaved. My heart stopped. I was shocked at the implication in her question. "No cookies!" Jordan chirped back.

As we walked back down the stairs to join the men, she informed me she would need to visit our home in Manhattan, to examine Jordan's bedroom, the supplies in the kitchen and fridge. She assured me that this was all part of the required protocol to ensure that the child was bathed, lived in a clean home, had enough food to eat.

When the investigator told me she could see that our family was closely bonded, it felt like things would be okay. Then she went on to ask me if it was possible my assessment of Anthony's parenting lacked the accuracy it would have had if I was present in the home on a regular basis, and what I heard, between the lines, made me want to ask, *You mean if I worked less?* I had been the primary breadwinner for most of my marriage, so not working was not an option. I expressed as much to her.

She nodded that she understood and kept writing her notes.

Another twenty-four hours went by, and we returned to the city, where I received a letter delivered to the front desk of my building. "This is to inform you that you are another person named in a report of suspected child abuse or maltreatment received by the NY State child abuse and maltreatment register on 8/29/16." I pulled out my laptop, and while one hand held on to my iPhone for a conference call, the other hand typed out an email to the head of the nursery school asking if we should come, as planned, for the first day of school, given the latest news. Throughout the previous year the school leadership as well as the families of the children at the nursery school had kindly tolerated the photographers outside the building and even used their bodies to block Jordan's face when we dropped him off. But what would these people say now? And what would the school administration say?

The school principal had been an educator for decades, one of the leaders in progressive early childhood development in New York, someone who would also be interviewed by Children's Services in their investigation of us. She emailed me back immediately. "Please call me." When I did, she simply said, "Your family has been in our thoughts. We are all focused on Jordan and what is best for him. When you all come, I expect grown-up problems to be left at the front door. Inside, it's all about your child. See you at school."

* * * *

In the immediate aftermath of the story breaking, I decided to stay off the road. It's not that anyone asked me to, but now that I'd told Anthony to leave, I had to reconfigure my situation at home. We had moved into a new apartment, a duplex, the year before. It was two small apartments that sat on top of each other with a staircase between. Without ever discussing it, Anthony had taken over the fifteenth floor, where there was one bedroom that also functioned as an office and playroom. Jordan and I took the two small bedrooms on the fourteenth floor. But now my mother, who had cut short her visit to New Jersey and moved in with me, took Anthony's bedroom on the fifteenth floor, while Anthony moved in with his own mother in Brooklyn. My mother was so heartbroken, so stunned by this latest behavior by a son-in-law she had grown genuinely fond of, that when he came to see Jordan I tried to ensure that she and Anthony remained on separate floors so she could avoid interacting with him. When she did see him she, like me, did her best to feign civility in front of her grandchild, but they would never have a real conversation again.

For the month of September, my mom would be helping take care of Jordan whenever I had to go to the office, and now I needed to coordinate his schedule and fill her in on all of the details of his life. I also had to pick up much of the responsibility of ferrying him to and from playdates, dropping him off at school in the mornings, and picking him up in the afternoon. Anthony still came over most mornings for breakfast and to help Jordan get ready for school because we wanted to keep things as normal as possible for him, but seeing Anthony was not easy for me. The light and laughter that had filled our home for much of the time since Jordan was born, even after Anthony's earlier transgressions, had disappeared, erased by feelings of rage on my part and guilt on his.

The first day of school came and went without incident, once the three of us moved past the crowd of photographers at our apartment and then at school. At a coffee gathering in the park a few blocks away, the parents of Jordan's classmates asked questions about him, about how we were getting through the days, how they could help. From time to time, their eyes wandered in the direction of Anthony, who was playing with the kids in the grass, making up games, goofing around to entertain them, while the rest of us sat on picnic blankets nearby.

A week and a half into our new routine, on September 9, after we talked through her schedule for the week, HRC told me she was not feeling 100 percent and that her doctor had diagnosed her with pneumonia. They wanted her to stay home for the week, or at least for several days.

"Stay home?! She can't do that!" I said to her doctor.

I wish I had thought more clearly about the seriousness of pneumonia, but this close to the election, we could only move forward through sheer will and the refusal to make any allowances for illness.

Two days later, on September 11, HRC was at the annual memorial service at Ground Zero. She had first visited the site on September 12, 2001, and had returned for the ceremony almost every year she was in the Senate, and whenever she could in the years thereafter, to offer her support and pay her respects to the survivors, the first responders, and the family members of those who had died.

I was home feeding Jordan breakfast when I got a text from Connolly: "fyi, we might leave early." I texted her back: "you cannot leave early. She has to stay for at least the two bells." These were the sounds that marked the time each tower fell. Connolly didn't respond. A few minutes later, I got another text: "She is leaving. I don't think she is feeling well. It's really hot here." I called Connolly, but her phone went to voicemail. Minutes later she called me back to tell me that HRC was definitely not well and that she had left. A second later, a text came from her Secret Service agent letting me know they were driving her to Chelsea's apartment. Then HRC herself texted me that she was fine and there was nothing to worry about.

I left Jordan with my mother and ran most of the nine blocks to Chelsea's apartment. When I arrived, I was the one hot and gasping for air, while HRC was standing at the front door looking perfectly well, in fact surprised, and even a little annoyed, that everyone had made it seem like such an emergency. "I am fine!" she insisted. She wanted none of us to worry.

She was a public figure trying to hold on to some shred of privacy. I understood how that felt, now more than ever. In this instance, though, she was in no position to do that. She was potentially the next president of the United States and had left an important event suddenly, with no explanation.

I texted Jen to tell her all was okay. Then video emerged showing

HRC seeming to fall faint as she climbed into her van with the help of staff and the Secret Service. This was going to be a problem. The question was, should we make it public that she had pneumonia—something no one else on the campaign knew—since that had so clearly played a role in her feeling unwell?

I consulted with HRC about what to do. Should we tell the world? Would they overhype it? Exaggerate it? We both knew the answer to all those questions was yes. "I'll think about it," she said, and I left her with her family. As I was walking back home, my phone pinged. "Go ahead." So I called Jen to tell her about the pneumonia diagnosis, and when the statement went out the world went nuts for weeks, as though she had some deep, dark illness that we were trying to conceal. It's not that she was trying to hide something. She had just worked right on through, even though she wasn't feeling well, and that is pretty much what she always did. This time, though, it got the best of her.

While HRC's poll numbers had gotten a boost post-convention, the high didn't last long, and as we headed into the fall, we knew that everything we did every single day was crucial. News cycles in 2016 had become less predictable, driven by the shorter-term virality of social media and the high volatility of everything that came out of Trump's mouth. Incidents like her pneumonia diagnosis were exaggerated, distorted, and reported on endlessly. We would spend weeks working on a plan for a policy rollout on issues that mattered in the lives of voters, only to have to contend with yet another story about her emails or Benghazi or another favorite target, the Clinton Foundation, which was regularly attacked despite the otherwise high marks it received from independent monitors for its pioneering global work.

Much of our effort went into showing the stark contrast between Trump and HRC. When he couldn't give a coherent answer to questions about his world views, we planned a foreign policy speech to allow HRC to lay out her plans for global engagement, in a setting that looked presidential. When Trump boasted about his success as a businessman, we organized press conferences with small-business owners Trump had failed to pay. How much of an impression it made was hard to tell, but we kept at it, hoping the message was getting across.

Yet we were operating in a bizarro universe where HRC's serious, thoughtful, and sober approach to the presidency was mocked and undermined by the inept show Trump was headlining. A world of false equivalence, where her use of a private email server was weighted more heavily than the obvious deficiencies Trump would bring to office. Was it a mistake to use a private email system? In retrospect, yes, one she had apologized for, and one for which she continued to be relentlessly hounded. Meanwhile Trump spewed lies and slurs and ignorance like a firehose, but these were met with a collective Trump-will-be-Trump shrug. A few days after the September 11 anniversary, Trump said at a rally in Miami that HRC's Secret Service protection should be disarmed. "Let's see what happens to her," he said. "Take their guns away, okay. It would be very dangerous."

There was no respite from the pressure at home either. On September 13, Children's Services came to our house before I left for work. In the two weeks since we had seen them on Long Island, they had interviewed my mother-in-law, our babysitter, the head of the school, Jordan's pediatrician, and Anthony's therapist. As they warned me they would, that day they opened all the doors and closets in the house, inspected Jordan's bed, examined his clothes, looked in the fridge. After they had completed their inspection and talked with Anthony and me separately, they made plans for a follow-up visit in another two weeks.

Ever since we had returned from Long Island, whenever I was alone with Anthony, he tried desperately to explain away the photo. That it was being misconstrued, that he didn't even remember taking it, that probably one of his many enemies had plotted to get at him to damage HRC's campaign. I didn't believe his excuses about the photo itself, but I did wonder how that image had leaked in the first place. HRC's opponents saw in Anthony a soft target to derail the campaign. One which would prove very effective.

IS IT AMERICA YET?

To prepare for her first debate against Donald Trump, HRC had asked campaign debate prep veterans Ron Klain and Karen Dunn to lead the sessions. Along with a small group of us from the campaign, they huddled with HRC for six to eight grueling hours a day. HRC would stand or sit at the podium and debate our stand-in for Trump. It was Philippe, who had thoroughly transformed himself with a too long red tie, a Trump-brand watch and cuff links, shoes with lifts in them, and a contraption around his ankles that made him lumber about stiffly. She'd take questions from the team, then try to answer them, while being interrupted constantly by "Trump."

During a break on September 21, Karen, who was also still my personal attorney, pulled me into a separate room. She had just heard about a story in a UK tabloid, the *Daily Mail*, alleging that Anthony had sexted with a teenage girl. It was only three weeks since the photo in the *New York Post* and our formal separation. Each time I thought Anthony had reached a new nadir, he shocked me by going even lower, but this was lower than anything I could have imagined. If the allegation was true, his behavior was not just intolerable, it would potentially have crossed a line into criminal.

When debate prep began again, I didn't join the rest of the group. I stepped outside into the parking lot to call Anthony. There was no point in asking him about the truth of the article, because by then I no longer had any faith that he would tell me the truth. The only thing I wanted to know was whether he had made any progress on finding a residential therapy program, which was what his therapist had recommended. I wanted him to be away somewhere where he could do no further damage to the campaign. But when I asked him, he hedged.

"What if I just stay in New York and go to therapy every day? This way I can still see Jordan every day."

"No," I insisted. It was clear that sessions in New York had not been enough. Not even close. I would not accept any other option than a residency program out of state. To make sure he went, I told him I would join the calls with the facilities he was considering. On debate prep breaks over the next few days, I stepped out into the parking lot and we made calls together. The place that his therapist recommended, the place where a lot of high-profile people went, was out of our financial reach. The place he ultimately selected would be partly covered by our insurance, and since it was the choice we could afford, we settled on it, and he prepared to leave in a matter of days.

The first weekend after Anthony left, I took Jordan for a walk to the park across the street from our apartment building. As we approached the crosswalk, Jordan put his hand in mine. For years it was always his daddy's hand he reached for first—an instinct borne of habit and custom, since Anthony was the parent who was always there. In that moment, I felt something so intense it is hard to describe. I was suddenly so overwhelmed by love, grateful that I could have this being in my life, who by the mere fact of his existence brought such unadulterated joy to each and every day.

A couple of days later, on September 26, I paced in HRC's driveway as we were preparing to leave for Hofstra University in Hempstead, New York, for her first debate with Trump. I was on the phone with the Children's Services investigator, who explained that they had received even more complaints from the public about us. They would be following up with me at our upcoming meeting in a few days.

Then I jumped into Scooby with HRC for the drive, trying to focus on the debate ahead. HRC was quiet during the ride, staring out the window when she wasn't looking at the notes in her binder. Once the debate began, it turned out that Philippe had embodied Trump so well in prep that all the flailing and heavy nostril-breathing that real-life Trump did felt entirely predictable, almost normal. HRC accused Trump of inciting the Russians to hack the DNC—an illegal national security threat. He criticized her for preparing for the debate, that she needed to stay home to get ready while he had been "all over the place" with the American people. She confirmed that she had prepared for the debate, just as she was "prepared to be president." HRC criticized him for his misogynistic rants about women's physical appearances, referring specifically to a Miss Universe he had called "Ms. Piggy." He huffed and scowled.

The next day, the mood at headquarters was jubilant, and our rally in North Carolina equally so. Most pundits agreed that HRC had trounced Trump in the debate. Days later Trump claimed he had won while also asserting that he'd had a "really bad microphone," which made us laugh, because during prep, Philippe-as-Trump would occasionally blame "the mic guy" for his poor performance. That's how thoroughly he had studied Trump!

Even on celebratory days like these, I felt a sense of dread about what the nights would bring. That's when Anthony would call. He had only been away a few days before threatening to come home.

"They've taken away my phone," he complained. "They only let me have it for a half hour a day."

I told him there was no chance he could come back and I would discuss the phone issue with the facility. He gave me the phone number of the man he said was responsible for him. Halfheartedly I called the number, mostly to ensure that Anthony would stay put. He had committed himself voluntarily and I wasn't certain anyone could force him to stay. When I reached the man, he was kind but firm.

"I'm sorry," he said. "We're only giving him this much access to it so he can check in with his family and his attorney, nothing more."

"Okay," I said, worried that Anthony would use this as an excuse to check out of the facility.

He then explained that Anthony's limited phone access was required given the nature of his addiction.

"Addiction?"

It was the first time a mental health professional had ever used the term addiction to describe Anthony's behavior. The 2011 diagnosis sitting in a folder at my home very clearly stated that he did not have a sex addiction. In very direct language, this man was confirming the thing that was now just obvious. This "personality disorder" that everyone had tiptoed around for so long had spiraled into something that Anthony could not control, and something impossible for the people around him to contend with, particularly those of us who were the collateral damage. Addiction seemed like the only possible explanation for online behavior that he couldn't "knock off," that worsened with every episode, along with its consequences.

"Keep him there as long as you can."

The problem was that this was just a temporary fix. He would only be able to stay there briefly, until his therapist could come up with a residential therapy plan that would take him away for a much longer period of time. In a panic at the idea of his returning anytime before the election, I called the New York therapist and left her a message saying I was prepared to do whatever necessary to address Anthony's mental health issues. A week after the *Daily Mail* piece was published, on September 28, I was headed back home on HRC's plane from a trip to Boston. Once we landed in New York, I picked up a voicemail from the therapist. She had calculated that the bill for the long-term treatment she was recommending for Anthony would total around $127,000. I almost dropped my phone from the shock. Who has $127,000 sitting around?

HRC looked across from her seat on the plane.

"Anything going on?" she asked. It was her standard question whenever we landed and people had had a chance to pick up their emails and retrieve their phone messages.

"Nope," I replied nonchalantly. I didn't want her to know how bad things were at home.

Sitting in the dark of my bedroom that night, contemplating the therapist's message, I thought about the fact that in the world I inhabited, there were actually a lot of people who had money to spare, people who would loan me the money if I asked. But there was no way I could ask any of them for help with this. I remembered the conversation I'd had with Oscar de la Renta when he couldn't understand why I hadn't reached out to him for help, asking why he had to read about my life in the newspaper. Then as now the thought of reaching out to a friend felt shameful, inappropriate. I just couldn't do it.

The next morning, on the way to drop Jordan off at school, he and I were accompanied by more than the usual number of photographers

and reporters, all of them shouting out questions—in front of a four-
and-a-half-year-old—with words like "underage" and "sexting" and
"arrested."

Afterward, I went to headquarters for a three-hour planning meeting to lay out the schedule for HRC and all the other principals—
including President Obama, WJC, Chelsea, and several other
important surrogates—for the rest of October. Alex, Jason, their deputies, and I had spent weeks preparing for this meeting.

That morning, as my team walked through the plan we had collectively come up with, I couldn't help but smile. These people were
rock stars. They had distilled the massive amount of information I'd
given them about what we needed to do and where we needed to go
in these final weeks of the campaign into a tightly organized series
of events that covered every base. Once the strategy was signed off
on, we focused on which messages and events to build out in which
cities: where to talk about healthcare; where best to push out HRC's
message on infrastructure, childcare, national security; which events
should be rallies, and which should be press conferences or roundtables; which local elected officials we would need to invite, and who
the other speakers should be. As we planned HRC's days, Dennis
tried to figure out whether we would be able to fit in fundraisers
in the various cities she'd be visiting. Would there be old friends of
HRC's to invite or new local groups to engage? De'Ara was on top of
that. How long could she be on the ground in Colorado, or Nevada,
or Ohio, or Florida before running into crew rest? Connolly was
thinking that through. Where and how and when did we need to
send the hundreds of advance staff? Jason was all over that. There
were thousands of big-picture questions and tiny details to address
and execute.

After work, I made it home just in time to meet with the waiting
Children's Services team. They did all the same things they had done
on the previous visit, spending two hours inspecting the apartment,
asking questions, and taking notes. They asked how I intended to
handle Anthony's return from his residential treatment program, if I
intended to have Jordan examined by a psychologist, whether we were
losing support from friends and family members in light of the recent

news about Anthony's communication with the teenage girl, what my long-term plans were.

It felt like I was constantly flipping the switch between work and home, between Jordan's needs and Anthony's recklessness, between lawyers and therapists, Children's Services investigators and teachers, preschool parents and colleagues, donors and staff. Then there were the reporters and photographers to contend with, the waves of email and text chains and ringing phones. Not to mention cooking, cleaning, and laundry. I looked at these women from Children's Services. I wanted to say, "My long-term plan just gets us to November 8, Election Day!" But I didn't. I assured them that Jordan's behavior hadn't changed, that he was doing well. Between my mother, my mother-in-law, and me, we'd been able to keep his routine intact and he was still happy at school and at home, playing with friends, running around at the playground, and leaving toys all over the apartment. Anthony and I had told Jordan that Daddy wasn't feeling well and he would be away for a little while, and that explained Anthony's absence well enough for him.

They nodded and said they would be back in a few weeks.

I worked from home the next day, September 30, because I needed to get everything ready for Jordan since I would be flying to Paris and London for the weekend that night. Months earlier I'd committed to doing fundraisers with Americans in Europe, and while I was torn up about leaving Jordan now that Anthony was gone, I knew these events would bring in millions of dollars and I couldn't cancel. Sitting at my kitchen table, I typed up details about Jordan's schedule for Anthony's mom, who had been staying with us since my mother left a few days before. Attached to the schedule was a page of information on who Jordan's current playmates were, how to reach their parents, what his favorite snacks and nighttime rituals were. Suddenly, I heard a knock and the sound of Anthony's mom opening the door and greeting someone upstairs. Several minutes later, a man in a trench coat came into the kitchen. It was raining outside, and he was dripping as he stood in front of the kitchen sink holding a black box he had taken from a hallway closet without my even knowing he'd gone into it. He said a short hello, then told me he was from Anthony's legal team and had come to retrieve evidence. The U.S. attorney for the Southern District had asked for Anthony's electronic devices to search for any messages that would be relevant to their investigation into Anthony's communications with the teen. He had gotten what he needed, he said. I had a flight to catch and a lot to do between then and now, so I just nodded that I understood. A moment after he left, I lost the internet. The man had pulled out the router.

When I walked out of my building a few hours later on my way to the airport, one of the doormen was standing by the revolving doors. "Huma!" he called out, "They are outside." I realized that I was leaving Jordan and his grandmother to fend for themselves against the photographers, and my heart began to ache. Until then, either Anthony or I had been able to accompany Jordan through the gauntlet, which was something we'd become used to. Was I a bad mother for leaving him now? The wonderful doorman must have sensed my fears. He told me not to worry. "We will protect your little guy. We love having you in the building." I gave him a hug and hurried to my waiting Uber to get to JFK for my flight.

In the United States, we had grown so accustomed to absorbing the latest outrages from Trump that we were almost numb to them, so it was interesting to see how much higher the alarm was in Europe. As I walked into my first fundraiser in Paris, a young American woman who was volunteering for the event pulled me aside.

"My family is from Iran. They fled during the revolution." She said she was worried Trump would lead a similarly totalitarian government. "I am scared," she said as her eyes welled up.

"We are doing everything we can to make sure he doesn't win," I said.

Then I walked into the event and spotted Anna Wintour, who was, as always, early. We were to be the two speakers. She and I moved into a little parlor to catch up as people checked in for the cocktail reception. She asked how Jordan was doing, how I was holding up. I told her he was fine and I was having a rough time but doing my best, and then just before I could update her on what was happening with Anthony, our hosts interrupted and told us it was time to begin.

We walked into the dimly lit living room, she made her speech,

439

and then I made mine. As I was in the middle of the Q&A afterward, I saw Anna slip out and was sorry I wouldn't get a longer chat with her—there was so much more I wanted to tell her about what I was going through. But we both had other events to attend and it would have to wait. When I finally got to the house where I would be spending the night, waiting in the entrance hall on a small round table was a beautiful arrangement of white flowers with a note that read, "I am thinking of you and sending much love, Anna."

After landing in New York at the end of the weekend, I stopped at the grocery store to pick up Jordan's current must-have staple, applesauce, and a few other items before getting home. My schedule was so frenzied that usually when I was out and about, something was awry. Either one of my earrings was missing, or the heel on my shoe was broken, or the streaks from my dry shampoo had not blended in, or my hastily applied lipstick had leaked beyond my lip line. Some days, I must have looked like a clown. On this day, as I stood in the checkout line, a woman tapped my shoulder. She pointed to a tabloid newspaper with an image of George and Amal Clooney on the cover. "Are you her?" she said, pointing at Amal. I laughed out loud as I shook my head. I walked out smiling. She had made my day.

* * * *

October 7 was a campaign news tsunami, and for the next thirty-one days, until the election, it would be a wall of waves crashing over us as we struggled to come up for air each time and then kept paddling.

The Department of Homeland Security and Office of the Director of National Intelligence released a statement that Russia was behind the leak of the DNC emails, confirming the points Robby had made three months earlier, and those that HRC had made at her first debate with Trump. The statement went on to say that the officials believed that Russia was also attempting to interfere with the U.S. elections.

About thirty minutes later, a news alert broke. It was the audio of Donald Trump from *Access Hollywood*. In the behind-the-scenes recording he boasted, using the kind of language that you have to silence in front of children, that he physically assaulted women and that they just let him do it because he was a star. Jen and I heard the news backstage at a rally where HRC was speaking.

"What do you think this means?" I asked her.

"Well, it's not good for him!" she said as we all tried to game out the impact this was going to have on the race.

About a half hour after that, everything changed again when Wikileaks released a batch of John Podesta's emails that had been hacked, the first of several installments they would leak over the days that followed, adding up to some twenty thousand pages.

On October 9, the day of the second debate with Trump, a call came in at 6:30 p.m. from Anthony. He was irate. "I'm getting out of here," he huffed. "Thirty minutes a day on my phone is not enough."

"You cannot come back," I said and hung up on him.

A few days earlier Anthony's brother had texted that he and his parents would take care of Anthony's legal fees. I thanked him for letting me know and let it go at that. I knew his family must be suffering too, but I didn't have the time to talk about their feelings with them or the bandwidth to try to imagine anyone else's emotional state. With only a month until the election, I was just trying to make it through each day.

* * * *

HRC endured the second debate with Trump glowering behind her like something out of a monster movie. Strutting about the stage, he dismissed the leaked *Access Hollywood* tape as "locker-room talk." After all the fireworks of the debate, it was generally conceded to have been a draw, since unlike the first debate, Trump had managed to utter a few coherent sentences, and the bar was low enough for him that he got a lot of credit for that.

We were uplifted at rallies like one in Ohio where our crowd of 18,500 people hit a new record. We were knocked on our backs by the public airing of our private emails through all of the hacks. My phone number had gone public, probably in one of the stolen emails, and I started to get crank calls and text messages. "You are dumb," or "Enabler," or "Hi, criminal." On the night HRC was about to walk on stage for her last debate, where Trump would call her a "nasty woman," a text came in that read, "You belong in jail," along with a photoshopped image of me in an orange jumpsuit.

When the reporters outside Jordan's school and our home became more aggressive, banging on the car windows or blocking our car to force me to stop so they could get a shot of us, Jordan began to be frightened—"It scares me when the men with the cameras shout at you, Mommy"—and I started to talk to him about his fears. Although it pained me to think about how much Anthony's absence impacted him, his daily FaceTime call with his father seemed to be enough. One night, as I was putting him to bed, he said, "I miss Daddy."

"Daddy loves you so much, Jordan. He needs to be away to get better, but he will be back soon," I said.

"When he comes back, will you take me to Disneyland?" he asked. I smiled at how quickly he pivoted.

"Yes, I promise, when the campaign is over, we will take you to Disneyland," I said.

"As soon as Hillary is president?" he asked.

"Right after Christmas. Deal?"

* * * *

On the night of October 24 I returned home to find the Children's Services investigator waiting for me. Had I considered what life would be like if Anthony went to prison? she asked. I must have looked blank because she then offered, as kindly as she could, "You seem perplexed." Perplexed didn't begin to describe it.

"I just need to get through the next fifteen days," I responded. "Just fifteen days. Then I can think about things like prison."

It may have sounded flip, but I really had no answers to this question—or to so many others. I just didn't. As usual, the meticulous note-taking continued. I had no idea what she really thought, and knew it wouldn't be appropriate to ask, so I didn't. She left, promising to be in touch soon.

A couple of days later on a campaign trip in Miami, I turned on the television in my hotel room and saw Rudy Giuliani on CNN. He indicated that the FBI in New York had information that was about to become public and that it was "big" and bad news for our campaign.

What was he talking about? And how would he know what the FBI was up to?

Turns out Giuliani knew a lot. On October 28, on a flight to Cedar Rapids, the reporters on board our campaign plane heard about a letter FBI director Jim Comey was sending to Congress announcing that the FBI was reopening the email investigation. When we landed, Jen and Nick were glued to their phones. In the holding area at our event, Jen walked over to me, still processing the information herself, and said that the investigation seemed to have something to do with some emails found on Anthony's laptop.

The instant she said "Anthony," my heart stopped. No, no, no. I had handled this, I had taken control of this. I had sent him away. It had cost us a fortune, I had cobbled together a life of relative normalcy for my son, I came to the office every day. This couldn't be happening now. But there was no time to linger on any of that. Jen and I caught up with HRC in a tented area, just as she was about to walk out to deliver her speech, to let her know about this latest development.

While her eyes opened wide with surprise, she shook her head, then simply said, "Okay, keep me posted," as though it was just another hiccup, and walked out on stage.

No matter how hard I tried, whether it was to help Anthony, to threaten him, to sympathize with him, to ignore him, to throw him out of my house, it was impossible to move on. This man was going to ruin me, and now he was going to jeopardize HRC's chances of winning the presidency, which would leave our country in the hands of someone dangerously unfit for the office.

On the plane after the event, Jen came over to update HRC. The letter Comey had sent to Congress was out. It confirmed what the reporters had heard. The Comey investigation was officially reopened. It turned out that the Southern District, which was prosecuting Anthony's case involving the teenager, had found emails of mine on his laptop and to this day I do not know where or how because I never knew they were there. They called the FBI's New York office, who then called the DC office, which meant the laptop ended up with Comey. They didn't alert Anthony's attorneys or mine. I watched HRC's face as she processed it. The moment she made eye contact with me, I just broke down.

I had held it together for months—through the night of the shock-ing photo, all the meetings with Children's Services, the paparazzi on the street, becoming a single parent overnight, the daily hate mes-sages, and even, until just a few minutes ago, the news about Comey's announcement to Congress. But now that I knew the investigation somehow involved my own email, tears flowed out of me. HRC stood up from her seat, came over to hug me, and then walked with me to the bathroom so I could compose myself. On a plane full of col-leagues, Secret Service agents, reporters, photographers—everyone with eyes simultaneously averted and questioning—she did that.

When I got home that night, heart pounding furiously, I called Anthony. I had never proactively tried to reach him since he had entered the treatment facility and I couldn't even remember the alias he was using. When I got someone on the phone, they said they would get him a message when they could.

"I need to talk to him immediately," I said, trying to keep my voice measured.

"It doesn't work like that here," the person said.

I hung up wishing I had screamed that this was about the future of our democracy, but I had restrained myself and sat by the phone until Anthony called about an hour later. It seemed he hadn't heard the news because he had no idea what I was talking about.

"How could your emails be on my laptop?" he asked. It was the question the entire world was asking, a question neither of us can answer to this day. Then he went into Anthony mode, where there is a solution to every problem: "I am sure it's a mistake and they will figure it out." His attitude was confident, almost dismissive, as though he didn't understand the magnitude of its impact.

"Anthony," I said, wanting to shake him through the phone, "if she loses this election, it will be because of you and me."

That night, I wrote one line in my notebook. "I do not know how I am going to survive this. Help me God."

I did know, however, what I had to do next. First, I figured out that, based on what we had in our bank account, I could go without a paycheck for about two months, maybe three.

That gave me a timeline. It was eleven days before the election. I went to work the next morning, ignoring the chaos and the nonstop texts from strangers that deluged my phone, gleeful messages reveling in my downfall. When I arrived at headquarters, the television screens all played images of Anthony on a loop, with scrolling chyrons featuring my name.

I walked into Robby's office to offer my resignation. He looked puzzled, like it was a joke. "I am not accepting your resignation! This is what happens in campaigns. We just need to strategize how to use resources and plot out this last week." He assured me we would be okay, that he was still feeling good, that we had comfortable margins in the battleground states. He told me not to worry. "I'm on it," he said. He smiled and hugged me, trying to cheer me up, but I just couldn't tell if he was more worried than he was letting on. Robby was always upbeat, no matter what.

As I left Robby, I saw Elan Kreigel, our analytics director, in the hall and asked if he had a minute to come to my office.

"What do you think?" I asked him. "Please be honest with me."

He was far more circumspect than Robby had been. Yes, our numbers were up and there was a buffer, but the margin was so small, any little blip could impact it and this had been an earthquake. He wanted to remain confident, but it was still too early to tell. They would be able to assess the damage in a day or two.

"But, if you're asking for my honest opinion, yes, I'm worried," he said.

I slid halfway down the wall I was leaning against, not bothering to fight back the tears any longer, and just said, "Thank you for telling me. I'd rather know now."

"I'm sorry," he said as he left the room.

I wiped my eyes. My assistant, Sawsan, cheerfully brought in a fresh cup of coffee and gave me an updated list of outstanding calls I needed to return. I wanted to hug her for the gesture, for keeping things normal, for not seeming to pity me. My entire team had come through during these last few nightmarish months, and I was so grateful to each and every one of them.

Next I called Mandy Grunwald, who I always believed knew all, and asked her what she thought. She also didn't sugarcoat the situation for me.

"This close to Election Day, every tiny thing makes a difference and this is a big thing. Just keep your head down, we are all doing our jobs, and hopefully we'll pull through."

It was that day that I believed we would lose. How, when the margins were so razor-thin, would we survive this nuclear bomb? I was too devastated, too traumatized to try to process how I felt. In fact, the very act of feeling anything for myself felt selfish. Instead of being the invisible person who made everything work behind the scenes, now I believed I had become only too visible and, in the process, somehow managed to tank the campaign singlehandedly.

Sawsan walked back in as I hung up with Mandy.

In her usual gentle manner, she told me that pictures of me from early that morning, before I was dressed, had just appeared in a tabloid. Someone with a long lens had taken photos of me standing at my kitchen sink from the sidewalk fourteen floors below.

"Maybe you should just keep your blinds down from now on," she offered. So much for going home and crawling into bed.

Nodding in acknowledgment, I replied in the only way I knew how, "Okay, thanks for the warning. Who's next on my call list?"

* * * *

Two nights later, Heba and her three boys came over for dinner. Jordan was standing at the top of the stairs with his cousin, lost his footing and fell headfirst toward Heba and me as we stood at the bottom. We jointly caught him before he could tumble all the way down, but only after his forehead right above his eye and lips had made impact with the edge of a step. The blood came gushing out of his mouth, and he was crying hysterically, taking in large gulps of air as the shock set in.

I held him tight in a kitchen chair, rocking him back and forth, and FaceTimed his pediatrician. My hands were shaking as I dialed the number.

"It was an accident, it was an accident," I kept repeating as I showed her his forehead and his mouth. She told me to monitor his condition for vomiting or dizziness or anything off that might indicate a concussion and to keep her updated. Children's mouths bleed a lot, Heba kept reminding me. She made an ice bag and pressed it gently against his mouth and eye. We gave him some children's Tylenol and he calmed down pretty quickly, thanks to having his cousins right there to distract him. Heba tried to put me at ease, reminding me that kids fall all the time.

It was an accident kept running through my mind as a shield against my biggest fear: that Children's Services would find out. They already had me labeled as an absentee mother. Now, even when I was present, I couldn't protect my son.

"What if they take him?" I blurted out to Heba. She seemed stunned, as though she hadn't understood what I was up against until that very moment, but still she said, "He is going to be okay."

That night, I stayed up in the white rocking chair in Jordan's room watching him to make sure he was breathing and not vomiting. Each time I dozed off, the scene of him falling flashed in my mind and jolted me back to alertness. Thankfully, Jordan slept well, woke up with a bump and a bruise, but was otherwise his usual self.

The next night, Philippe texted me after the campaign plane landed, "I'm coming over." I hesitated. "You can't say no. I have instructions from the boss."

"Should we order dinner?" I asked as I ushered him in, realizing I hadn't eaten anything the night before or all day and was now famished.

"Order whatever you want," he said.

I rarely used my own name to order anything in New York anymore, so I ordered online from an Italian restaurant I loved, using the name Sara. Pizza and pasta and an extra pizza just in case. While we waited, Philippe entertained me with stories from the road. When I started to tell him I was worried about Comey's impact on the election, he pulled out his iPad, which had an electoral college map that you could manipulate to see how each candidate got to the magic number to win.

"Click all the places you think she should win. Go ahead."

Whichever combination I played on the map showed HRC winning. Then Philippe started to play around with it too. In just about every iteration, she won. When our food hadn't shown up after an hour, I called and the restaurant said the order had been delayed; thirty minutes later, when it still hadn't come, I called again, and this time they said they never got the order and that it would be quicker if I just picked it up myself. So I placed another order for "Sara," for pickup instead of delivery, and Heba, who had joined us for dinner, offered to go get it. Philippe was shaking his head in disbelief.

"Listen, if there was ever a time you need to identify yourself, it is tonight! Tell them you are Huma Abedin, your life is a train wreck, and the least they can do is give you a damn pizza!"

* * * *

On Sunday morning, two days before the election, I was sitting in my office when I heard applause and cheering outside my open door from the expanse of desks crammed together in the shared workspace. When I looked up, Jake was standing in my doorway. He came over and gave me a hug. "It's over," he said. "They've closed the investigation again." When I walked outside, the entire headquarters staff was watching the television screens on high volume. The FBI had completed their review and determined that the emails on Anthony's laptop were duplicates of what they had already reviewed, and they were now done with the investigation.

I felt an equal measure of relief and of rage. Why did they have to "reopen" the investigation and announce it in the first place? And then close it with a similar dramatic flourish? Why, especially when they knew I would have cooperated with any request, as I had throughout the investigation? All it did was set off another seismic jolt two days before the election. From the campaign plane, Jen called a minute later. I could hear cheering in the background.

"Get back on the road, girl!" Jen said.

The biggest rally of the campaign was the next night in Philadelphia with the entire Clinton family, President and Mrs. Obama, and Bruce Springsteen, after which we would head to a last midnight rally in Raleigh, North Carolina, with Jon Bon Jovi and Lady Gaga. I wanted to be part of these culminating events, and I knew that I could be useful in juggling the hundreds of moving parts we'd set in motion, but I was still hesitant.

There was silence on the line before another voice joined. It was the boss. "We started this campaign together. We are going to end it together."

The next morning I told Jordan, who was his usual chirpy self, oblivious to grown-up problems, that Grandma Fran was going to take care of him for two days because the election was close and I needed to help Mrs. Clinton. He nodded that he understood.

"Mommy, the next time I see you, will Hillary be my president?"

"Yes," I said mustering every ounce of optimism in me as I kissed him goodbye, "she will."

*   *   *   *

On Election Day I stood in line outside my polling station on 13th Street in Manhattan. It was a beautiful morning, sunny and crisp.

"Don't you need to be somewhere else?" a man in line called out.

I didn't, actually. HRC had voted in Chappaqua early and the plan was to regroup mid-afternoon at the Peninsula Hotel in midtown Manhattan, where the campaign had booked rooms for the night so HRC, family, and staff could watch the election results come in. Once I got my ballot, I savored the moment when I filled in the blank circles by Hillary Clinton's and Tim Kaine's names. Still uncertain of victory, I held on to the encouraging news in the polls, which still had HRC winning by five points in a direct matchup with Trump and by four points if you considered the third party candidates, like Jill Stein, who were also in the race. Our team had set up multiple election-night locations. There was to be a small team at headquarters in Brooklyn, a boiler room for the political team tracking results at the Jacob Javits Center, where the victory speech would take place, and then a small boiler room down the hall from HRC's hotel suite for a handful of campaign leadership staff.

I walked into my room at the Peninsula Hotel late in the afternoon while on a call with someone from the transition team who was asking what time HRC might like to receive the presidential daily briefing the next day. This conversation made me uncomfortable because it seemed so presumptuous, but I was assured they were asking the same question of Trump and that they had already received a time from him in the afternoon. This was all part of the smooth transfer of power. Only the person who won would receive the presidential daily briefing, but each candidate had to be on the schedule. We settled on 11 a.m. the next day. I then wandered over to check in with Robby and Elan, who had set up their laptops on a small table covered with a white tablecloth. So far everyone was feeling cautiously optimistic but no one was cheering.

Early in the evening, I made one of my regular check-ins with HRC in her suite. There, at a long, dark rectangular table in the dining room, Jake and speechwriters Dan Schwerin and Megan Rooney were talking to HRC about her victory speech. The red curtains had been drawn shut. I could hear the television on low volume in the living room, where WJC had already begun his night-long watch for the results. Every thirty minutes or so Robby or Podesta would wander in to share the latest numbers as they came in. The rooms were very dim even when the lights were on the brightest setting, and our hotel advance, Opal Vadhan, seemed to be constantly bringing in extra floor lamps to plug in throughout the suite as dusk turned to dark. Opal, whom I had met when she turned up at a training session in New York in 2015, had become our star hotel advance on every trip. She had a work ethic and dedication that made her a core member of our travel team.

Around 6 p.m., Connolly and the Ralph Lauren team who had made HRC's election-night outfit arrived for a final fitting. They brought along outfits for her to consider for the next few days as well. There was a white suit for this night, a gray jacket with a purple collar to signify "unity" to wear on her first trip to Washington, another purple suit with matching coat, and a second simpler white suit as a surprise. They had intended to present it to her for the inauguration but it was ready early.

No matter what she wore, she would have looked presidential at the venue Greg, Alex, and Jason had built for the election-night speech. Over the past week, they had been building a stage in the glass-topped Jacob Javits Center on the far west side of midtown Manhattan. I had visited the site the day before and confirmed for myself that

HRC would indeed be standing under a glass ceiling. The site cost us more money than our frugal campaign manager had wanted to spend. But when we made the case for the budget—that our daughters, our granddaughters, our great-granddaughters, and girls throughout the centuries to come, would look at the pictures from that night and see in them the huge leap in progress our country had made—even Robby had to agree it was hard to put a price on history.

When I stood on the stage, built in the shape of a map of the country, and looked up through the glass ceiling, it was hard not to get emotional. How far I had come from the twenty-one-year-old fresh-faced advance rookie of two decades before. I turned to Greg. He was emotional too. "No, none of that. Let's save it for tomorrow," he said. We had shed so many tears together in those endless, miserable days of 2008 that we hardly dared to believe in the promise of this moment.

* * * *

With every state we won as the returns rolled in that night, we exchanged high fives. At 7 p.m. EST, Vermont. Then at 8 p.m. Maryland, Massachusetts, New Jersey, and Washington, DC. Then Rhode Island, then Illinois, then New York by 9 p.m. It was good news, sure, but these were all the obvious and expected victories. Every so often, Greg checked in with me to report on what he was seeing and hearing at the Javits Center. He and Connolly had recommended that since there was no good holding-room option on site, HRC should come only after the election was called.

Once the map started to become tricky, then downright challenging, the mood at the Peninsula darkened. I was sitting in my own room when Florida was called for Trump at 10:50 p.m. We had lost Ohio by then too, though we had won Virginia, which could have gone either way. I walked back into the Clintons' suite, where a small team of advisors was beginning to assemble along with the family. HRC had taken the initial surprise losses in stride, but with some key states about to be called, now she was saying, "Can someone explain to me what is happening?" When the team emptied out to get more updates on what was going on in the upcoming states, I followed her into the small office in the suite. She said to me, or maybe just to herself, "I'm not going to win." She wasn't angry, really. It was sheer disbelief. More like shock.

As the hours ticked on, contradictory things were happening. The Secret Service had brought in bulletproof glass, and other agents had stationed themselves along the hallway and stairwell outside the suite. But upbeat reports from the on-site boiler room became less and less frequent. I would walk into the eerie silence of the suite, and HRC, who was not watching the results because she never did on election nights, would ask, "What do we know now?" And it was always either nothing, or nothing good. Chelsea, her husband, Maggie Williams, and Cheryl sat on the sofa and watched TV with WJC, the volume still turned low. Robby and Podesta came in around midnight to say that we were still waiting for some crucial results from Pennsylvania, Wisconsin, and Michigan. It was becoming clear to all of us that HRC might not make it to the Javits Center that night.

It was past midnight when my phone rang with a call from Connolly. She had Greg on the line too, and he reported that the audience at Javits was getting antsy and agitated. It looked like it could be a very long night because the results were coming in much slower than we had hoped. I asked Greg to find out whether we'd be able to get into the Javits Center the next day if necessary. He called back. No Javits option available for the next day. If the crowd was to be addressed from there, it had to be that night. Upon hearing this, HRC decided that Podesta should go to Javits to tell people to go home until results were clearer. Soon after Podesta left the suite, Pennsylvania was called for Trump. In a speech that was carried live at 2:02 a.m., Podesta still relayed HRC's message to her supporters and the world though victory at this point was basically impossible.

As soon as Pennsylvania had been called at 1:35 a.m., all our phones had started ringing. Results from different boiler rooms, people calling in from various states, from Brooklyn, from across town at Javits, and from the hotel where Kaine and his team were staying. Some team members had new information, or updated vote count data that needed to be unpacked. Some of our campaign veterans called in to say we should do nothing, that we should stand by until counting could be completed in some of the key states; others said it was imperative to wait until we understood more about some of the numbers coming in from certain parts of the country which were inconsistent with what we were tracking. I was standing in the suite when my phone rang from a familiar number, one stored in my contacts for twenty-plus years, one that never changed. It was the White House Operator. I answered it. She was calling on behalf of the President.

I stepped into the hallway and told the operator HRC would call back shortly. There was no way I was going to put HRC on with President Obama without having a better sense of what she intended to do. While I'd been speaking to the operator, Robby was talking to the White House political director. Robby reported that the White House did not want this election to fester into the coming days. This was not to be 2000, when Gore conceded and then took it back when they saw that Florida's numbers were irregular. If we did not believe we could cross the electoral vote threshold, and as of that moment, it certainly did not seem likely, the White House team was prepared to congratulate the winner in the morning and to get ready for an appropriate transfer of power.

Robby and I walked into the suite so he could relay the message to HRC.

"I don't believe this," she said in a mechanical voice. Not a hint of emotion but also no suggestion she would fight the inevitable. It was like we were all on a slow-motion train that was about to crash into a mountain, and she had become resigned to fate, just as she had those years ago when we were on a descending plane with one engine down.

Less than thirty minutes after Podesta had addressed the world, at 2:29 a.m., the AP declared Trump the winner in Wisconsin, giving him enough electoral votes to claim victory, thus anointing him President-elect.

We had lost.

There was total silence in the room. It was the family, Robby, Cheryl, Maggie, Jake, Philippe, Capricia Marshall, and me. Someone said one word. "Comey." We all nodded slowly because what the heck else were we to do. Opal punctured the silence by loudly wheeling in a room service tray filled with scoops of ice cream that no looked at, let alone ate.

"Okay, make the call," she said to me.

"I am not calling anyone until I talk to Podesta." I had been trying to reach him, but so far hadn't succeeded. It wasn't as though Podesta was the Oracle, like he was going to give me an answer that I didn't already know, but I had to hear him say it. Just then, he called back, after he too had spoken with the White House. His voice was low but firm.

"She needs to concede tonight," he said. "And she should call Trump before she calls POTUS."

"Are you fucking kidding me?" I said.

"No" came the totally stoic reply.

I was months away from understanding what the moment must have meant for President Obama. He would have known then that a bomb had just been dropped on his legacy. The sense that I make of it now is that he quickly came around to doing what he was elected to do: lead. And our leader, our president, agreed it was over.

"*Call* them," HRC insisted. She had decided. Robby gave me Trump's campaign manager's number. Robby and Kellyanne Conway had agreed earlier in the day that the two sides would talk tonight regardless of the outcome, and also that both sides would agree to accept the election result as the AP called it. Since the AP had just called it for Trump, we knew that Trump was likely to declare victory very soon.

HRC didn't hand me her phone, so I started dialing from mine. We were automatons at this point. I dialed the number and exchanged pleasantries with Kellyanne, as if we were calling to arrange a lunch date. She handed Trump the phone and I heard a loud "Hello!"

"Mr. Trump, one moment please." I reached over to HRC to hand her the phone.

"Hello!" came the loud voice again. HRC looked at the phone and then at me.

"What am I supposed to say?"

How many times had we had this exchange over the years? How many times had I handed her a phone and prompted her? We had developed such shorthand that usually all that was required was one word to jog her memory. I'd say "Afghanistan" or "Ohio" or "Thank you," and she would grab the phone and launch into a detailed conversation with whoever was on the other end.

Tonight, I didn't even bother to whisper. Whatever steeled me in that moment was something I could only have learned from her.

"Say congratulations."

"Donald, it's Hillary. Congratulations," she began in a light voice before she told him that while they had vigorous differences, she would always support the sitting president. She had her game voice on. The call was short. Less than five minutes after AP called the election, she had already graciously conceded.

I then dialed the White House. As soon as the President got on, her back straightened. "I am so sorry, Mr. President." I could infer from her end of the conversation that he was trying to say something encouraging or supportive. She hung up the phone and sat back down at the dining room table. If she had teared up on the phone with Obama, I couldn't tell.

"Get Jake, Dan, and Megan in here. I need to work on my speech. We have to find a place to do it. Have you talked to any of the staff yet? How is everyone? Tell John to come in as soon as he gets back. I want Robby and Elan to give me the latest report on what we learned from the states, especially Michigan and Wisconsin." And on and on. I could barely keep up with her.

By 3 a.m. the rest of the senior team was gathered at the dining table. Once we had determined what needed to get done immediately, including the dozens of calls that had to be made to shocked supporters, people went to work. I called Alex to tell him to look for a hotel to deliver a concession speech. I was secretly relieved we could not go back to the Javits Center, because who wanted to be there anyway? It would only be macabre now. Alex was already working on it with Grady Keefe, one of our best advance aides, who was wandering into hotel lobbies, waking up concierges, asking about open ballrooms for an event later that morning. Once HRC had decided she would deliver the concession, she wanted to do it as soon as possible. I called Greg and tried to joke that at least he had predicted correctly there would be crying tonight.

I went back to my room, walked straight to the bathroom, and sat on the closed toilet seat. I wanted the tears to come—something, anything to show I had any feelings left—but they wouldn't. What I felt was pure rage. I found myself distracted by the travel-sized hotel bottles of Oscar de la Renta beauty products lined up on the shelf and thought about how perfect life had seemed when Oscar was alive. My phone was ringing. My team had found a site. I stood up, hurled all the little bottles to the floor, applied a fresh coat of lipstick and walked back to the suite to tell HRC we had a plan and we were prepared to do whatever she needed. Philippe later told me that I looked pale, stunned, and was spewing gibberish when he walked in a minute later with the rest of the senior team.

* * * *

On November 9, 2016, at 11:45 a.m. EST HRC delivered her concession speech. When it was done, she spent some time with all the staff, who had gathered in a back area near the exit. As she finally began to walk to her van, she called me over. "We need to help people find jobs. I have to help get our team back on their feet. Let me know what I can do." I nodded, and she told me to keep her posted. Then I stood with John and Jen as we watched her Scooby van drive away from us, our country's future slipping away as the lumbering van disappeared in the rainy distance. We could barely stand. None of us had slept. The exhaustion built up over the last sixteen months weighed heavily, the loss of the election far more so. We were shattered. We had failed the person we should be calling President-elect and we had failed our children.

As we walked across the street headed for the staff van, the crowd of reporters who had gathered called out to me, "Huma! Do you think your laptop cost her the election? Do you feel responsible for her loss?" I got into the van with Podesta, his daughter Mae, and Jen, and we made our way back to headquarters. But when we got stuck in traffic we jumped out of the van and walked to the nearest subway station.

As we stood on the subway platform waiting for a train, a woman approached me. "You know we Americans are a peace-loving people." I nodded. She continued, "So I just want to ask you . . ." I attempted a smile, not sure where this was going. "If you don't love this country, why don't you leave?" My legs began to shake, partly from the exhaustion, partly from the shock of her words, and I thought they might buckle under me. Podesta intervened.

"Today is not the day for this. Please leave her alone."

The woman was persistent. "No, I want to know if she loves this country. I want her to look me in the eye and tell me she loves this country. Can she do that?"

As an Indian, Pakistani, Muslim girl growing up in Saudi Arabia, my tremendous pride in being an American had never wavered. It was part of my identity, the same as any other American's. The same as hers. I didn't reply to this stranger who in one of the very darkest moments of my life questioned my love of country.

What I wanted to say, what I could have said, was *I love this country so much that I spent the last twenty years of my life in public service, working for the institutions that defend your right to stand here and say whatever the hell you want to me.* But I did not want to give her the satisfaction of a response. The train pulled in. I boarded, watched the sliding doors close, leaving her on the platform, then I dropped onto the orange bench. The forces unleashed by the dawning of the presidency of Donald Trump were here, out in the open, ugly and angry, hateful and spiteful, soon to be given voice from the most powerful pulpit in the world. Instead of Love Trumping Hate, now we had *this*.

TRUTH HURTS

Suffering has been stronger than all other teaching, and has taught me to understand what your heart used to be. I have been bent and broken, but—I hope—into a better shape.
—Charles Dickens, *Great Expectations*

Election night brought a judgment on HRC and the Democratic Party. We lost the White House, and despite Democrats winning two Senate and nine House seats, Republicans maintained control of both houses of Congress.

The judgment on me had yet to come. The day after the election, my attorney called with an update on the Children's Services investigation. I learned that a formal report was likely to be finalized in the coming months. What would be in it I didn't know. All the investigator had been willing to tell me during her visits was that "concerned citizens," people who read about us in the news, had expressed doubts about our capacity to care for our child—Anthony because of his behavior and me because of my absence.

Whenever they visited, they performed the same examination of the apartment, and asked many of the same questions, but revealed little about their findings. In the meantime, my lawyer had warned me to beware of any knock at the door. While ACS would typically alert parents before a visit, which until now they had always done, sometimes they didn't. If they got wind of a problem or new concern or if there was more breaking news, they could come without warning to take my son and place him in protective custody until the review was complete. What exactly did this mean? It was impossible to know. I just needed to sit tight and wait.

One night after I put Jordan to bed, I sat in the rocking chair in his room checking emails as he dozed off to sleep. I was tired myself after his bedtime routine, one that had almost exclusively been handled by his father until last August—the bath where it seemed more water ended up outside the tub than inside, the chase afterward to put on pajamas, the same books read over and over again, then up and down for a glass of water and any other excuse not to let the day end. When I finally saw his chest rising and falling with each breath, I tiptoed out to the kitchen to join a nightly campaign shutdown call.

Since our apartment had once been two small apartments stacked on top of each other, we used the fifteenth-floor door leading to the living room as the main entrance. We had never used the door to the fourteenth floor, which was right outside Jordan's bedroom. So that night I was startled when I suddenly heard knocking at the door by Jordan's room. Normally, the doorman would call before sending anyone up. I was momentarily confused until I realized who it might be, quickly hung up the call, and walked over to the hollow metal door, not even daring to look through the peephole. I sat on the floor with my back leaning against the door. I felt the vibration in my chest from the knocking; tapping that was soft at first, then increasingly louder and more insistent. It was not fear that motivated me that night but sheer defiance. *Let them even try to take this child.* I stayed there as the knocking slowed, the pregnant pauses between knocks growing ever longer, until mercifully there was silence.

* * * *

There was no Senate or State Department or ongoing campaign to go back to, so the days following the election lacked the urgency and purpose I'd grown accustomed to in my adult life. If I hadn't felt obligations to my campaign colleagues, my boss, and her supporters, and if I was not the mother of a five-year-old, I would probably have spent days in bed with the covers over my head. I didn't even notice how miserable I was feeling or how badly I was eating until Anna took me to dinner a week or so after the election, and I found myself rambling about nothing in particular and ordering two entrees and two desserts, stuffing my face while she sat next to me completely unfazed and singularly focused on how to help me get my life back on track.

There was still plenty to do to shut down the campaign, though, so each day I took my usual subway commute to our headquarters in Brooklyn. Robby had given the staff notice, with different timelines based on their roles in the process, and he promised to keep healthcare for everyone for as long as possible. For most people, employment would last only another handful of weeks, if that. A start-up that had been launched and built at warp speed the year before was crashing to a stop. It was like my marriage. What had started as a commitment, a dream, a leap into a grand adventure filled with excitement, energy, and endorphins, had morphed into a grinding, complicated mess of paperwork, and an uncertain future.

As the staff archived their work and packed up boxes of personal mementos, I could hear music playing from some of the office pods. The large TVs that had hummed with breaking news coverage every day were off or muted. The first week of shutdown, Robby would give a daily pep talk in the morning or afternoon, depending on when he sensed it was most needed. Our COO, Beth Jones, brought in buffet lunches and dinners so we could all eat as a community. Supporters sent baked good, snacks, stacks of pizzas, tubs of ice cream. One day, a cotton candy machine appeared and Sawsan walked into my office with a large pale pink ball of spun sugar on a stick. We organized a large staff thank-you party, where HRC encouraged all of us to stay positive, hopeful, and future-focused.

By the end of the first week, the happy talk was beginning to wear thin. One afternoon, just to see how everyone was doing, I wandered into a conference room where Rob Russo and other members of Team Vice Chair were packing up papers and organizing all the recent notes and gifts that had come in for HRC. Instead of responding to my usual question, Rob snapped back, "I don't want people to keep asking me if I am okay. *I* am not okay. *None* of us are okay! We gave up our lives for two years, working for someone who should be president right now and it ends like *this*?" He kicked the nearest box and it tipped over, the contents spilling onto the floor. The staff around us walked out to give Rob privacy, everyone's expression betraying that they felt just the way he did. I didn't have many comforting words. He was speaking for me too. I still felt deeply at fault for the loss myself.

I went to Chappaqua a few days after the election to catch up with HRC. She asked how everyone at headquarters was holding up. Then we went over the list we'd compiled of all the people she needed to call, write, or thank in some way. It numbered in the many thousands. She was still baffled by the reasons for her loss but had already set herself the task of unpacking what went wrong. She never once indicated that she blamed me. She said then that ultimately what had happened was her responsibility, and that made me feel even worse.

Other colleagues seemed to be second-guessing some of our strategic campaign decisions; whether the messaging had been off, if we should have pushed to do more interviews, if some explanation could be found as to why and how private and public polling had been so misleading. The list of possible explanations seemed endless. There was no way to tell how all the fake ads and posts that ran rampant on social media had affected people's choices. It was still too early to know the extent of the impact of Russian interference. The rumors we dismissed as full-on crazy—that she was seriously ill, that her Secret Service agent was actually a nurse carrying medication, that she had murdered people—seemed to have been believed by many people, or at least entertained as possibilities. Reporters were now privately telling Nick and Jen that they had been hard on her in the weeks leading up to the election because they all presumed she would win. The serial dumps of John Podesta's anodyne emails had been a factor too, because each time they were released and the media and thus the public focused on them, the daily messaging of the campaign got buried. The cumulative effect proved devastating. Then there was the fracturing between the moderate and more progressive wings in our party. And Comey. Always and ever it came back to Comey. It had all created a perfect storm. Still HRC had managed to win the popular vote by almost 3 million votes, but the narrow electoral college defeat made those votes moot.

During those days, I spent a lot of time hugging people on the street and on the subway. One day a woman touched my arm and told me she was so scared for our country's future now that Trump was headed to the White House and what a loss it was not to have HRC as president. Another day a young woman stopped me to tell me she was depressed and had had to start taking antidepressants. Just stepping out for the day, walking around Manhattan, I felt waves of emotion gush out from all corners.

While there was plenty of love on the street, the attention was not always positive. A few times, men passed me by and hissed "Where are all the missing emails?" or said something nasty about Anthony. One day I was walking between meetings, busy on a call, when a man in a gray suit, colorful bow tie, and round spectacles started walking alongside me. I assumed he was going to say something about the election.

Instead he said in a low voice, "There is a man following you."

"What?" I asked. The man put his hand on my elbow and steered me forward.

"Don't stop walking."

I turned and saw a man who did seem to be following quite determinedly behind us. Pale, with longish brown hair, wearing light-colored jeans, he had an expression on his face that I couldn't quite make out. *Is this what hate looks like?* I wondered.

"His behavior is odd and he has been following you for a few blocks and so I started following along too," the Good Samaritan continued. "Where are you going? I think I should escort you."

We started walking faster as we talked, his hand on my elbow the entire time. I told him I was walking some distance.

"Then I insist I put you in a cab. You cannot be on the street."

He hailed a cab, and helped me in. The minute the door closed, I felt a bang on the trunk and looked through the rear windshield at the smirking face of the man who had been following us.

"Sheesh," the cabdriver said, shaking his head, "people in New York are crazy. Oh, Huma! Nice to see you!"

Many yellow taxicab drivers in New York are South Asian, so I was often recognized. A few times during the campaign, I recorded videos for wives back home or took a selfie for a driver's mother.

All through November, the notes poured in for HRC from around the country and the world. Brooklyn headquarters and the midtown office where a small number of us would be relocating, were drowning in mail—hundreds of thousands of letters and emails that we would take turns opening, reading, and sorting. Many of the staff received notes too, and I cherished the messages that came to me. I'd pull them out to read from time to time, on days I felt low, which meant I was pulling them out a lot. One said, "Thank you for reminding us, no matter where we come from, we can all serve our country." The offers people made melted my heart. A woman said she had a lovely lake house in Maine where I could disappear with my son. That was tempting. A woman from Massachusetts suggested I drown my sorrows in a good crème brûlée and she knew where to get one. A man passed me a note in a coffee shop offering to buy me a meal because "you look like you need one." That one made me laugh. A friend's wife sent me a note with a small token of appreciation, a tube of red lipstick, an "effective Band-Aid" she wrote and I agreed. One note said, "Your fight for our country—and for your family—has not been unnoticed. Thank you for your courage, for your strength and for all of the work you do! Hang in there."

Was I fighting for my family? What was my family now?

* * * *

The morning after the unknown knock at the door outside Jordan's bedroom, as I headed back to my apartment after school drop-off, Danny, our considerate doorman, stopped me on my way in.

"A man left this for you," he said and handed me a piece of scrap paper with a handwritten name, phone number, and the words "process server" on it. "He was here last night and we had to let him up. I am sorry." I didn't ask why they hadn't called to warn me, assuming Danny had been unnerved by the visitor.

Danny threw his hands up apologetically. "He said he was required to give papers to you directly."

I must have let out an audible sigh of relief because he laughed, "I have never seen anyone look so happy to get served legal papers!"

He had no idea. I was on edge every night when I was home with Jordan, not knowing who was coming, when, or what they would do. The man did indeed return that night. I was being sued, along with John Podesta and others whose names I didn't know, accused of working together to rig the primary against Bernie Sanders. After skimming the first few pages of the thick stack of paper, I shoved it back into the envelope and left it on top of all my unopened mail, and started looking at a printout Heba had left with me on one of her visits. It was from the website for an indoor water park in Pennsylvania that she thought would be a good escape for Jordan and her boys. When she'd first mentioned it, I thought I couldn't afford to take the time away. Aside from shutting down the campaign and rebuilding some semblance of a private office for HRC, I was preparing for another FBI interview in early January, having been called in to officially confirm I had no knowledge of any emails being anywhere aside from my own computer. But now I decided a fun getaway would be good for everyone, including me. I needed a break from being paralyzed in my apartment, bracing for a knock on the door, or running away from smirking men.

The water park was about two hours away and I relaxed on the drive. It was only when we approached the park, nestled in the Pocono Mountains, and drove past a slew of Trump/Pence yard signs on the street leading to the entrance that I thought I might not get the most welcome reception if I was recognized. At the park, I began to notice other visitors poking each other and whispering as they stared at me, or clearing their throats as I walked by. Once upon a time, during outings with Anthony, this would have bothered me. I would grab his hand and walk faster, or I would stare back or even confront people directly, asking, "Can I help you?" Now I just ignored it all. On our first night, while I was sitting at one of the plastic tables with Heba, watching our kids splashing in the water, a woman approached me.

"I am sorry to bother you," she said. "I just never thought I would ever meet you in real life. My husband is doing to me now what your husband did." I reached for her hand as she continued with less composure. "And I just want to tell you that the mornings when I don't think I can get out of bed, I think of you. You have given me strength and I want to thank you for it."

I had lost count of the women (and some men too) who had approached me with their stories of personal betrayal, their struggles

HUMA ABEDIN

to decide what to tolerate, whether to stay, when and how to leave, how to navigate this sometimes torturous thing called love. I looked over her shoulder, and saw her husband a short distance away, staring at us. He was a handsome man in a bathing suit, watching over a toddler with arm floaties splashing in the water. To any casual observer, they looked like the perfect family. The 2017 me wanted to tell her to run. Run as fast as she could. But I didn't. For whatever reason, this woman had made a choice to stay—a choice she felt was right for her, and I was not one to stand in judgment. "I am with you," I said before we each went back to our children.

I knew from my own experience that the decision to run from a marriage was complicated; and that even leaving, as I had finally done, didn't mean this person was out of your life forever, especially if children were involved. Anthony had recently returned from forty days in residential therapy, having stayed there until the election was over—not that keeping him away had ended up making a difference. He was back at his mother's house in Brooklyn, but he still came over each morning to help get Jordan ready for school, and sometimes returned at night to help put Jordan to bed.

We kept our feelings to ourselves in those days. He didn't share his fears and I rarely vocalized the depth of my anger. From my attorneys, I knew he was still in serious legal jeopardy because of the nature of his communication with a teenage girl, and that he was preparing for a trial in the spring. One night, however, after Jordan was finally asleep, I told Anthony that I just wanted him to go away. "You sound like you want me to go to jail," he said. That's not what I wanted. It was too complex to explain. I just wanted him to disappear, not to exist, so I would not have to deal with his problems ever again.

* * * *

When the Children's Services investigation concluded in January, five agonizing months after it began, the hundred-page document was the hardest thing I had ever had to read. The sources they cited for their concern were letters of complaint from anonymous people who knew nothing about our family but challenged the ACS to investigate, saying they hoped that just because we were "privileged," the ACS

466

wouldn't go easy on us. Referring to me, one of the letters began with "What kind of woman . . ." The ACS also cited tabloid news stories, which they'd appended to the report, with no regard whatsoever to whether they were credible. This forced me to read salacious articles I would otherwise never have looked at.

The mental health professionals the investigators interviewed, including those treating Anthony, were unanimous: not one was concerned about Jordan's safety around his father. The ACS also concluded that while they had been "gravely" worried about my ability to protect my child, they were assured that I had the capacity to care for my son, presumably because I would now be home. I might still be guilty in the court of public opinion, but they had decided otherwise. Of course the one person who would have been most adversely affected by a negative finding was the little boy those anonymous people claimed needed protection.

HRC had lost the election. My consolation prize was that I would be allowed to keep my child.

The report was dated January 20, 2017, the day Donald Trump was inaugurated. I went to DC for the swearing-in. I didn't need to be there, but I wanted to show support for my boss. As bitter as it would be, the peaceful transfer of power in American democracy meant something profound to her.

I wore head-to-toe black. It was not a color I wore often but felt right that day. A few hundred steps away from me, outside, on the dais along the exterior of the U.S. Capitol building, HRC walked toward her appointed spot, on the arm of her husband, who had taken his own turn at that march twice before.

WJC looked sadder that day than I had seen him in a long time, maybe ever. HRC looked resplendent, almost defiant in her Suffragist white, one of the suits that had been prepared for her own inauguration. Some people might have found it too painful to wear such a haunting reminder of what could have been, but HRC is too practical to let something like that bother her.

My staff seat was in the nosebleed section on the riser, and since no one would notice if I didn't occupy it, I was afforded the mercy of hiding indoors, where I took refuge outside an office that served as the Clintons' holding room. It was far enough away from the ceremony that the sounds were muffled and low and I could almost pretend this day wasn't actually happening. After what seemed like no time at all, however, I heard footsteps approaching, echoing down the marble halls, until the group appeared a short distance away from me and began lining up on either side of the hallway in which I stood. To the left side were President and Mrs. Obama and Vice President and Dr. Biden. On the right stood Donald and Melania Trump and Mike and Karen Pence. Behind the principals, the congressional leaders followed, lining up by party affiliation on their respective sides. And clustered in a small circle nearest to me was the official POTUS package—the special agent in charge of the Secret Service, the doctor, the nurse, and the military aide carrying the "football" with the nuclear codes.

While everyone waited, mostly silent, to be told it was time to walk outside for the Obamas' final farewell, I tried to stay invisible. I saw Mrs. Obama turn around and begin talking to Dr. Biden in a low voice. She noticed me standing in the corner, smiled, and waved. Then President Obama saw me too, and walked over, giving me a quick hug and saying "hang in there," before resuming his place in line. Even on his last day as leader of the free world, he had not lost the easy, low-key manner that I had first encountered over a decade before when he was a junior senator, crouching in the back of the airplane.

Finally, the procession moved forward. It was only when I saw the core support package—especially the uniformed man with the codes to start World War III—move not left to follow Barack Obama, but right, in the clearest possible sign of the transfer of power, that I truly accepted that Donald Trump was the forty-fifth President of the United States.

LETTING GO

Fifteen to thirty years. Those were the reported mandatory minimum prison sentences Anthony could face for exchanging illicit material with a minor if he was found guilty in the case involving the teenager. When he came over to put Jordan to bed one night, I asked him what he intended to do. He said he understood that if he went through a jury trial and was found guilty, the judge would be required to work within whatever mandated guidelines. If he instead pled guilty, the sentencing would be left to the judge's discretion.

He told me he had initially thought that if he could explain his actions through the lens of his disease, which would be detailed by his therapist, the jury would take that into consideration. But his case was too much in the public sphere, and most people seemed to have decided how they felt about him. So he was leaning toward a guilty plea. He then asked if I would be willing to send a letter to the judge asking for leniency as he considered sentencing.

I was still so angry that I was reluctant to intervene on his behalf, but after Anthony left, those numbers kept flashing in my head. Jordan would be an adult or even have graduated from college by the time his father returned. Anthony would miss his entire childhood. I texted him late that night. "I'll do it." In my letter to the judge, I tried to convey what a long separation would mean for our son. Also, how important I believed it was that Anthony was now finally enrolled in a treatment program that seemed to be working, and how concerned I was about the risk of his regressing because of the lack of mental health support in prison. I hoped the letter would not fall on deaf ears.

After many nights of hearing me say, over and over, "I don't think I will ever fully understand what you did and why," Anthony responded with a question.

"Would you be willing to go through a disclosure with me?"

"What is that?"

Anthony explained that it was a multi-step process he had learned about in treatment, which would begin with my writing a letter detailing all the ways he had hurt me. I barely had the bandwidth to get through the day, and now I was supposed to do the emotional work for his misdeeds? No, thank you. I was too full of resentment to have room for anything else. I reiterated that I just wanted to formalize the separation I had initiated the previous August and go through the legal process of getting a divorce. Each time I had raised the possibility, however, the conversations ended the same way. In a stalemate. Anthony did not want a divorce. I have yet to meet anyone who can out-argue Anthony and I am no exception. I used to pray that a mystery arbitrator would stage an intervention or at least moderate a conversation between us that didn't end with Anthony telling me that I should seek therapy for my anger issues.

Now, though, I had clarity: for my own emotional well-being, I needed to proceed with the divorce, no matter how much Anthony argued against it. However, since I was hoping to avoid being the subject of any new press stories, I wondered if there was some way to file for divorce anonymously. Yes, I was told. I could file privately and remain anonymous. Many actual celebrities did it this way, and their names were never revealed. But just to make sure that I could keep it under wraps, I came up with the idea to file the same day as Anthony was scheduled for the court appearance at which he would plead guilty. I figured his plea would be the big news and maybe, just maybe, if I was lucky, I'd manage to keep my own news private. Sitting in a cold conference room, at a long white table in an attorney's office, I signed the papers that would be filed the next day. I was finally taking an action that would enable me to move on with my life.

After I dropped Jordan off at school the next morning, I went to work as usual and joined HRC for an 11 a.m. meeting in our conference room, trying not to be distracted. That was the hour when Anthony would plead guilty. Then noon came and went. If news of our divorce filing—news that I had shared with no one—did leak despite the assurances of anonymity, I didn't know how much time I would have before it became public. Turned out to be exactly thirty-four minutes. At 12:34 p.m., Opal, now my assistant, came into the meeting and slipped me a note from Nick, who had stayed on as HRC's personal communications director. It read, "Did you just file for divorce?" In a replay of the record that had been running for the last half decade, I was once again in the position of feeling terrible that my colleagues—first Philippe and now Nick—had to deal with incoming from reporters asking about my personal life and about what HRC had to say about it (which would be, as always, nothing).

I waited until the meeting was over, then stepped out and got a download from Nick on what had appeared in the press about my filing and also about what had happened to Anthony. He said it had been an awful morning to watch. During the open court hearing, in a courtroom filled not just with press but with members of the public, Anthony had read a statement apologizing for his behavior and had broken down crying. The judge, ignoring the circus this case had become, announced that he would review the case and sentencing would come that fall, four months away.

Jordan, now a five-and-a-half-year-old, was blissfully oblivious, and we wanted him to stay that way as long as possible. Anthony suggested an end-of-the-school-year pool party for Jordan's nursery school class. During the past two years, he had organized similar gatherings for Jordan and his classmates, all of which I had missed since I was always on the road for the campaign. The four towers of our apartment complex shared recreational facilities which included a swimming pool and a community playroom, so Anthony had been able to plan afternoons at the pool followed by pizza and ice cream in the playroom. He thought we could throw the same kind of party now. "Do you think anyone will come?" I asked, feeling that our place in the social world was even more uncertain than it had been for the last six years. "Only one way to find out," he said, seeming entirely confident. We set a date, texted all the parents, thinking maybe one or two would say yes and the rest wouldn't want to have anything to do with Anthony and me.

To our relief and Jordan's delight, the whole class accepted the invitation. I bought party supplies to decorate the playroom, ordered pizza, an ice cream cake, and filled goody bags. When everyone had arrived, the parents all caught up with one another on plans for the summer, Anthony made up pool games for the kids, and I went to my apartment to get the food. As I was heading upstairs, I walked past the front desk to find one of my neighbors complaining to the facility staff. She was an older woman who used the pool regularly, and was known to complain if she was inconvenienced in any way—if the floor by the pool was too slippery, if the water was too cold, if any kids were too noisy or had used the hot tub. She had her back to me as she spoke to the young woman at the front desk and I realized she was talking about us.

"But they should not be allowed to use the pool," she said.

The young woman responded, "They are tenants, they have paid for the lifeguard's time, they are entitled to use the facilities."

This seemed to anger the woman even more. "He is not even allowed to be around children! These people should be reported."

I approached the desk. "Is there a problem?"

The woman scowled at me and walked away as the attendant mouthed "I am sorry" to me. A minute later the woman and I were both waiting at the elevator banks. She kept her mouth pursed, her eyes not meeting mine. When the elevator came, we both entered, pushed our separate buttons and rode in silence on opposite sides of the elevator until we arrived at her floor. Before she exited, she turned to me and said, "Shame on you."

No. Not anymore. I had lived with shame long enough. I was done with shame eating away at me. Done with it having so much power. I had nothing to be ashamed of, didn't have to tolerate any of this, and so I just shook my head and smiled widely back at her. My son was about to lose his dad for who knows how long and I was going to make these last few months as stable and enjoyable for him as possible. If that was going to make my neighbor unhappy, so be it.

* * * *

In September 2017, Anthony was sentenced to twenty-one months in federal prison. We consulted with two child therapists about what to say to Jordan about why his father would be gone all those months. They suggested that we liken Anthony's absence to a "timeout," something he needed to do to take responsibility for a mistake he had made, and leave it at that. They recommended we not tell him anything until a week before Anthony would start his sentence, early in November.

The week before Anthony was to leave I went on a work trip to Chicago with HRC, who was on a publicity tour for her new book. On a crash deadline, she had researched and written *What Happened* in order to share with the public her motivations for running for president a second time, the guiding principles behind her campaign, what she saw and heard around the country during the campaign, how she had planned to help people, and her assessment of what had gone wrong. She was hard on herself in the book. She owned all the personal and political shortcomings she thought had contributed to the loss and took full responsibility for those. But she also carefully analyzed all the factors outside her control, from the disinformation on social media to Russian interference to voter suppression to Comey. In classic Hillary Clinton form, she ended on a hopeful, optimistic note. She wanted her loss to count for something, to motivate young people to participate in the public process—to organize, to vote, to run for office, to claim their own future.

Before an audience of several thousand people at Roosevelt University in Chicago, HRC was to be in conversation with the author Cheryl Strayed, both on stage and for a podcast that Cheryl was taping. Before the trip, in an email to me, Cheryl had mentioned that she would love to ask me some questions too. She thought it would be interesting for her listeners to hear about the power of female friendship. I was a huge fan of Cheryl and had gotten to know her a bit over the course of the campaign after she delivered a beautiful endorsement of HRC. But I balked.

In truth, I wasn't ready to do an interview or put myself before the public in any way. My goals for the moment were simple if not necessarily simple to achieve: to find a new normal where I was no longer bracing for the next unknown, to keep my son's life as secure and stable as possible, and to help HRC get back on track for whatever it was she wanted to do next—which included working on Onward Together, an organization she'd founded with Governor Howard Dean to encourage young progressive activists and leaders to organize, get involved, and run for office. That was all that I was up for at the moment, and doing interviews didn't fit into that picture.

Nonetheless, I decided to just play it by ear once the podcast started taping, without committing one way or the other. And then, as we were sitting backstage in the holding area, right before the taping was about to begin, my phone rang and I saw my home number flashing on the screen. It was Jordan, who was sick with a high fever, calling to say good night. His father would be gone in just over a week, though he didn't know it yet, and my heart hurt for him. Torn between my professional and personal responsibilities, I stopped briefly to talk to Jordan and saw HRC walking out of the room with Nick. By the time I hung up and swung open the squeaky door into the broom closet office they were using to record, the podcast recording had begun.

HRC was midway through answering a question. All eyes turned to me, before HRC simply said, "Huma, it's okay, you don't need to be in here." In that moment I realized, she was right, I *didn't* have to be there. My job was important, but it no longer had to be the primary thing that defined me. I closed the door and called Jordan back in time to listen in as his grandmother and father took turns reading him a bedtime story while he dozed off.

* * * *

The experts had told us that Jordan would make the adjustment so long as we kept his schedule as routine and predictable as possible. They said that a sense of time was beyond the grasp of a child that young, and it was true that after Anthony left in November, Jordan seemed to adapt seamlessly. I had taken him on the much-anticipated trip to Disneyland soon after the campaign ended, and now I promised to take him on many more adventures in the hopes of distracting him from his current reality.

Over the holidays that year, the Clintons had been invited to stay at a friend's house in Hawaii, and the friend also had an apartment nearby where WJC's deputy chief of staff, Jon Davidson, and Jordan and I could stay. For years I'd gone on every vacation with my boss because her vacations were always working trips. If Jordan came along, he would usually be left with his dad while I joined HRC.

Hawaii was going to be different, however, in that the little boy who had just turned six would be tagging along with us whether we were trying to make plans for Onward Together or mapping out HRC's schedule for the coming year. Since none of us had taken a full two weeks off ever, and we'd barely taken any time since the insanity of the election, we decided we would try to make this a real vacation, even if it was still a working vacation. Every few days, we would explore a little bit of the island or go on some kind of excursion.

The Clintons made all their plans with Jordan in mind. One day we went whale watching and witnessed a whale breach, which had Jordan squealing with delight. As we disembarked from the boat, Jordan asked the Clintons when he could see the whale "fly" again. A few days later, HRC said, "You know Bill loved whale watching so much, we thought about going again." So we did, and all the adults got just as much pleasure watching Jordan's face as watching the majestic mammals in the water. Another day we went snorkeling. One morning, the President asked if Jordan wanted to go golfing with him. Boy, did he ever. He was gone the whole day. When I went to pick him up, the sun was just beginning to set, the sky lit bright orange in the distance, and the golf cart swarmed by people taking pictures with WJC. This left Jordan with the clear impression that he was not a former president but a "really famous golfer." WJC took him golfing twice more. When HRC and I would meet at the house, Jordan would "help" the President with his many-thousand-piece puzzle. They indulged him in every way and included us in every meal. This continued even after one night when the President was talking about Xi Jinping's leadership in China and my six-year-old announced, "This is really boring." Throughout they were patient, caring, and inclusive.

Toward the end of our trip, Jordan and I went to dinner with a family we had met on the beach with a son the same age as Jordan. It had been a long day of playing Uno by the pool, splashing in the ocean waves, and building sand castles, so the kids were pretty tuckered out when dinner ended late. As we all stood to leave, Jordan's new little friend ran over to his dad, put his arms in the air, and was instantly scooped up. The little boy then rested his head on his father's shoulder. I saw Jordan's huge eyes pool with tears as he cried out, "I want my daddy!" I bent down quickly to pick him up myself, but it did little to soothe him.

I said a rushed good night to our new friends and walked back to our apartment as fast as I could, carrying my sobbing son, trying to calm him as I tottered in my too-high heels until I finally kicked them off and left them on the lawn. Once we got to our room, I climbed into bed and stayed with him until he fell asleep. Even as I write this today, the image of my little boy triggered by the sight of another father and son, everything that he felt had been taken away from him for reasons he couldn't understand, guts me. We were at an exclusive resort in Hawaii surrounded by luxury, by adoring adults, by plenty of playmates and activities, but nothing was going to fill the hole in his heart left by the absence of his father.

The next day, I received a call with an update on our divorce proceedings. The last thing we had done together before Anthony left for prison was show up in divorce court with our attorneys. It was a standard status hearing, usually done over the phone or in the judge's private chambers, but it turned into such a spectacle that at the last minute it had to be moved to a larger courtroom to accommodate "public interest." It was awful. But at least it felt like another step on the way to finally moving forward.

There were still more steps to get through, of course, because as anyone who's ever filed for a divorce knows, it's complicated. I had been waiting for news about the date for the next status hearing, and in the call that morning I was informed that the judge had rejected our request that the next hearing be conducted over the phone. He had determined it had to be in person, which would be impossible given where Anthony was. So the prison would have to allow Anthony to be video-conferenced into the hearing. If I wanted to ensure that the divorce proceedings continued, this was the way I had to do it.

As if there weren't enough awful images of Jordan's dad in the world, now we'd see one of him sitting in federal prison being video-conferenced into a hearing just so we could say we were still working on our divorce? The only other option was to withdraw the divorce petition and refile later. I was mad, livid actually, but I realized that

that was the option I had to choose if I wanted to do anything privately. And so I did.

During our entire time in Hawaii neither the President nor HRC nor Jon ever asked me about the judgment of the Children's Services investigation or Anthony's sentence or the status of my rocky divorce hearings. They were all just there for Jordan and me, and I was grateful.

* * * *

When Anthony went away, I had told him I would never allow our son to visit him in prison, that it would be too traumatic. But after the father-son scene made me realize how devastating the separation was, I promised Jordan I would take him to see his daddy. I also promised to take my son home. To my home. To a world I still felt deeply connected to. To my mother, his grandmother, whom I had seen and spoken with far too infrequently since all of the madness had descended on our lives. It had also been too long since I had visited Makkah and it was time to go there again. I needed it.

I planned our ten-day trip to Saudi Arabia for spring break 2018. Hadeel and her kids would be coming too. The trauma of my personal life, out in the public for the world to see and judge, shook my immediate family in a way nothing had since we lost Abbu in 1993. His death had been a devastation from which none of us were sure we could ever fully recover. And then, two decades later, I broke us again, in a searing, awful, degrading humiliation. All my family members had to withstand a nightmare for years—sleepless nights, calls from the press for comment, knocks on doors from unidentified strangers, mysteriously vandalized homes, nieces and nephews who had to put up with classmates whispering behind their backs. My family's endurance is testament to the esteem their own communities hold them in.

I've never sat everyone down and apologized for what my upheaval put them through. Are there words one can use in circumstances like these? If they exist, I don't know what they are. And it's not because I was afraid they'd say *we told you so*. They would never have said that. They would have said, *It's okay. We love you. It was God's will. Be grateful for what you have.* So all the words have been left unsaid, and the unconditional love remains.

477

I had long jokingly called my childhood home Miss Havisham's House. Like her house in Charles Dickens's novel *Great Expectations*, ours had been frozen in time for the last quarter century. As Mom's career flourished, as she worked every day to educate and advance opportunities for young women, she had left all the remnants of our family life before the death of my father intact. Everything from his empty "Three Nuns" tobacco tins to the many brown glass bottles of homeopathic medicine from England—it was all still there. During the brief visits I had made every few years in the past, I would take a stab at tackling the mountain of physical reminders, one year opening the mail sent the week after my father died, another throwing out the medicines in his cabinet. But there was still much to do.

On this trip, when my time was not so short and pressured, I went into my own room and did a radical purge. The dried flowers from my high school graduation, old cassette tapes, and posters of movie stars went directly to the trash. The clothes from the 1980s that were many sizes larger than anything I would wear now because we always wore looser, more modest looks back then, the pink ballet flats, the drawerful of scrunchies, the toys from my childhood—those things went into the donate pile. After all these years, the possessions I did still cherish were my books, each of them still numbered in the order my father had wanted me to read them—*Anna Karenina*, *Pygmalion*, *Great Expectations*, *The Turn of the Screw*, *The Portrait of a Lady*, *Animal Farm*, *Macbeth*, and of course, *Silas Marner*—and I packed up as many of them as I could to take home with me.

One day Hadeel and I went through my father's closet. I noticed that his undershirts, still neatly folded two decades later, were all spotted with small dark bloodstains. I pointed them out to my sister, now a long-practicing physician. She said it was to be expected given all the surgeries, the invasive procedures, the incisions, he had to endure. There could not have been a more stark reminder of how much constant pain he was in, all hidden by his perfectly tailored suits, his ever-present smile, his unfailing joy at the privilege of simply being alive. It took my breath away. How he found promise in life despite that pain might have been Abbu's final lesson for me, delivered twenty-six years later.

As planned, I took Jordan for his first trip to Makkah. Setting him in front of the Kaaba as I prayed in the cool evening breeze, I felt a catharsis one can only experience in a place devoid of all judgment. I was no longer the elephant in the room, no one was bothering to take my picture or scold me for some perceived misdeed I had committed or scream obscenities at me. I was just another supplicant asking for guidance and grace. I had arrived back at the place that was so central to my childhood. A place I had always visited to ask for whatever I wanted: a Barbie, a Walkman, a couture gown, a dream job. As I got older, I would ask for health for myself and my family, I would pray for my father's soul. On this night, I repeated the prayer that all Muslims make. I didn't ask for an amazing job, loving family, exciting lifestyle. I have had all those things. I have said that prayer, whispered it, thought it, maybe a million times, but this night I concentrated as never before on its meaning. *Rabana atina fiddunia hasana.* God, grant me in this life that which is good.

* * * *

As 2018 progressed, I began recapturing a part of myself that had been dormant for years. I now had control over every decision in my life, but this meant that I also had to take responsibility for all the details that someone else had handled for the past eight years. I paid my own bills, maintained my own apartment and car, and began looking for a new place to live. I scheduled playdates for Jordan, came up with weekend adventures, took him to places my parents had taken me when I was little. It felt good to be in charge. Not that single parenting was easy. If I told my mom or mother-in-law or babysitter I would be home by 5:30, I stood up at 5, even if we were in the middle of a meeting, and made my way out the door. People were surprised at first but quickly adjusted. I fell asleep each night utterly spent, but at least I felt I had found some version of myself that I could recognize again.

I made plans to be with family for meals and holidays, saw friends for lunches and Broadway shows and weekends away, and in some of these gatherings the tension that had been the norm for the last seven years simply evaporated with Anthony's absence. I was reclaiming some of my cherished friendships, while also enjoying the new friends

Anna had introduced me to, people who brought me into a world that wasn't obsessed with politics, and couldn't have cared less about the nitty-gritty behind each campaign decision. I began to tend to the friends in my life with the recognition that their time and companionship were gifts. I had learned a harsh but important lesson—that friendship is not unconditional. Like anything precious, you have to earn it. You cannot demand it, expect it, or take it for granted. The many years I would show up to meet friends for a meal or a movie or a catch-up only when it was convenient for me, only when I could dictate the when and where, had meant that my needs always took precedence over theirs and I was rarely present for them in times when they had needs of their own.

The people who had written me off in 2011 when I decided to stay in my marriage, or in 2013 when I managed to keep my job, continued to ignore or slight me—and still do—in meetings or at dinner parties or on email chains. For years, it hurt; I ached for their approval. Now I am okay without it. As I have gotten older and more self-accepting, I am no longer desperate to contort myself into the person they would like me to be. I have also learned that often the cause of their ostracism has more to do with something they may be struggling with in their own lives than with me, so I try not just to accept it but to meet it with forgiveness.

I could see signs of forward motion in the political world too. A year and a half after HRC's loss, I was thrilled to see all the women and young people and people of color who were running for office in the midterm elections, even more so when I saw how many of them went on to win. In the wake of Trump's election, other forms of power had begun coalescing, starting immediately with the huge women's marches that took place across the nation and around the world the day after his inauguration. Rage had propelled Trump's supporters to the polls on Election Day, carrying him to the tiniest of victories in the states where he needed them—Pennsylvania, Florida, Wisconsin, Michigan—and rage of a different kind, for equality, for justice, for respect, was now animating millions of women. They posted long essays about their shock and anger at the elevation of such a patently misogynistic, racist, xenophobic, as well as wholly incompetent, man.

Stories objecting to the impossible standards HRC had been held to also began to proliferate. The negative comments about her hair, her clothes, her voice, her ambition—it was all being questioned and analyzed. Women were now refusing to disguise their anger. They raised their voices and they recounted the experiences that had held them back, demeaned them, humiliated them. They drew a line between what had once been tolerated and what was now no longer acceptable. They wouldn't smile, apologize, or muzzle themselves anymore. They were declaring enough was enough.

Some of these women and young people have openly said that it was the inspiration of seeing what HRC achieved that propelled them to speak up. Others said they had no idea how hard it was or what she had been up against until they jumped in the ring themselves and found they had to overcome all kinds of ridiculous challenges and barriers. Still others were mad that this eminently qualified, measured, professional woman was repudiated in favor of a man who was so clearly none of those things. It opened their eyes to the reality that if democracy meant something to them, if they wanted their leadership to reflect their aspirations and beliefs, they needed to step up themselves. Too few people know that among so many other things, Hillary Clinton is also a "young leader incubator," as one of our Onward Together partners told me.

A friend who had been in politics a long time told me she believed there was a divine purpose to what happened in November of 2016. HRC had to lose for many Americans to wake up; to scare them, motivate them to stand up for the values they believed in. And they did.

I was proud to see the proliferation of Muslim and South Asian candidates, especially women, running for local, state, and federal offices. In some ways it was a response to the travel ban against Muslims that Trump announced a week after his swearing in. At the time, I couldn't help thinking about all the people I had met on the campaign trail who had shrugged off my "dramatic" warnings about what a Trump win would mean for Muslims. People who did not take him seriously or literally, but as a form of entertainment. Once the ban was announced, teams of lawyers had to swarm airports to assist families whose loved ones were now detained simply for being Muslim or coming from one of the banned countries, like Syria, Iraq, or Iran.

Even though we are only a small percentage of the American population, both the Muslim and South Asian communities have concentrations of citizens in battleground states like Michigan, Georgia, Nevada, Arizona, and North Carolina. In 2020, two polls would be conducted by the U.S. Immigration Policy Center at the University of California, San Diego showing that between them, the Muslim populations in Arizona and Georgia are large enough to make a difference in the electoral outcomes in presidential races—and that their interest and motivation to participate was higher than ever before. AAPI Data, which does research on Asian Americans and Pacific Islanders, would later determine that in 2020, AAPI voters supported Democratic candidates over Republicans two to one. No longer was I part of a minority in this country that didn't count, as my colleague had told me back in 2007. Like any minority, we need to keep raising our voices, claiming our place in the public discourse, defining ourselves instead of just gritting our teeth over malicious and unfounded accusations. We also have to make an effort to demystify our faith, our culture, our values and beliefs, and I am excited that all these new faces and voices are showing us the way.

* * * *

That June, for Father's Day, I kept my promise to my son and took him to see his daddy at the place where he was having his "timeout." Jordan, Anthony's mother Fran, and I drove three and a half hours to the federal prison in Ayer, Massachusetts. My heart was full of terror at what the experience would be like for my little boy. Oblivious to my fears, Jordan chattered excitedly during the drive, listing all the latest adventures he planned to share with his dad. Hoping that the visit would go undetected, I had decided I would not go inside with him and Fran. Besides, I was still so angry with Anthony that I didn't know whether I could restrain myself if I saw him in person. As we approached, I was reassured to see that the building itself was unimposing and nondescript, nothing too foreboding or obviously prison-like about it. After I dropped Fran and Jordan off out front, I drove a short distance to a local park, sat on a bench, and waited.

Two hours later, at the agreed-upon time, I returned to pick them up, my dread at what I might read in the expression on my son's face growing more intense with every moment I drew closer. When I pulled into the driveway and stopped the car at the entrance, I stared at the steering wheel for a moment, collecting myself, taking a deep breath, bracing, until I saw Fran and Jordan make their way toward me. Jordan was all smiles, and I immediately felt a weight lift off my chest. If my son had been animated on the way here, he was positively giddy on the three-and-a-half-hour return trip to New York. He had been able to play games with his dad, had shared all his milestones, and most exciting of all, he had eaten lunch out of a vending machine, and he'd counted the right number of coins for the slot without any grown-up help. For him, the afternoon wasn't traumatic or upsetting—it was a gift. He was on a high for days after that visit.

However, any hope I had had for keeping this visit private turned out to be futile. A tabloid photographer had captured Jordan and Fran as they walked toward the car, then as I drove the three of us back to Manhattan, then when I dropped Fran off. While it felt like another unfair intrusion, I had ceded control of that sphere so long ago that when concerned colleagues asked if they could call the tabloids to scold them for this gross violation of the privacy of a child, I told them not to bother because I knew it would be pointless.

Jordan went with his grandfather for another visit a few months later, and the picture taken of him with his dad from that trip was displayed in his room along with his other family photos. The prison uniform that I was anxious about sharing with the world in divorce court didn't mean a damn thing to my son—he was so proud of his daddy. Shame is what we teach our children, not something born of their own authentic experiences.

SUFFERING IS OPTIONAL

The cure for pain is in the pain.
                                        —Rumi

I was in the bowels of the New York City subway system on a weekday evening in late June 2019 when I received the "last" call. First a text from Anthony, "You free?" Seconds later, "We need to talk"—words I had learned to dread.

"The *New York Post* just called," I heard him say. "They have a—" and then the call dropped. When he'd run for mayor last time, he'd made the need for better cell service in the subway one of his campaign pitches, but the reception underground was still lousy. So I was left for the remaining twenty minutes of the commute with that familiar feeling. Heart racing, fire under my skin, anger rising from a core place in my gut. For the rest of the commute home I had to brace myself for whatever I was about to hear.

When Anthony completed his sentence in May 2019, he resumed going to the therapy sessions he hadn't had access to when he was incarcerated. He moved into an apartment in my building, trying to make up for lost time with our son, now seven and a half. Jordan happily welcomed his dad back into his life even if it was more as a playmate than a permanent fixture.

I was secretly worried about how Anthony would reacclimate to society, whether he could change his behavior, whether he could earn a living to help support his son, but I raised none of these concerns with him directly since I had made the choice to no longer allow his problems to be my problems. He attended recovery meetings often and he started spending time with people he met there. He told me it had been a long journey just to get to a place where he felt like he could talk about what he was struggling with, in a safe place, surrounded by a community of people who cared for him.

Our conversations about his mental health were amicable but less motivated, on my part, by concern for him; all I really wanted to know was that my son would have a healthy father, with good judgment. We had committed to each other that we would always be present for our son, and would try to keep our disagreements between ourselves.

For the most part, I managed to stick by my intention to remain civil; but I had my setbacks when Anthony's presence reminded me of all he had caused and all we had lost. Anthony, though, was unchanged. He seemed to have no problem going back to his pre-scandal state of mind. He whistled as he walked down the hall; he approached both friends and strangers as though he had not a care in the world. He immediately resumed being a fun and inventive dad with a new game or adventure every weekend.

Was this all about to be ruined again by another violation by him and another sordid headline?

When I made it aboveground, I called back, armored for the news. He said there was a photo of him with a woman and it was about to be reported. I had said many cruel things over the years in anger and despair, and I had given up on a healthy marriage, but I had always honored the fact that I was married in the eyes of God and the law. He had only been released for two months and was looking for work, trying to get his life started again. And now we had to deal with more stories about other women.

I was in the midst of one of the most difficult periods of my life. Trying to figure out what my next act should be, making efforts that just didn't seem to be going anywhere positive, struggling as a single mother—I was feeling hopelessly inadequate. In the past, during difficult moments in my life, I would visit my friend and the founder of the Child Mind Institute, Harold Koplewicz, and exclaim, "Harold, I am so depressed!" To which Harold would always reply, "Are you losing sleep at night?" No. "Are you unable to eat?" No, never. "Well, my friend, you might be dejected but you are not technically depressed!"

In those weeks during the summer of 2019, however, I had been losing sleep, waking up at 3, 4, then 5 a.m. every day, my mind racing with panic. And I couldn't eat, wasn't even interested in looking at food, worried constantly about my future and how to support my son. What was the purpose of all my efforts? None of it seemed to matter. I could get nothing right. I wasn't sure how or if I could climb out of this hole. Without the strong support structure that came with being in a big mission-driven office environment each day, or a best friend to confide all my worries in, and with most of my family so far away, I had fallen to the lowest point I had ever experienced. On my way home from work one night I had contemplated for a brief moment stepping off a subway platform. The very fact that I thought it, even if it was for only a second, terrified me.

Maybe this latest call was the wake-up I actually needed. I decided it would be the last time I would allow myself to live in fear of a bad news bulletin from Anthony.

Three hours after Anthony told me about the story that was about to be released, we met in my living room and I shared exactly how I felt. I didn't think the old way of relating to each other would work. Instead, I said I wanted us to go together to meet with his therapist. He responded that he had tried for three years to act differently, that he had long ago stopped expecting me to acknowledge, affirm, or even notice anything he did. That he had lived three years of hell. All that time he kept trying to take the next right action, even in prison. He had believed what I had always said, that my life without him was better, happier. His goal had become peace between us, nothing beyond that. He thought he had tried to be supportive and present, listen and be a good father. He confessed that he struggled with his disease, that he was lonely and alone, that he too was trying to get through as best as he could. He had thought about dating as something that would be healthy to do, normal. He chose not to tell me because he feared what it would bring up.

When he left that night, I took a can opener to the can of worms that I had never touched in our marriage. This new life of dating, being with other women, seemed to have come so naturally to him. In all the years that reporters and therapists had dug into our lives, the chasing, the hounding, the new stories about Anthony's trans-gressions, was it actually possible that he had begun having physical affairs?

I did something that night that any professional will tell you is a big mistake. I picked up his old phone which had been sitting in a drawer in my apartment and searched through old messages. That, as a friend later told me, is what we call *pain-shopping*. This time, unlike a decade earlier in Punta Cana, I found what I was looking for and I read it all. It took me eight hours. When I looked up, the sun was com-ing in through my bedroom window. I was still in my work clothes from the day before and the tears had long since dried on my cheeks.

None of the names in the messages had been in the news, none were women who shared their stories or tried to profit from their moment in the sun. There were hellos and thank-yous and deep conversations about the state of the world and love letters from Anthony to women not named Huma. This time it was not me imagining what might be happening. It was me seeing with clear eyes the writing in front of me. When we had walked out of his campaign office building on election night in 2013 and I had felt that tectonic shift in our marriage, he had felt it too, and he had acted on it. What had started as digital fantasy relationships at the beginning of our marriage had progressed into something more in a couple of instances. Women had been with my husband, in my house, surrounded by pictures of my family. Maybe they touched my clothes, tried on my jewelry, ate and drank from my fridge. Maybe they held hands with my husband while the two of them explored cities Anthony had traveled to in the course of his work.

All the exchanges followed the same pattern. They involved women whom Anthony was helping: writing their résumés, advising them about job interviews, giving suggestions on how to get their husband or boyfriend to treat them well (the irony of that was stunning), tell-ing those with physical insecurities how beautiful they were. He was problem solving for all of them, all in the midst of exchanging flirta-tious and totally inappropriate messages.

An hour into reading the messages, I thought, *What is wrong with these women?* But by the time the sun came up, my judgment had altered. These were professional women, some of them mothers; all with lives, challenges, and responsibilities of their own. Some of them clearly knew it was a game and were enjoying the parrying. Some of them, I suspected, genuinely cared for Anthony. Some of them compared themselves to me. Maybe some of them were addicts themselves, but I will never know and it is none of my business. I was struck both by how avidly many of them had pursued him and by his responses, which were equally fervent. Yet I could not find it within myself to hate any of them—or him. Anthony's behavior had clearly caused a lot of people to suffer. The two of us, our child, our families, friends, colleagues, and also at least some of these women.

I realized I had two choices: to continue to seethe in anger at yet more evidence of Anthony's transgressions or to try and understand. I had told Anthony for years that I hated him, when the reality was I hated what his illness did to us. Those are two different things. So the choice I made was to get the whole truth, process it, and finally move on; to be released from the PTSD that I had been diagnosed with a decade before.

The next morning, I told Anthony I wanted to proceed with the disclosure process that he had asked me to participate in years earlier. I didn't have rage or jealousy in the traditional sense. I knew I had been betrayed, but now I wanted to know exactly *how* I had been betrayed. There were so many lies in our past, I wanted Anthony to flex the new muscle he claimed to have been working on for three years: honesty.

One of our first steps toward honesty with each other was to acknowledge that we were codependent, that our lives were inextricably entwined. Trying to be good parents, trying to find long-term financial security, trying to navigate a not-so-forgiving society—we had to do this together. I began seeing a therapist on my own recommended by Anthony's regular therapist. I don't know if it was just that she was so good or that I was now more open to this path, but something shifted as soon as I sat in her office. For the first time, it felt like I was getting concrete answers to simple questions. I asked her if she thought Anthony could stay healthy and not relapse if I wasn't willing to work on our relationship. She didn't think it would be easy for him under those circumstances.

For years, I had asked therapists "what is wrong with him?" and "how can we fix it?" but I never got a satisfactory response. I learned that day that my frustration with them for not being able to "fix" him was grounded in the basic fact that what was required was far more complex than what I had understood. My father had been ill my whole life. He was diagnosed, he was treated, then he had surgery. A defined ailment with clear, actionable responses. That was my model for illness and treatment. But treating the mind requires patience and a lot of hard emotional work, the therapist explained to me. In our life, the secrets were so numerous, they had become cancers. On top of everything else, prison exacerbated the isolation and loneliness that had led Anthony to transgress in the first place. I walked out of that first session feeling remarkably less burdened.

Addiction, I discovered, is a powerful adversary. While people are in the throes of active addiction, I was told, they can rationalize behaviors that, when they are in their right minds, they would never even consider. It takes over all conscious, sensible thought, which is why even very good people, when in active addiction, can do terribly irresponsible and destructive things. It can be like dealing with a Dr. Jekyll and Mr. Hyde. I had always believed that the person doing those destructive things was not the man I had married, and all these years later, I learned that I was right.

After spending years being angry on behalf of my son, angry for the 2016 loss and our role in it, now, finally, I was able to wrap my head around his betrayal of *me*. It took a lot of time and a lot of painful work to process it all because there was so much to digest. The truth was hard, almost unbearable, but the road to healing felt much better than the road to nowhere, which was the road I'd been following for too long.

With the help of our two very qualified therapists who worked closely together, Anthony and I began an intricate and lengthy process that helped us communicate honestly and therapeutically, about all the ways his addiction had affected our lives. I say "process" because, as I learned, the "disclosure" was only one part of what needed to happen. I discovered that I needed a lot more—both from Anthony and myself—than just the data about "what happened." I told him everything his untreated addiction and out-of-control behavior had cost me, physically, mentally, emotionally, spiritually, the blows to my self-esteem, my relationships, my work, my hopes, and so much more. He worked for months exploring his entire romantic history and wrote it up in black and white so we could both look at it with the same painful clarity we would muster if we had to have a doctor give us the facts about a cancer diagnosis, its spread, its treatment, and its prognosis. I then had to really look at, and express exactly how I was being impacted by finally knowing the full truth. Finally, Anthony had to come up with exactly what he was going to do to restore what had been destroyed. He had to lay out a real, practical, and actionable plan that would be more than just words. It was a long and excruciating process. In many ways it strained our relationship even more. Ultimately, what this process did was give us the honest factual data that could be assessed along with all the emotions so we could make the hard decisions about a future that would affect above all else—our son's well-being. They were decisions that could not be made just on hopes, promises, or just on fears. They needed to be rooted in truth.

The process also led me to meet a few women who had been in my shoes, who understood. They told me I would feel foggy and dazed for a few weeks, or months, but that eventually it would pass and the picture would get clearer, the madness would start to make a certain kind of sense. They were right.

Once it dawned on me that hanging on to all of the bitterness and the anger wasn't constructive—especially if I was going to be a model for my son—Anthony and I almost immediately started a new phase in our relationship. Anthony began to share what he had learned in recovery: that while pain might be inevitable, even necessary, suffering is optional. It had been slowly killing me, and now I knew that I didn't have to give it that power. I had spent a decade of my life married to an addict, and I could either cower in shame and forever resent the loss of my previous life, or I could find my way to a new life. My marriage is over but my relationship with my child's father is not, and never will be. Together we have begun to find a new way of dealing with each other.

With our son, we have chosen to share some hard truths, because we can't protect him from them. We live in a world where any awful story or image can be accessed anytime, anywhere. When he was six, a playmate teased him about his father being in jail. He didn't cry or run to me, so I didn't intervene, although I was sitting in the next room listening to every word. He simply said, "At least he took responsibility for his mistake," and I marveled at the emotional intelligence he had managed to show in that moment. Then he went back to playing.

So what is on the other side? Of the weight and devastation of the 2016 result? Of the verbal assaults from strangers? Of having one's entire life laid out for the world to judge? Of crushing disclosure? Of the revelation of deeply painful truths? For one, resilience, as I have seen in my brave little boy. And maybe something else.

In 2018, I traveled with HRC and her close friend Susie Buell to Rajasthan, India, where Susie arranged for us to meet with an astrologer. Muslims are told not to seek out fortune-tellers because no human can possibly tell you your fate, that is for God alone to know. But I agreed to see him, more out of curiosity than anything else. There was nothing particularly earth-shattering or thought-provoking in what I heard, except this: the astrologer said that I seemed to spend a lot of my life seeking entertainment, but that there is a difference between entertainment, which makes you think you are happy, and the feeling of true bliss. I did have plenty of opportunities in my life to do entertaining things. I was often invited to fashion shows, to galas, to glamorous lunches and dinners, to social events around the world. I went to the theater with friends, tried new restaurants, enjoyed long hikes and the country houses of friends. I traveled every corner of the globe twice over.

But how exactly would I achieve this state called bliss? True believers in Islam are not expected to be passive supplicants. We are taught to pursue knowledge, to question, to push ourselves to greater understanding of the purpose in our lives. Even the *istikhara* prayers that we make aren't about blind faith. You are not making a prayer to just leave it all in God's hands. No, you make an intention. Whatever it is. Applying to law school, getting married, having a baby, finding a new job. You don't just sit there, you have to go out and get it. I am not sure how I will find my true bliss, and I doubt the man from Rajasthan knows either. I do know that I have walked through fire and it didn't destroy me. Each day I get to wake up healthy and whole. I get to love and laugh. To work and learn. To continue to explore the wonder and adventure that is motherhood. To welcome new relationships with an openness and excitement I never allowed myself before. Each day brings a new experience, a new challenge, a new opportunity, and a new level of happiness, satisfaction and yes, maybe even eventually—bliss.

* * * *

Stepping off the politics treadmill for the 2020 presidential cycle gave me the time and space to heal myself, to focus on my son, and to prepare for my next chapter. Not that it was easy. I missed the drama, the excitement, the sense of being at the center of the universe. There were days I became edgy and uncomfortable, frustrated by having to watch from afar, and nights when I would yell at the television screen during the candidates' debates and rallies and interviews. Jordan would wander by, slightly befuddled that I seemed so familiar with all these little people on the screen.

Though I spent many long hours trying to prognosticate the results of the Democratic primaries based on who had done well in the debates and what the polls meant, HRC was clear-eyed from the beginning, always responding to my theories: "It will be Biden. And when it is over, Kamala Harris will be his running mate."

Election night brought a collective sigh of relief for more than half our country. But if anyone thought the course had been entirely corrected with the victory of the Joe Biden and Kamala Harris ticket, they had to reconcile that comforting belief with the unsettling fact that even more people voted for Trump in 2020 than in 2016, when so many outside forces—Russian interference, hacked emails, and, most of all, the totally gratuitous reopening of the FBI email investigation—had tilted the election in his favor. Whether that support will wither as the country recovers from the Trump years, we will have to wait and see.

For a long time, Comey was a daily nightmare for me, and even now the thought of what he did sometimes creeps in to torture me. But I have slowly come to accept that I am not the sole cause of the 2016 election loss. One man's decision to play God forever changed the course of history. It should not be my burden to carry the rest of my life. It should be his.

From Hillary Clinton, I have learned all kinds of things. How to be confident, brave, unfailingly empathetic, future-focused, tough, and gracious. She and I have had countless adventures over the past twenty-five years and who knows what lies in the future, but I am still certain about one thing. Hillary Clinton would have been an exceptional President of the United States. Maybe one of the best presidents. I say that with even more conviction and resolve today than when I believed it as a starry-eyed young woman.

The overarching quest of her public life has always been how to help every man, woman, and child reach their full potential. That purpose drove every policy rollout, every bill in the Senate, every speech she delivered, every town and country she visited, every book she wrote. Her focus was always how to give each child the opportunity to grow and flourish, every parent the tools to raise healthy, educated children, every person the right to live in dignity, every worker the protections and rights to succeed and thrive. As president, she would have done the tough things, the right things, the messy but necessary things, she would have reached across the aisle and forced divergent opinions to the table to help all Americans. She would have served her country, not herself. Maybe it won't happen in her lifetime or mine, but I'm confident that history will remember her as one of the American Greats.

HRC's legacy lives on in all the girls and young women across the country who have a dream to do something bold, and in the boys who learn to value, not fear, women's power. If anyone believes all the effort wasn't worth it, they have only to look at the history-making election of Senator Kamala Harris as the first female, Black, South Asian Vice President of the United States. Witnessing her take that oath of office was both awe-inspiring and reaffirming. Still, Harris's task is not easy and never will be because she is in the club of "firsts." Her every move, every decision is judged against the same phantom ideal woman HRC was always compared to.

A week after the election, an older Indian friend called me. I assumed it was to gush about the history Harris had made. She was full of pride and praise, but she also asked me to pass on some ideas about the clothes the new vice president should now be wearing, and suggestions on how she should modulate her voice. For most of my professional life, I would have politely thanked her, and assured her that I would pass on the feedback. Not this time. I asked with some irritation, "Have you stopped to listen to what she has to say and seen the work she is doing?" After some throat clearing, the friend apologized for being so superficial, agreed she was focusing on the wrong things, and we moved on. Just as I was beginning to feel better about setting this friend right, as we were ending the call, she said, "Maybe you could at least mention to her sister Maya to help her." I had to bang my head against the wall. How are we to measure what success looks like for a "first"? What are the standards by which we are judging her? These types of "helpful" suggestions are not just about her looks or her clothes or the tone of her voice, of course. Those are proxies for what really irks detractors: her audacity to pursue ambitious goals, to hold a position of power. I wonder how long it will take for people to understand that the way many of us consciously and subconsciously approach women leaders must undergo a fundamental shift if we want the future—for women, for our children, for all of us—to change.

I wonder what my eight-year-old grandmother imagined about her own future when she hopped on that covered oxcart one hundred years ago. What was she feeling as she made that rickety trip to school each morning? What stories did she carry with her? What dreams propelled her forward? Where did she think this journey would lead her? Did she see a future filled with daughters and granddaughters who would carry her torch forward? Did it ever occur to her that one of us might write a book in part to honor her very aspirations?

I have never wavered from the belief that public service is a worthy profession, that the reward is worth the risk, that the stakes are too great to turn away from the calling. That fork in the road, a quarter of a century ago, when I left a family wedding to embark on the great unknown, turned into the most unexpected journey, the next step in a path my mother, grandmother, and great-grandmother had cleared for me. It took me to a place that was worth every ounce of effort, commitment, and sacrifice required to get there.

And if I had to choose to do it all over again, I would.

In a heartbeat.

ACKNOWLEDGMENTS

Someone once said it takes a village. In my case, it took a small army. Nothing I have succeeded at in my life was done alone and the birthing of this book is no exception.

First and foremost, to my parents, Saleha and Zainul Abedin. Those ever-important roots that you nurtured and reminded me to maintain made me who I am today. Because of you, I always believed I could be anything, do anything, say anything. You taught me to stay true to my values and principles, to have radical empathy for others, to live humbly and honorably. You said the greatest power was in my pen if I used it wisely, and I hope I have lived up to your expectations. To Hassan, Hadeel, and Heba—how far we have come from the days of driving down Tahlia Street for Wendy's, wandering through the Acropolis, getting lost on European road trips, running through monasteries in Crete, praying on the side of the road in the middle of nowhere. You have been there for me—rock-solid, unconditionally supportive, and I am lucky you are my siblings and to have all these incredible brothers- and sister-in-law, nephews and nieces. To my extended family—aunts, uncles, cousins—thank you for your love and support over the years. A special thanks to my cousin Farhan in India who provided me with a lot of early family history, and particularly to all my mom's sisters who shared family lore over the years.

My son Jordan Zain is my reason for living, the reason there will always be laughter and joy, hope and promise, and, above all—love. I

ACKNOWLEDGMENTS

have had so many words for Anthony Weiner—if you have read the book, you know many of them. In the end though, I want to thank Anthony for two things. First and foremost, for our extraordinary son. And, second, for giving me an experience where I felt like I was the most special person in any room. Perhaps because our moment of total bliss was so fleeting, it was all the more precious. To Fran, Mort, Linda, Jason, Almond, and Rive—thank you for always being there.

I wrote an entire chapter called Hillaryland but really it could have been two words: Ruby Shamir. It would be wrong to simply call Ruby my collaborator because she was and is so much more. In true Hillaryland fashion, she immediately picked up the phone when I called, signed on to help with the book without really knowing what she was getting into, and since then she has been my guide, my architect, my friend, my unfailingly positive partner, and increasingly the other half of my brain. She gave a narrative arc to all my long, rambling stories and ideas; a theme, a reason for what needed to be where, what needed to be said, what was missing. Even on the hardest days she pushed me to keep going, keep writing, and she made every single draft I gave her stronger, smarter, clearer, more coherent.

I want to thank my tireless and dedicated researcher Alina Husain for her excellent work in finding, confirming, and fact-checking such an overwhelming and massive document and making it a better whole than the parts I first gave to her. She was a crucial part of getting this book right. Thank you to Lona Valmoro for the many, many schedules she pulled up, reviewed, and shared and the reminders about trips and moments even I had forgotten. I am grateful for her patience, friendship, and steadiness through all our years together. Thank you to Opal Vadhan, my ultimate cheerleader and supporter in just about everything I have done in the last five years of my life, including all the help in preparing for this project. Even on days that it was most daunting, Opal was optimistic! I am so proud of her. Thank you to Grady Keefe for his endless dedication, unfailing good humor, positive energy, and especially for helping to research campaign photos and always being available whenever he was called on. Carley Felzer created all my paper and photo archives, then organized and compiled all the lists I never even knew I needed, which was a daunting task and she did a wonderful job.

ACKNOWLEDGMENTS

I want to acknowledge Carolyn Reidy, the late legendary president and CEO of Simon & Schuster, whom I first spoke with about writing my story four years ago and who I am truly sorry is no longer with us. I want to thank Jonathan Karp, Carolyn's successor, for believing in the story from day one. After all the years we worked together on HRC books, I never imagined one day it would be mine and it still feels surreal.

Most authors can only dream of having Nan Graham as their editor and I was lucky to have her as mine. Even when her notes were simply "write better," it made a huge difference because I never wanted to disappoint Nan! Her vision for what this book could be, her constant questions, suggestions, precise surgeon-like edits gave the book clarity and coherence. Sabrina Pyun diligently ensured all the trains ran efficiently and on time, never dropped the many balls she was handed to juggle, and did everything with a smile on her face. It would never have come together without her. I am so grateful to them, as well as to the team at Scribner who worked so hard throughout the process of perfecting every detail of this book from inception to completion. To Roz Lippel, Rebekah Jett, Brian Belfiglio, Paul Samuelson, Brianna Yamashita, Jaya Miceli, Jason Chappell, Erich Hobbing, Amanda Mulholland, Annie Craig, Elizabeth Hubbard, and Hilda Koparanian, a huge thank-you. I also want to thank Beth Rashbaum, who came in when we were dealing with a behemoth to help cut it down without losing its essence. She is a magician with words.

To my supportive team at CAA: Cait Hoyt, David Larabell, and Kate Childs. It has always been an adventure and they deftly guided me through a sometimes overwhelming process and I am excited about what is yet to come. I want to thank my attorney Tara Cole for her advice and guidance, for picking up her phone when I needed her most. She is a real class act.

I want to thank all the people who read parts or all of the material and provided their thoughts, insights, feedback, and constructive criticism throughout the process. Their time, effort, and commitment to help tell the story properly made it that much stronger. To Hassan Abedin, Saleha Abedin, Miriam Altshuler, De'Ara Balenger, Jon Davidson, Karen Dunn, Martha Goodman, Paul Kelly, Heather

ACKNOWLEDGMENTS

King, Imam Khalid Latif, Bari Lurie, Bernadette Meehan, Nick Merrill, Cheryl Mills, Farah Pandith, Lauren Peterson, Philippe Reines, Heather Samuelson, Dan Schwerin, Mike Taylor, Angel Ureña, Opal Vadhan, and Lona Valmoro.

This entire book is in its own way a thank-you to Hillary Clinton for allowing me the honor to serve my country. She was, is, and always will be my mentor, guide, and trusted friend. To President Bill Clinton, Chelsea Clinton, and the entire extended Rodham-Clinton families, thank you for welcoming me generously and wholeheartedly into your lives for the last quarter century.

Much of this book was written at Anna Wintour's home in Mastic—in the Roosevelt Cottage—and I could not have asked for a more perfect or inspiring place to do it or more supportive people to be around while I did. To Anna, my deep gratitude for giving me the gift of unconditional friendship. To her and the entire Wintour-Shaffer family—especially Bee and Francesco, Elizabeth and Charlie, Kathryn and Sam—thank you for welcoming Jordan and me into your many family meals, trips to the beach, games on the lawn, movie nights, tennis matches. They are all cherished moments.

To all the women and men I worked with in Hillaryland—from the White House to the Senate to 2008 to State to HFA 2016—I will never forget those many, many highs and the lows and all the historic moments we were fortunate to have shared. For my current Hillaryland and Onward Together colleagues, thank you for bearing with me through this process and for your leadership and friendship—Dennis Cheng, Nick Merrill, Jess O'Connell, Laura Olin, Lauren Peterson, Emmy Ruiz, Rob Russo, Ella Serrano, Astrid Silva, Lona Valmoro, Jessica Wen, and Liz Zaretsky. To all of Team WJC and CVC, led by Jon Davidson and Bari Lurie, it is never a dull moment, is it? I could ask for no better professional partners. To Philippe Reines and Nick Merrill, who fielded so much incoming on my behalf over the years, never saying it was too much or too annoying or my problem alone to deal with, you define what true friendship is. I promise to try to make your lives easier. As I have recalled in great detail, absolutely nothing would have come to life without the legions of incredible advance colleagues. Thank you for always making us look good.

ACKNOWLEDGMENTS

A special note of appreciation to Brigitte Lacombe, whose work is truly in a league of its own—what a thrill and honor to have my portrait taken by her. Thank you to Sonya Hebert, Barb Kinney, Paul Morse, Pete Souza, and Diana Walker for giving me the permission to use your beautiful photographs. These images capture moments in a way sometimes words never can and it's wonderful to be allowed to use your art in my book. Thank you to the William J. Clinton Presidential Library—to Bruce Lindsey, Stephanie Streett, and especially to John Keller and Herbert Ragan for their assistance in researching and sending some unforgettable memories from the Clinton White House years.

I never could have done my job without the support of my counterparts in the United States Secret Service and Department of State Diplomatic Security. Thank you for your service to our country.

Navigating the world of investigation after investigation was both stressful and overwhelming. I do not know how or if I could have managed without the wise counsel and friendship of Karen Dunn, Martha Goodman, Mike Brille, Josh Riley, and Miguel Rodriguez and I will be forever grateful. To David Boies and Jonathan Schiller, thank you for all you did for me.

Kathleen Kelley and Paul Kelly guided me through the hardest period in my adult life. They never gave up on me even when I was ready to give up on myself. Their professionalism, care, and experience were more than I could have ever hoped for, and thanks precisely to them, the world has begun to make sense once again.

I have been fortunate to have a wealth of female friendships my entire life. There were many who supported me on all my good days and even more on the bad ones. Each of these women came to every conversation with open ears and an open heart. I love you all. Thank you in particular to Margo Alexander, Samantha Barry, Dorothea Bongiovi, Binta Brown, Susie Buell, Georgina Chapman, Lynn de Rothschild, Bonnie Gold, Risa Heller, Sheree Hovsepian, Jill Iscol, Jodi Maggio, Sienna Miller, Cheryl Mills, Minyon Moore, Summer Nasief, Lisa Perry, Elaine Schuster, Allison Stein, Rory Tahari, Tanya Taylor, Ann Tenenbaum, Maggie Williams, and Whitney Williams. I want to especially thank Michael Kives, Stacey Bendet, Derek Blasberg, and Dasha Zhukova—for bringing me into your worlds, making me feel loved and welcomed, when my own had totally exploded. To the families at school whom Jordan and I spend so much of our life with and who have been the best and steadiest of friends—thank you for being part of our village and bringing us into yours.

To all the women who have inspired and motivated me to write my story and provided the most incredible words of support—I am so incredibly grateful. Thank you to Glennon Doyle, Cheryl Strayed, Cleo Wade—each of you are figures of wonder in your own right.

There were times over the last four years that I faced skepticism about this story, questions about what I could possibly add to the record, that no one wanted to hear any more about scandal. And yet I knew that I had a much broader story to share, and felt driven to put it all down. I am grateful I had the opportunity to do so and to have the support of all the people listed above to get to this place. All the opinions and observations I chose to share throughout are entirely my own and I take full responsibility for any inadvertent mistakes.

And finally, and perhaps most important, I thank Yahweh, God, Allah for giving me in life that which is good.

PHOTO CREDITS

Interior

Frontispiece: Courtesy of the author
p. 1: Courtesy of the author
p. 71: William J. Clinton Presidential Library
p. 207: Courtesy of Paul Morse
p. 377: Hillary for America/Barb Kinney

Photo Inserts

1. Courtesy of the author
2. Courtesy of the author
3. Courtesy of the author
4. Courtesy of the author
5. Courtesy of the author
6. Courtesy of the author
7. Courtesy of the author
8. Courtesy of the author
9. Courtesy of the author
10. Courtesy of the author
11. Courtesy of the author
12. Courtesy of the author
13. Courtesy of the author
14. Courtesy of the author
15. Courtesy of the author
16. William J. Clinton Presidential Library
17. William J. Clinton Presidential Library
18. William J. Clinton Presidential Library
19. Courtesy of the author
20. William J. Clinton Presidential Library
21. William J. Clinton Presidential Library
22. William J. Clinton Presidential Library

PHOTO CREDITS

23. Courtesy of Philippe Reines
24. Courtesy of the author
25. Diana Walker/ *Time*
26. Diana Walker/ *Time*
27. Courtesy of the author
28. State Department
29. Courtesy of Philippe Reines
30. Courtesy of Barb Kinney
31. Courtesy of Barbara Ries
32. Courtesy of Heba Abedin
33. Sonya Herbert/The Obama White House
34. Courtesy of Nick Merrill
35. Courtesy of Nick Merrill
36. McCain Institute
37. Hillary for America/Barb Kinney
38. Hillary for America/Barb Kinney
39. Hillary for America/Barb Kinney
40. Hillary for America/Barb Kinney
41. Courtesy of Derek Blasberg
42. Hillary for America/Barb Kinney
43. Hillary for America/Barb Kinney
44. Pete Souza/The Obama White House
45. Courtesy of Opal Vadhan

INDEX

INDEX

INDEX

INDEX

INDEX

Jews, Judaism, 14, 20, 22, 115, 116, 117, 215, 280, 339

JFK Airport, 144

Jinnah, Muhammad Ali, 248, 250

Johnson, Rebecca, 184

Jones, Beth, 461

Jones, Jim, 253

Jordan, 120, 128, 275

Jordan River, 327

Journal of Muslim Minority Affairs, 26, 49, 57, 64

Justice Department, U.S., 339

Kaaba, 22, 54, 479

Kahn, Louis, 395

Kaine, Tim, 418, 422–23, 449, 452

Kalamazoo, Mich., 4, 5, 6, 29, 32, 52, 61, 184

Karachi, 15, 17, 249–50

Kashmir region, 14, 18, 248

Kaur, Rupi, 87

Kavanaugh, Brett, 161

Keefe, Grady, 455

Keigher, Connolly, 389, 410, 430, 450, 451, 452

Kelley House (Edgartown), 211

Kelly, Ray, 345

Kennedy, Jackie, 79

Kennedy, Robert, 198, 199, 200, 420

Kennedy, Ted, 198, 212

Kennedy family, 199

Kenya, U.S. embassy bombing in, 155

Kerry, John, 174

Ketchem, Fred, 247–48

Ketubah ceremonies, 280

Khadijah (wife of Prophet Muhammad), 53

Khan, Ghazala, 421

Khan, Humayun, 402–3, 421

Khan, Khizr, 402–3, 421

Khan family, 402, 403

King, Heather, 148, 151, 213–14, 394

King, Martin Luther, Jr., 420

King Abdulaziz University, 6, 25–26, 45, 47, 48, 273, 274

Kirshner, Ricky, 420

Klain, Ron, 433

Kohl, Helmut, 147

Koplewicz, Harold, 486

Kors, Michael, 375, 407

Kosovo, 131

Kravitz, Lenny, 128

Kreigel, Elan, 445, 450, 455

Kurds, 176

Kuwait, 37, 114, 176

Lady Gaga, 448

La Grange, Zelda, 244

LaGuardia airport, 290, 291

Lahore, 247, 251, 283

Lambs Club, 375–76

Lazio, Rick, 135–36

Lebanon, 19–20

Lee, Matt, 304

"Let There Be Light" (S. Z. Abedin), 130–31

Lewinsky, Monica, 102, 104

Libya, 321
  Benghazi attacks in, 352, 353

Lincoln Memorial, 59, 232, 300

Little Rock, Ark., 77

Living History (H. Clinton), 189

Lodhi, Maleeha, 66

London, 38, 46, 53, 64, 142, 238, 260, 397–99, 438

Los Angeles, Calif., 403, 411

Love, Reggie, 190, 201, 229, 239

Lukens, Lew, 234, 245, 301, 305

Lurie, Bari, 201, 356, 425

Luzzatto, Tamera, 138–39, 146, 148, 152, 171

Macedonia, 130–32, 231

Macmanus, Joe, 233, 237

Madrid, 311

Mahfouz, Naguib, 47

INDEX

INDEX

ABOUT THE AUTHOR

Huma Abedin has spent her entire career in public service and national politics, beginning as an intern in First Lady Hillary Clinton's office in 1996. After four years in the White House, she worked in the U.S. Senate as senior advisor to Senator Clinton and was traveling chief of staff for Clinton's 2008 presidential campaign. In 2009, she was appointed deputy chief of staff at the U.S. Department of State. Huma served as vice chair of Hillary for America in 2016, resulting in the first woman elected nominee of a major political party. She currently serves as Hillary Clinton's chief of staff. Born in the United States and raised in Saudi Arabia, Huma moved back to the U.S. in 1993. She lives in New York City with her son, Jordan. This is her first book.